CHARLEMAGNE AND LOUIS THE PIOUS

CHARLEMAGNE.

Meissonier
D. J. Pound

THE LONDON PRINTING AND PUBLISHING COMPANY

TRANSLATED WITH
INTRODUCTIONS AND ANNOTATIONS
BY THOMAS F. X. NOBLE

CHARLEMAGNE AND LOUIS THE PIOUS

THE LIVES BY
EINHARD, NOTKER, ERMOLDUS, THEGAN,
AND THE ASTRONOMER

THE PENNSYLVANIA STATE UNIVERSITY PRESS
UNIVERSITY PARK, PENNSYLVANIA

Frontispiece: Charlemagne, Print Collection, Miriam and Ira D. Wallach Division of Art, Prints and Photographs, The New York Public Library, Astor, Lenox and Tilden Foundations.

Library of Congress Cataloging-in-Publication Data

Charlemagne and Louis the Pious : lives by Einhard, Notker, Ermoldus, Thegan, and the
Astronomer / translated with introductions and annotations by Thomas F.X. Noble.
　　　　　　p.　　cm.
Includes bibliographical references and index.
Summary: "Translations of ninth-century lives of the emperors Charlemagne
(by Einhard and Notker) and his son Louis the Pious (by Ermoldus, Thegan, and the Astronomer).
Presented chronologically and contextually, with commentary"—Provided by publisher.
ISBN 978-0-271-03573-4 (cloth : alk. paper)
ISBN 978-0-271-03715-8 (pbk. : alk. paper)
1. Charlemagne, Emperor, 742–814.
2. Louis I, Emperor, 778–840.
3. Holy Roman Empire—Kings and rulers—Biography.
4. France—Kings and rulers—Biography.
5. Holy Roman Empire—History—To 1517—Sources.
6. France—History—To 987—Sources.
I. Noble, Thomas F. X.

DC73.6.C44 2009
944′.01420922—dc22
2009012104

For BENJAMIN, NICHOLAS, *and* MATTHEW

CONTENTS

ACKNOWLEDGMENTS

This book has been an unconscionably long time in the making. Consequently, I owe more than the usual debts of gratitude to the gentle prodding and prodigious patience of Peter Potter and Sandy Thatcher. I began the book while I was completing twenty wonderful years at the University of Virginia. My teaching, reading, writing—and translating—were complicated during my last years there by course overloads and an onerous, albeit important and satisfying, set of committee responsibilities. In January of 2001 I moved to Notre Dame to assume the directorship of the Medieval Institute. The years since my move have been the most rewarding of my professional life, but they have also been, by far, the busiest. Various duties, challenges, and responsibilities have continually nudged this book aside.

I have made very good use of the delays, however, by testing some of these translations on my students and by obtaining close readings of some of them by generous friends. My students in The World of Charlemagne have made numerous perceptive suggestions for improvement in *The Life of Charles the Emperor*. Julia Smith and Mayke De Jong read Thegan and the Astronomer in early drafts. Eric Goldberg gave Notker a finely attentive reading. Conversations—in person and via e-mail—with John Contreni, Paul Dutton, David Ganz, Paul Kershaw, Rosamond McKitterick, Jinty Nelson, Julia Smith, and the late Patrick Wormald have helped me in countless ways. Two research assistants, Katie Anne-Marie Carloss and Phil Wynn, deserve special thanks. I owe particular debts to Erin Greb, who drew the map that graces this book, and to Keith Monley, who edited a difficult text with sensitivity and imagination. My gratitude to students and colleagues is exceeded only by what I owe to my family. By the time I set to work in earnest on this book, my children were grown and married. This means at least two things. First, I owe more than ever to the patience and understanding of my wife, Linda. Second, the years when I was working on this book brought new joys into my—into our—life, three grandsons, to whom I affectionately dedicate the volume.

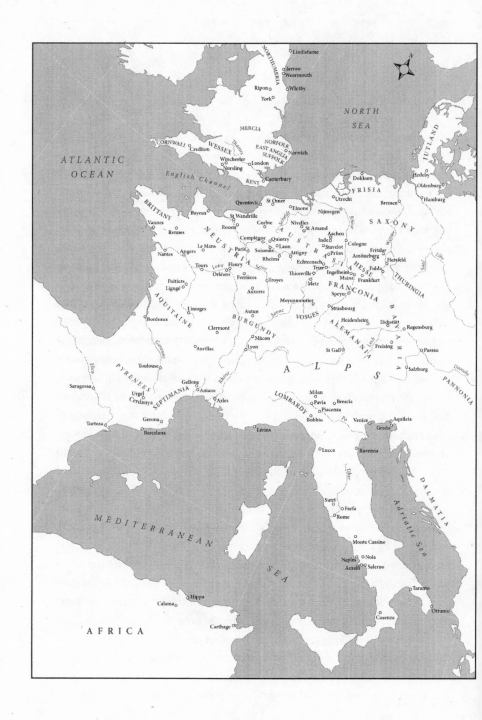

Introduction

Carolingian history has long been a staple of teaching and research, but the numerous and impressive histories written by the Carolingians themselves are only recently coming into their own as serious subjects of investigation. To be sure, for more than two centuries scholars in many lands have scrutinized Carolingian "sources" for information about the Carolingian period. To their painstaking labors we own much of our basic picture of what happened in the eighth and ninth centuries. Nevertheless, the sources have usually been treated as great quarries from which the building blocks of narrative, documentation, and corroboration have been hewn. Until recently, with some notable exceptions, too little attention has been paid to the sources themselves in their own right and to their authors. It is also worth remarking, in a volume of English translations of Carolingian historical texts, that most of the old scholarship and much of the new exists in languages other than English. Undergraduates, beginning graduate students, and the elusive "general reader" who have no Latin are unlikely to read French, German, or Italian.

To be sure, source criticism of the solid, traditional variety can still sometimes bring important new insights. Two examples will suffice. Surely, one of the most familiar facts of Carolingian history is the famous question sent by Pippin III to Pope Zachary asking whether it was right that those in Francia who had the name of king had no power, while those who had power had not the name of king. Zachary allegedly responded that this situation contravened "order," and soon thereafter Pippin was acclaimed as king by the Franks. Rosamond McKitterick has looked carefully at all the surviving evidence for this exchange and has come to the conclusion that it was a later

---

1. "The Illusion of Royal Power in the Carolingian Royal Annals," *English Historical Review* 460 (2000): 1–20; "Constructing the Past in the Early Middle Ages: The Case of the Royal Frankish Annals,"

invention.[1] Although one may disagree with McKitterick's reading of the evidence, her arguments are forceful and intriguing. Another well-known issue in Carolingian history involves Charlemagne's famously contentious relations with Duke Tassilo of Bavaria. Matthias Becher has looked carefully at the *Royal Frankish Annals,* a semiofficial account begun in close association with the Carolingian court around 790, and he has concluded that the *Annals* were composed largely, if not exclusively, to create a justification for Charlemagne's conquest of Tassilo's duchy. Becher calls into question the *Annals'* account of critical events of 757 and 763 that supposedly provided the basis for Charlemagne's moves in 788.[2] Like McKitterick, Becher interprets a key source as constructing earlier historical narratives to serve later needs.

Still, what is most impressive about current research is the way that it looks at Carolingian histories as key sites for the exploration of ideology, political thought, social ideals, educational attainments, and their emulation of classical models, to mention only some prominent areas of investigation.[3] Scholars have looked at what sources do not say as a way of contextualizing what they do say and of gauging the intentions of authors.[4] And if the production of historical texts has attracted sustained attention, so too has the reception of those texts.[5] It is clear that there were courtly and aristocratic audiences for history and that, in consequence, histories were often written to advance particular arguments or to promote particular individuals. In short, while details still matter, historians are learning to appreciate the artistry and intentions of the authors who provided us with those details.

Transactions of the Royal Historical Society, 6th ser., 7 (1997): 101–29; and, more briefly, *History and Memory in the Carolingian World* (Cambridge, 2004), 133–45, with references to her earlier articles.

2. *Eid und Herrschaft: Untersuchungen zum Herrscherethos Karls des Grossen,* Vorträge und Forschungen 39 (Sigmaringen, 1993), 21–77. See also Stuart Airlie, "Narratives of Triumph and Rituals of Submission: Charlemagne's Mastering of Bavaria," *Transactions of the Royal Historical Society,* 6th ser., 9 (1999): 93–119.

3. Suggestive examples of these and other approaches may be found in Yitzhak Hen and Matthew Innes, eds., *The Uses of the Past in the Early Middle Ages* (Cambridge, 2000); Guy Halsall, ed., *Humour, History, and Politics in Late Antiquity and the Early Middle Ages* (Cambridge, 2002).

4. One example: Johannes Fried, "Papst Leo III. besucht Karl den Großen in Paderborn oder Einhards Schweigen," *Historische Zeitschrift* 272 (2001): 281–326.

5. Among countless contributions, the following may be cited as exemplary: Rosamond McKitterick, "The Audience for Latin Historiography in the Early Middle Ages: Text Transmission and Manuscript Dissemination," in *Historiographie im frühen Mittelalter,* ed. Anton Scharer and Georg Scheibelreiter, Veröffentlichungen des Instituts für Österreichische Geschichtsforschung 32 (Vienna, 1994), 96–111; Janet L. Neslon, "History-Writing at the Courts of Louis the Pious and Charles the Bald," in ibid., 435–42; and eadem, "Public *Histories* and Private History in the Work of Nithard," *Speculum* 60 (1985): 251–93.

One kind of history is biography. In various forms—individual texts, collections, and panegyrics—biography flourished in antiquity. During the long centuries of late antiquity, however, a distinctive Christian form of biography, hagiography, the life of a holy man or woman, supplanted secular biography almost entirely. The gentleman bishop Sidonius Apollinaris (ca. 430–ca. 486) penned a sharp portrait of the Visigoth Theoderic II (r. 453–66), a text that may have been known to Charlemagne's biographer Einhard, but he stopped short of a full biography in any sense of that term.[6] Bishop Julian of Toledo (ca. 644–90) wrote a *History of King Wamba* (r. 672–80), but this text is patchy and episodic and was apparently unknown in the Carolingian period.[7] Major early medieval historians such as Gregory of Tours (538/39–590), Bede (673–735), and Paul the Deacon (ca. 720–ca. 800) did not write biographies but did create many memorable portraits of individual rulers, as well as of queens, holy men and women, bishops, and monks. Their works were certainly known in the Carolingian period, and their influences can occasionally be traced. Conditions at the dawn of the ninth century portended no stunning rebirth of secular biography, but that is exactly what happened. Indeed, biography has long been recognized as one of the brightest bands in the spectrum of Carolingian historical writing. That said, it is important to realize how novel and impressive was the achievement of the authors whose works are gathered together in this volume.

This volume presents for the first time in one place the five royal/imperial biographies written in the Carolingian period. Chronologically the texts begin with Einhard's *The Life of Charles the Emperor* and Ermoldus Nigellus's poem *In Honor of Louis,* continue with Thegan's *Deeds of Emperor Louis* and the Astronomer's *Life of Emperor Louis,* and conclude with Notker's *Deeds of Emperor Charles the Great.* Although Einhard is rightly credited with reviving the tradition of secular biography (meaning, on the one hand, the biography of a layman and, on the other hand, a biography that is fundamentally secular in scope and outlook), Ermoldus's poem may have preceded Einhard's *Life* by a year or so if the dates of composition offered below in the introductions to each text are accepted. Be that as it may, there is no evidence that either Einhard or Ermoldus knew or reacted to the other's work. And

6. Sidonius Apollinaris, *Poems and Letters,* ed. and trans. W. B. Anderson, Loeb Classical Library (Cambridge, Mass., 1936), letters, bk. 1, no. 2, 1:335–45.

7. *The Story of Wamba: Julian of Toledo's Historia Wambae Regis,* translated with an introduction and notes by Joaquin Martinez Pizarro (Washington, D.C., 2005).

Ermoldus' poem treats only the period from the 780s to 826; Louis the Pious lived until 840.

I have not presented the texts in strict chronological order of composition. That is, I offer first Einhard and Notker on Charlemagne (748–814) and then Ermoldus, Thegan, and the Astronomer on Louis (778–840). I introduce each text briefly and with a few basic points in mind: The introductions supply essential details, insofar as they are known, about the authors themselves, along with information about the date and context of each life. In addition, the introductions offer some details on matters of style, the sources used by the authors, and the influence, if any, exerted by the texts. Finally, I suggest some themes and issues in each text that deserve the reader's attention. I have tried hard not to say so much about each text that I would overdetermine the reader's experience.

Each introduction concludes with a list of "Essential Reading." In some cases I have cited almost everything there is on a particular author and text. In other cases, most notably Einhard, I have made choices. The reader will notice that much of the scholarship is not in English. Accordingly, my introductions attempt to synthesize for nonspecialist readers the best current thinking on the various texts. I have been reading, thinking about, and teaching these texts for many years, and each introduction contains some of my own ideas. The reading lists also point out "Collateral Sources." Here I supply references to relevant contemporary texts in English translation. I hope that these lists will spur student reading and research and that medievalists who do not specialize in the Carolingian period will find them helpful.

I shall confine myself to just a few words on the translations. Any translation is at once an interpretation and a betrayal of an author's work. I have tried to be as literal as possible in rendering these ninth-century Latin texts into twenty-first-century English. In four cases I have endeavored to give the reader a "feel" for the original version. For example, I hope that readers of this volume will be able to perceive the difference between Einhard's classicizing Latin and Thegan's biblical, annalistic style. The Astronomer and Notker were both good Latinists and could write in flowing periods. That is, they could write in what someone not schooled in Latin would consider very long, looping sentences. Occasionally, I have rendered these long sentences as they stand in the original. In many cases, however, I have broken up these sentences into two or three manageable English ones. In quite a few cases I have silently turned pronouns into proper names because Latin syntax provides clear signals that are lost in English. I have standardized the spelling of personal and place-names within each text and across all the texts.

I suppose that every translator allows himself the hope that his version is better than the existing ones. For there are many existing versions, particularly of Einhard. I am confident that my version of Einhard is better than Lewis Thorpe's[8] and at least as good as any of the other existing versions, with the possible exception of Paul Dutton's[9]—the one I would use had I not been using my own for some years.[10] I believe that I have improved on the J. R. Ginsburg and Donna Lee Boutelle translation of Thegan[11] and on Allen Cabaniss's often paraphrased rendering of the Astronomer.[12] These are the only translations into English known to me of these two works. My Notker, I think, is once again better than the familiar version of Lewis Thorpe.[13] Other versions of Notker have not been in print in recent years, although there is a version on the Internet that I find to be rather clumsy and archaizing.[14] My translation of Ermoldus is, I believe, the first in English to appear in print. But mine is not the first English translation of Ermoldus. The first one constituted one part of a Berkeley doctoral dissertation, and the second, part of the dissertation of my former student Carey Delores Fleiner.[15] Fleiner's version has many fine qualities, but in the end I decided to prepare my own. I have betrayed Ermoldus badly, however, by turning his verse into prose. In the end, I make only two claims for this volume: completeness, in that all the texts are here together, and consistency, in that one translator tackled them all.

Just one or two words are called for on the annotations to each text. First and foremost, I have not prepared these notes for specialists. That is, I have

8. *Einhard and Notker the Stammerer: Two Lives of Charlemagne* (Harmondsworth, Middlesex, 1969), 51–90. This was the widely read Penguin edition. It has been replaced by a translation by David Ganz (2008).

9. *Charlemagne's Courtier: The Complete Einhard* (Peterborough, Ont., 1998), 15–39.

10. The new Penguin translation of Einhard and Notker by David Ganz appeared too late for me to take account of it.

11. This text began life as an appendix to Boutelle's unpublished 1970 University of California dissertation and was reprinted by Paul Edward Dutton in his *Carolingian Civilization: A Reader,* 2nd ed. (Peterborough, Ont., 2004), 159–76.

12. *Son of Charlemagne: A Contemporary Life of Louis the Pious,* translated with an introduction and notes by Allen Cabaniss (Syracuse, 1961).

13. See Thorpe, *Einhard and Notker the Stammerer,* 93–172.

14. www.fordham.edu/halsall/basis/stgall-charlemagne.html.

15. I have never seen the translation by Donna Lee Boutelle, "Louis the Pious and Ermoldus Nigellus: An Inquiry into the Historical Reliability of In Honorem Hludowici" (Ph.D. diss., University of California, Berkeley, 1970). Carey Delores Fleiner, "In Honor of Louis the Pious, a Verse Biography by Ermoldus Nigellus: An Annotated Translation" (Ph.D. diss., University of Virginia, 1996).

not provided running historical commentaries to each text. What *have* I done? I have identified all people not sufficiently identified in the texts themselves. I have explained technical terms and phrases with which a nonspecialist might reasonably be expected to be unfamiliar (my students have been especially helpful in this regard). I have occasionally clarified historical points that the texts left murky. Finally, I have supplied reasonably full cross-references between the five texts.

One last word on references: In the notes to the introductions, the reader will find both complete and abbreviated references. The abbreviated references are to works included in the list of "Essential Reading" for each introduction, where the reader will find complete bibliographic information. All other references are given full documentation in the notes themselves.

Einhard, The Life of Charles the Emperor

INTRODUCTION

Einhard was born around 770 in the Maingau, that is, in the central Rhineland north of the confluence of the Rhine and Main Rivers.[1] His parents, possibly named Einhard and Engilfrit, seem to have been noble and to have possessed lands around Mulenheim. When he was still a boy, Einhard's parents sent him to the monastery of Fulda, but he never professed as a monk. In the early 790s Abbot Baugulf, who was by no means alone in functioning as a kind of talent scout for Charlemagne, sent Einhard to the court, less on account of his nobility than his intelligence. Einhard remained there until Charlemagne's death, in January of 814. Abundant testimony demonstrates that Einhard was wise, discreet, and much loved by all who knew him. He served as Charlemagne's personal envoy to Pope Leo III in 806 for sensitive consultations on the royal succession. In 815 Louis the Pious granted estates at Michelstadt and Mulenheim to Einhard and his wife, Emma. This donation may have been a reward for Einhard's influence in getting Louis recognized as his father's sole heir in 813.[2] Emma seems to have been from a family of some consequence; she was probably a good deal younger than Einhard. It is not known when Einhard and Emma were married, but most likely after Charles's death. Einhard never mentions Emma until around the time of her death, in 836, when he refers to her as "once his most trusted wife but now my most beloved sister and companion." They seem to have had a son, Vussin, about whom nothing is known.[3] Under Louis the Pious, Einhard became a reasonably wealthy man,

---

1. The best manuscript evidence suggests that his name should be spelled Einhart, but I retain the coventional Einhard.
2. See Ermoldus, page 143.
3. Letter no. 30, in *Charlemagne's Courtier*, ed. Dutton, 143.

holding, in addition to the lands already mentioned, lay abbacies and estates at St.-Peter and St.-Bavo in Ghent, St.-Servais at Maastricht, St.-Cloud near Paris, St.-Wandrille (Fontanelle), Pavia, and Fritzlar. Einhard was one of the few of Charlemagne's courtiers who remained prominent under Louis. He provided advice on many occasions and served as tutor to Louis's oldest son, Lothar.[4] The quarrels among Louis's sons seem to have dispirited Einhard, who, in the late 820s, withdrew from the court and tended more to his own properties, to various writings, and to his own spiritual life. Still, through letters and messengers, he remained involved with the court. Einhard died in March of 840.[5]

Although best known for the *Life of Charles,* Einhard wrote other works. Between late 828 and late 830 Einhard wrote, probably in stages, a substantial treatise, *The Translation and Miracles of the Blessed Martyrs Marcellinus and Peter.*[6] In 826 Abbot Hilduin of St.-Denis, who was fast becoming a key adviser of Louis the Pious, secured from Pope Eugenius II the body of Saint Sebastian. In 827 Einhard sent his trusted man Ratleic to Rome to secure relics for his churches at Mulenheim and Michelstadt. The *Translation* is full of intrigue but recounts in detail the acquisition of the relics, their transport to central Germany, the distribution of fragments to various churches, and the miracles associated with them. In 836, in response to a query by Abbot Lupus of Ferrières, Einhard wrote a short treatise, in the form of a letter, titled *On the Adoration of the Holy Cross.*[7] This little work is as much a reflection on prayer as it is a discussion of the appropriate reverence to be shown to the cross. More than sixty letters written by Einhard also survive, almost all of them from the last fifteen years or so of his life.[8] These letters reveal his personal, political, and spiritual interests and put his far-flung connections on display. It seems that Einhard came to court with some reputation as a poet. Scholars have argued whether he may have authored the *Paderborn Epic,*[9] a poem that treats the

---

4. Letter no. 34, in *Charlemagne's Courtier,* ed. Dutton, 145–47.

5. For basic biographical details, see Fleckenstein, "Einhard"; *Charlemagne's Courtier,* ed. Dutton, xi–xli; Störmer, "Einhards Herkunft"; Schefers, "Einhard und die Hofschule"; Smith, "Einhard: The Sinner and the Saints"; eadem, "Emending Evil Ways."

6. Eng. trans. in *Charlemagne's Courtier,* ed. Dutton, 69–130; Latin text, MGH, SS 15.1:239–64.

7. Eng. trans. in *Charlemagne's Courtier,* ed. Dutton, 171–74; Latin text, MGH, Epistolae 5:146–48.

8. Eng. trans. in *Charlemagne's Courtier,* ed. Dutton, 131–64; Latin text in MGH, Epistolae 5:105–42.

9. Dieter Schaller, "Interpretationsprobleme im Aachener Karlsepos," *Rheinische Vierteljahrsblätter* 41 (1977): 160–79; idem, "Das Aachener Epos für Karls den Kaiser," *Frühmittelalterliche Studien* 10 (1976): 136–68; Peter Godman, *Poetry of the Carolingian Renaissance* (London, 1985), 22–24; Wilhelm

encounter between Charlemagne and Pope Leo III at Paderborn in 799. From this work only one book of an original four survives; no other extant poetry may plausibly be attributable to Einhard.

At Charlemagne's court most of the key figures were assigned biblical or classical nicknames. Einhard was called Bezaleel. The name derives from Exodus 31:1–5: "The Lord said to Moses, 'See, I have chosen Bezaleel, son of Uri, son of Hur, of the tribe of Judah, and I have filled him with divine spirit of skill and understanding and knowledge in every craft: in the production of embroidery, in making things of gold, silver or bronze, in cutting and mounting precious stones, in carving wood, and in every craft."[10] In his verse epitaph for Einhard, Hrabanus Maurus says "he was skillful in many things" and "by means of him [Charles] accomplished many fine works."[11] It is conceivable that Einhard had a hand in many aspects of the construction and decoration of the palatine complex at Aachen, but no source documents such work explicitly. Einhard did indeed design and build two impressive and partially extant churches at Steinbach (outside Michelstadt) and at Seligenstadt (Mulenheim). A seventeenth-century drawing now in the Bibliothèque Nationale de France in Paris shows an eleven-inch-high cross base made of silver plate over a wooden frame and depicting biblical scenes. The dedication panel says, "Einhard, a sinner, strove to set up and dedicate to God this arch to support the cross of eternal victory."[12] It is a shame that more cannot be known about the crafts to which Einhard applied himself.

Einhard's fame rests chiefly on the *Vita Karoli,* the *Life of Charles.* Three fundamental problems stand in the way of any attempt to read and understand this remarkable text. When did Einhard write it? Why did he write it? What sort of a work is it? With regard to this last, the *Vita* seems so different from Einhard's other literary productions that some consideration of his oeuvre as a whole, to gain some perspective on the man behind the texts, seems necessary to any assessment of the *Vita* in specific.

First, when did Einhard write the *Life of Charles?* All scholars who have grappled with this problem agree on two points: the *Life* must have been

---

Hentze, ed., *De Karolo rege et Leone papa,* Studien und Quellen zur Westfälischen Geschichte 36 (Paderborn, 1999), 66–72.

10. All biblical quotations are from the NAB unless otherwise noted.

11. Eng. trans. in *Charlemagne's Courtier,* ed. Dutton, 10; Latin text MGH, PLAC, 2:237.

12. Reproduced in *Charlemagne's Courtier,* ed. Dutton, 63–67. Karl Hauck, ed., *Das Einhardkreuz: Vorträge und Studien zum der Münsteraner Diskussion zum arcus Einhardi* (Göttingen, 1974).

written after 817 because Einhard mentions a rebellion of the Slavic Abotrits as well as the collapse of the wooden porticus at Aachen, which are known to have occurred in that year;[13] and it was probably written before about 830 because a letter of Lupus of Ferrières from approximately that year makes admiring reference to the text.[14] Although the date of Lupus's letter cannot be determined securely, other evidence nevertheless strongly suggests that Lupus read the *Life of Charles* while he was studying at Fulda between 827 and 829, or possibly in 829–30.[15] So the *Life* was probably in existence by then.

In recent years there have been two attempts to date the *Life* early in the reign of Louis the Pious. One attempt places the *Life* in the context of the grants to Einhard mentioned above, seeing them perhaps as a reward connected with a commission to write the text, and of the succession scheme known as the *Ordinatio Imperii*, of 817.[16] Another attempt dates the *Life* to the early 820s because two documents from 823 bear both verbal and contextual resemblance to the *Life* and fall near in time to the birth that same year of Louis's son Charles.[17] Both of these arguments are learned but ultimately circular and not persuasive. What is more, Einhard speaks warmly (c. 19) of Charles's designation of Bernard as king of Italy in succession to his father, Pippin, who had himself been named king of Italy in 781. Bernard, caught up in a rebellion in 818, was blinded in punishment and died from his wounds.[18] Louis did public penance for his treatment of Bernard, and for other failings too, in 822 at Attigny. A curious text, *The Vision of the Poor Woman of Laon*,

13. *Life of Charles*, cc. 12, 32, below. In chapter 12 Einhard merely remarks that the Abotrits, "who had earlier allied with the Franks, were suffering from constant attacks," but the *Annales regni Francorum*, anno 817, ed. Kurze, 147 (Eng. trans. by Scholz, 103), date the Abotrit rebellion securely. In chapter 32 Einhard tells of portents announcing Charles's demise, mentioning among them the collapse of the porticus. Once again, the *Annales*, 146, date this event to 817. There is no evidence that such an accident occurred during Charles's reign.

14. Ep. no. 1, in Loup de Ferrières, *Correspondance*, ed. Léon Levillain (Paris, 1927), 6 (Eng. trans. by Regenos, 1). The problem here is that the date of the letter has occasioned some controversy: it could date anywhere between 829 and 834 or even 836. For a discussion of the dating of the letter, see Löwe, "Entstehungszeit," 89–93.

15. Löwe, "Entstehungszeit," 96–101 (for 827–29), and Tischler, *Einharts Vita Karoli*, 121–22 (for 829–30). Arguing on different grounds, Krüger, "Neue Beobachtungen," 126–29, insists that Lupus read the *Life*, perhaps in Gaul and not in Fulda, well before 829.

16. McKitterick, *Charlemagne*, 11–14; McKitterick and Innes, "The Writing of History," 203–7.

17. Krüger, "Neue Beobachtungen," 138–45.

18. Jörg Jarnut, "Kaiser Ludwig der Fromme und König Bernhard von Italien," *Studi medievali*, 3rd ser., 30 (1989): 637–48; Thomas F. X. Noble, "The Revolt of King Bernard of Italy in 817: Its Causes and Consequences," *Studi medievali*, 3rd ser., 15 (1974): 315–26.

severely censures Louis for his treatment of Bernard.[19] Whatever one makes of this text, its existence demonstrates contention over Bernard continued well into the 820s. It is difficult to believe that Einhard could have written chapter 19 before these divisive issues had been settled. In what has been an influential study, Heinz Löwe assigned the text to the years 825 or 826 without raising specific arguments and largely, it seems, by halving the difference between earlier attempts to find a date.[20]

Several hints converge to suggest a date around 828 or 829. Near the end of his prologue Einhard says, "Here you have a book . . . in which there is nothing for you to admire." Scholars have in the past neglected this "you." A London manuscript of the *Life* bears this heading: "Einhard to his dearest G., greetings." This "G.," as David Ganz has argued, is almost certainly Gerward, Louis's palace librarian. Accordingly, Gerward must be "you." There is evidence, albeit not conclusive, that Gerward left the court in 829 or 830; but he was certainly still the librarian in 828.[21] Gerward wrote a set of dedicatory verses for the copy of the *Life* that was presented to Louis the Pious.[22] He is the first known recipient of the work.

In turning to the question of why Einhard wrote the *Life,* I will have more to say about when he wrote it. But it seems right to begin with Einhard's own stated reasons for taking up his quill. In his prologue he offers three reasons for writing the *Life:* he was there and could give a trustworthy account; he was not confident that anyone else would write Charles's life; and he owed a great personal debt to Charles for fostering him and to Charles's children for befriending him. Sentiments like these have more than a whiff of literary convention, but that does not make them false. The problem is that such reasons for writing would have existed from the moment when Charles died. Was there

19. Hubert Houben, "Visio cuiusdam pauperculae mulieris: Überlieferung und Herkunft eines frühmittelalterlichen Visionstextes," *Zeitschrift für die Geschichte des Oberrheins* 124 (1976): 31–42 (new ed., 41–42). Eng. trans. in Dutton, *Carolingian Civilization,* 2nd ed. (Peterborough, Ont., 2004), 203–4.

20. "Entstehungszeit."

21. Ganz, "Preface to Einhard's 'Vita Karoli,'" 309; idem, "Einhard's Charlemagne," 41; Tischler, *Einharts Vita Karoli,* 1:157–68; Schefers, "Einhard und die Hofschule," 93.

22. Insofar as these verses constitute the first known reaction to the *Life,* they are worth quoting in Dutton's fine translation (*Charlemagne's Courtier,* 4):

For you, O greatest prince, Gerward, your obedient servant
  Produced these little verses for your
Eternal praise and memory. For good reason
  He raises your distinguished name to the stars.
You, O reader, being wise know that magnificent Einhard
  Wrote this account of the deeds of Charles the Great.

a particular time when knowledge and gratitude were urgent prods to write what others had not or what others might say or have said very differently?

In fact, some evidence, circumstantial to be sure, points again to the late 820s. In the opening years of Louis's reign, criticism of Charles was given free rein. Louis sent *missi* throughout the realm to look for injustices, and they discovered a "numberless multitude" of oppressed people.[23] As late as his public penance at Attigny in 822, Louis was admitting culpability for both his own failings and his father's.[24] Criticism of Charles then took a rather bizarre turn. In 824 Heito, then a simple monk at Reichenau but formerly abbot of the house and bishop of Basel, wrote down the deathbed visions of a Reichenau monk, Wetti. To his shock and dismay, Wetti had seen Charles in purgatory, where animals were gnawing on his genitals to punish him for his voracious sexual appetite.[25] In 827 Walahfrid Strabo set Wetti's text to verse and sent it to the court.[26] At around the same time, the vision of the "poor woman" of Laon began to circulate as well as another vision experienced by a mysterious Rotchar.[27] The poor woman also saw Charles suffering afterworldly torments, whereas Rotchar encountered Charles after he had been released from his punishment. Einhard may have been responding to this criticism, especially after it got personal and salacious.[28]

In the *Translation and Miracles* Einhard says that he was called to court for the assembly of 828.[29] Momentous events took place there, chief among them the sacking of three major officials.[30] Einhard himself was at that time embroiled in a bitter quarrel with Louis's archchaplain Hilduin.[31] While Louis was at court, a messenger arrived from Mulenheim with a booklet bearing revelations that the archangel Gabriel, disguised as Saint Marcellinus, had given to a blind man, with instructions that they be given to Einhard for transmission to Louis. The booklet contained severe criticisms of the failings of Louis's

23. Astronomer, c. 21; Thegan, c. 13; Ermoldus, page 147. *Annales regni Francorum,* anno 814, ed. Kurze, 140–41 (Eng. trans. by Scholz, 97).

24. *Annales regni Francorum,* anno 822, ed. Kurze, 158 (Eng. trans. by Scholz, 111).

25. Heito, *Visio Wettini,* ed. Dümmler, MGH, PLAC, 2:267–75.

26. David A. Traill, *Walahfrid Strabo's Visio Wettini: Text, Translation, and Commentary* (Frankfurt, 1974).

27. For the poor woman, see note 19 above; for Rotchar, see Wilhelm Wattenbach, "Aus Petersburger Handschriften," *Anzeiger für Kunde der deutschen Vorzeit* 22 (1875): 73–74.

28. Paul Edward Dutton, *The Politics of Dreaming in the Carolingian Empire* (Lincoln, 1994), 61–75; Noble, "Greatness Contested and Confirmed."

29. *Translation and Miracles,* 3.12, trans. Dutton, in *Charlemagne's Courtier,* 100.

30. *Annales regni Francorum,* anno 828, ed. Kurze, 174 (Eng. trans. by Scholz, 122).

31. Smith, "Emending Evil Ways," 202–5.

regime, but, Einhard says, Louis failed to act on it. A little later, another report reached Einhard concerning a devil, Wiggo, who had possessed a young girl. When the devil was exorcised, he related that he and his companions had been sowing discord for some years because of the wickedness of the people and the sins of the rulers. "Friends do not trust friends," Wiggo says, "brothers hate brothers and fathers do not love their sons."[32] If Einhard had begun composing the *Translation and Miracles* in 828, then the disturbances of that fateful year and Louis's failure to heed salutary warnings might have prompted him to send his *Life of Charles* to key courtiers. Whether he did so from the confines of the court in 828 or early 829 or sent the book to the court from home after leaving the court in 829 is difficult to say.[33] Be that as it may, much evidence points to a date for the *Life of Charles* in 828 or 829.

So, it is safe to say that Einhard wrote the *Life* partly to stanch the flow of criticism of Charles, partly out of frustration at the disastrous course of events in the late 820s, and partly to teach the new generation better ways by showing them the highlights of the previous one. And yet each of these explanations, no matter how plausible, touches only the externals of the *Life*. Surely the form, language, and intellectual foundations of the *Life* also have information for us about why Einhard wrote it.

What kind of a work is the *Life*? It is important to be clear on the shape of the work as it left Einhard's writing table. Walahfrid Strabo admits that he inserted the chapter numbers. The original text of the *Life* constituted a single, uninterrupted block. This much is clear. Less clear is whether Einhard expected his prologue to be a permanent part of the *Life*. It is possible that it was addressed to Gerward and neither to Louis the Pious nor to posterity. One class of manuscripts does lack the prologue and instead begins with Gerward's dedicatory verses. Yet the majority of the manuscripts have Einhard's prologue, the *Life*, and Charles's testament. The latter document seems to have been a constituent of Einhard's text. Einhard's title appears to have been *The Life of Charles the Emperor*, not *The Life of Charles the Great*. If, therefore, Einhard expected his readers to encounter both his prologue and the *Life*, then those readers may draw testimony from both segments of the whole text in an

<hr/>

32. *Translation and Miracles*, 3.13–14, trans. Dutton, in *Charlemagne's Courtier*, 101–5.

33. The last datable miracle recorded in the *Translation and Miracles* (4.18) falls in August 830. Obviously the work was not finished before that date. But when was it begun? See Smith, "Emending Evil Ways," 205; Tischler, *Einharts Vita Karoli*, 172–78; Dutton, "Preface to Einhard," in *Charlemagne's Courtier*, xxv–vi.

attempt to capture a sense of Einhard's intentions and purposes.[34] It is interesting to note as well that Einhard does not identify himself as the author and that Walahfrid takes some care to stress that Einhard was indeed the author. Walahfrid was not the first to do so; Gerward also specified that the work he was transmitting to Louis was Einhard's. That Einhard wrote the *Life* must have been an open secret, but one cannot help wondering why there should have been any question about the matter.

In his prologue Einhard lays down a number of explicit and implicit statements about his work. He says that he plans to write about the "life and character" (*vitam et conversationem*) and "no small part of the accomplishments" (*ex parte non modica res gestas*) of Charles. He defends the writing of contemporary history and condemns those who write to ensure their own fame rather than to record the justly famous deeds of the truly great. He notes that he aims to write succinctly. Finally, he stresses the importance of eloquence, specifically of Ciceronian eloquence, but once again because the subject demands it, not simply because he can do it; indeed, Einhard insists that he is barely up to the task.

The sources Einhard used, and the uses he made of those sources, reveal important things about the nature of the *Life*. As he says, he was an eyewitness. Memory played a role. The *Royal Frankish Annals* provided details, especially for the chapters treating wars. In his prologue Einhard signals his own familiarity with Sulpicius Severus's (ca. 360–ca. 430) *Life of Saint Martin of Tours* (ca. 396); most likely he expected his readers to spot the allusions.[35] Nevertheless, Einhard wrote the first significant secular biography since antiquity. The *Life* is secular in two respects: it is the life of a layman, and its values and outlook are rigorously secular.

Writing in a world where saints' lives had served as biographical fare for centuries, Einhard had no readily available models for the kind of book he wished to write. Accordingly, he turned to Suetonius. Gaius Suetonius Tranquillus (ca. 70–ca. 130) around 110 wrote his best-known work, *On the Life of*

---

34. Ganz, "Preface to Einhard's 'Vita Karoli'"; idem, "Einhard's Charlemagne," 38–39; Tischler, *Einharts Vita Karoli*, 78–101, 113–22.

35. Hellmann, "Einhards literarische Stellung," 168; Beumann, "Topos und Gedankengefüge bei Einhard"; Wolter, "Intention und Herrscherbild," 296–303; Berschin, "Einhart," 206–9; Ganz, "Einhard's Charlemagne," 41–42; Hageneier, *Jenseits der Topik*, 54–56, 104–13. The key elements are Sulpicius's dedicatory epistle and preface: *Vita Martini*, ed. Jacques Fontaine, Sources chrétiennes 133 (Paris, 1967), 248–52 (Eng. trans. by F. R. Hoare, in *Soldiers of Christ*, ed. Thomas F. X. Noble and Thomas Head [University Park, 1995], 3–5.

the Caesars, a set of twelve more or less biographical accounts of the Roman emperors from Julius Caesar to Domitian. Suetonius's work was not widely known in the Carolingian period. Einhard may have encountered it at Fulda, where there was a manuscript that is no longer extant. Lupus of Ferrières may have seen this same manuscript and may well have spotted Einhard's debts to the classical historian.[36] As far as is known, no one else recognized Einhard's use of Suetonius until the French scholar Isaac Casaubon (1559–1604), who prepared an edition of the *De vita caesarum* in 1595. Far from being praised for making use of a classical source, Einhard was for a long time pilloried as a slavish imitator, as the author of the "thirteenth caesar."[37] Then the scholarly pendulum began to swing in the other direction.[38] Several points have emerged from this reassessment of Einhard's use of Suetonius. He was artful and selective in drawing from his source. Broadly speaking, Suetonius supplied Einhard with an organizational model. Suetonius divided his lives into two main sections, one on character and one on statesmanship. Einhard adapted this structure so as to create three sections, one on wars, one on character, and one on administration. Because Suetonius sought to reveal character more than to tell a story, he provided Einhard with a model for writing biography instead of history. Suetonius crafted his imperial portraits with reference to one or another of the classical virtues. Einhard adapted this feature of Suetonius's work as well, so as to portray a Charles who measured up to classical, and secular, standards of conduct and excellence. In addition to these kinds of general influences and inspirations, Einhard borrowed words and phrases from various imperial lives in creating his memorable physical description of Charles and in limning his character.[39] Rosamond McKitterick has recently made a persuasive argument for Einhard's use of Tacitus's *Agricola.* In A.D. 96 or 97 Tacitus, the superb and crafty historian of early imperial Rome, wrote an account, partly historical and partly biographical, of his father-in-law, Agricola, who had served as governor of Britain. The structure of *Agricola* and some of the *kinds* of information it contains suggest that Einhard was influenced by it.[40]

36. Innes, "The Classical Tradition in the Carolingian Renaissance." See also Meyers, "Éginhard et Suétone." The oldest surviving manuscript was written at Tours in the mid–ninth century.

37. Halphen, "Einhard, historien de Charlemagne."

38. Hellmann's "Einhards literarische Stellung" was the epoch-making study.

39. In addition to Hellmann, see Ganshof, "Einhard"; Berschin, "Einhart," 212–13; Ganz, "The Preface to Einhard's 'Vita Karoli'"; idem, "Einhard's Charlemagne"; Hageneier, *Jenseits der Topik,* 59–64.

40. *Charlemagne,* 17–20.

Recently Einhard's considerable debt to Cicero has been recognized too. In his prologue he says that to treat his subject properly he would need "the gifts of a Cicero," and he mentions Cicero's *Tusculan Disputations*. Surely it is significant that this is one of only two books mentioned by Einhard, the other being Augustine's *City of God,* from which Charles enjoyed hearing readings at dinner time (c. 24). But Einhard also seems to have been familiar with Cicero's writings on rhetoric and oratory; at any rate, Lupus of Ferrières requested the loan of several Ciceronian works on these topics.[41] From Cicero Einhard derived certain organizational principles derived from the rules of oratory.[42] For example, the prologue captures the reader's attention and benevolence, and the body of the work is brief, exciting, and memorable, while the overall effect is to convey a persuasive image of a remarkable man. Einhard also knew Alcuin's work on rhetoric and may have had in mind his friend's words on how to open a speech or on why to read ancient books.[43] Even more important than these structural borrowings are the Stoic virtues that Cicero brought to Einhard's attention and that Einhard applied to Charlemagne. Chief among these are magnanimity, patience, courage, and perseverance.[44]

A recent study provides a penetrating analysis of Einhard's chapter 16, where he treats all the foreign embassies sent to Charles's court.[45] In the past, scholars noticed and criticized Einhard's seeming inattention to basic historical accuracy in this chapter. In fact, it appears that Einhard was here employing his command not only of Suetonius but also of the ancient biographical and panegyrical tradition so as to make a point about Charles's Roman-like universality. In view of Einhard's famous chapter 28, where he describes in less than enthusiastic terms Charles's imperial coronation in Rome at the hands of the pope, it is important to see how he could make Charles similar to the Romans of old without making him a Roman. Einhard would have expected his readers to perceive Charles's uniqueness and Frankishness without straining their credulity.

From these diverse sources and inspirations, then, Einhard created a fascinating portrait of Charles. His Charles was virtuous and vigorous, always restless and on the move. He was a great warrior who expanded his realm and

41. Ep. no. 1, in Loup de Ferrières, *Correspondance,* ed. Levillain, 8 (Eng. trans. by Regenos, 3).

42. Kempshall, "Some Ciceronian Models"; Berschin, "Einhart," 208–9.

43. An important discovery by Ganz, "Einhard's Charlemagne," 39, 45, referring to *The Rhetoric of Alcuin and Charlemagne,* ed. and trans. Wilbur Samuel Howell (1941; repr., New York, 1965), c. 20, pp. 96–98 (Latin), 99–100 (English); c. 37, pp. 130–36 (Latin), 131–37 (English).

44. Hellmann, "Einhards literarische Stellung," 210–14; Kempshall, "Some Ciceronian Models," 18–22; Ganz, "Preface to Einhard's 'Vita Karoli'"; Morrissey, *Charlemagne and France,* 25–27.

45. Latowsky, "Foreign Embassies and Roman Universality."

promoted peace and justice within. Einhard, born east of the Rhine, presents Charles as a proud Frank—note that when he tells of Charles's imperial administration, he mentions additions to the Germanic law codes and preservation of the cultural patrimony but does not say a word about government.[46] Charles's greatness attaches to his personality, to his character, not to his royal or imperial office. Einhard's Charles is never an abstraction. He is a flesh-and-blood human being. Charles is never a God-appointed ruler, and the Lord does not lead his armies or confer victories upon him. Charles is personally pious, but he is not portrayed as a church reformer or as an ecclesiastical statesman. Suetonius delighted in telling amusing and informative anecdotes about the caesars. Einhard eschews this approach. If Walahfrid is correct in saying that Charles told Einhard his secrets, then we are disappointed by Einhard's failure to tell them to us. Charles speaks only four times in the *Life* (cc. 19, 24, 26, 28). We rarely feel close to him.[47]

To what extent can we believe Einhard? He himself insists that he was there, that he knew very well the things he recorded. Given that he sent his work to the court in the first place and that many people were still alive in the late 820s who could remember equally well the days of Charles, it seems unlikely that Einhard fabricated large parts of his account. As the notes to this translation point out from time to time, Einhard did sometimes conceal and sometimes misrepresent things. From Louis Halphen in the early twentieth century down to, say, Roger Collins in 1998, the persistent tendency has been to argue that whenever Einhard cannot be corroborated, he should be disbelieved.[48] In my view and in the view of other recent commentators, this hypercriticism goes too far.[49] As I have been arguing, Einhard was a literary craftsman and a man with an argument to advance. His selectivity is more a matter of interpretation than of misrepresentation. Most of what Einhard tells us can in fact be found in other contemporary sources—sources, let it be said, available to us and to Einhard's contemporaries. Therefore, we actually read Einhard for his interpretations more than for his details. It is his *portrait* of Charlemagne that demands our scrutiny.

What, in conclusion, can be said about Einhard himself? He was learned; that is clear. He commanded an elegant and exact Latin prose style, but as the

---

46. Especially emphasized by Wolter, "Intention und Herrscherbild," 303–7.
47. Ganz, "Einhard's Charlemagne."
48. Halphen, "Einhard, historien de Charlemagne," esp. 96–98; Collins, *Charlemagne*, 1–2.
49. McKitterick, *Charlemagne*, 7–20; Ganz, "Einhard's Charlemagne."

Translation and Miracles shows, he could write a rough-and-ready Latin as well. He was devoted to his wife and devastated by her death. He was extremely well connected for many years and virtually alone came unscathed through a change of regime and bitter political quarrels. His survival may owe something to the esteem in which he was held but probably owes more to his discretion. He could create an utterly secular portrait of Charles, but his other writings show him to be a conventionally religious man of his times.[50] Interestingly, Einhard opens the *Translation and Miracles* by saying the point of writing such a text is to set forth examples that people can follow, but in the prologue to the *Life* he says that Charles's deeds are almost inimitable. Einhard opens the *Translation and Miracles* and many of his letters this way: "Einhard, a sinner."[51] Perhaps this is how he should be remembered, since, after all, he says he wrote the *Life* to commemorate Charles, not to draw attention to himself.

ESSENTIAL READING

Éginhard. *Vie de Charlemagne.* Edited by Louis Halphen. Les classiques de l'histoire de France au Moyen Âge 1. Paris, 1938; repr. 1967. (I have translated from this edition. The other standard edition is edited by Oswald Holder-Egger, *Vita Karoli Magni,* MGH, Scriptores rerum Germanicarum in usum scholarum separatim editi 25 [Hannover, 1911]. A more recent edition, with facing-page German translation, has not yet found wide acceptance: Einhard, *Vita Karoli Magni imperatoris: Übersetzung, Anmerkungen und Nachwort,* ed. Evelyn Scherabon Firchow [Stuttgart, 1981].)

Collateral Sources

(Each of the other works translated in this volume is relevant. Thegan, the Astronomer, and Ermoldus all have important information in their earlier sections.)

Carolingian Chronicles: Royal Frankish Annals and Nithard's Histories. Translated by Bernhard Walter Scholz. Ann Arbor, 1970.
Charlemagne: Translated Sources. Edited and translated by P. D. King. Lambrigg, 1987.
Charlemagne's Courtier: The Complete Einhard. Edited and translated by Paul Edward Dutton. Peterborough, Ont., 1998.
The Lives of the Eighth-Century Popes (Liber Pontificalis). Translated, with an introduction and commentary, by Raymond Davis. Translated Texts for Historians 13. Liverpool, 1992.

50. Smith, "Emending Evil Ways," 190; Wolter, "Intention und Herrscherbild," 296–97.
51. Preface to *Translation and Miracles,* in *Charlemagne's Courtier,* ed. Dutton, 69. In the same volume, see letters 2, 3, 4, 10, 17, 25, 29, 43, 46, 48, 59, 60, and 64 for *Einhardus peccator.* See Ganz, "Einhardus peccator," and Smith, "Einhard: The Sinner and the Saints."

The Lives of the Ninth-Century Popes (Liber Pontificalis). Translated, with an introduction and commentary, by Raymond Davis. Translated Texts for Historians 20. Liverpool, 1995.

Lupus of Ferrières. *The Letters of Lupus of Ferrières*. Translated, with an introduction and notes, by Graydon W. Regenos. The Hague, 1966.

Poetry of the Carolingian Renaissance. Edited and translated by Peter Godman. London, 1985.

The Reign of Charlemagne: Documents on Carolingian Government and Administration. Edited and translated by H. R. Loyn and John Percival. Documents of Medieval History 2. London, 1975.

"The Time of Charlemagne (768–814)." Chap. 2 in *Carolingian Civilization: A Reader*, 2nd ed., edited by Paul Edward Dutton, 23–154. Peterborough, Ont., 2004.

Charlemagne

Barbero, Alessandro. *Charlemagne: Father of a Continent*. Translated by Allan Cameron. Berkeley and Los Angeles, 2004.

Becher, Matthias. *Charlemagne*. Translated by David S. Bachrach. New Haven, 2003.

Collins, Roger. *Charlemagne*. Toronto, 1998.

Dutton, Paul Edward. *Charlemagne's Mustache and Other Cultural Clusters of a Dark Age*. New York, 2004.

Favier, Jean. *Charlemagne*. Paris, 1999.

Hägermann, Dieter. *Karl der Grosse: Herrscher des Abendlandes*. Munich, 2000.

McKitterick, Rosamond. *Charlemagne: The Formation of a European Identity*. Cambridge, 2008.

Scholarship on Einhard

Berschin, Walter. "Einhart." In *Biographie und Epochenstil im lateinischen Mittelalter*, vol. 3, Quellen und Untersuchungen zur lateinischen Philologie des Mittelalters 10:199–220. Stuttgart, 1991.

Beumann, Helmut. "Topos und Gedenkengefüge bei Einhard." *Archiv für Kulturgeschichte* 33 (1951): 337–50.

Collins, John F. *Einhard "Vita Karoli Magni."* Bryn Mawr Latin Commentaries. Bryn Mawr, 1984.

Fleckenstein, Josef. "Einhard." In *Lexikon des Mittelalters*, vol. 3, cols. 1737–39. Munich, 1999.

Ganshof, François-Louis. "Einhard: Biographer of Charlemagne." In *The Carolingians and the Frankish Monarchy*, 1–16. Translated by Janet Sondheimer. Ithaca, 1967.

Ganz, David. "Einhard's Charlemagne: The Characterization of Greatness." In *Charlemagne: Empire and Society*, edited by Joanna Story, 38–51. Manchester, 2005.

———. "Einhardus peccator." Chap. 3 in *Lay Intellectuals in the Carolingian World*, edited by Patrick Wormald and Janet L. Nelson. Cambridge, 2007.

———. "The Preface to Einhard's 'Vita Karoli.'" In *Einhard: Studien zu Leben und Werk; Dem Gedenken an Helmut Beumann gewidmet*, edited by Hermann Schefers, Arbeiten der Hessischen Historischen Kommission, n.s., 12:299–310. Darmstadt, 1997.

Hageneier, Lars. *Jenseits der Topik: Die karolingische Herrscherbiographie.* Historische Studien 483. Husum, 2004.

Halphen, Louis. "Einhard, historien de Charlemagne." In *Études critiques sur l'histoire de Charlemagne,* 60–103. Paris, 1921.

Hellmann, Siegmund. "Einhards literarische Stellung." In *Ausgewählte Abhandlungen zur Historiographie und Geistesgeschichte des Mittelalters,* edited by Helmut Beumann, 159–229. Darmstadt, 1961 (orig. 1932).

Hoffmann, Heinrich. *Karl der Grosse im Bilde der Geschichtschreibung des frühen Mittelalters (800–1250).* Historische Studien 137. Berlin, 1919.

Innes, Matthew. "The Classical Tradition in the Carolingian Renaissance: Ninth-Century Encounters with Suetonius." *International Journal of the Classical Tradition* 3 (1997): 265–82.

Kempshall, Matthew. "Some Ciceronian Models for Einhard's Life of Charlemagne." *Viator* 26 (1995): 11–37.

Krüger, Karl Heinrich. "Neue Beobachtungen zur Datierung von Einhards Karlsvita." *Frühmittelalterliche Studien* 32 (1998): 124–45.

Latowsky, Anne. "Foreign Embassies and Roman Universality in Einhard's *Life of Charlemagne.*" *Florilegium* 22 (2005): 25–57.

Lehmann, Paul. "Das literarische Bild Karls des Grossen." In *Erforschung des Mittelalters,* 154–207. Leipzig, 1941.

Lintzel, Martin. "Die Zeit der Entstehung von Einhards Vita Karoli." In *Kritische Beiträge zur Geschichte des Mittelalters: Festschrift für Robert Holtzmann,* Historische Studien 238:22–42. 1933. Repr., Vaduz, 1965.

Löwe, Heinz. "Die Entstehungszeit der Vita Karoli Einhards." *Deutsches Archiv für Erforschung des Mittelalters* 39 (1983): 85–103.

McKitterick, Rosamond, and Matthew Innes. "The Writing of History." In *Carolingian Culture: Emulation and Innovation,* edited by Rosamond McKitterick, 193–220. Cambridge, 1994.

Meyers, Jean. "Éginhard et Suétone: À propos des chapitres 18 á 27 de la *Vita Karoli.*" In *Les historiens et le Latin médiévale,* edited by Monique Goullet and Michel Parisse, 129–50. Paris, 2001.

Morrissey, Robert. *Charlemagne and France: A Thousand Years of Mythology.* Translated by Catherine Tihanyi. Notre Dame, 2003.

Noble, Thomas F. X. "Greatness Contested and Confirmed: Remembering Charlemagne in the Ninth Century." In *The Legend of Charlemagne in the Middle Ages: Power, Faith, and Crusade,* edited by Matthew Gabriele and Jace Stuckey, 3–21. New York, 2008.

Schefers, Hermann. "Einhard und die Hofschule." In *Einhard: Studien zu Leben und Werk; Dem Gedenken an Helmut Beumann gewidmet,* edited by Hermann Schefers, Arbeiten der Hessihcen Historischen Kommission, n.s., 12:81–93. Darmstadt, 1997.

Smith, Julia M. H. "'Emending Evil Ways and Praising God's Omnipotence': Einhard and the Uses of Roman Martyrs." In *Conversion in Late Antiquity and the Early Middle Ages,* edited by Kenneth Mills and Anthony Grafton, 189–223. Rochester, 2003.

———. "Einhard: The Sinner and the Saints." *Transactions of the Royal Historical Society* 13 (2003): 55–77.

Störmer, Wilhelm. "Einhards Herkunft—Überlegungen und Beobachtungen zu Einhards Erbesitz und familiärem Umfeld." In *Einhard: Studien zu Leben und Werk; Dem*

Gedenken an Helmut Beumann gewidmet, edited by Hermann Schefers, Arbeite der Hessischen Historischen Kommission, n.s., 12:15–39. Darmstadt, 1997.

Tischler, Matthias. *Einharts Vita Karoli: Studien zur Entstehung, Überlieferung und Rezeption.* 2 vols. Schriften der MGH 48. Hannover, 2001.

Wolter, Heinz. "Intention und Herrscherbild in Einhards Vita Karoli Magni." *Archiv für Kulturgeschichte* 68 (1986): 295–317.

THE LIFE OF CHARLES THE EMPEROR

Einhard

The Prologue of Walahfrid Strabo to the Life of Charles the Great

It is accepted that it was Einhard who wrote as follows in purest truth about the life and deeds of the glorious emperor Charles the Great. He was a man most worthy of praise among all the palace officials of his time, not only for his accurate knowledge—his testimony gains strength because he was an eyewitness to almost everything—but also for the complete honesty of his mores. He was born in eastern Francia in the district called Maingau. He received the basic elements of his education as a little boy in the monastery of Fulda, the house established by the martyr Saint Boniface. He was soon transferred by Baugulf, the abbot of the aforesaid monastery, to Charles's palace, not so much on account of his noble birth as because of the gift that was so marked in him, namely the exceptional ability and intelligence that even then gave promise of the remarkable knowledge that later shone so greatly in him. For of all kings Charles was most eager to seek out wise men so that they could think deeply in full comfort and improve with every science the darkness—or, as I might say, the widespread blindness—of the kingdom committed to him by God and bring back to this barbarian realm the light up to then largely unknown, with God illuminating and watching. Now, however, the light of knowledge is, on the contrary, perishing again because learning is less cherished and fewer possess it.

So this little man—for he was awfully short—attained such a growth of fame for his wisdom and probity in the court of Charles, who was himself a lover of knowledge, that among all the ministers of his royal majesty there was no one with whom the king, the most powerful and wise of those days, would share his private affairs with greater confidence. And this was entirely right, for not only in the time of Charles himself but—and this is even more amazing—under Emperor Louis, when different and numerous disturbances stirred up the Frankish state and things were collapsing in many ways, he knew how to look out for himself, with God looking over him, in a certain marvelous balance that was surely divinely provided. His lofty reputation, which for many brings envy and a fall, did not desert him, nor did his reputation subject him to irremediable dangers.

We say these things so that no one will have any doubts about his words just because he did not know him. The particular praise for his beloved patron might provoke the curiosity of the reader about his farseeing truthfulness.

I, Strabo, have inserted titles and divisions into this little work, as it seemed fitting to do, so that whoever seeks out individual points may find more easily whatever he pleases.

Einhard's Prologue

After I conceived the idea to set forth the life and character and no small part of the accomplishments of my lord and foster father[1] Charles, the most excellent and justly famous king, I carried out the huge task as briefly as I could. I neither omitted anything about those matters that had come to my attention nor offended with a long-winded narration those who find new things distasteful—if, indeed, it is actually possible to avoid offending with a new work those who find disagreeable even the old masterpieces composed by the most learned and eloquent of men.

Still, I do not doubt that there are many, devoted to leisure and letters, who do not think that the conditions of the present age should be neglected or that everything that happens now is unworthy to be remembered and should be consigned to silence and oblivion. Even so, seduced by their love of immortality, they prefer to insert into whatever they are writing the well-known deeds of other people rather than, by writing nothing, strip the fame of their own names from posterity's memory. Nevertheless, I did not see any reason to hold back from a book of this sort, because I was aware that no one could write these things more truthfully than I, since I was there and I knew confidently, as they say, what I saw going on around me. And I simply did not know whether these events would be recorded by anyone else. I judged it better to

---

1. *Nutritor:* Einhard signals that he owed his upbringing to Charles.

hand on to posterity my remembrances, along with the common reports of other writers, than to permit the distinguished life and tremendous deeds, virtually inimitable by men of these days, of this most excellent king, in his time the greatest of all, to be veiled by the darkness of oblivion.

There remains one more reason, a perfectly reasonable one, I think, that might by itself have impelled me to write these things down: the fosterage that he bestowed upon me and also my unceasing friendship with him and with his children from the time when I began to associate with them in the court. He so won me over and put me in his debt, in both life and death, that I would seem, and indeed actually be, ungrateful if, unmindful of so many kindnesses lavished upon me, I passed over in silence the remarkable and distinguished deeds of this man who deserved the best from me, and if I allowed his life to remain without a written account or its due praise, as if he had never lived. To write and explain such a life it is not my scant skill, which is meager and small, practically nonexistent, that is needed, but the gifts of a Cicero.

Here you have a book with a memorial of the most distinguished and greatest of men, in which there is nothing for you to admire except his deeds, unless perhaps you think that a barbarian, modestly equipped in the Roman language, has been able to write something aptly and properly in the Latin language. Indeed, I rushed forth with such great impudence as I think Cicero was condemning when he was speaking about Latin authors in the first book of his *Tusculan Disputations:* "for someone to put down his thoughts in writing when he can neither organize nor clarify them, nor attract a reader with a certain charm, is an extravagant waste of time and effort."[2] This opinion of the famous orator might have deterred me from writing except that I had already decided it was better to write this book, incur the condemnations of some men, and accept some damage to my little reputation than to spare myself by passing over the memory of such a great man.

[The Life of Charles the Emperor]

(1) The family of the Merovingians, from which the Franks had been accustomed to make their kings, is considered to have lasted right down to King Childeric,[3] who was deposed, tonsured, and forced into a monastery on the

---

2. *Tusculan Disputations,* 1.3.6.
3. The third of this name. He reigned from 743 to 751.

order of the Roman pontiff, Stephen.[4] Although it might appear that the family came to its end in him, actually it had possessed no vitality for a long time already and could boast nothing better for itself than the empty title of king. Indeed, the resources and power of the realm were in the hands of the prefects of the palace, who were called mayors of the palace and to whom the highest authority belonged.[5] In fact, nothing was left to the king except to be happy with the royal title and to sit on his throne with his flowing hair and long beard and to behave as if he had authority, hearing envoys who came from all over and dismissing them with answers that he had been taught, or even commanded, to give. Apart from the empty name of king and a precarious stipend that the prefect of the court extended to him as he wished, he had nothing else of his own except one estate with a tiny income, a house, and a small number of servants, who obeyed him and provided for his basic needs. When he had to travel about, he went in a cart pulled by yoked oxen and led by a plowman in the country fashion. Thus he used to go to the palace or to the public meeting of his people that was held annually for the benefit of the kingdom. The prefect of the court managed everything that had to be done or organized at home or abroad for the administration of the kingdom.

(2) Pippin, the father of King Charles, was already acting in that capacity as if by hereditary right when Childeric was deposed. For his father, Charles,[6] used to discharge quite capably the very same magistracy that his own father, Pippin [II],[7] had left to him. It was Charles who crushed the tyrants who were claiming dominion for themselves throughout all of Francia,[8] and as for the Saracens who were trying to occupy Gaul, he so defeated them in two great battles, one in Aquitaine near Poitiers and the other near Narbonne on the River Berre, that they were compelled to return to Spain.[9] The people generally did

4. Pope from 752 to 757. He visited Francia in 754, but it was Pope Zachary (741–52) who, according to most sources, authorized the Franks to make Pippin their king in 751.

5. Einhard uses several different terms for the office that historians usually call the mayor of the palace: *palatii praefectos, maiores domus, praefectus aulae*. Einhard may be trying to vary his style, or it may be that since the office was abolished by the Carolingians when they became kings, its precise name had been forgotten. Or maybe it never had a single "official" name.

6. Charles Martel, mayor of the palace from 714 to 741, although securely only after 717.

7. Pippin II "of Herstal," mayor of the palace first in Austrasia and then in the whole Frankish realm. He died in 714. Pippin had at least two sons by his first wife, Plektrude. Both had died by 714, but one had a son whose cause his grandmother championed. Charles Martel was born of a second wife, Alpaida. To secure his own tenure of the mayoral office, he had to circumvent Plektrude, her grandson, and various Frankish magnates.

8. This curious remark relates to the intense political turmoil that followed the death of Pippin II in 714.

9. The first in 733 and the second in 737.

not give this office to anyone except those who outshone others in the distinction of their birth and the size of their fortune.

Pippin, the father of King Charles, held this office for a few years as if he were under that above-mentioned king.[10] The office had been left to himself and to his brother Carloman by their father and grandfather, and they shared it in the greatest harmony. But then his brother Carloman, for some unknown reason, although it seems that he was inflamed by a desire for the contemplative way of life, abandoned the burdensome cares of the earthly kingdom, went to Rome to seek his peace, and there changed his garments and became a monk. He built a monastery on Monte Soratte,[11] near the church of St. Sylvester, and with the brothers who came there to join him, he enjoyed for a few years the calm he so desired. But when many of the nobles from Francia solemnly visited Rome to fulfill their vows, they did not wish to miss seeing this man who was once their lord. Their constant visits disrupted the leisure in which he took such delight, and compelled him to move. When he finally saw that a throng of this sort was going to interfere with his aims, he left Monte Soratte and went away to the monastery of St. Benedict located at the fortress of Casino[12] in the province of Samnium. There he passed the earthly time that was left to him by fully embracing the religious life.[13]

(3) Pippin, however, who was prefect of the palace, was made king on the authority of the Roman pontiff, and he ruled the Franks alone for fifteen years or more.[14] Having brought to an end the Aquitainian war, which, once begun, he waged for nine straight years against Duke Waifar of Aquitaine, Pippin died of edema[15] in Paris. He left behind two children,[16] Charles and Carloman, to

10. Actually, the Merovingian throne was left vacant between 737 and 743 and then filled because some people, especially in frontier regions, who had often resented obeying the Merovingians, objected even more to having to obey the Carolingians.

11. A small town about twenty kilometers northeast of Rome.

12. Einhard says "in castro Casino" where one might have expected "in monte Casino."

13. In fact, Carloman was drawn by some of Pippin's opponents into the politics of the Frankish change of dynasty in 753–54. Some sources even say that King Aistulf of the Lombards prevailed upon the abbot of Monte Cassino to send Carloman to intervene. Carloman did travel to the north and died there in 754.

14. In fact, 751–68. Einhard holds to the family line in insisting that the papacy commanded Pippin to be made king. The Carolingians were, after all, usurpers. Some scholars doubt this papal role.

15. An excessive accumulation of fluid beneath the skin, formerly called dropsy: *morbo aquae intercutis.*

16. Einhard says *liberis,* which literally means "children," even though only sons are named here. But the boys had a sister, Gisela, so there were at least three "children." Another son, Pippin, died in 761.

whom the succession to the kingdom passed by divine will. The Franks, indeed, having gathered in a general assembly, solemnly made both kings after setting forth this condition: the entire kingdom was to be divided equally, with Charles receiving that portion which his father Pippin had ruled and Carloman getting the portion their uncle Carloman had once ruled. These conditions were acceptable to both, and each received the portion of the kingdom allotted to him by the plan.[17] This harmony persisted, but only with the greatest difficulty, because many of Carloman's supporters were trying to drive the heirs apart and some were actually scheming to commit them to war. The way things actually turned out showed that there was more suspicion than danger in the situation, for when Carloman died, his wife[18] and sons and a number of his chief nobles sought refuge in Italy. For no reason at all, and having spurned her husband's brother, Carloman's widow placed herself and her children under the protection of Desiderius, the king of the Lombards.[19]

(4) I think it would be useless to try to write about his birth, infancy, or boyhood, since nothing is written down anywhere, and there is no one alive who says he has any information about those times. Leaving aside what cannot be known, I intend to pass on to the deeds, habits, and other aspects of his life that ought to be explained and set forth. Nevertheless, so that I pass over none of those things that are worthy or necessary to know, I shall begin by telling of his deeds at home or abroad, move on to his habits and interests, and finish with his governance of the kingdom.

(5) Of all the wars he waged, he began with one in Aquitaine, started but not completed by his father, because he thought it could be finished quickly. His brother was still alive then and was even asked for his assistance. Although his brother disappointed him by denying aid, he carried out the campaign with the greatest energy once it got under way, for he did not wish to stop what he had started or to abandon what he had begun. Charles struggled with determination and persistence to achieve his goals completely. He compelled Hunold, who tried to take over Aquitaine after Waifar's death and to stir up a war that was almost finished, to abandon Aquitaine and head for Gascony.

17. Einhard is not accurate here. He seems to repeat what is known of the division of 741 effected by Charles Martel between his sons Pippin and Carloman. Many aspects of the division of 768 remain unclear, but it appears that Charles got a great arc of lands running from central Germany, along the North Sea coast, and southward along the Channel and Atlantic coasts to Gascony. Carloman got a core of lands running from the Paris basin to Provence.

18. Gerberga was her name.

19. Reigned from 757 to 774.

Charles, however, was not willing to let him stay there, so he crossed the broad Garonne and commanded Duke Lupus of Gascony to hand over the fugitive, and to do it quickly or run the risk of war. Lupus, following the wiser plan, not only handed over Hunold but also submitted himself and the province over which he ruled to the authority of Charles.

(6) After affairs in Aquitaine were settled, the war there was brought to a conclusion, and his partner in rule[20] having departed the cares of the world, Charles, stirred up by the request and pleas of Hadrian,[21] the bishop of the city of Rome, began a war against the Lombards. This war had been begun by his father on the request of Pope Stephen, but only with the greatest difficulty, because some of the most important Franks, with whom Pippin was accustomed to consult, struggled against his plan to such a degree that they loudly pronounced themselves willing to desert from his army and go home. Nevertheless, at that time, the war was started and finished very quickly against King Aistulf.[22] Whereas it seemed that he and his father had similar, or rather the same, reasons for going to war, the wars were scarcely alike in the effort expended in them or in their outcomes. For Pippin, after besieging Pavia for only a few days, had forced King Aistulf to hand over hostages, to restore the towns and fortifications he had taken from the Romans, and to swear an oath that he would not recapture what he had returned.[23] Charles, however, once he had started his own war, did not stop until he had worn down King Desiderius in a long siege and received his submission. Adalgis, the king's son on whom all the hopes of the Lombards seemed to rest, was expelled from the kingdom and even from Italy. He [Charles] restored everything that had been taken from the Romans. He also crushed Duke Rotgaud of Friuli,[24] who was plotting a new uprising, and in order to submit all of Italy to his command, he made his son Pippin king.[25]

At this point I could describe how difficult the crossing of the Alps and the entry into Italy was, and how the Franks struggled to overcome trackless

20. His brother, Carloman.

21. Reigned from 772 to 795.

22. Reigned from 749 to 756.

23. Einhard compresses his account a bit: Pippin fought two campaigns in Italy, in 755 and 756, and concluded peace with Aistulf twice, demanding on the second occasion substantial indemnities.

24. Einhard calls Rotgaud *Forojuliani ducatus praefectum* (the one presiding over the Duchy of Friuli) instead of *Forojuliani ducem* (duke of Friuli), which suggests that he may have been trying to call his legitimacy into question. Rotgaud rebelled in 776.

25. Here again Einhard compresses things. Charles's siege of Pavia lasted from the autumn of 773 to the late spring of 774. The rebellion of Rotgaud happened in 776. Pippin was made king in 781.

mountains, peaks that reached up to the sky, and sharp rocks, except that it is my plan in the present work to relate the manner of his life more than the events of his wars. The outcome of this war was that Italy was conquered, King Desiderius was sent into perpetual exile, his son Adalgis was deported from Italy, and the properties snatched by the Lombard kings were restored to Hadrian, the rector of the Roman Church.

(7) After the end of this war, the one against the Saxons, which seemed merely to have been interrupted, was begun again.[26] No other war undertaken by the Franks was longer, fiercer, or more difficult than this one because the Saxons, like almost all the peoples who live in Germany, were ferocious by nature, devoted to the cult of demons, hostile to our religion, and did not consider it shameful to defile or transgress divine or human laws. There were always issues that could disturb the peace on any day, particularly because our borders and theirs touched almost everywhere in open land, except for the few places where substantial forests or mountain ridges traced precise limits between both our lands. Murder, robbery, and arson never ceased on either side. The Franks were so irritated by these incidents that they decided the time had come to stop responding to individual incidents and to open a full-scale war against the Saxons.

So a war was begun against them, and it was fought for thirty continuous years with great hatred on both sides, although with more damage to the Saxons than to the Franks. The war could have been ended sooner had not the perfidy of the Saxons prevented this. It is very hard to say how many times they were beaten and handed themselves over as suppliants to the king, made promises relating to the conduct that was required of them, turned over without delay the hostages that were demanded of them, and received the envoys that were sent to them. Several times they were so beaten and weakened that they promised they would abandon the cult of demons and willingly submit to the Christian religion. But just as they were sometimes inclined to do these things, so too they were quick to go right back to their old ways, such that it was not easy to decide which of these ways of acting was actually easier for them. Indeed, after the beginning of this war there was scarcely a year without a reversal of this kind. Yet the king's greatness of spirit and constant determination, in both good times and bad, could not be overcome by any changeability, nor did he tire of any task once he had begun it. For he was

---

26. Einhard is acknowledging, without details, that Charles had warred with the Saxons in 772 before breaking off those hostilities to go to Italy.

never willing to tolerate with impunity people who perpetrated such things, and he avenged their treachery and exacted a suitable punishment either by leading an army against them or by sending one under his counts, right up to the point when, with all of those who were used to resisting him either struck down or else returned to his power, he transported ten thousand of the men who lived along the Elbe, along with their wives and little children, and dispersed them in little groups in various places in Gaul and Germany. So the war that was drawn out for so many years was seen to be brought to a conclusion, on terms proposed by the king and accepted by the Saxons. They had to abandon the cult of demons and let go of their ancestral rites, receive the sacraments of the Christian faith and religion, and unite themselves to the Franks so that they might become one people with them.

(8) Although this war dragged on for a very long time, he himself joined battle with the enemy not more than twice, in a single month with only a few intervening days, once near the mountain that is called Osning in a place called Detmold and again on the River Haase. In these two battles the enemy were so crushed and conquered that subsequently they did not dare to provoke the king or to resist his approach unless they were protected by some fortification. Many nobles and holders of high office, both Franks and Saxons, perished in that war. It was finally brought to a close in its thirty-third year, but in the meantime many great wars against the Franks broke out in various parts of the land. The king managed them with such ingenuity that anyone who looked into the matter might well wonder whether it was more appropriate to marvel at the king's determination or his good fortune. Although this war began two years before the Italian one and was waged without cease, nevertheless nothing was overlooked in the wars that had to be waged elsewhere, nor was there anyplace a cessation of hostilities because of that burdensome struggle. For the king, of all those who ruled over peoples in his time, was the wisest and most outstanding in the greatness of his soul. No effort could deter and no danger shake him from beginning anything or bringing it to a conclusion. He learned to size up and to bear each situation on its own terms. He simply would not yield to adversity, nor, in good times, would he succumb to the false flattery of good luck.

(9) While he was carrying out the war with the Saxons persistently, indeed almost continuously, he established garrisons at appropriate places and set out for Spain with the greatest military force he could muster. After crossing the Pyrenees, he received the submission of every town and fortification that he

approached, and his army came back safe and sound except that on his return, in the heights of those very Pyrenees, it happened that he had a brief taste of Basque treachery. With his army stretched out and advancing in a long column, for that was all that the narrowness of the area permitted, the Basques laid their ambush right on the tops of the mountains. The area is especially suited to ambushes because of the dense and very deep forests. They fell upon the last part of the baggage train and those who were protecting the troops at the very back of the column, as well as those who had gone on ahead into the valley below. Having joined with them in combat, the Basques killed practically every one of the Franks. Protected by night, which was just falling, they snatched up the baggage and as quickly as possible scattered in every direction. The Basques were much assisted in this battle by the lightness of their arms and the lay of the land, whereas the heaviness of their arms and the unevenness of the land rendered the Franks utterly unequal to the Basques. Among many others who fell in this battle were Eggihard, the overseer of the royal table, Anselm, the count of the palace,[27] and Roland, the prefect of the Breton March.[28] Charles could not take revenge at that time because, after the attack, the enemy scattered, leaving no hint of where in the world they might be sought.

(10) He also subdued the Bretons, who lived along the seacoast in the westernmost part of Gaul. He heard that they were not subject to him, so he sent an expedition against them that compelled them to hand over hostages and to promise to do whatever they were told.[29]

He himself afterward set out for Italy with an army and, marching right through Rome, approached the Campanian city of Capua, where he pitched camp and threatened the Beneventans with war unless they submitted to him.[30] Anticipating the struggle, Arichis, the duke of these people, sent his sons, Romuald and Grimoald, to the king with a great deal of money and asked him to accept them as hostages. He promised that he and his people were ready to do what the king demanded, except for one thing: he did not

27. The count of the palace was the chief judicial officer and performed various other duties. He should not be confused with the mayor of the palace, which the Carolingians suppressed.

28. It is not clear that the Breton March, a triangle of land running from Rennes to Nantes to Vannes, effectively under martial law, had been formally organized this early. But the kings of the Franks had been trying to guard the Breton frontier since the sixth century. Roland is the hero of the later (ca. 1100) *La chanson de Roland*. Interestingly, there is one class of Einhard manuscripts (the "B" class) that omits mention of Roland.

29. This campaign took place in 786.

30. These events took place in 787.

want to be forced to meet with the king. Thinking more about the interests of the people than the stubbornness of their duke, the king accepted the hostages that had been offered to him, agreed that in return for a large gift he would not make the duke appear before him, and, retaining one of Arichis' sons, the younger one, as a hostage, sent the older one back to his father. He also left legates with Arichis to demand and to receive an oath of allegiance from the Beneventans. Charles then went back to Rome, and after he had spent a few days there venerating the holy places, he returned to Gaul.

(11) And then, in Bavaria, a war both broke out suddenly and was quickly brought to an end. The haughtiness and foolhardiness of Duke Tassilo stirred it up. He was egged on by his wife, who was a daughter of King Desiderius and thought she might be able to avenge her father's exile through her husband.[31] She urged him, after he had made a pact with the Huns,[32] who were the neighbors of the Bavarians to the east, not only to refuse the king's commands but even to start a war with him. The king's boldness simply could not bear the duke's surpassing defiance. And so he collected his forces from all over and got ready to invade Bavaria. Charles himself, with a great army, arrived at the River Lech, the river that separates the Bavarians from the Alemans.[33] Having pitched his camp on the bank of the river, he decided that, before he entered the province, he would see if he could gauge the duke's thinking by means of envoys. Tassilo thought it over and concluded that nothing useful was to be gained by him or his people through further obstinacy, so he submitted humbly to the king, handed over the hostages that were demanded, including his son Theodo, and, what is more, swore an oath that no matter who might try to persuade him, he would not defect from the king's power. And so that war, which looked like it was going to be immensely protracted, was brought to an end very quickly. Tassilo, after he had been summoned to the king, was

31. Her name was Liutperga. Einhard's account here is intriguing. Desiderius had four daughters and a son. One daughter, Anselperga, became abbess of the convent of San Salvatore in Brescia. Another daughter, Adelperga, was the wife of Arichis of Benevento and the mother of his sons. A portion of chapter 10 above is devoted to them. Einhard says later, in chapter 18, that Charles himself was briefly married to and then repudiated yet another daughter, whose name was probably Gerperga. Recall, too, that when Charles took Pavia (c. 6 above), he exiled not only Desiderius but also his son, Adalgis (c. 6 above). Einhard thus provides the key facts about, but no explanation of, this remarkable family constellation that Charles systematically dismantled.

32. Actually not Huns, but Avars, a people from the frontier regions of China and Mongolia who, like the Huns before them, traversed the Russian steppes and settled in the middle Danube basin in the mid–sixth century.

33. The people of southwestern Germany who inhabited the region more familiarly known as Swabia.

not permitted to go home, and the province he had held was not given to another duke but instead was assigned to counts to rule.[34]

(12) So, these rebellions having been put down, war was carried to the Slavs,[35] whom we customarily call Wilzi but who are properly, that is, in their own language, called Welatabi. In that war, the Saxons fought as auxiliaries, just like the other peoples who followed the royal standard and command, although their obedience was feigned and less devoted. The cause of the war was that the Abotrits, who had earlier allied with the Franks, were suffering from constant attacks, and the Wilzi could not be compelled to stop by commands.

A certain bay extends to the east from the Western Ocean.[36] It is of unknown length, and its width never exceeds one hundred miles and is often much narrower. Many peoples live around it. The Danes and Swedes, whom we call Northmen, hold the northern shore and the islands along it. Slavs, Estonians, and various other peoples live along the eastern shore. The Welatabi were the most prominent among them, and it was against them that the king was commencing a war. In just one campaign, which he waged himself, Charles so smashed and dominated them that they never again thought of refusing to obey his commands.

(13) The war he initiated with the Avars, or Huns, was the greatest of all the wars he waged, except for that against the Saxons, to which this one succeeded.[37] He managed this war with more spirit and greater preparation than any other. Still, he himself made only one expedition into Pannonia, the province that those people then inhabited, and he left the rest to be accomplished by his son Pippin, by the prefects of the province, by counts, and even by envoys. The war was prosecuted by them with the greatest energy and was brought to an end in its eighth year. How many battles were fought in that

34. Einhard makes a hash of Charles's encounter with Tassilo. In 787 Charles did march three armies against Bavaria. Tassilo submitted, but in 788, perhaps indeed on his wife's prompting, broke his oaths. Charles went to Bavaria again, and this time Tassilo was sentenced to death, and Bavaria was assigned to counts, and later to a prefect, Gerold, who was the brother of one of Charles's wives, Hildegard. Tassilo's death sentence was commuted to exile, and he was sent to a monastery in Francia, where he lived out his days. It is possible that Einhard deliberately compressed this story and that his account is further evidence for the *damnatio memoriae* visited by the Carolingian court on the family of Tassilo.

35. In 789.

36. He is referring to the Baltic Sea.

37. This war went through several stages from 788 to 805, with the major campaigns in 791 and 796.

war, and how much blood was shed, is revealed by the fact that Pannonia was emptied of human inhabitants and the place where the khagan's palace used to be was so deserted that it left no trace of human habitation. The entire nobility of the Huns perished in that war, and their whole reputation collapsed. All the money and treasure they had accumulated over a long time was pillaged, and the mind of man could not recall any war in which the Franks were so endowed with booty and wealth. Indeed, up to then they had seemed almost poor, but so much gold and silver was found in the palace, so many spoils hauled off in battles, that one might well think that the Franks had justly snatched from the Huns what the Huns had previously and unjustly snatched from other peoples.

Only two of the foremost Franks fell in that war, Eric, the duke of Friuli,[38] who was killed in Liburnia, near the maritime city of Tersatto, in an ambush by the town's residents, and Gerold, the prefect of Bavaria, who was killed in Pannonia along with two escorts—it is not known by whom—when he had arranged his troops for battle and they were riding along encouraging each man. For the rest, this war was almost bloodless for the Franks, and it had a most advantageous outcome even though it dragged on for a long time, owing to its importance.

Subsequently, the Saxon war received a conclusion that was well suited to its long duration. The Bohemian and Linonian wars,[39] which arose later on, did not take very long and were both brought to an end quickly under the leadership of the younger Charles.[40]

(14) The last war he began was against the Northmen who are called Danes. They initially practiced piracy and then devastated the shores of Gaul and Germany with a large fleet. Their king, Godfred, was so puffed up with vain ambition that he claimed for himself control over all of Germany; indeed, he used to think of Frisia and Saxony as if they were his own provinces, and he had already drawn his neighbors, the Abotrits, under his authority and made them pay him tribute. He even boasted that he would soon arrive with a large army before Aachen, where the king held his court. Although vain as they could be, his words were not entirely disbelieved, because it was thought that

38. Eric died in 799 in events unconnected with the Avar war.

39. The Linones were an obscure group who lived near the Abotrits, mentioned in chapter 12 above and chapter 14 below.

40. That is, Charles's eldest son. The Bohemian campaign took place in 805. There were two campaigns against the Linonians, in 808 and 811.

he might venture something like this, until a premature death prevented him from doing so. For he was killed by one of his followers, and both his life and his planned war came to a swift end.[41]

(15) These are the wars that the most powerful king waged in various parts of the world with great wisdom and good fortune over forty-seven years—for that is how long he reigned.[42] The kingdom of the Franks, which he had received from his father, was large and powerful, but by these wars he admirably expanded it and almost doubled its size. Originally no more land was occupied by those Franks who are called eastern[43] than that part of Gaul which lies between the Rhine and the Loire, the Ocean,[44] and the Balearic Sea, and that part of Germany situated between Saxony and the Danube, the Rhine, and the Saal, the river that divides the Thuringians and the Sorbs. What is more, the Alemans and Bavarians used to submit to the authority of the Frankish kingdom.[45] In the wars just mentioned, he first added Aquitaine and Gascony and the whole range of the Pyrenees right up to the Ebro River, which rises in Navarre, flows across the extremely fertile fields of Spain, and joins the Balearic Sea under the walls of the city of Tortosa. Then he took all of Italy, which extends more than a thousand miles from Aosta to lower Calabria, where the border runs between the Beneventans and the Greeks. Next, he conquered Saxony, which is not a small part of Germany and is about twice as wide as the land occupied by the Franks and similar to it in length.[46] After that he added both parts of Pannonia,[47] Dacia beyond the Danube,[48] Istria, Liburnia, and Dalmatia, except for the maritime cities, which, on account of friendship and of the treaty he had concluded with the emperor at Constantinople,[49] he permitted him to keep. Moreover, he so dominated all the ferocious and

41. Godfred attacked the Abotrits (Frankish allies against the Wilzi, as noted in c. 12 above) in 808, ravaged the Frisian coast with a large fleet—two hundred ships—in 810, and was murdered later in that same year.

42. Pippin III died September 24, 768, and Charles died January 28, 814.

43. It is hard to say what Einhard has in mind here. "Eastern" Franks would presumably have been the inhabitants of Austrasia, the old Merovingian realm that ran from the Paris basin to the Rhine. Since Charles's family were Austrasian Franks, Einhard seems to attribute to them rule over all the Frankish lands.

44. Here Einhard is referring to the North Sea.

45. Einhard has already treated Bavaria with a circumspection that verges on dishonesty. The Franks defeated the Alemans in a bloody battle at Cannstadt in 746, and Alemannia was not fully reconciled to Frankish rule until well into the ninth century.

46. Einhard seems to be referring to Franconia and not to all the lands ruled by the Franks.

47. That is, the areas both north and south of the Danube.

48. "Beyond" (in *in altera Danubii ripa*) means "north of."

49. Nicephorus I (802–11). Presumably the year is 810.

barbarous peoples who lived between the Rhine and Vistula rivers, and between the Ocean[50] and the Danube, peoples who were pretty similar in language but very different in customs and character, that he made them pay tribute. The most important among these were the Welatabi, Sorbs, Abotrits, and Bohemians, with whom indeed he had armed conflict, but he received the submission of the others, whose number was much greater.

(16) He also increased the glory of his kingdom by building friendly relations with certain kings and peoples. Indeed, Charles so won over King Alfonso[51] of Galicia and Asturias that whenever Alfonso sent him letters or envoys, he commanded that in the king's presence he should be called the king's own man.[52] By his generosity, he so bent the kings of the Irish to his will that they never called him anything but lord and themselves his subjects and servants.[53] Letters sent by them to him survive and reveal feelings of this sort toward him on their part.

He had such friendly and harmonious relations with Harun,[54] the king of the Persians who held virtually the whole East except for India, that Harun preferred his goodwill to that of all the other kings and princes in the world and judged him alone to be worth cultivating by respect and generosity. So it was that when Charles's envoys, whom he had sent with gifts to the most Holy Sepulchre of our Lord and Savior and to the place of his resurrection, appeared before Harun and announced to him the will of their lord, he not only agreed to what they asked him but even decreed that that holy and life-giving place should be assigned to Charles's authority. Harun added his own envoys to Charles's returning ones and sent him immense gifts, among which were robes, perfumes, and rich treasures from eastern lands. A few years earlier Harun had sent him the only elephant he then possessed, simply because the king asked for it.[55]

50. The Baltic Sea.

51. Alfonso II, "the Chaste," reigned from 791 to 842.

52. In translating this sentence I have supplied proper names, whereas Einhard uses only pronouns. One embassy from Alfonso II is known to have come in 797.

53. This passage is puzzling, for there is no evidence of relations between Charles and Irish kings.

54. Harun al-Rashid, the Abbasid caliph of Baghdad, 786–809.

55. Einhard compresses and confuses events here. In 799 Charles sent gifts to the Holy Land and was sent the keys to the Holy Sepulchre and a banner, a symbol of authority, by the patriarch of Jerusalem. In 801 a delegation from Harun arrived in the West accompanied by a Jew named Isaac whom Charles had sent to Baghdad in, probably, 797. This delegation brought the elephant, whose name was Abul Abbas. Other sources mention another Eastern embassy in 802 and then another in 807, this one laden with gifts.

The emperors of Constantinople, Nicephorus, Michael, and Leo,[56] were seeking even more than friendship and an alliance and sent numerous legations to him. For they strongly suspected that since he himself had received the imperial dignity,[57] he might wish for that very reason to seize the empire from them. Nevertheless, he concluded a very strong treaty with them so that no cause of offense would remain on either side.[58] The Romans and the Greeks had always had suspicions about Frankish power, whence the Greek proverb: "If you have a Frank for a friend, he is surely not your neighbor."[59]

(17) Even though he showed his greatness in expanding his kingdom and subjugating foreign peoples, indeed in constantly occupying himself with such efforts, he nevertheless in many places initiated numerous projects bearing on the attractiveness and convenience of his kingdom. He even finished some of them. It is just to think that the finest among them are the basilica of the Holy Mother of God at Aachen, built in the most marvelous way, and the bridge at Mainz over the Rhine, which was a half mile long, for that is the width of the river there. The bridge burned down a year before his death, and he was not able to rebuild it, on account of the suddenness of his death, although he had been thinking about replacing the wooden one with a stone bridge. He also began impressive palaces, one not far from Mainz, on the estate[60] of Ingelheim, the other at Nijmegen, on the river Waal, which flows along the south side of the island of the Batavians.[61] It came particularly to his attention that sacred buildings all over his kingdom were falling into ruin because of their age, so he commanded the bishops and fathers who had charge of them to restore them, and he took care through his envoys to see that his commands were carried out.

He also worked on a fleet against attacks by Northmen, having ships constructed for this purpose near the rivers that flowed from Gaul and Germany into the North Sea. Because the Northmen were constantly laying waste the Gallic and even the German coast with constant attacks, he set up military

56. Nicephurus I (802–11), Michael I (811–13), Leo V (813–20).

57. Einhard says *imperatoris nomen*.

58. Serious and lengthy negotiations there were, but they were not yet concluded when Charles died in 814. Moreover, Nicephurus always regarded Charles as a usurper and refused to negotiate with him seriously about the imperial office.

59. Einhard gives this proverb in Greek.

60. Einhard uses the word *villa*, which suggests he means, technically, "royal estate," that is, Carolingian royal property.

61. Such is Einhard's way of referring to what is not at all an island but in fact the east-central region of the modern Netherlands (province of Gelderland).

posts and watchmen in every port and in the mouth of each river that appeared capable of admitting ships, so that by such defense works he could prevent the enemy from escaping. He did the same thing in the South, along the coast of the province of Narbonne and of Septimania, and along the whole Italian coast right down to Rome, against the Moors, who had recently been making pirate raids. As a result, in his day, Italy did not suffer any serious damage from the Moors, nor Gaul and Germany from the Northmen, except that the Etrurian city of Centumcellae was seized and destroyed by the Moors through treachery, and in Frisia certain islands lying off the shore of Germany were ravaged by Northmen.

(18) It is agreed that he protected, expanded, and adorned his kingdom in such ways. From now on I shall begin to speak about his gifts of mind, of his supreme determination, no matter whether things turned out well or poorly, and of other things pertaining to his private and domestic life.

After the death of his father, when he was sharing the kingdom with his brother, he bore his rivalry and jealousy with such patience that it seemed remarkable to everyone that he could not be provoked to anger by him. Then he married the daughter of King Desiderius of the Lombards on the urging of his mother, but he repudiated her after a year—it is not clear just why— and married Hildegard, a woman of the most distinguished nobility of the Swabian people.[62] By her he begot three sons, namely Charles, Pippin, and Louis, and a like number of daughters, Rotrude, Bertha, and Gisela.[63] He also had three other daughters, Theoderada, Hiltrude, and Rothaide, two of them by his wife Fastrada, who came of East Frankish, that is to say, German, stock, and the third by a certain concubine, whose name escapes me at the moment. After Fastrada died,[64] he married the Alemannian Liutgard, who bore him no children. After her death,[65] he had four concubines: that is, Madelgard, who bore him a daughter, Ruothild; Gersvinda, a Saxon, who had a daughter named Adaltrude; Regina, who bore him Drogo and Hugo; and Adallinda, by whom he begot Theodoric.

His mother grew to a great old age in his presence and was held in high honor. He treated her with such respect that no discord ever arose between

62. She died in 783.
63. Actually, Hildegard bore four sons—Louis had a twin, Lothar, who died very young—and five daughters, Hildegard and Adelaide also having died young.
64. In 794.
65. In 800.

them except when he divorced the daughter of King Desiderius, whom he had married on her prompting. She finally died after the death of Hildegard, after she had seen three grandsons and an equal number of granddaughters in her son's house.[66] He had her buried with great honor in the same basilica where his father had been laid to rest, St.-Denis.

He had only one sister, named Gisela, who was dedicated to the religious life when she was still a girl. He loved her, just like his mother, with great tenderness. A few years before his own death, she passed away in the very monastery where she had been professed.[67]

(19) He thought that his children ought to be educated, both his sons and his daughters, and that in the first place they should be trained in the liberal arts, to which he had applied his own effort. He required that his sons, as soon as they were old enough, be taught to ride in the Frankish way, to use weapons, and to hunt. He ordered that his daughters become adept at working with wool, with both distaff and spindle, so that they would value work and cultivate every virtue rather than grow lax through leisure.

Of all these children, he lost only two sons and one daughter before he died: Charles,[68] who was his firstborn, Pippin,[69] whom he had made king of Italy, and Rotrude,[70] his eldest daughter, whom he had betrothed to Constantine, the emperor of the Greeks.[71] Among these children, Pippin left behind one son, Bernard, and five daughters, Adalhaid, Atula, Gundrada, Bertahida, and Theodorada. The king showed a special mark of his affection for them when, after the death of Pippin, he ordered that his grandson[72] should succeed his father and that his granddaughters should be brought up with his own daughters. Despite the preeminent greatness of his spirit, he was deeply touched and driven to tears by the deaths of his sons and daughter, for affection was no less one of his distinguishing traits.

66. She died in 786.

67. The important convent of Chelles, of which she was abbess.

68. Died 811.

69. Died 810.

70. Died 810.

71. The title accorded to Constantine VI is interesting, insofar as no emperor at Byzantium ever added an ethnic dimension to his name except "Roman" or "of the Romans." For Einhard to call him emperor of the Greeks was the Frankish way of saying that the Byzantines were not uniquely the heirs to the Roman Empire and that a Roman Empire was not the only imaginable one. There is also an implied insult here: Constantine is "merely" the emperor of the Greeks.

72. Bernard I was king of Italy until he was deposed in 818, after participating, in somewhat mysterious circumstances, in a rebellion in 817. See Thegan, c. 22, and Astronomer, c. 29.

When the death of the Roman pontiff Hadrian,[73] whom he held in a special bond of friendship, was announced to him, he wept as if he had lost a brother or a deeply cherished son. For he was careful in making friends, although he made them easily, and when he joined someone to himself in this union, he kept him steadfastly and loved him devotedly.

He was so concerned about the raising of his sons and daughters that he never dined without them when he was at home and never went on a journey without them. His sons rode along beside him, while his daughters followed behind. A number of his closest associates were assigned to the end of the line of march to protect them. Although his daughters were very beautiful and deeply loved by him, it is strange to report that he never wished to give any of them to anyone, not to one of his own and not to a foreigner, as a bride. Instead, he kept them all with himself in his house right up to his death, saying that he could not possibly forgo their company. And on account of this situation, although he was fortunate in other ways, he experienced the blows of bad luck. Nevertheless, he just pretended that no suspicion of immorality had ever arisen against any of them and that no rumors had ever circulated.[74]

(20) He had a son named Pippin, born of a concubine,[75] whom I declined to mention among his other children. He was handsome but a hunchback. When his father was wintering in Bavaria, after having begun his war with the Huns,[76] he feigned sickness and conspired against his father with some of the leading Franks, who won him over with the empty promise of a kingdom. After the plot was detected and the conspirators condemned, he was tonsured and permitted to take up the religious life he had long desired in the monastery of Prüm.[77]

Earlier, there had been another powerful conspiracy against him in Germany.[78] All of the ringleaders were sent into exile, some having been blinded and some without physical punishment. Only three of the conspirators were

73. In 795.
74. As noted above, Rotrude had been affianced to the Byzantine heir in 781, but Charles broke off the marriage alliance in, probably, 788. King Offa of Mercia requested one of Charles's daughters as a bride for his son, but he was refused. Other matrimonial possibilities are unrecorded. Rotrude had a son named Louis by count Rorgo of Maine. Bertha lived openly at court with the gifted poet Angilbert. They had several children, one of whom was the historian Nithard. When Louis succeeded his father in 814, one of his first acts was to dismiss his sisters from court.
75. Other sources, which Einhard knew, say her name was Himiltrude.
76. In 792.
77. See Notker, 2.12, who says that Pippin was sent to St. Gall.
78. In 785–86. The leader was named Hardrad. The rebellion was concentrated in Thuringia.

killed. They had drawn their swords to defend themselves so they would not be captured, and they had killed a few men. They were themselves put to death because there was no other way of restraining them.

It was widely believed that the cruelty of Queen Fastrada was the cause and reason for these conspiracies. In both cases, the conspiracies against the king arose because it seemed that, in giving in to the cruelty of his wife, he had departed sharply from the kindness of his nature and his customary gentleness. Throughout the entire rest of his life he was held in the highest affection and favor by everyone, both at home and abroad, and not the slightest hint of unjust cruelty was alleged against him by anyone.

(21) He loved foreigners and took great care in receiving them, such that their very number seemed not unjustly to be a burden for his palace and his kingdom. He himself, however, because of the greatness of his spirit, was untroubled by burdens of this kind, since he was compensated for this substantial expense with praise for his generosity and with the reward of a good reputation.

(22) He was big and strong in body, very tall, but not more than seemed right, for his height was seven times the length of his own feet.[79] The top of his head was round, his eyes were very large and lively, his nose was a little longer than normal, his hair attractively gray, his face charming and cheerful, and, what is more, the authority and dignity of his bearing were very great whether he was standing or sitting. Although his neck was thick and short and his belly stuck out a bit, the shapeliness of his other members concealed these features. His step was firm, and the whole bearing of his body was manly. His voice was clear but less strong than suited the size of his body. He was very healthy except that, before he died, in the last four years of his life, he suffered from frequent fevers, and at the very end he went lame in one foot. Even then, he took many actions of his volition rather than on the advice of doctors, whom he virtually detested because they were urging him to give up meals of roasted meat, to which he was accustomed, and to get used to eating boiled meat.

He used to ride and hunt all the time, which came naturally to him. Indeed, scarcely any people can be found to equal the Franks in this skill. He took delight in the steam produced by natural hot springs, and he kept his body fit by regular swimming, at which he was so accomplished that no one

---

79. Those who examined Charles's remains in the nineteenth century estimated his height at 6′ 4″.

could be considered better than he. It was indeed on account of this that he built his palace at Aachen and that he lived there constantly in the last years of his life and right up to his death.[80] He invited not only his sons into the bath but also his luminaries and friends, and sometimes even his personal followers and his bodyguards, so that on occasion there might be a hundred or more men bathing together.

(23) He wore ancestral, that is, Frankish, clothing. Next to his body, he wore a linen shirt and linen drawers, then a tunic ringed with silk fringe, and stockings. Then he wrapped his lower legs in cloth bands and put shoes on his feet. In winter he covered his chest and shoulders with a jacket made from otter or ermine skins, put on a blue cloak, and always girded himself with a sword, whose hilt and belt were either gold or silver. Sometimes he used a jeweled sword, but only on very important feast days or when the envoys of foreign peoples arrived. He rejected foreign clothing, even if very beautiful, and never put up with wearing it except at Rome, when once on the plea of Pope Hadrian, and again on the request of his successor, Leo, he wore a long tunic and chlamys,[81] and shoes made in the Roman fashion. On feast days he walked around wearing clothes woven with gold thread, gemmed shoes, a cloak fastened with a gold pin, and a golden crown with jewels. The rest of the time, his dress was hardly different from that of the common people.

(24) He was moderate in food and drink, more moderate indeed in drink, since he detested drunkenness in any man, but especially in himself or one of his followers. He just could not abstain from food, however, and he often used to complain that fasts were bad for his body. He banqueted very rarely and only on very important feasts, but then with a large number of people. His daily meal was served in four courses apart from the roast, which he enjoyed more than any other food and which his hunters used to carry in on a spit. During the meal he listened with pleasure to some recitation or reading. He took delight in the books of Saint Augustine and, among them, particularly those entitled *The City of God*.

He was so sparing in drinking wine and every other drink that he rarely drank more than three times at dinner. In summer, after his midday meal, he ate some fruit, drank once, then took off his clothes and shoes, just as he did

---

80. It seems that construction of the Aachen complex began in 788 and that Charles began residing there regularly, although not quite exclusively, as implied here, in 794.

81. A short mantle fastened at the shoulders, worn by men in the Greek East since ancient times.

at night, and rested for two or three hours. He used to sleep at night in such a way that he interrupted his sleep four or five times not only by awaking but even by getting up. When he was getting dressed and putting on his shoes, he not only used to admit his friends but also ordered, if the count of the palace said there was any case that could not be decided without his order, litigants to be admitted, and just as if he were sitting in a court of law, he listened to the case and pronounced a decision. And not only this, but at that time he would also handle whatever tasks needed to be done that day and would give orders to any of his officials.

(25) He was prolific and enthusiastic in conversation, and he could express very clearly whatever he wanted to say. He was not satisfied with his native tongue alone but worked hard to learn foreign languages as well. Among these, he learned Latin so well that he could speak it as well as he could his own language, but he could understand Greek better than he could speak it. Indeed, he was so accomplished that he was eager to speak.

He cultivated the liberal arts most zealously, and he endowed with big rewards those teachers whom he greatly respected. To learn the rules of grammar, he listened to the old deacon, Peter of Pisa.[82] In the other disciplines he had as his teacher Alcuin, called Albinus, likewise a deacon, a man of the Saxon people from Britain, the most learned man anywhere.[83] He put in a great deal of time and work with him in learning rhetoric and dialectic and especially astronomy. He learned the art of calculation and probed with acute exertion and great curiosity the course of the stars. He also tried to write, and for this purpose he used to put tablets and booklets under the pillows on his bed, so that if he had any free time, he could train his hand at forming letters. His effort met with little success, for instead of early, he began late in life.

(26) He cherished the Christian religion, in which he had been brought up since childhood, most reverently and with the greatest devotion. For this reason, he built at Aachen a basilica of the greatest beauty, and he adorned it with gold and silver, with lighting fixtures, and with balustrades and doors of solid bronze. Since he was not able to obtain columns and marbles for its

---

82. A minor poet and grammarian of modest attainment, Peter may have been teaching in Pavia as early as 767. He died before 799. Charles probably summoned him to Francia after the fall of the Lombard kingdom.

83. Alcuin (735–804) entered Charles's court in 786, remained there until 790, returned in 793, and stayed until he retired in 796 as abbot of St.-Martin of Tours. He was a prolific author and renowned teacher. Many of his pupils became famous scholars and teachers in the ninth century.

construction anywhere else, he managed to have them brought from Rome and Ravenna. As far as his health permitted, he went eagerly to church morning and evening, and also for night prayers and for Mass. He was especially concerned that everything that was done in the church be carried out with the greatest dignity, and he regularly warned the sacristans not to permit anything unseemly or dirty to be brought into the church or to remain there. He procured such an abundance of gold and silver sacred vessels and of priestly vestments that not even the doorkeepers, who rank last in the ecclesiastical orders, would be deprived of the garb suited to their ministry. He corrected most diligently the manner of reading and singing psalms. He was himself highly accomplished in both, although he never read publicly and sang only in a low voice along with everyone else.

(27) He was so devoted to supporting the poor, with that form of spontaneous generosity that the Greeks call alms,[84] that he took care to practice it not only in his own country and in his kingdom but even over the sea in Syria and Egypt and even in Africa, Jerusalem, Alexandria, and Carthage. When he discovered Christians living in poverty, he was moved by their want and used to send them money. It was for this reason especially that he sought the friendship of the kings of realms beyond the sea, so that some relief and solace might benefit the Christians living under their authority.

Above all other holy and venerable places, he loved the church of the blessed apostle Peter at Rome, on which he heaped up as donations an immense quantity of money in both gold and silver, and even gems. Many, indeed countless, gifts were sent to the popes. In his day, he considered nothing in his whole realm more important than that, by his efforts and work, Rome would shine forth as before, with all its ancient authority, and that through him the church of St. Peter would be not only safe and defended but also adorned and endowed before all other churches. Even though he was so dedicated to Rome, he went there during the forty-four years of his reign only four times,[85] to fulfill his vows[86] and to pray.

(28) His last visit to Rome was not only for these reasons but also because the Romans attacked Pope Leo and inflicted many injuries on him; to wit, they

84. Einhard writes *eleimosynam*.
85. In 774, 781, 787, and 800.
86. It is not quite clear whether Einhard means that Charles was fulfilling religious vows to visit the holy places or keeping his promise to protect the popes. Note that in the next chapter Einhard says that Leo III called on Charles's *fidem*. In fact, each of his visits to Rome was occasioned by territorial or political issues in central Italy.

tore out his eyes and cut out his tongue and forced him to invoke the king's loyalty. Therefore, he went to Rome to remedy the condition of the church, which had been so disturbed, and he spent the whole winter there. It was at that time that he received the name of emperor and augustus. At first he was so opposed to this that he affirmed that he would not even have entered the church[87] that day, although it was a most important feast, if he had known what the pope was going to do. He bore with great patience the anger of the Roman emperors,[88] who were indignant at the title that he had received. He overcame their stubbornness by his magnanimity, which was beyond a doubt far greater than theirs, by sending them frequent legations and by calling them brothers in his letters.[89]

(29) After he received the imperial name, he realized that his people's laws were deficient in many ways, for the Franks had two laws,[90] which differed sharply in many respects. He resolved to supply whatever was lacking, to reconcile the differences, and to correct whatever was badly or even falsely promulgated. But of this plan nothing else was done by him except that he added a few chapters to the laws, and these were incomplete. Still, he did command that the unwritten laws of all the peoples under his authority be written down. He also commanded that the native and very old songs, in which the deeds and wars of the old kings were sung, be written down for posterity.[91] He also began a grammar of his paternal tongue.

He also created words for the months in his own language because up to that time, among the Franks, the names were pronounced partly in Latin and partly in the native language. He also assigned names to the twelve winds, since previously no more than about four of the winds could be discovered to have names. With respect to the months, then, he named them this way: January *winteramonath* [winter month], February *hornung* [antler-shedding month; the month when the year turns or changes], March *lentzinmanoth*

87. That is, the basilica of St. Peter. When the Franks visited Rome, they stayed in the vicinity of St. Peter's, which was outside the city.

88. That is, the Byzantines.

89. It had for centuries been an imperial prerogative to address other rulers as "sons," thereby implying inferiority and submission. In addressing the Byzantine emperors as "brothers," Charles seems to have been asserting their equality with him.

90. The Salian and the Ripuarian.

91. The epic tradition was alive: the word "sing" appears in the first line of both the *Iliad* and the *Aeneid*. Here we have *carmina* and *canebantur*. Whether or not these songs, or poems, were actually collected and copied, we now have no trace of Charles's work. Cf. Thegan, c. 19, who says that Louis the Pious as an adult despised the songs he had learned as a boy.

[Lent month; the weeks preceding Easter in the Christian calendar], April *ostarmanoth* [Easter month], May *winnemanoth* [month of joy], June *brachmanoth* [plowing month], July *heuuimanoth* [hay month], August *aranmanoth* [literally "ear month," the month of ripening grain], September *witumanoth* [wind month], October *windumemanoth* [wine month], November *herbistmanoth* [harvest month], December *heiligmanoth* [holy month].[92] The winds he actually named this way: the east wind *ostroniwint,* the east-south wind *ostsundroni,* the south-east wind *sundostroni,* the south wind *sundroni,* the south-west wind *sundwestroni,* the west-south wind *westsundroni,* the west wind *westroni,* the west-north wind *westnordroni,* the north-west wind *nordwestroni,* the north wind *nordroni,* the north-east wind *nordostroni,* the east-north wind *ostnordroni.*

(30) At the very end of his life, when he was weighed down by sickness and old age, he summoned his son Louis, the king of Aquitaine, who was the sole remaining son of Hildegard.[93] He solemnly assembled all the leaders of the Franks from his whole realm, and with the advice of all of them, he made his son consort in all his kingdom and heir to his imperial dignity. He crowned him and ordered that he be called emperor and augustus.[94] His plan was accepted with great pleasure by all who were present, for he seemed to have been divinely inspired to look out for the well-being of his kingdom. This action enhanced his kingdom's grandeur and struck foreign peoples with no little trembling.

After letting his son go back to Aquitaine, he himself, in his accustomed fashion and despite being worn out by old age, went hunting not far from his palace at Aachen. He spent what was left of the autumn in this activity and went back to Aachen around the first of November. While he was spending the winter there, he was seized by a strong fever and took to his bed. He immediately decided, as he usually did when he had a fever, to abstain from food, thinking that this fasting might drive away his illness or surely relieve it. But, in addition to his fever, he got a pain in his side that the Greeks call pleurisy. Still, he kept to his fast and sustained his body only with an occasional

92. Notice how the names of three of the months reveal Christian influences, while the others pertain to natural phenomena or agricultural pursuits.

93. Compare the accounts in Astronomer, c. 20; Thegan, c. 6; Ermoldus, page 141.

94. Einhard's terminology is interesting here. These events took place in September 813, well after the imperial coronation. Yet all territorial references are to the "kingdom" (*regnum*), while references to the office that Louis was receiving make him coruler of the "kingdom," heir of the "imperial dignity" (*imperialis nominis*), and have him "called" (*iussit appellari*) "emperor and augustus."

drink. On the seventh day after he took to his bed, he died, after receiving Holy Communion. He died on the twenty-eighth of January, at nine o'clock in the morning. He was in the seventy-second year of his life and the forty-seventh of his reign.[95]

(31) His body was washed and prepared in solemn fashion and carried into the church[96] and buried amid immense weeping by all the people. At first there was some doubt about where he ought to be laid to rest, because, while he was alive, he had provided no instructions on the matter. Finally, everyone agreed that no place would be more fitting for his burial than in that basilica, which he had built in that very place at his own expense, for the love of God and of our Lord Jesus Christ, and for the honor of his Blessed and Ever Virgin Mother. He was buried there on the same day he died, and a gilded arch with an image and inscription was erected over the tomb. That inscription was written out this way:

UNDER THIS MONUMENT LIES THE BODY
OF CHARLES, THE GREAT AND ORTHODOX EMPEROR,
WHO NOBLY EXPANDED THE KINGDOM OF THE FRANKS,
AND WHO RULED SUCCESSFULLY FOR FORTY-SEVEN YEARS.
HE WAS OVER SEVENTY WHEN HE DIED IN THE YEAR OF THE
    LORD 814,
IN THE SEVENTH INDICTION, ON THE TWENTY-EIGHTH OF
    JANUARY.[97]

(32) There were many omens as his death approached, so that not only others but even he himself knew it was coming. For three straight years at the end of his life there were frequent eclipses of the sun and moon, and a certain dark spot could be seen on the sun for a period of seven days. The porticus[98] that he

95. Einhard's numbers put Charles's birth in 742 and the inception of his reign in 767. Scholars now believe that Charles was born April 2, 748. His reign began in 768.

96. That is, the Palatine Chapel at Aachen.

97. *Anno Domini* dating was popularized by the Anglo-Saxon monk Bede in the early eighth century and was only just beginning to gain wide use by Charlemagne's time. Consequently, Carolingian documents often have several complementary dating systems. Indiction years go back to the Roman Empire. In 287 the government began announcing annual tax assessments and then gradually extended those assessments over five- and finally over fifteen-year periods. The tax year began on September 1. From 312 the fifteen-year tax cycles became formalized as a dating system (alongside others, of course).

98. A covered passageway.

had built with such great labor between the basilica and the palace suddenly collapsed right to its foundation and was ruined on the day of the Lord's ascension.[99] Likewise, the bridge over the Rhine that he had built of wood in ten years, with immense labor and impressive skill, so that it looked like it would last forever, accidentally caught fire and was burned up in three hours. Not a splinter of it remained except what was under water.

He himself, when he was conducting his last campaign in Saxony against Godfred, the king of the Danes, was just beginning to leave camp before sunrise when he suddenly saw a meteor of tremendous brilliance fall from the sky and flash across the clear air from right to left. As everyone was wondering what this sign could possibly mean, the horse on which he was sitting suddenly lowered its head and fell down and threw him so heavily onto the ground that the clasp of his cloak was broken and his sword belt was torn off. The attendants who were present rushed to him and lifted him up disarmed and disrobed. Even the spear that he had been holding tightly in his hand went flying and wound up twenty or more feet away.

On top of this, frequent tremors shook the Aachen palace, and the ceilings of the rooms in which he lived constantly creaked. The basilica, in which he was later buried, was struck by lightning, and the golden apple, which was on top of the roof, was thrown onto the bishop's house,[100] next to the basilica. There was in that same basilica, running along the cornice between the upper and lower arcades inside the building, an inscription written in red that gave the name of the builder of that very same temple. At the end of the verse,[101] one read: KAROLUS PRINCEPS. It was noticed by some in the same year that he died, a few months before his death, that the letters which spelled out PRINCEPS were so faded that they could scarcely be seen any more. Yet he either paid no attention to all these things or else rejected them as if they had nothing at all to do with him.

(33) He planned to draw up a will so that his daughters and his illegitimate sons could be his heirs to some extent, but he began late and was not able to

---

99. The collapse of the porticus actually occurred in 817. Writing later, Einhard may have wished his readers to see the collapse as a comment on Charles's death more than a portent of Louis's troubled reign.

100. Aachen did not become a bishopric until 1802. The "bishop's house" was the residence of the archchaplain, the head of the palace clergy and of the writing office. Usually this important person was a bishop. At the end of Charles's life it was Hildebald of Cologne. The Carolingians got papal permission for these bishops to reside away from their dioceses for long periods.

101. Late antique buildings often had verse inscriptions. The practice was adopted at Aachen.

finish it.[102] Nevertheless, three years before he died, he did divide his treasure, money, clothing, and furnishings in the presence of his friends and officials. He asked them to testify that, after his death, the distribution that he himself had made would, with their help, remain in force. Whatever he wanted to happen to the goods he had divided he set forth in a short document. Its plan and text is as follows:

In the name of the Lord God Almighty, Father, Son, and Holy Spirit, this is the inventory and division that was made by the most glorious and pious lord emperor Charles, in the eight hundred and eleventh year after the incarnation of our Lord Jesus Christ, in the forty-third year of his reign in Francia, and the thirty-sixth year in Italy, in the eleventh year of his imperial reign, and in the fourth indiction.[103] With pious and prudent reflection and with the Lord's help, he resolved and he actually did make this division of whatever treasure and money was to be found in his chamber on that day. In this division, he wanted especially to ensure that generous almsgiving, which Christians solemnly give from their own possessions, would be carried out in an orderly and reasonable fashion for his own benefit and from his own money, but also that his heirs, every doubt having been banished, would know clearly what ought to belong to them and that they would be able, without litigation or strife, to divide his money among themselves in suitable shares.

With this plan and purpose in mind, he divided, first of all into three lots, all the treasure and furnishings that could be found on that day in his chamber. Then he subdivided those three lots, making twenty-one shares out of two of them and keeping the other one whole. The reason why he made twenty-one shares out of those two parts is that, as is known, there are twenty-one metropolitan sees in his kingdom. Each one of those shares was to reach each metropolitan through the hands of his heirs and friends in the name of alms, and the archbishop, who was then seen to be the rector of each church, should share in this way with his suffragans the portion that was donated to his church and that he received: one-third for his church and two-thirds to be divided among the suffragans. The divisions that were created, as is known, from the first two parts according to the names of the twenty-one metropolitan cities

102. In the course of this long chapter Einhard speaks of *testamenta, breviario, constitutionem,* and *ordinationem.* Inside the text itself, as Einhard quotes it, the only words that name the document are *descriptio atque divisio,* translated here as "inventory and division."

103. The fourth indiction began September 1, 810. Since the twelfth year of Charles's imperial reign—using the Roman system of reckoning that counts both ends of a series—began on December 25, 810, this will was drawn up in the autumn of 810.

were separated distinctly from one another and were put aside and stored in their own chests. The names of the metropolitan cities to which these alms, or generosity, were supposed to be given are as follows: Rome, Ravenna, Milan, Friuli [Cividale], Grado, Cologne, Mainz, Juvavum (that is, Salzburg), Trier, Sens, Besançon, Lyon, Rouen, Reims, Arles, Vienne, Moutiers-en-Tarantaise, Embrun, Bordeaux, Tours, and Bourges.[104]

His thinking with respect to the one part he wished to be kept whole was that, with two parts distributed into shares as mentioned above and set aside under seal, this third part would be dedicated to his daily needs, such that it would seem to be property touched by no vow of obligation and never alienated from the property of its possessor. This arrangement was to last as long as he remained alive or judged that he had need or use for it. After his death or his voluntary withdrawal from worldly cares, that part was to be cut into four shares. One was to be added to the above-mentioned twenty-one portions; the second was to be divided in a just and reasonable partition among his sons and daughters and among the sons and daughters of his sons; the third, as is usual for Christians, was to be assigned to the benefit of the poor; the fourth, in a similar fashion and by way of alms, was to be distributed for the support of the male and female servants in the palace.

To this third portion of the total, which just like the others consisted of gold and silver, he wished to add everything that could be found that day in his chamber or wardrobe, vessels and utensils of bronze or iron or other metals, arms and clothing, and any other furnishings for various uses whether valuable or common, such as curtains, bed covers, carpets, mattresses, leather goods, and saddles. In this way, even bigger shares could be created, and the gift of alms could reach more people.

He ordained that the chapel, that is, the ecclesiastical service of the palace, with respect to both what he had made or put there and what it had inherited from his father, should be kept intact and not suffer any division. If, however, any vessels or books or other ornaments should be discovered that he did not indisputably give to the chapel, anyone who wished to have them might purchase and possess them after meeting a price that was deemed fair. Likewise, concerning the books, of which he had collected a great number in his library, he decreed that those who wished to have them could secure them at a fair price and that the money should be distributed to the poor.

104. For some reason Narbonne is omitted from this list.

It is known that among the other treasures and money were three silver tables and another gold one of remarkable size and weight. Concerning them, he determined and decreed that one of them, which was square and had a map of the city of Constantinople, should be added to the gifts that were assigned to Rome for the basilica of blessed Peter the Apostle. The second, which was round and adorned with an image of the city of Rome, should be given to the bishop of Ravenna. He decided that the third, which outstripped the others by far in the beauty of its workmanship and its sheer weight and contained a representation in careful and tiny drawing of the whole world in three connected circles,[105] along with the fourth, namely the gold one, should be added to the third part, for his heirs and for those who would share alms.

He made and established this decree and ordinance[106] in the presence of bishops, abbots, and counts who could then be present and whose names are written here.

> Bishops:[107] Hildebald* [Cologne], Riculf* [Mainz], Arn* [Salzburg], Wolfar* [Reims], Bernoin [Clermont], Leidrad* [Lyon], John* [Arles], Theodulf [Orléans], Jesse [Amiens], Heito [Basel], Waltgaud [Liège].
>
> Abbots: Fridugis [St.-Martin of Tours], Adalung [Lorsch], Angilbert [St.-Riquier], Irmino [St.-Germain-des-Prés].
>
> Counts: Wala, Meginher, Otulf, Stephan, Unruoch, Burchard, Meginhard, Hatto, Rihwin, Edo, Ercangar, Gerold, Bero, Hildiger, Hrocculf.

After he had looked over this short document, Louis, his son who succeeded him on God's command, took care to fulfill with the greatest devotion all these things as soon as he could after his father's death.

---

105. Doubtless a forerunner of the familiar medieval *mappae mundi* that showed Asia, Africa, and Europe, usually with Jerusalem as the center of the world.

106. Einhard says *constitutionem atque ordinationem,* which is very formal and technical sounding considering that, as he himself says, Charles never got around to drawing up a proper will.

107. Archbishops, those metropolitans who benefited from Charles's bequests, are marked with an asterisk. Theodulf of Orléans was also an archbishop, but as sometimes happened in the Carolingian world, this was a purely personal honor, since Orléans was not a metropolitan see.

INTRODUCTION

Notker Balbulus ("the Stammerer") was born around 840, orphaned very young, and raised for a time by a foster father, Adalbert, who gave him as a child oblate to the monastery of St. Gall. Notker died in April 912. He seems to have come from a prominent, landed family, and he kept company with men of power and influence. He tells us (in the preface to book 2) that Adalbert served in the wars with "his lord Gerold." Gerold, a renowned paladin of Charlemagne's, was a brother of the king's second wife, Hildegard. Notker received a fine education at St. Gall and in his turn became a famous teacher in the monastery. Future abbots and bishops were among his pupils. He also wrote documents for the monastery and served at different times as librarian and guestmaster. There is no evidence that Notker held high offices outside the monastery or that he was a confidant of rulers.[1]

Although Notker is best known as the author of *The Deeds of Emperor Charles the Great,* he wrote other works as well. He produced in prose a continuation, from 840 to 881, of Erchanbert's *Breviarium,* a modest historical work. He also completed, in 890, for his former pupil Bishop Salomon III of Constance, a collective volume containing a guidebook to significant Christian writers along with formulas for preparing monastic and episcopal documents. He also left a small letter collection with seven prose and ten verse epistles. In about 896 he made a start on a martyrology. In verse, Notker finished, in 884, his justly famous *Book of Hymns,* a collection of fifty sequences dedicated to Bishop Liutward of Vercelli plus a few other hymns. Finally, he authored a *Life of St. Gall.* This work was a *prosimetrum,* that is, a book in both prose and

---

1. For basic biographical details, see Haefele's introduction to *Taten Kaiser Karls des Grossen.*

verse. Notker holds a distinguished place in the history of medieval music, and no less an authority than Max Manitius called him one of the finest poets of the Middle Ages. Notker's Latin is less classicizing than that of Einhard, but it is correct, vigorous, and artful.[2]

The text of the *Deeds* as it survives is incomplete. Book 1 has thirty-four chapters on Charles's educational, religious, and ecclesiastical activities. Book 2 has twenty-two chapters on military and diplomatic affairs. Chapter 22 breaks off in midsentence. It should be added that the chapter divisions are supplied by modern editors, not by Notker. In the preface to book 2 Notker says, "In the preface to this little book I promised that I would follow three informants. . . . the most important of them, Werinbert, died seven days ago." Whether "the preface to this little book" was a preface to book 1 or a general preface to the whole work cannot be ascertained, but no such preface survives. In two places in book 2 (cc. 11 and 16) Notker implies that he is going to come eventually to a discussion of Charles's habits and private life. Perhaps it is a sign that the work was never properly edited that chapters 26 to 34 of book 1 treat military and diplomatic affairs, Charles's construction projects, and Frankish dress and arms. Occasionally these chapters treat wayward clerics, and very often they explicitly discuss aspects of Charles's character. These topics might well have been moved to book 2 or the never written book 3. That is, it is a fair presumption that the *Deeds* was to have comprised three books. It is reasonable as well to suppose that Notker's three informants each supplied information for one book. In the preface to book 2 Notker also says that the following book on Charles's wars was informed by Adalbert. Book 1, therefore, must have been informed by Werinbert, Adalbert's son. Who was the third informant? There is no way to say for sure, but on the basis of what Notker implies (1.8) about Grimald, the abbot of St. Gall from 841 to 872, it has been hypothesized that Grimald was in fact the third source.[3] There is absolutely no evidence that the rest of book 2 or book 3 was ever written.

Some clues about why Notker left his book unfinished, as well as about what kind of a book it is, derive from the period of the work's composition. Traditionally the years 883 and 887 have bracketed Notker's supposed period of composition. In the former year Charles III "the Fat," to whom the work is addressed (see 2.9–11, 14, 16, 17, 19), visited St. Gall for three days, and in

---

2. The major work on Notker's writings remains von den Steinen, *Notker der Dichter.* See also Manitius, "Notker der Stammler."

3. Innes, "Memory, Orality, and Literacy," 19–20.

November of the latter year Charles was deposed. Recent research demonstrates that Notker could have received a commission to write the book any time *after* 883, not necessarily *in* 883.[4] In 2.10 Notker mentions the death of Abbot Hartmut, which occurred in December 883. As just noted, Notker says that Werinbert had died "seven days ago." In fact, Werinbert died in May 884. In 1.30 Notker makes a reference to his inability to describe Aachen, and this remark may be related to a charter Charles III issued in late 884 for the Maria chapel at Aachen. Charles was in Regensburg at that time and had never visited Aachen. Thus his "notaries" (*cancellarii*) must have supplied the detailed information contained in the charter. Hence, Notker tells Charles, the addressee of his *Deeds*, his notaries can inform him about Aachen. In 2.13 Notker conflates the Danish kings Godfred I and III. The latter was active in the Moselle region in mid-885. Notker's *Notatio*, his annotated list of books that a bishop should know, was completed in 885 and bears similarities to central themes in book 1 of the *Deeds*. In 1.30 Notker appears to refer to a fire in Mainz that took place in March 886. Book 1, therefore, was probably finished in the spring of 886, but it could have been begun any time after the beginning of 884. There is only one secure clue for the terminal date. In 2.10 Notker refers to grants given to St. Gall by Louis the German in 873, which he very much wished to see confirmed. On May 30, 887, Charles III did issue that confirmation, but the *Deeds* betrays no knowledge of this. Notker must have been finished by then.

If we know when Notker wrote, we still do not know why he stopped writing.[5] Perhaps, however, court politics and the succession crisis combined to discourage Notker from bringing his work to completion and sending it to Charles. Notker maintained cordial relations with Bishop Liutward of Vercelli, who became archchaplain when Charles III succeeded in 882. Liutward replaced the redoubtable Liutbert of Mainz, who was possibly the most important churchman in the East Frankish kingdom from the 860s to the 880s. There is evidence that Liutbert seethed at his demotion. This evidence takes on added significance in light of chapters 16 through 19 of book 1. These viciously humorous chapters attack the bishop of Mainz, albeit not by name. In 1.18 Notker implies that Charles invited this kind of criticism, and states

---

4. What follows depends on MacLean, *Kingship and Politics*, 201–4, where the older literature is cited and evaluated. For the traditional arguments see Haefele, introduction to *Taten Kaiser Karls des Grossen*, xii–xvi.

5. MacLean, *Kingship and Politics*, 158–60, 205–7, 218–22, 229; Löwe, "Das Karlsbuch Notkers," 286–87.

openly that he feared incurring enemies. In 885–86 Charles attempted to per-suade key bishops and Pope Hadrian III to permit him to divorce his wife, Richgard, and to legitimize his minor son, Bernhard. Liutbert thwarted this plan. Meanwhile, Notker lamented (2.11) the fact that Charles had no "little Louis or Charles" at his side, in other words, no legitimate heir. Notker also lamented Bernhard's youth (2.11, 14). Notker was quite prepared to see Charles turn to his brother Carloman's illegitimate son, Arnulf, but Charles resolutely refused to take this course of action (although it cannot be said that he directly opposed Notker in taking this tack). By 887 Notker's hope for a continua-tion of the male Carolingian line in a legitimate or even illegitimate heir was dashed. What is more, in May of 887 Liutward was removed from office and Liutbert replaced him. Under the circumstances, it is easy to see why Notker did not send his *Deeds* to court, where criticisms of Charles might have been unwelcome and criticisms of Liutbert might have been dangerous. If it is not difficult to see why a combination of discretion and disillusionment might have caused Notker to set down his quill, it is remarkable to think that his fragmentary work survived at all.

That Notker was well informed about and acutely alert to the great politi-cal issues of his day is one crucial clue to what kind of a book he meant to write. Notker, after all, was a skilled and memorable teacher, and as such intended to teach Charles III and to steer him though the difficulties of his challenging time. Notker elected to use the deeds of Charles's great-grandfather to make his case. On one level, Notker's Charles the Great is a literary invention made from a bundle of anecdotes designed to teach lessons, but Notker was a cun-ning writer who worked on several levels simultaneously.

One of those levels concerns sources and how Notker built up his story. He certainly knew and made use of Einhard, the *Royal Frankish Annals,* and the continuations of those annals in *The Annals of Fulda.* He seems to have known the lives of Louis the Pious. Hagiographical sources provided Notker with his basic thematic, nonnarrative framework. The Bible was a constant influence.[6] Yet Notker acknowledges only the three oral informants mentioned above (whom he calls *auctores,* which must mean "authorities" more than "authors"). Numerous scholars have argued that Notker's work has about it the feel of an oral background.[7] It may be that the epic memory was already

---

6. On sources generally, see Berschin, "Der sanktgallische Universalbiograph Notker," 390–96; on the importance of the Bible, Ganz, "Humor as History," 176–78.

7. Innes, "Memory, Orality, Literacy," explores these issues fully.

at work when Notker set out to commemorate Charles. His approach is "It is said . . ."[8] He does not, indeed could not, pretend to be an eyewitness. But he claims to cite eyewitnesses. Granted that he was highly selective in the stories he chose to relate, are Notker's anecdotes to be dismissed as sheer invention? There is no reason to insist that Notker made up all these stories. But that is not the same as saying that they are true. Probably the safest course is to say that Notker retailed stories that were well known by his time, that had entered the common stock of tales about Charles. The same cannot be said with equal confidence about the numerous instances of direct speech. Charles may actually have done many of the things Notker says he did, but it is unlikely that Notker, or anyone else, knew what Charles said on various occasions. In the end, one should not press too hard a distinction between a learned, written work and a popular, oral one. The *Deeds* clearly possesses elements of both. The fundamental fact is Notker's guiding intelligence.[9]

Another level concerns Notker's literary devices. As noted, he proceeds by heaping up anecdotes. His work has no chronological, narrative flow. Nevertheless, the *Deeds* is by no means a disorganized grab bag. The work is deeply didactic; it intends to teach moral lessons. Stories are chosen for precisely this purpose. To a degree that has only recently come to be appreciated, humor is absolutely central to Notker. The stories about, say, the stuffed mouse or the dandified nobles and their spoiled clothes would surely have elicited hearty laughter in Notker's time, as they still do now. Humor does not, however, compromise Notker's seriousness of purpose. On the contrary, biting humor helps him to make some of his most effective, most serious points. There is no reason why a work that is sometimes humorous cannot also be seriously didactic.[10] If Einhard keeps us at a respectful distance from Charles, Notker's style accords his readers a kind of intimacy with his subjects. And it is important to realize that there are subjects. The *Deeds* almost becomes a collective biography, treating as it does Charles but also his son Louis and his grandson Louis the German, not to mention a few revealing asides about Charles III.[11] Einhard talks about Charles alone. But Notker, by bringing several characters into the *Deeds,* telling stories about them, putting words into their mouths,

8. Morrissey, *Charlemagne and France,* 28.

9. Lehmann, "Das literarische Bild," 169–72; Löwe, "Das Karlsbuch Notkers," 271–72.

10. MacLean, *Kingship and Politics,* 228–29; Ganz, "Humor as History," 171.

11. Berschin, "Der sanktgallische Universalbiograph Notker," 398; Löwe, "Das Karlsbuch Notkers," 277–78.

digressing often, creates a pleasing air of spontaneity. Readers will surely tire of Notker's endless superlatives—and they make hard work for translators, too!—they may sound tones of sarcasm or irony or regret. It is important to realize that Notker was a master of multiple meanings.[12]

One more level involves Notker's central themes, or even arguments. That is, if didacticism was one of his key devices, what was he trying to teach? And who was he teaching? In several respects Notker appears to have been responding directly to Einhard's presentation of Charles.[13] Einhard begins with wars and diplomacy, turns to personal qualities and domestic life, and concludes—more or less—with administration. His portrait is rigorously secular. Notker never gets around to personal life as a separate topic, although he does include many revealing observations. Nevertheless, he begins with God; indeed he does so with his opening words. He then turns directly and at length to Charles's religious and ecclesiastical activities and treats wars and diplomacy in his second book. Charles is for Notker a God-willed priest-king. Control over and protection of the church were fundamental royal duties.[14] Einhard never cites the Bible, but Notker does so often, and the biblical text is always Notker's subtext.[15] Whereas Einhard put some stress on Charles's surrounding himself with scholars, Notker reveals his own emphasis by telling three stories about teachers, education, and wisdom at the very beginning of his first book. Fulfilling God's appointed objectives for Notker is a matter of instilling the right ideas in those who would teach or learn.

To the extent that he was trying to "teach" Charles III and his court, then, religious ideals and responsibilities topped his syllabus. But Notker had other lessons to teach as well. At the beginning of book 1 Notker not only mentions God but also employs two images, the Roman of iron with earthenware feet and the Frankish with a golden head, to announce a new era in which the Franks have implicitly and explicitly become the people of God, the New Israel.[16] As

---

12. Morrissey, *Charlemagne and France,* 27–38; Kershaw, "Laughter After Babel's Fall"; Berschin, "Der sanktgallische Universalbiograph Notker," 401–4; Ganz, "Humor as History," 182–83; Folz, *Le souvenir et la légende,* 13–15.

13. Berschin, "Der sanktgallische Universalbiograph Notker," 390–91, 400–410; Ganz, "Humor as History," 176.

14. Goetz, *Strukturen,* 60–62, 98–99, 102–5; Berschin, "Der sanktgallische Universalbiograph Notker," 400–401.

15. See note 6 above.

16. MacLean, *Kingship and Politics,* 223–26; Berschin, "Der sanktgallische Universalbiograph Notker," 390–91; Ganz, "Humor as History," 174; Goetz, *Strukturen,* 81–82, 102–5; Löwe, "Das Karlsbuch Notkers," 279–80; Eggert, "Zu Kaiser- und Reichsgedanken"; Siegrist, *Herrscherbild und Weltsicht.*

he develops his picture of Charles, Notker mentions other Frankish rulers as well. For Einhard Charles was inimitable, whereas for Notker Charles's genius inhered in his descendants. But not in all his descendants. Notker ignores the West Frankish kingdom and assigns the legacy of Charles to the East Frankish kingdom and its rulers. In other words, Notker does not present his readers with a monumental Charles the Great who is to be admired but who cannot be emulated. Instead, he presents a living Charles embodied in his extended East Frankish progeny.[17]

Notker's keen sense of the social and political realities of his own day led him to be particularly sensitive to issues of rank, order, and hierarchy. Notker seems to be saying that the advice and support of the lay and clerical nobility is essential to the smooth functioning of the government.[18] He admires those who act selflessly and honorably. He repeatedly contrasts good and bad bishops and counselors. His commitment to the biblical precept of humbling the proud and exalting the humble comes through again and again. Notker's treatment of Queen Hildegard is revealing in this respect. Perhaps he intended his comments about her to stand as an implicit criticism of Charles III's queen, Richgard. Perhaps, however, she simply stands for the good counselor who always has in mind the king's and the realm's best interests.

The great French historian Louis Halphen once quipped that reading Notker for information about Charles is like reading Alexandre Dumas's *Three Musketeers* for information about Louis XIII. Halphen missed the point. The key issue is not whether Notker supplies new or accurate information. Rather, we read Notker to see how Charles was coming to be remembered and to see how he could be used as a symbol.

---

17. Eric Goldberg, *Struggle for Empire: Kingship and Conflict Under Louis the German, 817–876* (Ithaca, 2006), 341–42; Goetz, *Strukturen*, 75–80.

18. MacLean, *Kingship and Politics*, 205; Morrissey, *Charlemagne and France*, 31–38; Löwe, "Das Karlsbuch Notkers," 272–75, 282–84.

ESSENTIAL READING

Notker der Stammler. *Taten Kaiser Karls des Grossen.* Edited by Hans F. Haefele. MGH, Scriptores rerum Germanicarum 12. Berlin, 1962.

Collateral Sources

(Each of the sources included in this volume contains valuable material. Notker made use of Einhard, Ermoldus, and Thegan. The *Royal Frankish Annals* are once again relevant.)

The Annals of Fulda. Translated and annotated by Timothy Reuter. Ninth-Century Histories 2. Manchester, 1992.

The Annals of St. Bertin. Translated and annotated by Janet L. Nelson. Ninth-Century Histories 1. Manchester, 1991.

The Saxon Poet's Life of Charles the Great. Translated by Mary E. McKinney. New York, 1956.

"The Time of Charlemagne (768–814)" and "The Time of Charles the Fat (878–888)." Chaps. 2 and 6 in *Carolingian Civilization: A Reader,* 2nd ed., edited by Paul Edward Dutton, 23–154, 505–41. Peterborough, Ont., 2004.

Scholarship on Notker

Berschin, Walter. "Der sanktgallische Universalbiograph Notker." In *Biographie und Epochenstil im lateinischen Mittelalter,* vol. 3, Quellen und Untersuchungen zur lateinischen Philologie des Mittelalters 10:388–416. Stuttgart, 1991.

Eggert, Wolfgang. "Zu Kaiser- und Reichsgedanken des Notker Balbulus." *Philologus* 115 (1971): 71–80.

Folz, Robert. *Le souvenir et la légende de Charlemagne dans l'empire germanique médiévale.* Paris, 1950.

Ganz, David. "Humor as History in Notker's *Gesta Karoli Magni.*" In *Monks, Nuns, and Friars in Mediaeval Society,* edited by Edward B. King, Jacqueline T. Schaefer, and William B. Wadley, 171–83. Sewanee, 1989.

Goetz, Hans-Werner. *Strukturen der spätkarolingischen Epoche im Spiegel der Vorstellungen eines zeitgenössischen Mönchs: Eine Interpretation der "Gesta Karoli" Notkers von Sankt Gallen.* Bonn, 1981.

Haefele, Hans. Introduction to *Taten Kaiser Karls des Grossen,* by Notker der Stammler, MGH, Scriptores rerum Germanicarum 12:vii–xlvi. Berlin, 1962.

———. "Studien zu Notkers *Gesta Karoli.*" *Deutsches Archiv für Erforschung des Mittelalters* 15 (1959): 358–92.

Halphen, Louis. "Le moine de Saint-Gall." In *Études critiques sur l'histoire de Charlemagne,* 104–42. Paris, 1921.

Innes, Matthew. "Memory, Orality, and Literacy in an Early Medieval Society." *Past and Present* 158 (1998): 3–36.

Kershaw, Paul. "Laughter After Babel's Fall: Misunderstanding and Miscommunication in the Ninth-Century West." In *Humour, History, and Politics in Late Antiquity and the Early Middle Ages,* edited by Guy Halsall, 179–202. Cambridge, 2002.

Lehmann, Paul. "Das literarische Bild Karls des Grossen." In *Erforschung des Mittelalters,* 154–207. Leipzig, 1941.

Löwe, Heinz. "Das Karlsbuch Notkers von St. Gallen und sein zeitgeschichtlicher Hintergrund." *Schweizerische Zeitschrift für Geschichte* 20 (1970): 269–302.

MacLean, Simon. *Kingship and Politics in the Late Ninth Century: Charles the Fat and the End of the Carolingian Empire.* Cambridge, 2003.

Manitius, Max. "Notker der Stammler." In *Geschichte der lateinischen Literatur des Mittelalters,* vol. 1, bk. 2, 354–67. Munich, 1911.

Morrissey, Robert. *Charlemagne and France: A Thousand Years of Mythology.* Translated by Catherine Tihanyi. Notre Dame, 2003.

Siegrist, Theodor. *Herrscherbild und Weltsicht bei Notker Balbulus: Untersuchungen zu den Gesta Karoli.* Geist und Werk der Zeiten 8. Zurich, 1963.

von den Steinen, Wolfram. *Notker der Dichter und seine Geistige Welt.* 2 vols. Bern, 1978.

THE DEEDS OF EMPEROR CHARLES THE GREAT

Notker the Stammerer

Book 1

(1) The almighty ordainer of affairs, the one who sets in order realms and times, when he had crushed the iron, or even earthenware, feet of that amazing image he had erected among the Romans, raised up another, no less admirable image among the Franks through the illustrious Charles, this one with a golden head. When he had begun to reign alone in the western regions of the world, and the study of letters was almost everywhere forgotten, and even the worship of the true God had become tepid, two Scots from Ireland, men incomparably learned in both secular and sacred writings, appeared on the coast of Gaul with British merchants. Although they offered nothing for sale, they regularly cried out to the crowds who gathered to buy things, "If anyone is keen for wisdom, let him come and get it from us." They insisted that they had wisdom for sale—because they saw that the people had come to trade in what was for sale, not what was for free—so that they might stir up all who were coming to wisdom before everything else or, as subsequent events were to prove, they might turn them to astonishment and wonder by their cries. When, in the end, they had cried out this way for a long time, their claims were borne by those who admired them, or perhaps by those who thought them crazy, to the ears of King Charles, who always loved and most eagerly

sought wisdom. After he summoned them into his presence in all haste, he asked them if it were true, as the story had it, that they had brought wisdom along with themselves. They said, "Yes, we have it, and in the name of the Lord we are ready to give it to those who seek it worthily." When he asked them what they would seek in return for wisdom, they answered, "Only suitable dwellings and eager minds, food and clothing, for without these things our mission cannot be completed."[1] On hearing this, he was filled with immense joy, and right away he kept them both with himself for a short time. After a while, when urgent military affairs required him, he instructed one of them, whose name was Clement, to reside in Gaul, and he assigned to him a good many boys of the nobility, of the middling sort, and of the lower classes. Moreover, he demanded that they be furnished with such food as they might require, and he provided them with suitable dwellings. The other, whose name was [. . .],[2] he sent into Italy, and he set him over the monastery of St. Augustine in Pavia so that anyone who wished to do so could gather around him there to learn.

(2) When Alcuin,[3] an Englishman, heard how Charles, the most religious of kings, received wise men with delight, he took ship to meet him. He was, beyond all men in recent times, well practiced in the whole range of scriptures, inasmuch as he was a pupil of the most learned Bede,[4] the finest commentator after Saint Gregory.[5] Charles kept him with himself continuously until the end of his [that is, Alcuin's] life, except when he had to go off frequently to fight, such that he wished to be called Alcuin's pupil, and Alcuin to be called his teacher. He gave him the abbacy of St.-Martin of Tours so that when he

---

1. Notker would almost certainly have expected his readers to catch an allusion to Proverbs 8:1–4, 19: "Does not Wisdom call, and Understanding raise her voice? On the top of the heights along the road, at the crossroads she takes her stand; By the gates at the approaches of the city, in the entryways she cries aloud: 'To you, O men, I call; my appeal is to the children of men.'. . . My fruit is better than gold, yes, than pure gold, and my revenue than choice silver." See Ganz, "Humor as History," 175–76.

2. The manuscript has a lacuna at this point. Some have suggested that Dungal was the individual referred to, but others have though it was an Andreas. There is no way to decide. In any case, Clement and Dungal did appear at the court in the early ninth century, and Dungal was made bishop of Pavia by Louis the Pious in about 825. There was no monastery named for Augustine in Pavia, but the monastery of San Pietro in Ciel d'Oro in Pavia was sometimes called St. Augustine's because of the presence there of some of the saint's relics. This whole moralizing tale (see further c. 3) is probably apocryphal.

3. Ca. 735–804.

4. This is not true, although Alcuin was a pupil of Bede's student Egbert, who was archbishop of York from 735 to 766.

5. Gregory I the Great, 540–604, pope after 590.

himself had to be away, Alcuin could rest there and put himself to teaching those who would come to him.[6] His teaching flourished to such an extent that today's Gauls or Franks may be considered equal to the Romans or Athenians.

(3) When the most victorious Charles returned to Gaul after a long time, he ordered the boys whom he had commended to Clement to come to him and to offer him their letters and poems. Those of the middling and lower sort offered works adorned, beyond his expectations, with every sweet sign of wisdom. The noble boys, however, handed over flimsy works that were wholly silly. Then Charles, the wisest of men, imitated the justice of the eternal judge and, having set those who performed well at his right hand, addressed them with these words: "My sons, you have earned great favor with me because you have tried very hard to fulfill my command and to do what was useful to yourselves as far as you were able. Now, therefore, be eager to do even better, and I will give you bishoprics and splendid monasteries, and you will always have great honor in my eyes." Then he turned with great intensity to those on his left and, contorting his face and piercing their consciences with a flashing look, threw at them ironically these terrible words that sounded more like thunder than speech: "You nobles, you sons of magnates, you delicate and pretty boys, you who trust in your birth and wealth, setting aside my command and your own advancement, you neglected the study of letters, and you indulged in luxury, games, idleness, and useless pastimes." After he said this, he turned his august head and his unconquered right hand to heaven and hurled an oath at them in his customary fashion: "By the king of heaven, I give no weight to your nobility and good looks even though others may esteem you. Know this beyond any doubt: unless you make up for your earlier negligence by diligent study, you will never obtain anything of value from Charles."

(4) From the poor boys we just mentioned, Charles brought into his chapel one who was especially good at composing and copying. The kings of the Franks used to call their own sanctuary by that name on account of the cape [*cappa*] of Saint Martin, which they always carried with them into battle for their own protection and the defeat of their enemies.[7] When King Charles, abundant in foresight, was told that a certain bishop had died, he asked

---

6. Alcuin, although only a deacon, was abbot of Tours from 796 to 804. He was at Charles's court from 786 to 790 and 793 to 796. See Einhard, c. 25.

7. This account refers to a famous scene in the life of Martin of Tours (ca. 336–397) in which Martin, on encountering a poor man, divided his cloak with him only to discover that the man was Christ. The story is told by Sulpicius Severus in his *Life of Martin*, c. 3.

whether he had set anything aside from either his resources or his works before he had passed away. The envoy responded, "Lord, no more than two pounds of silver." Now, that very boy of whom I was speaking let out a sigh and, unable to contain the ardor of his mind, blurted out in the king's hearing: "That is pretty small provision for a very long, indeed eternal, journey." Then Charles, the most measured of men, reflected for a short time and said to him, "Do you think that if you were to receive that bishopric, you would take care to set aside more for that long journey?" With these words hanging in the air, the boy devoured them like ripe grapes falling into the mouth of someone hankering for them and said, "Lord, this lies in the will of God and in your power." So the king said to him, "Stand behind this curtain at my back and listen to see if you will have any supporters in gaining this honor." The palace officers who were always looking out for the misfortunes or deaths of others, when they heard of the demise of the bishop, did everything they could through those people closest to the emperor to press their own interests, to chafe at delays, and to inveigh against one another. But the king, persisting in the determination of his plan, denied them all, saying that he had no intention of betraying his word to that young fellow. Finally Queen Hildegard[8] sent some of the key nobles of the realm and later approached him herself to seek that bishopric for her own cleric. Charles received her request with every mark of courtesy and said he neither could nor would deny her anything unless it would cause him to disappoint his own little cleric. As it is the design of every woman to wish to put her own plan and desire before the rules of men, she hid away the anger welling up in her mind, softened her loud voice, and said to him, while trying to mollify his unshaken views with gentle gestures, "O, my king, what has that boy got to lose if he does not get that bishopric? I beg you my lord, my glory, and my sweetest refuge, that you give it to a faithful member of your household, to my cleric." At that point the young boy whom the king had ordered to stand behind the curtain, in front of which he himself was sitting so that he could hear what each person might request, reached out and embraced him, wrapping the curtain around him as he did so, and cried out, "Lord King, be brave, do not let anyone snatch from your hands the power that God has given you." Then the king, the strongest possible lover of the truth, called him to come out in the open and said to

8. Ca. 750–783, Charlemagne's third wife, or second if one discounts Himiltrude, the young woman Charles set aside to marry the daughter of the Lombard king Desiderius. Note, too, the presumed influence of the queen. See Einhard, c. 18.

him, "You shall have that bishopric. Take every precaution that you lay aside greater provisions for that long and irrevocable journey that lies before you, and before me, too."[9]

(5) There was a certain poor and low-born cleric in the entourage of the king who was not well enough instructed in letters. The most pious Charles took pity on his poverty, and even though everyone else disdained him and tried to get rid of him, the king could not be persuaded to send him away or to separate him from his following. It happened, however, that on the vigil of Saint Martin[10] the emperor was informed that a certain bishop had died.[11] When he heard this, he called to himself one of his clerics, a man of no little nobility and learning, and gave him that bishopric. Joyful beyond restraint, the newly appointed [bishop] summoned a great many of the palace officials to his house and even received with immense arrogance a good number of those who had come from his new diocese. He ordered a magnificent banquet to be prepared for everybody. Utterly weighed down by the food, almost drowned in the strong drink, and nearly dead from the wine, he failed on that holiest of nights to come to the night Office. There was of course a custom according to which the master of the school would, on the day before, assign each person the response that he was to sing the next night. To the one who was now practically holding a bishopric in his hands, he assigned this response: "Lord, if I am still useful to your people." Since the one of whom we have been speaking was absent, there ensued a long silence after the reading, and everyone urged everyone else to raise up the response, but one after another said he would only sing his own response. Finally the emperor said, "Someone sing." Then a man of humble estate was comforted by God's spirit and, strengthened by His authority, made the response. Soon the most merciful king, thinking that he would not know how to sing the whole thing, ordered someone to help him. Then everyone began to sing, and that unhappy soul was not able to get the verse from anyone. So he started singing, quite properly,

9. The reader may take two points from this charming tale: first, the king could appoint whom he pleased to a bishopric and often selected new bishops from among his palace entourage; second, as in the case of Einhard's (c. 20) attribution to Fastrada of some of Charles's missteps, so too here Notker reveals a tendency to see women's influence as evil.

10. The feast of Saint Martin of Tours is November 11. Liturgically, the vigil begins at sundown on the previous day (in this case November 10). If we are to take this report as accurate, the news therefore came on November 10.

11. This is the first time Notker has referred to Charles as emperor. This might mean that this anecdote postdates December 800, but Notker is not careful enough to make this a certainty.

the response to the Lord's Prayer. Now everyone wanted to stop him, but Charles, the wisest of all, wanted to see how it would come out and prevented anyone from disturbing him. He concluded his verse with these words, "Your kingdom come," and the others, whether they liked it or not, were compelled to respond, "Your will be done." On the conclusion of Matins,[12] when the king went back to his palace, or actually to his bedroom, to warm himself and to dress for the great feast,[13] he ordered that old member of his household (but brand new cantor) to be summoned, and he said to him, "Who ordered you to sing that response?" Scared to death, he answered, "Lord, you gave the order 'Someone sing.'" And the king said—for that was the name commonly used for the ruler among the men of olden days—"Good." And he went on, "Who showed you that verse?" On God's prompting, so it was believed, he answered right away with words that inferiors used to use to honor or soften up or flatter their betters. He got all worked up and said, "O joyful Lord, O king who makes men joyful, when I could not learn that verse from anyone, I though hard about how I would offend you if I came out with something inappropriate, so I decided to sing the last part of what usually comes at the end of the response." At that the emperor, most measured in all his ways, smiled and said to him in the presence of his magnates, "That cocky fellow will lose that bishopric, since he neither feared God nor honored his most partic-ular friend so that he might check his luxurious habits for even one night and at least be present right away to sing the response that, I hear, he was assigned. You take care to rule it with canonical and apostolic authority, now that God has given it to you, and I have concurred."

(6) Another bishop also died, and the emperor put a certain young man in his place. He came forth full of joy, and his servants brought out his horse, along with a step for mounting, to maintain the seriousness of his episcopal office. He was indignant, thinking that they considered him to be infirm, and jumped from the ground right up on the horse, but he could not balance him-self on the animal and practically fell off the other side. The king was watch-ing from the railing of the palace balcony and right away demanded that he be summoned to him, and he addressed him this way: "Good man, you are swift and agile, active and nimble, and you yourself know that the peace of our empire is disturbed on every side by many military disorders. I certainly

12. The traditional morning prayer of the Western church (albeit sung in the middle of the night), usually preceding but sometimes joined with Lauds.
13. That is, Saint Martin's Day.

have need of such a cleric in my entourage. Stick around for the time being and lend a hand in our work while you can still leap on a horse so quickly."

(7) When I was telling about the arrangement of the responses, I forgot to mention the arrangement of the readings, and I ought to say a little on this topic. No one in the basilica of the most learned Charles ever indicated to anyone else what readings were to be recited; no one set a wax seal where he left off or even made a tiny sign with his fingernail. But each one took such care to acquaint himself with what had to be read that whenever they were unexpectedly commanded to read, they were found to be blameless in his presence. He pointed out the one he wished to read by pointing with his finger or his stick or by sending someone from his side to those who were sitting farther away. He indicated where he wanted the reading to end by making a sound with his throat. Everyone waited so intently for that indication that whether it came at the end of a sentence or in the middle of a clause or even a subclause, no subsequent reader dared to begin either further back or further ahead no matter how peculiar the beginning or end might seem. In this way it came about that all the readers in his palace were excellent even if they did not always understand.[14] No outsider, even a well-known one, dared to enter the choir unless he knew how to read and sing.[15]

(8) Once when Charles was traveling about his realm, he came to a large basilica. A certain wandering cleric who was ignorant of the routine in Charles's choir entered the choir, and because he had never learned anything of the sort, he had to stand silent and frantic in the midst of those who were singing. The choirmaster raised his wand and threatened to strike him if he did not sing. The cleric, not knowing what to do or where to turn and not daring to run outside, twisted his neck almost in a loop and, mindless of the trouble he was in, opened his mouth wide and tried as hard as he could to imitate the actions of a singer. While everyone else simply could not keep from laughing, the ever brave emperor, who could not be moved from his train of thought even by great events, paid no attention to his fakery and waited for the end of Mass in the most solemn fashion. Finally he called the miserable fellow before himself and took mercy on his struggles and difficulties, consoling him with these words, "Many thanks, good cleric, for your singing and your efforts." To lighten his poverty he ordered him to be given a single pound of silver.

14. The point is that people could be taught to read Latin aloud correctly without necessarily being able to understand what they were reading.

15. Cf. Einhard, c. 26.

I must not forget, or seem to neglect, what I know about his [Alcuin's?] industry and his merits, because no one remains, among his pupils, who did not become either a very holy abbot or bishop.[16] At his knee my lord G[17] studied the liberal arts, first in Gaul and then in Italy. Those who are knowledgeable in such matters may accuse me of lying in saying that there was no exception, for in his school were two sons of millers who served the monastery of St. Columbanus, whom it would not have been fitting to raise to a bishopric or the governance of a monastery but who nevertheless, because of the merits of their teacher, served most effectively, one after the other, as provost of the monastery of Bobbio.[18]

(9) And so the most glorious Charles saw that the study of letters was flourishing throughout his realm, but he was sad that it had not reached the stature attained by the fathers of earlier times despite his superhuman labors. Irked, he bellowed out: "Would that I had twelve clerics as learned as were Jerome and Augustine." At this the very learned Alcuin, who considered himself rather unlearned in comparison to these, grew powerfully indignant but refrained from showing it. He responded, "The Creator of heaven and earth does not have many equal to these, and you want twelve?" No other mortal man would have dared to speak at all in the sight of the terrible Charles.

(10) Right now I must relate something the men of our time will actually find hard to believe, for I who write these words would barely believe it, on account of the immense difference in singing between the Romans and ourselves, except that the truth of the fathers is more credible than the falsity occasioned by the laziness of modern times.[19] Therefore Charles, that indefatigable lover of divine service, although he was grateful that he had achieved as much as he could in the knowledge of letters, was nevertheless sad that all the provinces, regions, and cities differed from one another in divine praises, that is, in the strict measures of their singing. So he asked Pope Stephen III

16. Translators have usually supplied Alcuin's name here, but only two manuscripts give it; the rest have no name, making the sentence appear to relate to Charles himself. This reading, however, makes what follows difficult to understand.

17. This must mean Grimald, abbot of St. Gall (841–72), even though some manuscripts give Gallus, the famous seventh-century monk after whom the monastery is named. It is unlikely that Grimald was a pupil of Alcuin. Notker is thinking rather liberally of the "school" of Alcuin. It is possible that this Grimald was the third of Notker's informants.

18. An important monastery in northwestern Italy founded in 612 by Columbanus, an Irish monk who, after coming to the Continent, argued with Merovingian rulers, promoted church reform, and founded monasteries.

19. Compare Einhard's prologue on the ancients and the moderns.

of blessed memory, the very one who deposed and cut the hair of that most inactive king of the Franks, Childeric [III], and who had anointed him to the governance of the realm according to the ancient custom of his people, to send some clerics who were particularly accomplished in divine song.[20] The pope readily assented to his divinely inspired good wish and zeal, and he sent to him in Francia from the apostolic see twelve clerics, according to the number of the apostles, who were deeply knowledgeable about singing. Now then, what I have named Francia is all the cisalpine provinces, for, as it is written, "in those days ten men from all the tongues of the gentiles shall take hold of the fringes of a Jewish man," so in those days, on account of the excellence of the most glorious Charles, the Gauls and Aquitainians, the Aeduans[21] and the Spanish, the Alemans and the Bavarians, rejoiced at being so favored that they deserved to be called by the name "servants of the Franks."[22] When the above-mentioned clerics were setting out from Rome, they were overcome by envy of the glory of the Franks, as all Greeks and Romans always are, and they plotted among themselves how they might so vary their instruction in song that unity and agreement would bring no rejoicing in his kingdom and province. When they reached Charles, they were received honorably and dispatched to highly distinguished places. Each one in his own place was able to contrive as corruptly as possible, and they strove to sing and to teach others in many different ways. When the most perceptive Charles was celebrating the feasts of

20. The account given here is severely confused. In July 754 at St.-Denis, Pope Stephen II (752–57) anointed Pippin III, Charles's father, and likewise anointed Pippin's sons Charles and Carloman. The pope also forbade the Franks ever to choose a king from another family. This was not an ancient custom of the Franks, although Pippin had been made king in 751 perhaps with the approval of Pope Zachary (741–52) and certainly on the election of the Franks. Pippin's was the first royal anointing among the Franks. Pippin did indeed request Roman chant masters, from Pope Paul I (757–67). There does not seem to be any reason to connect this story with Pope Stephen III (768–72), who was indeed reigning when Charles became king in 768. Charles himself sought chant masters from Rome in the 780s. When Zachary died in 751, a man was elected pope, took the name Stephen, and immediately died. A new election produced the Stephen II who is the subject here. Right down to modern times there has sometimes been confusion about the numbering of the Stephens. Usually, the momentary pope in 751 is not counted; when he is, each subsequent Stephen is, as it were, one number higher. It is difficult to say how Notker was enumerating his Stephens.

21. The Aeduans were Celtic inhabitants of central Gaul. It is not clear why Notker used contemporary names for everyone but them.

22. The biblical quotation is from Zechariah 8:23. Notker makes a hash of it. Compare: "In those days, wherein ten men of all the languages of the Gentiles shall take hold and shall hold fast the skirt of one that is a Jew [saying: We will go with you, for we have heard that God is with you]." The point is ideological, of course. Notker's *fimbriam* I have translated as "fringes," from the fringes, or tassels, that Deuteronomy 22:12 required all Jewish men to affix to the edges of their outer garments. Modern biblical translations use "garment," "sleeve," and "skirt."

Christmas and Epiphany[23] at Trier and Metz, he most vigilantly, indeed acutely, paid attention to, or rather reflected deeply on, the force of the singing. In the next year he passed these same solemnities at Paris and Tours, and he heard nothing that sounded like what he had listened to so intently the year before in the above-mentioned places, and as time went by, he discovered that those whom he had sent to other places also differed from each other. He brought the matter to the attention of Pope Leo of holy memory, Stephen's successor.[24] Leo called them back to Rome, condemned them to exile or perpetual imprisonment, and said to Charles, "If I send you others, they will be blinded by envy like the earlier ones, and they will not neglect to deceive you. But I shall take care to satisfy your zeal in this fashion: give me two exceptionally discreet clerics who will not tip off the people around me to the fact that they belong to you, and they will attain, God willing, a perfect knowledge in respect of that learning you have requested." Behold, after a little while, he sent them back to Charles superbly instructed. Charles kept one with himself and on the request of his son Drogo, the bishop of Metz, sent the other to that very church.[25] Not only did his hard work accomplish much in that city, but it began to have an impact through all of Francia, such that right down to our own days, among those who use the Latin language, ecclesiastical singing is called "of Metz," whereas, among us who speak the Teutonic, or German, language, it is called *mettisca,* either from the vernacular *met* or *mette,* or by using a word derived from Greek.[26]

(11) Charles, who was profoundly religious and temperate, had this custom: during Lent he would take food at the eighth hour of the day, after he had completed the celebration of Mass along with Vespers; therefore he would not violate the fast according to the Lord's precept if he should eat an hour early.[27] A certain bishop, who was very just but completely stupid, foolishly reprehended him, against the counsel of wisdom. Charles, however, the wisest of all, concealed his anger and received his admonition humbly, saying,

23. December 25 and January 6.

24. Leo III (795–816).

25. Drogo (801–855) was an illegitimate son of Charles, but he did not become bishop of Metz until 823, nine years after Charles died. His birth is mentioned in Einhard, c. 15. Metz did indeed become a major school of musical studies, and this story is a garbled account of that school's beginning.

26. Readers familiar with earlier translations would expect here several lines on the second chant master, Peter, who was allegedly sent to St. Gall to institute a school of musical studies. That passage is a later interpolation.

27. Vespers followed the ninth hour of the day; thus the Lenten fast would normally have extended well into the evening.

"You have counseled well, my good bishop, and I therefore instruct you to eat nothing before the least of the officials who are in my court have been fed." When Charles was eating, the leaders and rulers and kings of various peoples waited on him. They ate after Charles had his meal, and counts, prefects, and nobles of various dignities served them. When these people finished eating, the soldiers and scholars took their nourishment. After these, the masters of every sort of office, then the officials, and finally those who served the officials, so that the last did not eat before the middle of the night. When Lent was nearly over and the above-mentioned bishop had continued in his punishment, the most merciful Charles said to him, "I think, bishop, you have discovered that it is not out of intemperance but out of care for others that I eat before the hour for Vespers in Lent."

(12) When Charles sought the blessing of another bishop, the bishop blessed the bread, took some for himself, and then wished to give some to the most honorable Charles, who said to him, "You keep all that bread for yourself." The bishop was left confused when Charles did not wish to accept his blessing.

(13) No one having greater foresight than Charles, he never assigned more than one county to any of his counts except for those who were established along the boundary with or even in the land of the barbarians, nor did he ever permit any of his bishops an abbacy or churches belonging to the royal demesne,[28] unless there were particular reasons for doing so. When he was asked by his advisers or members of his entourage why he acted this way, he answered, "With that revenue or estate, with that little abbey or church, I can make a faithful man, a good vassal, or even a better one than that count or bishop is." For particular reasons, however, he would assign multiple honors to certain men, as, for example, to Udalrich, the brother of the great Hildegard, the mother of kings and emperors.[29] After Hildegard's death Charles deprived him of his honors on account of something that he did. A certain jester proclaimed in the hearing of the most merciful Charles, "Now Udalrich has lost his honors in the East and in the West, his sister having died." Saddened by these words, Charles had him restored to his former honors.[30] When

28. In chapter 30 below, Notker refers to *regales ecclesiae*, which I translate "churches belonging to the royal demesne." The Latin here is *ad ius regium*, which I take to be synonymous.

29. Hildegard (ca. 750–783) was the mother of his sons Charles, Pippin, and Louis. Pippin was king of Italy until his death in 810; Charles was evidently Charles's choice as his successor, but he died in 811, and Louis succeeded him as emperor.

30. Udalrich is known to have been count in Linzgau and Argengau between 802 and 809.

justice dictated, he opened his hands most liberally to holy places, as will become apparent in what follows.

(14) There was a certain bishopric right in Charles's path when he was traveling, such that he could scarcely avoid it. The bishop of that place was so keen to please Charles that he lavishly placed everything that he possessed at his disposal. When, however, on a certain occasion the emperor arrived unexpectedly, the bishop was shaken, rushing here and there like a swallow, so that he had the basilicas and houses, and even the courtyards and streets, swept and cleaned. Powerfully hurt and displeased, he rushed out to meet him. When the deeply pious Charles noticed this state of affairs, casting his eyes in various directions and looking closely at each thing, he said to the bishop, "You are always the best host. You have cleaned everything well for our arrival." The bishop bowed down, grasped and kissed his unconquered right hand, hid his anger as much as he could, spoke as if divinely inspired, and said, "It is right my lord that whenever you come everything should be cleansed right down to the bottom." Then the wisest of kings, culling some information from others, spoke to him, "If I know how to empty, I also know how to fill." And he added, "You may have that fiscal property[31] next to your bishopric, and all your successors may have it for all time."

(15) While on that same journey he also came unexpectedly to a certain bishopric established where he had to pass by it. He did not wish to eat the flesh of four-footed animals or of birds on that day, which was Friday, and that bishop, on account of the nature of the place, could not provide fish on the spot, so he ordered some excellent cheese that was white because of its richness to be placed before him. Everywhere a model of self-control in all respects, Charles spared the bishop embarrassment and asked for nothing else. Charles took up his knife and started to eat the white cheese after he threw away the skin, which seemed nasty to him. The bishop, who was standing nearby like a servant, drew closer and said, "Why are you doing that Lord Emperor? You are throwing away the best part." Then Charles, who was incapable of deception and thought that no one could deceive him, took up the bishop's suggestion and put a bit of the skin in his mouth and, after chewing it slowly, swallowed it like butter. Having tested the bishop's advice, he said, "You have spoken the truth, my good host." Then he added, "Do not neglect

---

31. A fiscal property was an estate belonging to the king. In earlier times, fiscal properties were, strictly speaking, Roman public lands taken over by the Merovingian rulers. By the Carolingian period the line between public properties and private estates belonging to the Carolingian family had blurred.

to send me at Aachen every year two wagons loaded with cheeses like that."
The bishop, deeply disturbed at the impossibility of the task and, he thought,
in danger of losing his rank and office, proposed to Charles, "Lord, I can get
my hands on cheeses, but I have no idea which ones are like these and which
ones are otherwise, and I fear that I will be found displeasing to you." Then
Charles, from whom unusual, even unknown, things never escaped or were
concealed, said to the bishop, who was claiming ignorance of the very knowledge in which he had been brought up, "Cut them all down the middle. Put
the ones you find to be like those back together with a sharp skewer, place
them in a tub, and send them to me. Keep the others for yourself, your clergy,
and your household." This happened for two years, and the king ordered that
such gifts be accepted discreetly. In the third year the bishop himself came
and took pains to explain in his own words how much work it was and what
a long time it took to gather up the cheeses. Charles, who was extremely
fair, took pity on his cares and efforts and gave to that bishopric a very fine
estate from which the bishop and his successors could meet their needs for
grain and wine.

(16) Since we have told how the exceptionally wise Charles exalted the
humble, let us also say how he humbled the proud. A certain bishop was
vainglorious and most avid for worthless things. Because the eminently wise
Charles saw through the bishop, he instructed a certain Jewish merchant, who
was accustomed to go to the Holy Land and to bring back from there to these
lands across the sea many precious and unfamiliar things, to deceive and cheat
that very bishop however he could. He caught a household mouse, embalmed
it with different spices, and offered it for sale to the above-mentioned bishop,
telling him that he had brought this most costly and never before seen animal
from Judea. The bishop was so filled with joy at such an item that he offered
three pounds of silver if only he might have that cherished object. The Jew
responded, "What a fitting price for so desirable an object! I would rather
throw it into the sea than have any man acquire it for so cheap and shameful
a price." The bishop, who possessed much but never gave the poor anything,
promised him ten pounds so that he could get that incomparable object.
That clever man feigned anger and said, "The God of Abraham does not wish
that I lose my effort and also the cost of my journey." So that greedy cleric,
gape-jawed at such a desirable object, suggested twenty pounds to the Jew.
Still angry, the Jew wrapped the mouse in a very valuable silk cloth and prepared to leave. The bishop, deceived and at the same time the sort of man

who deserved to be deceived, called him back and offered him a full measure of silver if he could only get his hands on that extremely valuable object. Finally, that merchant, with a show of phony reluctance, gave in to his many entreaties and, having accepted the silver, went off to the emperor and told him everything that had happened. A few days later the king called all the bishops and nobles of his realm to his assembly, and after many urgent items had been dealt with, he ordered all the silver to be brought out and put right in the middle of the palace. Then, raising up his voice, he said, "You, fathers and stewards, our bishops, you ought to minister to the poor, or to Christ in the poor, not hanker after worthless things. Now, on the contrary, you turn everything into vanity, and you are greedy beyond all mortal men." And he added, "One of you gave this much silver to a certain Jew for a painted household mouse." The guilty bishop, who had been deceived in such a shameful manner, threw himself at Charles's feet and begged forgiveness for the offense he had committed. Charles upbraided him appropriately and let him depart in a state of distress.

(17) The same bishop was left as guardian of the glorious Hildegard when the great warrior Charles was engaged in battle against the Huns.[32] He became so full of himself on account of his familiarity with the queen—and his impudence reached such heights—that the wicked man asked if, instead of his episcopal staff, he might carry around the incomparable golden scepter that Charles had had made for use on feast days as more fitting to his status than an officer's rod.[33] She put him off shrewdly, saying that she did not dare to give it to any man whatsoever, but finally she persuaded him that she would bring his claim before the king. When Charles came back, she told him humorously what the senseless bishop had requested. The king playfully assented to his request and promised that he would do even more for the bishop than he had asked. When virtually all of Europe had assembled to celebrate Charles's victory over such a people, he spoke these words in the hearing of the greater and

32. Read Avars. Carolingian writers frequently referred to the Avars as Huns.

33. This passage reveals a good deal about Carolingian symbols of office. The episcopal staff (*ferula*) evolved into the crosier (the hooked shepherd's staff) as a typical sign of the episcopal office. It may have evolved from a simple walking stick or, more remotely, from the rod (*baculus*) used by Roman augurs when they officiated at divinations. Notker does not use the word *festuca*, but this was also a rod used chiefly by judicial officers. The rod, then, was a secular symbol of power that in late Roman times served as a sign of office for men carrying out various public tasks. That Charles shifted from the use of a rod to that of a scepter (*virga*), a symbol of rulership, is significant as a mark of his increasing sense of the dignity of his office. Charles's wife at the time of the Avar campaign was Fastrada.

lesser: "Bishops ought to be contemptuous of the things of this world and to provoke others to seek heavenly things by their own example. Now, however, they are corrupted more than all other mortals by such ambition that one of them, not content with his bishopric—for he holds a see in Germania Prima—wanted to claim for himself, without our knowledge, our gold scepter, which we customarily carry around as a sign of our rulership."[34] The guilty man acknowledged his fault, obtained forgiveness, and departed.

(18) I greatly fear, O Lord Emperor Charles,[35] that even as I am anxious to fulfill your command, I shall offend against all professed religious and especially against the bishops. But I do not care too much about all that as long as I do not lose your support. Charles, the most religious emperor, commanded that each of the bishops throughout the breadth of his realm should preach in the basilica of his ecclesiastical see before a predetermined day that he had appointed; if anyone failed to do so, he would lose the honor of his bishopric. But why do I say "honor" when the apostle insists, "If anyone desires a bishopric, he desires a good work"?[36] For in truth I confess to you privately that there is great honor in that office, but good work is hardly required. Therefore, the bishop I was speaking about above was shaken by this command, for he knew nothing except accumulating and taking pride in delights, and he was afraid that if he lost his bishopric, he would be deprived of his luxuries at the same time. On a feast day he called two of the high officers of the palace and, after the reading of the Gospel, ascended the steps as if he were going to speak to the people. Everyone assembled there was quite amazed at such an unexpected development, except for one poor little man with striking red hair who had put a boot on his head because he did not have a cap and was embarrassed by the color of his hair. The bishop, who held his office in name but not in truth, said to his doorkeeper, or usher, a man whose office or ministry was called by the name of aedile among the ancient Romans, "Bring me that man with a cap who is standing next to the door of the church." Hastening to comply with the command of his lord, he took hold of the poor fellow and began to drag him to the bishop. He was greatly afraid that he would be punished with severe blows because he had presumed

34. Riculf was archbishop of Mainz between 787 and 813, but there is no evidence that he was a person of the sort caricatured here. Almost certainly Notker was making sport of Liutbert of Mainz; see the introduction to this text.

35. The reference here is to Charles the Fat (839–888, emperor after 881), to whom Notker dedicated this work; see the introduction to this text.

36. 1 Timothy 3:1.

to stand in the house of God with his head covered. He struggled with all his might to avoid being led before the judgment of so stern a judge. Then from his lofty position the bishop preached, crying out at the top of his voice, now addressing his flock, and now upbraiding this poor little guy, "Bring him here, be careful that he does not get away. For you have to come here whether you want to or not." Subdued either by fear or by force, he drew closer, and the bishop said, "Come closer! Approach!" Finally he snatched off the captive's headgear and proclaimed to the people, "Behold, people, you can see that this wicked fellow here is redheaded." Then he turned back to the altar and celebrated the solemnities, or pretended to do so. With such a Mass having been brought to its conclusion, they walked to the bishop's hall, which was adorned with various carpets and wall hangings of every sort, where they had a sumptuous banquet, replete with vessels of gold and silver, even with jewels, that might well have evoked disgust or nausea in those partaking of it. For his part the bishop himself, decked out in the most precious silks in the imperial purple, sat on the softest feather cushions; he lacked only the scepter and name of king. He was surrounded by a troop of richly clad soldiers in comparison to whom those palace officials, that is, the nobles of the unconquered Charles, seemed to themselves extremely poor. After that amazing banquet, itself unlike those to which kings were accustomed, the officials sought permission to leave. But the bishop, in order to make even clearer his grandeur and glory, ordered the most expert singing masters to come forward with every kind of musical instrument. Their voices and sound could have softened the hardest heart or turned the fast-flowing Rhine to ice.[37] Drinks of every possible sort, mixed with hues and dyes, crowned with herbs and flowers, which drew to themselves the sparkle of the gems and gold and imparted their own colors to these beverages, grew tepid in their hands as their stomachs were already stuffed. All the while bakers, butchers, cooks, and poulterers were preparing every sort of exquisite treat to tempt their full bellies. This sort of banquet had never been presented to Charles. When morning came and the bishop sobered up a little bit, he was horrified at the luxury that he had displayed the day before in the presence of the emperor's followers. He ordered them to be brought back into his presence, bestowed upon them gifts worthy of a king, and urged them please to tell mighty Charles about his good and modest life and that he had preached publicly in church in their hearing. When they got

37. Is he still making sport of Liutbert?

back, the emperor asked why the bishop had summoned them, and throwing themselves at his feet, they said, "Lord, so that in your name he could honor us beyond our measure." And they added, "He is most faithful to you, the best of all your bishops, and the most worthy of the highest priesthood. For, should you deign to believe base men such as us, we confess to your excellence that we heard him preach in highly polished fashion." Since the emperor was not unaware of his incompetence, he asked about his manner of preaching. Because they did not dare to deceive him, they laid out everything in detail. Then Charles understood that it was because of fear of him that the bishop tried to say something rather than neglect his command. Unworthy though he was, Charles permitted him to keep his bishopric.

(19) A little while later, when a certain youth who was a relative of the king sang the Alleluia excellently on a particular feast, the emperor said to that same bishop, "That cleric of ours sang very well indeed." On account of his stupidity, he took those words as a joke and, not knowing that the singer was a relative of the emperor, replied, "Yes, yes, every farmer can roar like that when he is out in the field working with his oxen."[38] After this badly ill-considered response, the emperor turned on him, glared like lightning, and threw the astonished man to the ground.

(20) There was another bishop of a tiny little town who, while he was in the flesh, did not wish to be considered an intercessor with God like the apostles and martyrs but instead desired to be honored with divine cult himself. He worked hard to hide his arrogance so that he could be called a holy man of God and not be judged hateful by everyone, along with the idols of the ordinary people. He had one vassal, by no means a low-class resident of his town, a man who was strong and hard working, to whom I would say he neither bestowed any benefice nor ever said a kind word. He did not know what he could do to placate the bishop's harsh spirit. He thought that he might gain the bishop's goodwill if he could show that some sign had occurred in his name. Therefore, when he was disposed to go to the bishop, he took along two little dogs, called greyhounds in the Gallic language, which, owing to their agility, easily captured foxes and other small animals and often fell swiftly on quails and other birds as they were rising to flight. Going down the road, he saw a fox sitting on a wall. In this unexpected opportunity, he kept dead silent

---

38. This sentence is hard to translate because it contains two words, *perriparii* and *vetrenere*, that never appear elsewhere. One manuscript glosses the former with *pastores*. Haefele (*Taten Kaiser Karls des Grossen*, 25 n. 2) renders the latter *vordröhnen*.

and loosed his dogs on it. They rushed after the fox with the swiftness of flight and caught it in the space of one bowshot. He himself followed along the course marked out by the dogs and extracted the fox alive and well from the teeth and claws of the dogs. Hiding his dogs where he could, and bounding away joyfully to his lord with that gift, he entered and said submissively, "Behold, Lord, what a gift a poor little fellow like me has been able to get for you." The bishop laughed a little and asked how he had captured it in good shape. He drew a little closer and, swearing on the good health of his lord, said that he would not conceal the truth from him. "Lord, I was riding through that field when I spotted this fox not far away. I relaxed the reins and began to ride after it. When the fox ran farther away so swiftly that I could scarcely see it any longer, I raised my hand and called to it, saying, 'In the name of my Lord Recho, stay put and don't move any farther.'[39] And, behold, it stood fixed in that spot as if bound by chains, and I picked it up as if it were a lost sheep." Then the bishop, puffed up with unwarranted exaltation, said in the presence of all, "Now my sanctity is made manifest; now I know who I am; now I recognize what I am going to be." From that day forward he cherished that detestable man above all other members of his household.

(21) Since the opportunity presents itself, I am inserting this tangential story, laid out in official style, which does not seem too unlike the others that are worthy of memory in our times. There was a bishop in New Francia[40] marvelous for his holiness and self-control and incomparable for his generosity and compassion. The ancient enemy, who hates every kind of justice, was utterly frustrated by this bishop's goodness, so he provoked in him a great desire to eat meat during Lent. The bishop thought he was going to die right away unless he renewed himself with a repast of that kind. He was encouraged by the advice of many holy and venerable priests that he could take meat to recover his health. Meanwhile he had been growing weaker throughout a whole year in his normal way. So that he would neither be disobedient to them nor betray his way of life, he ceded to their authority and, constrained by the ultimate need, put a little bit of meat in his mouth. When he began to chew and to get a little taste of the meat on his palate, he was seized by such dislike, disgust, even hatred (not only for meat but for every kind of food, and for light itself and this present life), and by despair for his salvation, that he no

---

39. Recho was bishop of Strasbourg (783–815). Strasbourg was not a "tiny little town," so Notker is being playful.

40. Apparently the region of Franconia extending eastward along the Main River from the Rhine.

longer wished to eat or drink anything. He confidently placed his hope in the Savior of lost souls. At the end of the first week of Lent, the above-mentioned fathers suggested to him that since he had to know that he was deceived by a diabolical delusion, he should strive by harsher fasts, by grief, and by an abundance of alms to bear away, to diminish, or to wash away that momentary lapse. He had been advised very well. He obeyed their counsel so as to confound the devil's malice and to obtain pardon for his offense from the restorer of innocence. He punished himself with two- and three-day fasts, dispensed with the rest of sleep, ministered daily with his own hands to the poor and pilgrims, washing their feet and supplying them with clothes and food to the best of his ability, although he wished to do even more. On the holy Sunday of Easter he asked for lots of jugs from the whole town, and he set about providing hot baths for all the poor from morning to evening. With his own hand he shaved the necks of individuals, and with his fingernails he removed festering sores and matted hair from their hairy bodies. He anointed them with unguent and dressed them in white garments as if they had been reborn. When sunset approached and no one was left who had not received such loving attention, the bishop himself entered the bath. When he emerged, his conscience was purified, and he was wearing an immaculate linen garment so that he could celebrate the solemnities for the people with the approval of the holy bishops. As he was approaching the church, his sly adversary wished to upset his plan such that against his vow the bishop would have left one poor man without a bath. The devil stood right in his way on the step of the church, having assumed the look of a tremendously stinky and ugly leper with flowing blood and ragged clothes stiff with gore, trembling and staggering with every step and hoarse like a real wretch. God inspired the holy bishop to take a step back so that he could think about how it was that he had recently given in to the enemy. He took off his white garments, ordered water to be heated without delay, and placed the poor fellow in it. He picked up a sharp knife and began to shave the really foul neck. When he had shaved the throat from one ear to the middle, he began on the other side with the idea of proceeding from there to the middle again. Amazing to relate, he found, when he got there, that the long whiskers he had already cut had grown back again. He did this again and again; indeed he did not stop shaving. And then—it terrifies me to tell the story—an eye of enormous size began to appear in the middle of the devil's throat. Frightened by such a monstrosity, the bishop jumped back and signed himself in the name of Christ with a huge scream.

After the bishop called on Christ, the phony guest could not hide his deception any longer, and he vanished like a puff of smoke. As he took his leave, he said, "This eye kept a close watch on you when you ate meat in Lent."

(22) In the same area there was another bishop of incomparable holiness. As though unaware of the female sex, he permitted extremely young nuns to speak with him with undue freedom for the sake of learning, no less than very mature priests. On the very feast of Easter, after the Divine Office, which dragged on past midnight, he indulged himself too freely with an Alsatian wine from Siegoldsheim as well as with an even stronger Falernian. In his weakened state he conjured up the image of a very beautiful woman who behaved like a harlot. When the others retired, he summoned her to his bed plaintively and debauched himself. As the morning sky reddened, he rose quickly and, after the fashion of the gentiles, washed away his nocturnal emission before proceeding with his stained conscience before the eyes of the inescapable true deity. On the completion of the first songs, he ought to have sung the angelic hymn in accord with his office, but, terrified, he was rendered senseless. He put the vestments of his sacred ministry on the altar, turned to the people, and confessed his offense. Then falling at the base of the altar, he was washed in an unimaginable flood of tears. The people urged him to get up and obliged themselves with a mighty oath that on that special day they would not allow the holy Mass to be celebrated except by their own pastor. But he could not be moved from that spot, and this standoff persisted for about three hours. Finally the merciful creator took pity on the vows of the devout people and the contrite heart of the bishop. Thus, lying on the floor, he put on his vestments again. Having been assured of his own forgiveness, he mercifully revived and stretched out his hands to the heavens to perform his awesome ministry as an example of true penitence and a warning that never and nowhere in this world is there safety, for always and everywhere security is but a shadow.

(23) In that part of Francia which is called Old Francia,[41] there was yet another bishop who was stingy beyond all measure. Once, in a very unusual year, the barrenness of all the produce of the land caused the whole region to become depopulated. At that time that greedy dealer rejoiced at the dire straits of all the mortals, really of all those who were dying, and ordered his storehouses to be opened and their contents sold at a terribly dear price. Just then a demon, perhaps a ghost, whose special skill was causing men to idle away

---

41. Franconia lying along the Rhine: see note 40 above.

their time in games and deceits, plied his custom by visiting the house of a certain blacksmith at night to play with his hammer and forge. When the head of the household tried to fortify himself and his possessions with the life-giving sign of the cross, the hairy creature said, "My dear friend, if you want to stop me from playing in your workshop, then put your little drinking pot here, and every day you will find it full." That wretched fellow feared bodily want more than the loss of his eternal soul, and he gave in to the promptings of the adversary. The demon broke into the cellar of Bacchus or Pluto,[42] picked up a huge flask, and, having accomplished his theft, let the rest flood all over the floor. When a great many vessels had already been emptied in this way, the bishop figured out that he was suffering from the wiles of demons. He sprinkled the cellar with holy water and protected himself with the sign of the unconquered cross. When night fell again, the sly agent of the ancient evil spirit came with his flask. When he did not dare to touch the wine vessels because of the sign of the cross and, what is more, was prevented from leaving, he was found in human form by the custodian of the house and bound tight. He was hauled before the people as a thief, and at the moment of his public execution he cried out, saying only, "Woe is me, woe is me, for I have lost my dear friend's flask." I have told this story—may it be true!—so that it will be known that when someone swears an oath in secret in times of need, nevertheless the invocation of the divine name is still powerful, even if it is not summoned for good reasons.

(24) While I have focused my eyes on the head of the Franks and surveyed its members, I have left to the rear the rest of the people both great and small. So I must now come to our neighbors the Italians, separated by a tremendous wall. In Italy there was a certain bishop who was extremely fond of useless things. The devil noticed this and appeared in human form to a certain poor man who had not been able to empty himself of greed, and promised to enrich him handsomely if he would hand himself over in a perpetual bond of partnership. When the miser did not decline to take advantage of the offer, the clever enemy said, "I am going to change into a very fine mule. Get on me and ride to the court of the bishop. When he begins to gape at this mule, drag the matter out, delay, decline his price, exaggerate, pretend to be angry, and withdraw a little. Then inevitably he will send after you and promise you many things. Finally, persuaded by his entreaties and loaded down with an

---

42. He means the bishop.

infinite sum of money, give him the mule, not willingly but as if you were compelled to do so. Then rouse yourself and run away to find a hiding place somewhere." And so it happened. The bishop, unable to wait until the following day, climbed on that prancing mule right in the midday heat, arrogantly rode through the city, went flying out into the fields, and hurried to a river to refresh himself. To his delight a long time passed, and they traced a whirling path, a speedy circle, looking very much like swimming dolphins. Behold, that ancient Belial, as if suffering neither bridle nor reins and raging with the fire of Gehenna, threw himself into the depths of the swirling waters and began to take the bishop with him. The bishop was barely extracted by a band of soldiers and the energy of the fishermen who were boating nearby.

(25) The adversary, skilled in sudden attacks, is accustomed to lay snares in the path we are walking, sometimes hiding traps here, sometimes taking advantage of another shortcoming there. The crime of fornication was alleged against a certain priest—in such a case the name of the bishop must be suppressed. This had already gained such wide attention among the people that it became known, on account of people's talking about it, to the bishop[43] of the bishops, to the most religious Charles. He was so wise that for quite a while he pretended to ignore the report, not wishing to grant credence to frivolous words, for nothing is swifter than a report of evils,[44] growing from the size of a tiny titmouse to a size beyond that of an eagle, so that it can never be concealed. Charles, the strictest possible seeker after justice, sent two of his palace officials, who were setting out that very evening for a place near the city, so that the next morning they could come to the priest unexpected. They were to demand that he celebrate Mass for them, and if he should make excuses, they were to oblige him in his name to celebrate the sacred mysteries himself. The bishop did not know what to do, for that same night he had sinned before the eyes of the heavenly watchman, yet he did not dare to offend against the officials. Nevertheless, fearing men more than God, he bathed his violently shaking limbs in an exceedingly frigid bath and went forth to offer the awe-inspiring Sacrament. But behold, either his conscience laid hold of his heart, or the water entered his veins, for he was seized by such a chill that he could not be helped by the ministration of any doctor. Indeed, he was carried

43. *Episcopus* (bishop) literally means "overseer."

44. Notker is here quoting Virgil, *Aeneid* 1.174, but not quite correctly. Virgil wrote "Fama, malum qua non aliud velocius ullum," whereas Notker has "fama malum quo non velocius ullum." Haefele (*Taten Kaiser Karls des Grossen,* 34 n. 1) also has "quo," not "qua."

right to death by a fever of the most immense strength and forced to yield up his soul by the decree of the severe and eternal judge.

(26) It is comforting for the rest of mortals, deceived by these frauds and others like them perpetrated by the devil and his agents, to think about the word spoken by the Lord when he confirmed the rock-solid[45] confession of Saint Peter—"For you are Peter, and upon this rock I will build my church, and the gates of hell will not prevail against it"[46]—and to stand unshaken and firm even in these exceedingly dangerous and wicked times. Since jealousy always rages among rivals, the Romans through the ages had a solemn custom that they all could at any moment be hostile, or instead violent, to anyone raised to the apostolic see. Thus it happened that some of them, blinded by envy, accused Pope Leo of holy memory, of whom I have spoken above, of a mortal crime and fell upon him in an attempt to blind him.[47] Truly, by God's will, they were struck with fright and fell back. They did not cut out his eyes, but they did slash him right down the middle with knives. He had word of this sent secretly through his household servants to Michael, the emperor of Constantinople, but he refused him any help, saying, "That pope has a kingdom of his own, one greater than our own. Let he himself gain vindication from his enemies."[48] So the holy man followed the divine plan and asked the unconquered Charles to come to Rome so that he who was already the ruler and commander of many nations might obtain more gloriously by apostolic authority the name of emperor,[49] of caesar and augustus. Charles, who was always on campaign and girded for war, set out without a moment's delay, even though he had no idea why he had been summoned—the leader of the world to the former capital of the world—with his advisers and a troop of young soldiers. When those extraordinarily wicked people became aware of his unanticipated arrival, they hid in various hiding places—cellars and dens— just as the birds called sparrows usually hide themselves from their master. But they could not avoid his energy and insight anywhere under heaven, and, caught and chained, they were led to St. Peter's basilica. There the undefiled father Leo picked up the Gospel of our Lord Jesus Christ and put it above his

45. The Latin has *firmissimam,* which I have translated as "rock-solid" to complete the pun with "rock."

46. Matthew 16:18.

47. Leo III (796–816). The attack took place April 25, 799.

48. There is no evidence that Leo appealed to Byzantium. Michael I in any case did not become emperor until 811. Is Notker confused, or was such a story circulating in the late ninth century?

49. *Nomen imperatoris* again: see pages 37, 143, 197.

head in the sight of Charles as well as his advisers and soldiers, and his persecutors too, and swore in these words: "So that I may share in the good news
on the day of the great judgment, I am innocent of the crimes falsely charged
to me by these men."[50] And right away the awe-inspiring Charles said to
his own people, "Be careful that none of them escapes." And he condemned
all the captives to various capital punishments or to perpetual exile. While,
however, the army was staying there for a few days for the sake of resting, the
apostolic bishop summoned whatever people he could from the neighboring
territories, and in their presence and that of the unconquered associates of the
most glorious Charles, who anticipated no such thing, he pronounced him
emperor and protector of the Roman Church.[51] Charles could not decline,
because he believed that it had come about through God's will, but he did not
receive the office gladly, because he thought that the Greeks would be inflamed
to even greater envy and that they would hatch an even more disagreeable plot
against the kingdom of the Franks. Perhaps they would be even more vigilant,
since the story was then going around that Charles would show up unexpectedly to subject their kingdom to his empire. The great-souled Charles was
already thinking in particular of how the Byzantine envoys of the king[52] would
come to him from their lord and tell him that he wished to be his faithful
friend and how, if they were to be neighbors, he would put him in the position of a son and relieve his poverty. Unable to calm the raging fire within
his breast, he burst forth with these words, "Would that this little sea did not
stand between us! Perhaps we could either divide the riches of the East or hold
them in common and share equally." This is what those who know nothing
about the poverty of Africa are accustomed to tell about the king of the
Africans.[53] The donor and restorer of health confirmed the innocence of the
Lord Pope Leo such that, after that criminal and terribly cruel slash, He gave

50. Some manuscripts at this point contain a later addition: "There were many among the captives who requested that they be permitted to absolve themselves of this crime at the tomb of Saint
Peter. But the pope, not unaware of their wiles, said to Charles, 'Do not, I beseech you, unconquered
servant of God, assent to their cunning. For they know that Saint Peter is especially generous to
sin. Search out among the tombs of the martyrs an inscription about a thirteen-year-old boy named
Pancras. If they will swear to you on it, you can treat them as safe.' It was done according to the pope's
wish. A good many people came forth as if to swear faithfully, but some of them fell down dead, while
others suddenly went mad."

51. This took place on December 25, 800. Cf. Einhard's treatment of these events, c. 28.

52. Note that Notker calls the Byzantine emperor king.

53. See 2.9 below and Einhard, c. 16, with note 55. The *Royal Frankish Annals* report under the
year 801 that envoys arrived from the Emir Ibrahim ibn al'Aghlab of Fustat in Egypt. Somehow this
story seems to be what Notker has in mind here. See note 114 below.

him back his eyes even sharper in sight than before, except that as a sign of his virtue He decorated his dovelike eyes with a beautiful scar, white as snow, in the form of a very thin line.

(27) Lest I be called uninformed by the ignorant because I said that the great emperor himself called the body of water that lies between us and the Greeks a "little sea," anyone who wishes to do so can learn that the Huns and Bulgars, and many other fierce peoples, were still whole and intact along the land road to the Greeks. Afterward the most warlike Charles cut some of those people down to size, such as the race of Slavs and the Bulgars, or virtually eradicated them, such as the ironlike and rock-hard people called Huns. I will tell you about this soon, but first I want to remind you a little, or at least enough, about the buildings that caesar augustus, the emperor Charles, so marvelously constructed at Aachen following the example of wise old Solomon as a resting place for God and for himself, for all his bishops, abbots, counts, and all the rest who came from all over the world.

(28) When Charles, the most active of emperors, was able to get some rest, he did not desire the idleness of leisure but rather the abundance of divine service, so he took pleasure in building in his own land and on his own plan a basilica finer by far than the works of the ancient Romans.[54] And once he started, he saw his wish fulfilled in short order. He summoned for the project, from all the lands across the sea, masters and builders who were skilled in every relevant art. He set above them an abbot who was the most skilled of all in completing such work, even though he did not know of his penchant for fraud. When the emperor withdrew, this abbot began right away accepting cash and let anyone who wished go home. If anyone could not meet his price or could not get free of their lords, then just as the Egyptians once afflicted the people of God with unjust work, so he oppressed them with immense labors and never permitted them to rest even a little. From this shifty behavior he collected an uncountable store of gold and silver, and silk cloths. He hung up the meaner items in his room, but he shut away the more precious ones in boxes and chests. Behold, he was suddenly informed that his house was on fire. He was all stirred up and went rushing right through the balls of flame

54. From the time of Pippin III Aachen was an occasional residence of the Frankish kings. Charles began to stay there regularly in 788 and in 794 decided to make it a more or less permanent capital, perhaps emulating the emperors in Constantinople and the caliphs in Baghdad. Einhard may have had a hand in the construction, but the chief architect was Odo of Metz, who created the chapel and allied buildings between 796 and 805. The story told here appears to be sheer invention. Cf. Einhard, cc. 17, 22, 26.

into the small chamber where the chests full of gold were kept. After getting in there, and not wanting to leave with only one, he put one on each of his shoulders and started to depart. Just then an enormous beam, having been burned through by the fire, fell on him. It burned his earthly body with ordinary fire as it transmitted his soul to the fire that never ceases. Thus did divine judgment keep watch over the most religious Charles when he himself could not pay attention because he was occupied with the business of the kingdom.

(29) There was another artisan, more skilled in every work with bronze and glass than all the others. When Tanco, a monk of St. Gall, forged a fine bell and caesar greatly admired its sound, that outstanding yet most unfortunate worker in bronze said, "Lord emperor, order a great deal of copper to be brought to me, and I will melt it down until it is pure. Then give me as much silver as I need instead of tin—a hundred pounds right away—and I will make you a bell next to which this other one will seem mute."[55] Then that most generous of kings, to whom vast riches flowed even though he never set his heart on them, easily commanded that everything the craftsman was seeking be brought. That wretch took everything and departed gleefully. He smelted and refined the bronze, but in place of the silver he substituted purified tin, and in no time he made a bell much finer by far than the one with impure metals. He tested it and presented it to caesar. Charles admired it greatly on account of its incomparable shape, and once an iron clapper had been installed, he ordered it to be hung in the bell tower. This was done without delay, and the watchman of the church, the rest of the chaplains, and a troop of boys who were loitering nearby tried one after another to make the bell sound, but they could not accomplish a thing. Finally, the author of the work and contriver of this unheard-of fraud, beside himself, grabbed the rope and yanked at the bell. Behold! The metal, having slipped from its moorings, fell on his head, with its evil schemes. It passed through his already dead corpse and landed on the ground with his guts and testicles. When that mass of silver about which we spoke was found, Charles, the most just of all, instructed that it be distributed among the poor servants of the palace.

(30) It was the custom in those days that whenever some work had to be accomplished on the emperor's orders, whether bridges, ships, or fords, or else the cleaning, surfacing, or improvement of muddy roads, the counts could fulfill these tasks through their vicars and officials insofar as they were minor

55. Bronze is a compound of copper and tin.

works. With respect to major works, and especially new constructions, no duke or count, and none of the bishops or abbots, might be excused in any way. There are still witnesses to this fact in the arch of the bridge at Mainz, a job that all of Europe[56] completed together and in most orderly fashion, although it was burned as a result of the shameful behavior of certain wicked people who wished to extract illegal tolls from ships passing under it.[57] If there were any churches belonging to the royal demesne that had to be decorated with paneled ceilings or wall paintings, local bishops and abbots looked after this. But if new churches had to be constructed, all the bishops, dukes and counts, abbots and anyone who presided over a church belonging to the royal domain, along with all of those who held benefices from the king, worked on them urgently from the laying of the foundation right up to the roof. Proof of this is still to be seen not only in the divine but also in the human basilica[58] at Aachen, and in the houses for every man who held an office, which were so constructed around the palace, on the plan of the most perceptive Charles, that he himself could see through the balustrade of his balcony what anyone who was entering or leaving was doing, as if he were right there with them. And so also the little dwellings of all the nobles were built well above the ground so that not only the soldiers of his army and those who served them but also every sort of man could protect himself under them from the discomforts of rain and snow, cold and heat, and yet never be able to escape the eyes of the exceptionally clear-sighted Charles. I am shut away, so I leave a description of this construction to your notaries who are free, and I shall come back to explaining the judgment of God that occurred there.

(31) Richly endowed with foresight, Charles ordered any magnates established nearby to take care to support the workers he had appointed and to provide everything they needed for the job. Those who came from a long way away he commended to Liutfrid,[59] the prefect of his house, who was to feed and clothe them at public expense and always to supply them diligently with everything that pertained to that construction project. With Charles there in residence with him, he did little enough, but when Charles left, Liutfrid ceased

56. Compare his use of "Europe" here to that in c. 17.

57. This bridge burned in 813. Einhard, c. 32, saw this as one portent of Charlemagne's death. There was another fire in Mainz in 886, to which Notker may be making reference.

58. He is referring to the *capella regia* (the octagonal royal chapel, which was called basilica by honor) and the *aula regia* (the royal hall, which was basilican in shape and perhaps modeled after Constantine's majestic basilica in Trier).

59. Otherwise unattested as far as I can determine.

completely, and the prefect amassed so much money from the oppressed wretches that Pluto and Dis[60] would not have been able to carry his ill-gotten gains to Hell except with a camel. And this is how he was found out by ordinary men. The most glorious Charles used to go at night to Lauds wearing a long and flowing cloak whose use and name have now slipped away. When the morning hymns were finished, he returned to his chamber and put on his imperial garb for a while. All the clerics used to come to that predawn Office and wait watchfully for the emperor either in the church or in the porticus, which was then called the little court, as he was going to the solemnities of the Mass. If anyone needed to, he would rest his head for a little while on the breast of a companion. A certain poor little fellow among them used to visit the house of the above-mentioned Liutfrid, as the least of the palace servants needed to do, to have his clothes, or really rags, washed and patched up. He was snoozing on the knee of his friend when he saw a giant taller that Saint Antony's adversary[61] crossing from the royal courtyard over the stream and hurrying to the house of the prefect, pulling along a huge camel weighed down with a burden unimaginably enormous. Astonished by what he had seen in his sleep, he asked him where he came from and where he wanted to go. He answered, "I pass from the house of the king to the house of Liutfrid so that I can put him on top of all these bundles and take him down to Hell with them." The cleric was startled awake by this vision and terrified by an even greater fear, namely, that the awe-inspiring one would discover him sleeping. He quickly raised his head and, calling the others to vigilance, spewed these words, "If you wish to hear about my dream, it seems to me that I saw that Polyphemus[62] who, while walking upon the earth, bumped into the stars on high and crossed the Ionian Sea without wetting his steep sides. He was rushing from that courtyard to Liutfrid's house with a heavily laden camel. When I asked him the reason for his passage, he said, 'I plan to put Liutfrid on top of this baggage and take him down to Hell.'" He had not yet finished this story when a girl who was very well known to all came from Liutfrid's house and threw herself at their feet, pleading that they might deign to keep her friend Liutfrid in memory. When they asked her what her problem was, she said, "My Lords, he went out to the

60. Names for the ancient gods of the underworld.
61. A reference to Athanasius's *Life of Antony*, c. 66, probably via the Latin translation of Evagrius of Antioch.
62. The giant cyclops who, in Homer's *Odyssey*, kept Odysseus and his companions prisoner until they tricked and blinded him and escaped.

latrine in good health, and when he stayed there a rather long time, we went out and found him dead." When the emperor learned of his sudden death, and his stubbornness and greed were freely described by the workmen and the household staff, he ordered his treasure to be inspected. When a countless number of goods were discovered, Charles, after God the most just judge, knew with what wickedness they had been assembled, and he pronounced in the presence of all, "Nothing so dishonestly acquired will be of any use to the soul of that wretch. Let all his possessions be divided among the workmen on this project and poorer folk among our palace servants."

(32) Two more things still need to be discussed that happened in the very same place. There was a certain deacon who, after the fashion of those from beyond the Alps, used to fight against nature. He went to the baths, got the closest possible shave, had his skin polished and his nails trimmed, and got his hair cut so short that it looked like it had been turned on a lathe. He put on linens and a brilliant white shirt, and because he could not avoid it, or rather so that he might appear even grander, he proceeded willingly to read the Gospel in the presence of almighty God and his angels and in the sight of the most stern king and his nobles. That his conscience was not clean became clear from what followed. While he was reading, a spider descended quickly on a thin thread from a beam, touched his head, and went back up rapidly. When Charles, always most attentive, saw this a second and third time, he pretended not to notice. The cleric did not dare to protect himself on account of fear of Charles, especially because he thought he was being pestered by flies and not attacked by a spider. He finished the reading from the Gospel and completed the rest of the Office. On leaving the basilica, he right away fell to the ground, and within the space of an hour he was dead. Charles was so deeply religious that he punished himself with public penance as if he were a murderer for what he had seen but did not stop.

(33) The incomparable Charles had a cleric who was also incomparable in every way, of whom a story was told that had never been told of any mortal, namely, that he excelled all others in the knowledge of secular and divine letters, in ecclesiastical and popular singing, in the composition and singing of new songs, and above all in the broad sweetness of his voice and in the immeasurable pleasure he gave.[63] When indeed the wisest lawgiver[64] himself—

63. In the next lines Notker compares the person he has just mentioned to a series of biblical figures who properly acknowledged God as the source of their gifts.
64. That is, Moses.

he was inspired by God—insisted that his voice was thin and his tongue was slow, he used the authority of God that dwelt in him—God who commands the heavenly bodies—to consult with Eleazar.[65] Our Lord Christ did not even permit him, of whom it was said that there was none greater born of woman, to perform any sign while he was still alive.[66] And he wished him[67] to marvel at the wisdom of Paul even though he had acknowledged him on the Father's prompting and he gave him the keys to the kingdom of heaven.[68] He even let the disciple[69] he loved above all the others fall into such trepidation that he would not dare to enter his burial place even though weak women went there all the time.[70] But as the Scripture says, "To him who has everything, it will be given."[71] Those who know whence they have the little they possess will succeed. That one who does not know the source of his gifts or who, knowing, does not give thanks appropriately to the author of the gifts has likewise lost everything. Now, when that one was standing right next to the glorious Charles like one of his closest associates, he suddenly vanished. The unconquered Charles was dumbstruck at such an unheard-of and incredible thing, but on recovering his composure, he crossed himself and then discovered, on the very spot where the cleric had been standing, a nasty lump of burned-out coal.

(34) That flowing cloak the augustus wore at night brings us back to his military gear.[72] The dress and equipment of the old Franks was as follows: boots gilded on the outside and decorated with laces three cubits long, interlaced leg wrappings and under them, from the hips to the shins, linens in the same color and skillfully decorated; very long leather strips were crisscrossed over these wrappings, inside and outside, front and back; then a bright white linen shirt over which was fastened a sword belt; the sword was placed first in a scabbard, second in some sort of leather holder, and third in a shining white linen holder stiffened with wax and worn with its cross-shaped hilt at the ready for attacking pagans; the outfit was completed by a cloak of white or blue formed in a double square, so that when it was put on the shoulders, it hung

65. See Exodus 4:10 and Numbers 27:18–21.
66. John the Baptist: see Matthew 11:11.
67. Peter.
68. Matthew 16:19.
69. John.
70. Luke 24:1–10.
71. Matthew 25:29.
72. Cf. Einhard, c. 23.

to the feet in front and back but on the sides barely touched the knees. A stick of applewood was carried in his right hand; it had even knots, was hard and menacing, and had an attached handle of gold or silver covered with symbols.[73] I am a rather lazy fellow, slower than a turtle, and I never went to Francia, but I did see the chief of the Franks in the monastery of St. Gall resplendent with two flowers, each with a golden crest, extending from his thighs so that, when he walked, the one in front was as tall as he was and the one in the back extended upward little by little until it covered his head and adorned it with the greatest glory.[74]

But as the way of human nature has it, when the Franks were fighting with the Gauls and saw them looking smart in their short striped cloaks, taking pleasure in the novelty and abandoning their ancient custom, they began to imitate them. For a time the strictest of emperors did not stop this, because he thought that outfit better suited to military pursuits. But when the Frisians abused his permission and began to sell those little cloaks for the same price as they had sold the bigger ones, he instructed that no one should buy from them at the customary price anything except the big, long, broad cloaks. And he added, "What good are those little tiny things? I cannot cover myself with them in bed, and when I am riding, I cannot protect myself from the wind and rain, and when nature calls, I cannot keep my legs from freezing."

Here Ends Book 1.

Here Begins the Preface [to Book 2].

In the preface to this little book I promised that I would follow three informants.[75] But because the most important of them, Werinbert, died seven days ago, and today, May 30, we, his sons and disciples, must commemorate his life, let this book on the religiosity and ecclesiastical concerns of the lord Charles end here, since it came from the mouth of that very same priest.[76] The one that follows, on the military affairs of the fierce Charles, has been composed

---

73. Compare what he says in 1.17 above about symbols of office.

74. Scholars have long puzzled over this passage. It might refer to some grandiose garments worn by Charles III when he visited St. Gall in 883. The flowers may symbolize hoped-for progeny. It might refer to Louis the German, who visited in 857 or 859, and the flowers may refer to his sons, Carloman (or Louis the Younger) and Charles III. Finally, the passage may refer to some sort of image of Charlemagne, with the flowers symbolizing two of his sons.

75. Notker's word is *auctores,* which would normally mean "authors," but it is clear from what he says that he was not using written texts.

76. Werinbert died in 884. Little is known about him.

from the telling of Adalbert, the father of that very Werinbert.[77] He was present at the wars with the Huns,[78] Saxons, and Slavs with his lord Gerold.[79] When he was already very old and I was a little child, he used to tell me about these things; actually, he forced me to listen, because I resisted and ran away all the time.[80]

Here Ends the Preface.

Here Begins Book 2 of the Deeds of Charles.

(1) Since I shall build on the report of a layman who had little learning in the language of Scripture, I think it not beside the point to recall a little about our ancestors from the witness of writers. When in the Persian War heaven struck down Julian, who was hateful to God, not only did provinces across the sea fall away from the kingdom of the Romans but also neighboring ones such as Pannonia, Noricum, Rhaetia, or Germania, and also the Franks and Gauls.[81] The kings of the Gauls or Franks began to slide backward on account of the death of Saint Desiderius of Vienne[82] and the expulsion of the foreign holy men, that is, Columbanus[83] and Gall.[84] The Huns used to go around like bandits in Francia and Aquitaine, even in Gaul and Spain.[85] When they set out all together, they devastated everything like a huge fire, and they hauled off to

77. Not much more is known about Adalbert than is told here.

78. Avars.

79. Gerold, who died in 799, was the brother of Charlemagne's wife Hildegard. Cf. Einhard, cc. 12, 13, and note 34.

80. It was Haefele's decision to make this section the preface to book 2. In earlier editions and translations, this section falls at the end of book 1. Its wording makes it ambiguous whether it concludes book 1 or opens book 2. Note that just below, in chapter 1, he says "report."

81. Julian "the Apostate" died in 363 after attempting a pagan revival. Notker severely compresses the next century and a half of history into one rapid set of events allegedly following upon Julian's demise. He did not get this account from any single book.

82. Desiderius was bishop of Vienne from at least 594. Deposed by Queen Brunhilde in 602/3, he soon recovered his see, only to be arrested again and executed for relentless criticism of the queen. His *vita* was written by Sisebut, and Notker may have known it.

83. Columbanus (ca. 543–615) was an Irish monk and missionary who arrived in Gaul ca. 590, founded a number of monasteries, including an important one at Luxueil, criticized the reigning kings, and eventually settled at Bobbio in Italy, where he founded an important monastery. See note 18 above.

84. Gall (ca. 550–645) was an Irish monk who accompanied Columbanus to Gaul, settled with him at Luxueil, and became a hermit after Columbanus's departure for Italy. He did not found the great monastery that honors his name, although tradition attributed the foundation to him.

85. The Huns did wreak havoc on the West in the fifth century, but Notker has conflated the Hunnic menace at that time with the threat posed by the Avars in the late eighth and early ninth centuries. Compare Einhard's treatment of the conquest of the Avar rings and the distribution of their treasure, c. 13.

their extremely safe hiding places whatever remnants survived. The above-mentioned Adalbert used to tell me what these hiding places were like. "The lands of the Huns," he used to say, "were circled about by eight rings." And since I could not think of any rings except woven fences, I would ask, "What on earth was that, my Lord?" He said, "It was fortified by nine hedges." And since I could not imagine any other sort of rings except those which usually grow around our grain fields, I pursued that matter and he said, "One circle was so wide that it included within itself as much land as there is between Tours and Constance, and it was built out of logs of oak, beech, and fir. It was twenty feet wide from one side to the other, as tall as it was high, and its internal space was filled with hard stones and extremely dense clay; the space between the walls was covered over with fresh sod. Between the edges of the walls were planted little trees, which, as we often see, were pruned and tilted forward to present tops of branches and leaves. Between these constructions households and villas were placed such that the human voice could be heard from one to another. Opposite those dwellings, between the impregnable walls, they set up narrow gates through which people from the inside and the outside used to rush to carry out raids. Likewise from the second ring, which was built just like the first, to the third one was a distance of twenty Teutonic miles, that is, forty Italian miles. And so right up to the ninth, although each circle was a little smaller than the one before it. From one circle to another the holdings and dwellings were so organized with respect to one another that the sound of a horn could signal each one of any important development.[86] Into these fortifications they gathered for two hundred years and even more all the wealth of the entire West, at the very time when the Goths and Vandals were disturbing the peace of mortal men and leaving the West virtually empty. But the unconquered Charles overthrew them in eight years, such that he scarcely permitted tiny remnants of them to remain. He also drew back his hand from the Bulgarians because they no longer seemed to threaten the kingdom of the Franks once the Huns had been defeated. Moreover, he distributed the booty uncovered in Pannonia most generously among the bishoprics and monasteries."

(2) In the Saxon war, however, in which he has engaged for quite a long time,[87] certain private men, whose names I would specify except that I wish to avoid a hint of conceit, formed a turtlelike protective shell and fiercely destroyed the walls of a well-defended city or rampart. On seeing this, the

---

86. This is the only extant description of the famous "Avar rings."
87. Cf. Einhard, c. 8.

most just Charles established the chief of them, with the agreement of his lord Gerold, as prefect between the Rhine and the Italian Alps.

(3) On the same occasion, when two sons of military leaders were supposed to be guarding the king's tent, they were lying about like dead men after over-indulging in drink. At the same time, Charles, since it was his custom to be vigilant all the time, was going around the camp quietly with almost no one recognizing him, and then he returned to his tent. When morning arrived, he summoned all the leading men of the kingdom and asked what punishment was worthy for someone who would have handed the chief of the Franks into the hands of the enemy. The military leaders mentioned above were com-pletely unaware of what had happened and condemned such men to death. Charles, however, lashed them with stern words but let them go, admonished yet unharmed.

(4) There were also two bastards born in a gynaeceum[88] in Colmar. When the emperor noticed that they fought most bravely, he asked them who they were and where they were born. When he learned, he summoned them to his tent one day about noon and spoke to them as follows, "My good young men, I desire you to serve me and no one else." They testified that they had come to him for that very purpose and that they would be satisfied to be last in his retinue. He said to them, "You ought to serve in my chamber." They said they would gladly do it, even though they hid their indignation. When the emperor began to take his rest, they seized the opportunity to go out to the enemy's camp, where they stirred up a commotion and washed away the taint of servi-tude in their own blood and that of the enemy.

(5) Even in the midst of preoccupations of this kind, the great-souled emperor did not in any way neglect to send men bearing gifts and letters to one king after another of the most far-off lands, and they sent back to him the honors of all their provinces. Consequently he sent envoys to the king of Constantinople from the seat of the Saxon war. The king asked him whether the kingdom of his son[89] Charles was peaceful or if it faced attacks from neigh-boring peoples. The leader of the embassy declared that everything was paci-fied except that a certain people who are called Saxons disturbed the Frankish frontiers with frequent raids. That man, who was soft from leisure and useless in the business of war, said, "For heaven's sake, why does my son struggle

88. The place on an estate where women worked. Carolingian moralists expressed concerns about sexual laxity in the gynaecea; there was some suspicion that in Italy they were actually brothels.
89. See 1.26 above.

against such a puny foe, one with no reputation and no strength? You may have that people along with everything that belongs to it." When they got back and reported to the most warlike Charles, he laughed and said, "That king would have done much better by you if he had given you a single linen wrap for your leg on such a long journey."

(6) The wisdom which that very same envoy showed to a Greek wise man must not be concealed. When in the autumn he and his traveling companions had arrived at a city that was once royal, they separated from each other, and he was commended to a certain bishop who burdened himself ceaselessly with fasts and prayers. The bishop practically killed that envoy by giving him almost nothing to eat, but on the first smile of spring he presented him to the king. The king asked him what he thought of the bishop. Drawing a deep sigh from the bottom of his gut, he said, "The bishop of yours is as holy as a man can be who is wholly without God." To which the flabbergasted king said, "How can anyone be holy 'without God'?" The envoy answered, "It is written 'God is love' and that one has none."

The king then summoned him to his banquet and sat him down amid his nobles. Among these people a law had been established whereby no one at the king's table, whether a native or a foreigner, should turn over any animal or piece of meat on its other side. He was to eat from the top part. A spicy river fish was brought in and put in his dish. The guest, ignorant of their custom, turned that fish over, and everyone jumped up and shouted to the king, "Lord, you have been dishonored as none of your ancestors ever were." The king let out a groan and said to the envoy, "I cannot stand in their way, and I must hand you over to death right away. But ask for something, whatever you like, and I will do it." The envoy thought for a while, and then, in the hearing of all, he came out with these words: "I beseech you, Lord Emperor, that according to your promise you grant me one little request." The king said, "Demand whatever you like, and you will get it, except that I cannot grant you your life against the law of the Greeks." So the envoy said, "Here is the request of the man who is about to die: let anyone who saw me turn over that fish be deprived of his eyes." Although dumbstruck at such a proposition, the king swore in Christ's name that he had not seen this but that he had merely believed those who said it was so. Right away the queen began to make excuses for herself, "By holy Mary, the joy-bringing Mother of God, I did not see it." Then the rest of the nobles, one right after another, wishing to get themselves out of such a dangerous predicament, tried to absolve themselves from this accusation, one by the keeper of the keys of heaven,[90] one by the teacher of the gentiles,[91] the rest by the powers of all the choirs of angels and saints. So that wise Frank overcame the cocky Greeks in their own house and, victorious and well, returned to his homeland.

Some years passed by, and the tireless Charles sent to Greece a certain bishop, a man of exceptional mind and strong body, and gave him as a companion an eminent military leader.[92] They were held up for a very long time, finally led to the king in unpresentable clothes, separated from each other, and sent to completely different places. In the end they were permitted to leave, and they returned home, having spent a great deal on their ship and expenses. Just a little later that same king sent his own messengers[93] to the most glorious Charles. By chance it happened that the same bishop and the above-mentioned leader were with the emperor. When the pending arrival of the envoys was announced, they suggested a plan to the very wise Charles: he ought to have them led around and around in the Alps. When they had used up or eaten everything and had fallen into complete want, he should compel them to come into his sight. When they had arrived, the bishop and his ally made the constable[94] sit down on a high throne in the midst of his subordinates. No one could have believed that he was anyone else but the emperor. When the envoys saw him, they rushed forth, wishing to stretch themselves out on the ground to adore him.[95] The servants prevented them from doing so and forced them to draw farther back. They reached a place where they saw the count of the palace in the midst of a group of nobles. Thinking he must be the emperor, they prostrated themselves on the ground. The men who were there drove them away with blows, saying, "This is not the emperor." They moved along a little farther and found the master of the king's table with his elegant staff. Thinking that he must be the emperor, they plopped themselves down on the ground again. Driven from there, they discovered the keepers of the king's private chambers along with their master in a meeting. There

90. Saint Peter.

91. Saint Paul.

92. Some manuscripts name this companion: Hugo. This would be Count Hugh of Tours. The bishop was Heito of Basel. The embassy took place in 811.

93. *Legatarios.* Everywhere else in his text Notker uses forms of *missus* or *legatus.*

94. *Comes stabuli,* literally the "count of the stable."

95. The scene is not as odd as it might seem (or as it might have seemed to Notker!). Ritual proskynesis, usually taking the form of prostration before the emperor, was called for in many settings in Byzantium. These and some other Persian customs had crept into Roman imperial ceremonial in the late third century.

seemed to be no doubt that this one was, among all mortals, the prince. But he denied it, although he promised that he would try very hard to get the nobles of the palace to lead the envoys into the presence of the most august emperor, if that should be possible. Finally some men were sent from the emperor himself to introduce the visitors honorably. Charles, the most glorious of kings, was standing by a particularly bright window, shining like the sun on its rising and radiant with gems and gold. He was leaning on Heito, for that was the name of the bishop he had once sent to Constantinople. Standing around him on all sides, like a copy of the heavenly militia, his three young sons, who had already been given a share in his realm;[96] his daughters and their mother,[97] adorned no less with wisdom and beauty than with necklaces; bishops, incomparable in appearance and virtues and most distinguished in nobility and holiness; abbots, and such commanders as Joshua when he appeared in the camp at Gilgal,[98] or such an army as made the Syrians and Assyrians flee from Samaria.[99] If David had been there, he would quite rightly have sung out, "Kings of the earth and all people, princes and all judges of the land, boys and girls, old and young, rejoice in the name of the Lord."[100] The envoys of the Greeks were deeply distressed. Their spirit failed, counsel left them, mute and lifeless they fell on the floor. But the gentlest of emperors raised them up and tried to breathe a little life into them with consoling words. Just as they were recovering, they saw Heito, who had once been so hatefully abused by them, in such glory that they were once again terrified and rolled around on the ground. Right away the king swore to them by the king of heaven that he in no way meant them any harm. That assurance strengthened them a little, and they began to behave a little more confidently. They went back home and never again came to our land. It seems worth repeating that the most distinguished Charles employed the wisest men in all cases.

(7) After the Lauds were celebrated for the emperor on the morning of the octave of Epiphany,[101] the Greeks privately sang the psalms in their own

96. Notker has completely abandoned chronology and accuracy here. By 811 or 812 only Louis, of Charles's legitimate sons, was still alive.

97. The story is wildly implausible on many grounds, and by 811 all of Charles's wives were dead.

98. Joshua 10:6–10.

99. Compare 1 Kings 20 (= 3 Kings 20 Vulgate), where Achab defeats Benadad the Syrian and drives him from Samaria (but Assyrians are not mentioned).

100. Psalm 148:11–12 (= 147:11–12 Vulgate).

101. That is, January 13. In liturgical practice the octave was the eighth day after a feast, counting the feast day itself (in this case January 6). Sometimes a major feast was celebrated throughout its octave; sometimes just on the octave.

language. The emperor concealed himself nearby and was delighted by the sweetness of the singing. He informed his clerics that nothing would be more to his taste than that they should present him with those same antiphons[102] translated into Latin. So it happens that all the tones are the same, and in one of them *conteruit* is found to have been substituted for *contrivit*.[103] These same envoys brought with them every kind of organ and various other things. All these were inspected very carefully, yet discreetly, by the craftsmen of the most wise Charles, and then reproduced, especially that extraordinary organ of the musicians, with its great bronze tanks, leather bellows filled with air, and amazing bronze pipes with their rumbling air that could equal the roaring of thunder, the tinkling of a lyre, or the sweetness of a cymbal. But this is neither the time nor the place to tell where it was placed, how long it lasted, or how it perished, along with other things, after the catastrophe.[104]

(8) At the same time, envoys of the Persians were sent to him.[105] They did not know where Francia was located and considered it a real accomplishment when they were able to reach the coast of Italy, on account of the fame of Rome, over which they thought he then ruled. And when they explained the reason for their arrival to the bishops of Campania or Tuscany, Emilia or Liguria, Burgundy or Gaul, they were treated to dishonest information or else driven off. Finally, after a year had passed, they, weary and worn out from their journey, met Charles, famous for all his virtues, at Aachen. They arrived there in the last week of Lent. They were announced to the emperor, but he put off seeing them until the eve of Easter. On the special feast that incomparable man was decked out incomparably, and he ordered the people from the race that had once seemed terrible to all the world to be introduced. To them the most excellent Charles seemed amazing before all others, as if they

102. Antiphons are sentences taken from the Bible and sung after the psalms and canticles of the Divine Office—the daily rounds of prayer observed by monks and sometimes priests.

103. The common form of the third-person singular, perfect indicative, of *contero* is *contrivit*, but there is a rare form *conteruit*. The customary form has three syllables; the rare form, four. The antiphon appears to be "Caput draconis Salvator contrivit in Iordane flumine" (The Savior cast the head of the dragon into the Jordan River). Bear in mind that Notker was a liturgist and musician, so he would have been interested in stories like this one.

104. Constantine V did send an organ to Pippin III, and the caliph Harun al-Rashid sent one to Charles. One of them, at least, was still in the palace in the 820s (see Ermoldus, page 183).

105. After settling the affairs of Pope Leo III, Charles left Rome in April 801. While traveling for some time in northern Italy, Charles received news that envoys of Caliph Harun—neither he nor they were Persian—had landed in Pisa. Notker's "Campania" would suggest that they landed south of Rome. Charles had them summoned to court somewhere between Vercelli and Ivrea. Notker certainly knew the *Royal Frankish Annals,* but he nevertheless mangles the details of this story.

had never seen a king or an emperor. He received them kindly and bestowed on them this gift: as if each were one of his children, they had permission to go wherever they wished, look over anything whatsoever, and ask about or investigate anything. They jumped excitedly at the chance to be near him, to look upon him, to admire him; they valued this more than the riches of the East. They climbed up to the gallery that ran around the basilica, and looked down on the clergy and soldiers, but, coming back again and again to the emperor, they were unable to keep from laughing, on account of their immense joy, and they clapped their hands, saying, "Before we have only seen men of clay, but now we have seen men of gold."[106] After this they approached each of the nobles and admired the novelty of his clothing or arms, but they kept coming back to the augustus, who seemed more marvelous still. They spent that night and the following Sunday together in the church, and on that holiest of days they were invited to the sumptuous banquet of the most opulent Charles with the nobles of Francia and of Europe. They were so struck by the wonder of what they beheld that they arose almost as if they had been fasting.

After Aurora left the saffron bed of Tithonius and sprinkled the earth with the sun's light,[107] behold Charles, unable to tolerate idleness or leisure, prepared to go hunting in the forest for bison or wild oxen, and to take along the Persian envoys. When they saw those huge animals, they were struck with terror and turned in flight. But the hero Charles was unperturbed and sat on his bold horse as he approached one of them, drew his sword, and tried to cut right through its neck. But his blow was in vain. The monstrous beast tore through the boot and leg wrap of the king and grazed his leg with the tip of his horn, rendering him a little slower than he was before.[108] Stirred up by its slight wound, the beast fled safe and sound into a valley made tough by trees and rocks. Just about everyone in the service of the lord wanted to take off their leggings, but he stopped them, saying, "I should go to Hildegard[109] just as I am." Isambard[110] followed the beast. He was the son of Warin, the persecutor of your patron Otmar.[111] Since he did not dare to get too close, he hurled his

106. Note the echo of the first sentence of book 1.

107. Notker is here combining bits of three lines from Virgil's *Aeneid:* 4.6, 4.584–85. Aurora is dawn, and Tithonius is her consort.

108. Cf. Einhard, c. 32, where there is a very different account of Charles's equestrian mishap.

109. Hildegard died in 783, long before the caliph's envoys arrived.

110. He was a count in the Thurgau, last mentioned in 806, and a benefactor of St. Gall.

111. Otmar, or Audomar (ca. 689–759), was abbot of St. Gall. Warin was one of the Frankish counts who worked under Pippin III to introduce Carolingian influence into Alemannia. Their efforts

spear, pierced the beast to the heart, between its shoulder and throat, and brought it still quivering to the emperor. But he seemed not to notice, gave the carcass to his companions, and went off home. He summoned the queen, showed her his torn leggings, and said to her, "What is suitable for the one who freed me from the enemy who inflicted this on me?" She answered, "Every good thing." The emperor then told her everything in detail, and having had the enormous horns brought in as evidence, he drove his lordly lady to sigh and beat her breast. And when she heard that Isambard, who was then hated and had been deprived of all his honors, had saved the emperor from such a foe, she threw herself at the emperor's feet, asked him to give back everything that had been taken from Isambard, and to give him even more besides.

The Persians also brought the emperor an elephant, monkeys, balsam, nard, and various ointments, spices, perfumes, and different medicines to such an extent that the East seemed emptied and the West filled.[112] After they had begun to become extremely familiar with the emperor, one day they were a little sillier than usual, heated up with strong wheat beer, and they spoke these words in jest to Charles, who was always armed with seriousness and sobriety: "Your power, O Emperor, is very great but much less than the report of your power that is spread in the eastern kingdoms." On hearing this, Charles concealed his considerable indignation and asked them with a smile, "Why do you speak so, my sons? Or why do things seem so to you?" So they went back to the beginning and told him everything that had happened to them in these lands across the sea, saying, "We Persians, or Medes, and Armenians, Indians, Parthians, Elamites, and all the peoples of the East, fear you much more than our own ruler Harun.[113] What should we say about the Macedonians or Achaeans? Nowadays they fear the pressure of your greatness more than they do the waves of the Ionian Sea. The peoples of all the islands through which we passed on our journey were as ready and determined in your service as if they had been raised in your palace and honored with huge favors. The nobles of your own lands, it seems to us, don't think much about you unless they are in your presence. For when we approached them more or

---

provoked quarrels with powerful local interests, including the abbot of the eminent monastery of St. Gall. Around 830 Gozbert wrote a *vita* of Otmar, and a few years later Walahfrid Strabo revised it. Charles III, for whom Notker wrote his book, had a particular devotion to Otmar.

112. On the elephant Abul Abbas, see Einhard, c. 16. The elephant seems to have arrived in late 801. In 807 the "king of Persia" sent sumptuous gifts again. Notker has confused the two embassies and their gifts, exchanging items between them, adding a few items, and omitting others.

113. Harun al-Rashid, Abbasid caliph (786–809). Notker writes "Aaron."

less as pilgrims and asked them to show us, for love of you, some kindness because we were looking for you, they did not listen and sent us away empty-handed." At that the emperor stripped away all the honors of the counts and abbots near whom the envoys had passed on their journey. The bishops, however, he punished and condemned to a vast fine. He ordered the envoys to be led back to their land with great security and respect.

(9) Messengers also came from the king of the Africans, bringing a North African lion and a Numidian bear, red dye from Spain and purple from Tyre, and other exceptional products of those same regions.[114] The most generous Charles lifted the Libyans from the yoke of poverty with the riches of Europe. Extending a generous hand, he provided them with grain, to be sure, wine, and oil, not only at that moment but for the rest of his life. He retained them as subjects and loyal followers and received from them a not inconsiderable tribute. Next, the indefatigable augustus sent to the emperor of the Persians Spanish horses and mules; white, gray, red, and blue Frisian cloths, which were rare in those parts and brought a high price; also dogs, distinctive for their agility and ferocity, which he himself had requested for catching or chasing away lions and tigers. Later on, Harun looked over the rest of the gifts without much attention but did ask his envoys what wild animals and beasts these dogs were accustomed to hunt down. He got this answer: they would immediately tear to pieces any wild animal they encountered. "The outcome," he said, "will show if this is true." Behold, the next morning there arose a great shout from the shepherds, fleeing a lion. When it was heard in the king's hall, he said to the envoys, "O, my Frankish friends, mount your horses and ride after me." They immediately followed after the king eagerly as if they had never suffered anything from effort or weariness. When they got to where they could see a lion, albeit at a distance, the satrap[115] of satraps said, "Set your dogs on the lion." They fulfilled his order and rushed forward as fast as possible. The Persian lion was caught by the German dogs, and the Franks killed it with their swords, hardened by the blood in the veins of the Hyperboreans.[116] Having seen this, Harun, the most powerful man to have inherited this name, perceived from small matters just how much more powerful Charles

114. Again Notker has confused the embassies of 801 and 807. The "king of the Africans" is likely to have been one of the two "Persian" envoys, namely the envoy of Emir Ibrahim ibn al'Aghlab of Fustat, who had been appointed by Harun ca. 800.

115. Satraps were governors of territories under the ancient Persian empire.

116. Hyperboreans were mythical peoples living in the far north. Presumably Notker is referring to Saxons.

was, and he blurted out these words on his behalf: "Now I know how true are the things I have heard about my brother Charles. By hunting so assiduously, and by exercising his body and mind with unflagging zeal, he is accustomed to dominating everything under heaven. What therefore can I possibly give him worthily, since he has taken such care to honor me so? If I give him the land promised to Abraham and shown to Joshua, he cannot defend it from the barbarians, because he is so far away; or if he undertook to defend it with his greatness of soul, I fear that the provinces bordering on the kingdom of the Franks would fall away from his command. So in the end I am tempted to make good on his generosity in this way: I will give the land into his power, and I will be his advocate over it. He himself, whenever it shall seem most opportune, may direct envoys to me, and he will find me a most faithful steward of the income of this very province." And so what the poet said was impossible actually happened: "Either the Parthian shall drink from the Saône, or Germany from the Tigris."[117] On account of the industry of the most vigorous Charles, the departure and return of his envoys and the dispatch and return of the envoys of Harun, young men, boys, and old men, from Parthia to Germany or from Germany to Parthia, were not only possible but seemed on the whole easy. And it does not matter how the grammarians take "Arar" [Saône], whether one takes it as flowing into the Rhone or another as flowing into the Rhine, because they are ignorant about these places.[118] I will call all of Germany to witness to this fact, that in the time of your most glorious father, Louis, every single farm in royal possession had to pay a single penny, which was given for the redemption of the Christians living in the promised land. They pleaded in the name of mercy for this money on account of the former dominion of your great-grandfather and your grandfather.

(10) Because an opportunity has presented itself, an honorable mention ought to fall about your indescribable father, perhaps to recall the prediction that, as is well known, the very wise Charles expressed about him.[119] When he was six years old and had been raised most carefully in his father's house, he seemed, quite rightly, to be far wiser than men who were sixty years old. His most indulgent father had very little expectation that he might actually

---

117. Virgil, *Eclogues*, 1.63. Thegan, c. 52, cites this same aphorism, albeit in a different context.

118. It is hard to tell whether Notker is being pedantic or is himself confused by the Arar (the Saône), which flows into the Rhone, and the Aare, which flows into the Rhine to the east of Basel.

119. To make the following clear: Notker is addressing Charles III, who was the son of Louis the German, himself the son of Louis the Pious, Charlemagne's son and successor.

bring him into the presence of his grandfather. But he took him—still a boy—
from his mother, who had raised him most tenderly, and began to instruct him
on how seriously and respectfully he should conduct himself in the emperor's
presence, and if by chance he was asked a question, he should answer it and
also show deference to his father. So he took him to the palace. On the first or
second day the emperor spotted him with some curiosity among the rest of the
attendants, and he said to his son, "Who is that little boy?" Your grandfather
answered, "He is mine, and yours if you wish it so." Your great-grandfather
spoke up and demanded, "Bring him to me." That done, the most serene
augustus kissed the little boy and sent him back to his former position. Right
away your father sensed his own status and disdained to stand second to anyone after the emperor. Having collected his wits and arranged his posture
most gracefully, he stood on the same step next to his father. When the farseeing Charles saw this, he summoned his son Louis and told him to ask his like-
named son why he did that, that is, with what assurance he presumed to make
himself equal to his father. He gave the following clever response: "When,"
he said, "I was your vassal, I stood behind you, among my comrades-in-arms,
as was fitting. Now, however, I am your ally and comrade, and so I quite
properly regard myself as your equal." When Louis told this to the emperor,
he came out with a statement to this effect, "If that little boy of yours lives,
he will know greatness." I have inserted these words, once used of Ambrose,
because what Charles said cannot be translated precisely into Latin.[120] I have
rightly adapted the prophecy about Saint Ambrose to Louis because, except
for those kinds of dealings and affairs without which earthly business cannot be conducted, marriage for example, and the use of weapons, he was very
much like Ambrose in everything. Indeed, in both the power of governance
and the zeal for religion, so to speak, Louis showed himself to be somewhat
greater than Ambrose, Catholic in faith, an extraordinary worshiper of God,
a tireless ally, guardian, and defender of the servants of Christ. And this is
true. For instance, when his faithful man, our abbot Hartmut,[121] who is now
your hermit, informed him that the tiny endowment of St. Gall had been
gathered together not from royal benefactions but from little bitty donations by private individuals, that it had no privilege like other monasteries, or
the rights common to all peoples, and no one could be found to serve as its

120. Paulinus, in his *Life of Saint Ambrose,* had related the same prophecy about the saint. Evidently the banter at court was in German.

121. Abbot of St. Gall (872–83).

defender or advocate,[122] he opposed himself to all our adversaries and did not blush to speak out effectively on behalf of our wretched state in the presence of his leading men. At the same time, he sent a letter to your own fine self [saying] that through your authority and on a compulsory oath we should be able freely to ask for anything we need. But alas, how stupid I am, for, taking thought a little for my personal pleasure, I have digressed on account of the special kindness Louis showed us, and I have not paid attention to his general and inexpressible goodness, his greatness and magnanimity.

(11) And so Louis, king, or emperor,[123] of all of Germany, Rhaetia, and Old Francia, and also Saxony, Thuringia, Noricum, Pannonia, and even all the northern nations, was grand in stature, handsome and dignified, with eyes that sparkled like stars and a clear manly voice. His wisdom was distinctive, and he could call upon an unusually keen intelligence. He never ceased to return again and again assiduously to the Scriptures. He was particularly adept in anticipating and overcoming all the attacks of his enemies, concluding the quarrels of his subjects, and providing every useful thing for his faithful followers. He did all this with unmatched liveliness. He grew more and more terrifying to all the peoples surrounding his realm than his ancestors had been up to that time. He earned his reputation, for he never pronounced a false judgment or stained his hand by shedding Christian blood, except when absolutely necessary.[124] But I do not dare to tell that story before I see a little Louie or Charlie[125] standing next to you.[126] After that slaughter[127] he felt unable ever again to condemn anyone to death. Subsequently, he used to punish disloyalty or conspiracy this way: he deprived the guilty of their honors and then never softened his judgment or let them return to their former rank either for any reason or after the passage of a long time. He was, beyond all men, so intent on devotion to prayer, dedication to fasting, and concern for divine

122. An *advocatus* was a layman appointed by the ruler, in consultation with the head of a religious establishment, to represent that establishment before the public authorities.

123. Louis the German was never crowned emperor. It was a fairly common Carolingian perception that one who was ruler over many peoples was eligible to be an emperor.

124. Some manuscripts have "unam et ultimam quidem necessitatem" (except once and only when absolutely necessary). It may be that Notker is referring to the ruthless suppression of the Stellinga Revolt in Saxony in 841–43, but it is more likely that he is speaking about the bloody battles of Ries and Fontenoy.

125. *Parvulum Ludowiculum aut Karolastrum.*

126. Note Notker's assumption that a royal Carolingian will be named Louis or Charles. These were the commonest Carolingian names, but in the ninth century there were Carlomans, Lothairs, and Pippins as well. Indeed, Charles III, who is referred to here, had brothers named Louis and Carloman.

127. See note 124 above; Notker's narration is a little confusing here.

service that following the example of Saint Martin he always seemed to be praying to God as if he were present, no matter what else he was doing. On specified days he abstained from meat and elegant foods. When the litanies were celebrated, he used to follow the cross barefoot from the palace to the episcopal church[128] or else to St. Emmeram[129] if he were in Regensburg. In other places, he accepted the practice of those with whom he was staying. He built new churches of admirable work in Frankfurt and Regensburg. When, on account of the size of the construction, there were not enough stones, he ordered the walls of the city to be torn down.[130] In cavities in the walls he found the bones of ancient men surrounded with so much gold that he not only decorated the basilica with it but he also had whole books written and covered with the same material almost to the thickness of a finger. No cleric could serve with him or even come into his presence if he did not know how to read and to sing. He despised monks who violated their vows as much as he loved with all his heart the ones who kept them. He always showed himself to be so full of good humor and sweetness that if anyone came to him sad, he departed happy just from getting a look at him or hearing him speak a little. If by chance something sinister or stupid suddenly happened in his sight, or if he happened to learn of such a thing elsewhere, he fixed everything with a simple glance, just as it is written of the eternal judge who sees within, "The king who sits on his throne dispels all evil with a glance."[131] There is no doubt that this power far exceeded in him what is conceded to ordinary mortals. I have said all this briefly as a short digression, but I vow to write more about him if I have time and divine favor.[132]

(12) Now we must get back to our subject. Meanwhile, because Emperor Charles was staying at Aachen a little too long on account of frequent incursions or even the invasion of the unconquerable Saxons or the piratical brigandage of the Northmen or Moors, the war against the Huns was being waged by his son Pippin, and barbarian nations came down from the North and ravaged a good part of Noricum and eastern Francia.[133] When he learned of this,

128. St. Peter in Regensburg.

129. Monastery in Regensburg named for the early eighth-century missionary/martyr who had come to Bavaria from Aquitaine.

130. Archaeological research confirms this statement.

131. Proverbs 20:8

132. Notker is here flattering Charles III with this glowing portrait of his father, Louis the German. It is interesting to compare what Notker says about Charlemagne with what he says about Louis the German.

133. Cf. Einhard, cc. 12–14, which Notker seems to have confused badly.

he struck them all down himself, and he even instructed that their boys and children should be measured against a sword, so that whoever exceeded that measure was to be decapitated. Out of this deed there emerged another that was much greater and more significant. When your imperial majesty's most holy grandfather died, certain giants, like those who, according to the Scriptures, were on account of God's anger born through the sons of Seth from the daughters of Cain,[134] were puffed up with pride, and no doubt just like those who said, "What share have we in David, or what inheritance in the son of Jesse?"[135] These men, each despising the excellent character of his offspring, tried to snatch away the government and bear the crown for himself. Then God inspired some of the lesser people to protest that just as the renowned emperor Charles had once measured the enemies of Christians against a sword, so should his progeny rule over the Franks, nay more, over all of Germany, as long as any could be found who was as long as a sword. That devilish faction was slammed as if struck by a thunderbolt and driven in all directions.[136] Although Charles was victorious over his foreign foes, he was beset by his own people in a remarkable but finally failed plot. Having returned to his queen from the land of the Slavs, he was almost captured and condemned to death by his son, born of a concubine, whom he had originally distinguished with the name of glorious Pippin, and would have been so if Pippin had had it in him.[137] But the conspiracy was discovered this way. When, having gathered the nobles together, Pippin had taken counsel in the church of St. Peter concerning the death of the emperor, and the session had been concluded, fearing absolutely everything, he ordered an investigation to see if anyone might have been hidden away in a corner or under the altars. And behold, just as they feared, they found one cleric hidden under the altar. They took hold of him and forced him to swear an oath that he would not betray their movement. To save his life he swore as they demanded. As soon as they left, he spurned his oath as a sacrilege and hurried to the palace. With the greatest difficulty he passed through seven bolted doors until he finally got to the emperor's chamber. He knocked on the door, provoking the greatest wonder in the always vigilant Charles about who would dare to disturb him at that time. He instructed

134. An imprecise derivation from Genesis 6:1–4?

135. 1 Kings 12:16 (= 3 Kings 12:16 Vulgate).

136. This narration is nonsense on its face but may be a garbled account of the immediately following story, which has a basis in fact even though Notker confuses the details.

137. Cf. Einhard, c. 20, and Astronomer, c. 6. This conspiracy took place in 792.

the women who were usually around to serve his wife and daughters to go out and see who was at the door and what he wanted. They went out and spotted a wretched character, bolted the door with great laughter and jeering, and, covering their mouths with their clothes, tried to hide themselves in a corner. But the wisest emperor, whom nothing under heaven escaped, diligently asked the women what was going on and who was knocking at the door. He got the answer that it was a certain shaved tramp, silly, out of his mind, dressed in a linen shirt and underwear, asking to see him without delay. He ordered him to be admitted. The cleric threw himself at Charles's feet and told everything in detail. All those conspirators, suspecting nothing at all, received suitable penalties before the third hour of the day, either being sent into exile or punished. Pippin himself, a dwarf and hunchback, was brutally whipped, tonsured, and sent for a little while as punishment to the cell of St. Gall, which then seemed to be poorer and smaller than all other places of the immense empire.

A little later some of the Frankish nobles desired to lay hands on the king.[138] This hardly eluded him, but he really did not want to lose them, because if they had wished him well, they could have been a great benefit to the Christian people. He sent his envoys to that same Pippin to ask him what would be best to do about them. They found him in a garden with the older brothers, the younger brothers being engaged on more important tasks. They found him digging up nettles and annoying plants with a pitchfork so that useful plants would be able to flourish. They explained to him the reason for their coming. He drew a sigh from the depths of his gut, for deformed people tend to be more irritable than healthy ones, and responded with these words: "If Charles thought my advice was worth anything, he would not be punishing me so. I have nothing useful to say to him. Tell him what you have found me doing." They were afraid to go back to the formidable emperor without some concrete answer, so they asked him again and again what they should tell their lord. So he said, peevishly, "I send him no message except what I am doing. I am pulling out worthless crap so that useful herbs will be able to grow freely." They departed very sad because they had nothing sensible to report. When they got back to the emperor and were asked what message they had, they complained that after so much effort and travel they could not say a single thing. With the wisest of kings asking them one thing after another—where

---

138. This rebellion took place in 786 and was led by a certain Hardrad. Cf. Einhard, c. 20.

they found him, what he was doing, what answer he gave them—they said, "We found him sitting on a rustic stool weeding an herb garden with a pitchfork. We went over the reason for our journey again and again, and even with the most earnest requests we could extract from him only this response: 'I have nothing else to say to him except what I am doing. I am pulling out worthless crap so that useful herbs will be able to grow freely.'" On hearing this, the augustus, who was not lacking in cunning, indeed brimming with wisdom, rubbed his ears, breathed out through his nose, and told them, "Best of vassals, you have brought back a reasonable answer." Whereas the envoys thought themselves in mortal danger, he himself learned from the gist of the report what to do. He removed all those conspirators from the midst of the living and gave his faithful followers places to grow and spread out, places formerly occupied by those fruitless men. One of his adversaries, who had chosen for himself the highest hill in Francia and whatever he could see from it, Charles ordered to be hung from a high beam erected on that same hill. He told his bastard Pippin to choose how he wished to live his life. Given the opportunity, he picked a place in a certain monastery that was then the noblest but is now, for reasons that are not unknown, destroyed.[139] But I will not tell that story before I see your little son Bernhard with a sword strapped to his thigh.[140]

Great souled though he was, Charles was angry that he was provoked to go out and fight those barbarian nations when one or another of his military leaders seemed suited to the task. That this was so I can prove by the action of one of my countrymen. There was a certain man from the Thurgau, Eishere, whose name meant "the great part of a terrifying army." He was so tall that one might believe him descended from the tribe of the Anakim,[141] except that so much time and space intervened. Whenever he came to the river Thur, swelling and flooding with Alpine torrents, and he could not get his huge horse into the stream—perhaps I should not call it a stream, since it was not even quite liquid—he grabbed hold of the reins and made the horse swim behind him, saying, "By the Lord Gall, you will follow me whether you want to or not." When he was in caesar's entourage, he cut down Bohemians, Wilzi, and Avars the way you would cut grass, and he skewered them on his

139. Prüm, which was sacked by Vikings in 882.

140. Bernhard was an illegitimate son of Charles III, whose twenty-year marriage produced no legitimate heirs. Charles's struggle to legitimize Bernhard is at issue here.

141. Deuteronomy 2:10.

spear after the fashion of a birdkeeper. When he came home victorious, he was asked by the layabouts how he liked it in the land of the Wends. He spoke as follows, both disdainful and angry: "What are those tadpoles to me? I used to run through seven or eight or even nine of them with my spear, and they muttered I don't know what as I carried them here and there. The lord king and I wasted our time fighting against worms like those."

(13) At the same time as the emperor was putting the last touch to the war with the Huns and he had received the submission of the above-mentioned peoples, the Northmen showed up and caused a great disturbance for the Franks and Gauls.[142] The unconquered Charles came back and tried to invade their territory by the land route, although it was very tight and without roads. But either the providence of God stopped him—as, according to the Scriptures, "these served to put Israel to the test"[143]—or our sins got in the way, but every one of his attempts failed. For example, one night, to the disadvantage of the whole army, fifty pairs of oxen belonging to one abbot were struck dead by a sudden disease. Therefore Charles, the wisest of men, gave up what he had begun, so that he would not disobey Scripture: "Do not try to rush against a flowing stream."[144] When Charles was traveling across his very wide empire for a good long time, Godfred, the king of the Northmen, stirred up by his absence, crossed the frontier of the Frankish kingdom and selected the Moselle region for his seat.[145] When he was calling his falcon off a duck, his son, whose mother Godfred had recently abandoned to take another wife instead of her, pursued him and cut him in two. At this, just as when Holofernes was slain, no one dared to trust in his courage or arms but sought protection in flight alone;[146] and so, lest on the example of the ungrateful Israel anyone vaunt himself against God, Francia was freed without his effort.[147] Charles, unconquered without even having to conquer, gave glory to God for such a judgment, but he complained a great deal because some of them had escaped on account of his absence. "I am really upset," he said, "that my Christian hand did not get to play with those dog-headed people."

142. These events took place in 810–11. Cf. Einhard, c. 14.

143. Judges 3:4.

144. Sirach 4:32 (= Ecclesiasticus 4:32 Vulgate).

145. Notker has here conflated the Danish attacks of 810 (Godfred I) and 885 (Godfred III). The latter did in fact ravage the Moselle region.

146. Judith 13:1–8, 15:1–3.

147. Judges 7:2.

(14) It happened that when Charles was traveling about, he arrived unexpectedly at a certain coastal city in Narbonnese Gaul. He was eating his breakfast without being recognized when Norman pirates made a scouting visit to its port. When the ships were sighted, some said they were Jews, some Africans, and some British merchants. Very wise Charles, from experience and cleverness, perceived that they were enemies, not merchants, and said to his men, "Those ships are not packed with merchandise; they are filled with fierce foes." On hearing this, one man after another, wishing to be first, rushed headlong to the ships. But in vain. For the Normans, having discovered that Charles the "Hammer," as they used to call him,[148] was there, evaded by a never-seen-before withdrawal not only the swords but even the eyes of those who might follow them, so that their entire fleet would not be defeated or chopped up in tiny pieces. Charles, religious, just, and reverent, rose from the table and stood at the east-facing window. For a long time he shed countless tears, and no one dared to press him on the matter. Finally, he explained to his war-hardened nobles his behavior and weeping. "Do you know," he said, "my faithful followers, why I have been weeping so bitterly? It is not that," he said, "I am afraid that these nobodies can harm me in any way. But I am very sad indeed that they have dared to attack this coast while I am alive, and I am torn up with particular grief because I foresee how much trouble they will cause for my successors and their subjects." May the protection of our Lord Christ keep this from happening, and may your[149] sword, already hardened with the blood of the Normans, stand in their way, and may the sword of your brother Carloman, already tinged with their gore, be joined to yours—even though it is now turned to rust, not on account of inactivity but because of a lack of resources and the barrenness of the land of your most faithful Arnulf.[150] But it ought to be possible to bring that sword back to its sharpness and sheen on the order and will of your power. From the prolific root of Louis this little branch alone, along with that delicate twig Bernie,[151] flourishes under the shelter of your protection. Meanwhile let's insert something into the history of your like-named ancestor about your great-great-grandfather

---

148. In fact, it was Charles's grandfather, also named Charles, who was called "the Hammer" (Martellus).

149. Notker switches here from talking about Charlemagne to addressing Charles III.

150. Carloman was Charles's elder brother. He died in 880. Arnulf ("of Carinthia") was Carloman's illegitimate son. He succeeded Charles as East Frankish king in 887 and became emperor in 896.

151. Bernhard again; Notker calls him Bennolini.

Pippin[152] so that, should divine mercy allow, it may be imitated in your own little Charles or Louis.[153]

(15) When the Lombards and other enemies were attacking the Romans, they sent envoys to that same Pippin to see if, for the love of Saint Peter, he would deign to come as quickly as possible. Having subdued these enemies, Pippin entered Rome as a victor to pray and was received by the citizens with this praise: "The fellow citizens of the apostles and the household of God have come together today bearing peace and making the fatherland shine brightly, to give peace to the nations and to free the people of the Lord."[154] Some people who do not know the meaning and origin of this song usually sing it on the feast day of the apostles. He actually returned quickly to Francia because he feared the ill will of the Romans or, as I should say, of the Constantinopolitans. Pippin discovered that some of the nobles of his army were accustomed to complain about him disrespectfully in private, so he called for a bull of terrifying size and indomitable spirit to be brought in and then for an extremely ferocious lion to be set on it. The lion rushed upon the bull in an exceptionally powerful attack, grabbed it by the neck, and threw it to the ground. Then the king said to those who were standing around, "Pull the lion off the bull and kill him on top of it." Those who were watching were frozen with fear, gasping, and in their terror barely able to mutter these words: "Lord, there is no man under heaven who would dare to try that." At which Pippin quite confidently rose from his throne, drew his sword, cut right through the necks of the lion and of the bull at the shoulders, put his sword back in its sheath, and sat back down on his throne. "Does it seem to you," he said, "that I am capable of being your lord? Have you not heard what little David did to that giant Goliath, or that pip-squeak Alexander to his noble followers?"[155] Then, like men struck by lightning, they fell on the ground, saying, "A man would have to be crazy to deny your right to rule over mankind."

Not only did Pippin show himself to be such a foe to beasts and men, but he also struggled in an unheard-of way against spiritual wickedness. For when the baths had not yet been built at Aachen and the hot and healthy springs were bubbling rapidly, he ordered his chamberlain to see if the spring had

152. Pippin III, king of the Franks, 751–68.
153. *Karolaster aut Ludowiculus:* Here, and in 2.11 above, Notker uses somewhat unusual diminutives, perhaps affecting a kind of tender intimacy.
154. Pippin III never visited Rome. The phrase is in part a paraphrase of Ephesians 2:19.
155. Pippin III was nicknamed "the Short."

been purified and if any unknown person had been hanging around there. When this was done, the king took his sword and hurried to the bath in his shirt and slippers, at which time the ancient enemy suddenly attacked as if to kill him. The king bared his sword, made the sign of the cross, and turned against the phantom in human form. He ran his unconquered sword right through it and into the ground such that it took him a long time and a real struggle until he was able, barely, to pull it loose. The phantom was of such nastiness that it fouled the spring with its hideous slime and gore. Unperturbed, the unconquerable Pippin said to his chamberlain,[156] "Pay no attention to such things. Let that fouled water flow, because when it runs pure again, I will take my bath without delay."

(16) I had originally intended, O August Emperor, to weave together my short little story about your great-grandfather alone—you know well everything that he did.[157] But when an opportunity presented itself or recollection urged it, I judged it wrong to leave completely untouched the deeds of your most glorious father, Louis, called "illustrious," and of your most religious grandfather nicknamed "Pious," or of your extremely warlike great-great-grandfather Pippin the Younger, about whom there has been all but silence in recent times on account of the laziness of people nowadays.[158] Now, about Pippin the Elder the deeply learned Bede fashioned almost a complete book in his ecclesiastical history.[159] All these things having been commemorated a bit too fully, I must now go swimming back like a swan to your illustrious namesake Charles. But if I do not leave out something of his military exploits, I will never get around to reflecting on his daily activity.[160] I will now relate whatever occurs to me at the moment as briefly as I am able.

(17) After the death of the ever victorious Pippin, when the Lombards were again disturbing Rome, the unconquered Charles, although he was extremely busy with affairs on our side of the Alps, took route for Italy without delay

156. Here is a good example of Notker's apparent carelessness with titles. He begins this section talking about the chamberlain (*camerarius*), an important person in the palace hierarchy, but then he switches to *cubicularius,* meaning, basically, a servant in the bedchamber.

157. This chapter comes as close as Notker ever comes to spelling out the reasons for his *Deeds.*

158. Cf. 1.10 above and Einhard's prologue.

159. Notker is doubly wrong here. Bede mentions Pippin only briefly (*Ecclesiastical History of the English People,* 5.10–11) in connection with the Anglo-Saxon missionary Willibrord, and the Pippin Bede mentions is not Pippin II ("the Elder") but the very Pippin III ("the Younger") about whom Notker has been speaking. Bede (673–735) was an enormously learned Northumbrian monk who spent almost his whole life in the monasteries of Wearmouth and Jarrow.

160. Notker is here anticipating the third book, which it seems he never wrote.

and in a bloodless battle, or even by spontaneous submission, received the humiliated Lombards into his service. To confirm that they would never fall away from the kingdom of the Franks or bring any damage to the lands of Saint Peter, he married the daughter of prince Desiderius of the Lombards.[161] A little while later, because she was bedridden and incapable of having children, she was put aside as if already dead on the judgment of the most holy priests.[162] Her father was angered and demanded an oath from his people, shut himself up within the walls of Pavia, and prepared to revolt against the unconquerable Charles. When he learned all this with certainty, Charles took to the road with speed.[163] It happened that a few years before, one of his foremost princes, Otker by name,[164] incurred the anger of the terrifying emperor and, on account of that, took flight to that same Desiderius. When they heard of the approach of the fearsome Charles, they climbed up the highest tower so that they could see anyone coming, far and wide. When the baggage animals came into view, moving along more swiftly than those of Darius or Julius Caesar, Desiderius said to Otker, "Is Charles in the midst of that great army?" Otker answered, "Not yet." When he saw distinctly the army of ordinary soldiers gathered from the immense breadth of the empire, he spoke to Otker, "Surely Charles takes delight in these troops," but Otker answered, "Not yet, not yet." Then Desiderius began to get hot under the collar and said, "What will we do if more men come with him?" Otker said, "When he comes, you will see what he is like. I do not know what is going to happen to us." While they were talking, Charles's personal attendants came into view, men with no knowledge of resting. Seeing them, Desiderius was stupefied. "That is Charles," he said. But Otker replied, "No, not yet, not yet." Then they perceived the bishops and abbots and the chaplains with their associates. On seeing all of them, Desiderius was almost dead and could scarcely bear the light of day. He babbled with sobs, "Let's go down and hide in the earth in the face of the fury of so terrible an adversary." Otker was scared silly too and thought back to happier times when he was knowledgeable about and

161. Charles had married one of Desiderius's daughters (Gerperga?) after his mother, Bertrada, had attempted to patch up peace between the two kingdoms in 770. By the time of his campaign in Italy in 773–74, he had already repudiated her. Cf. Einhard, c. 18. Note that Notker does not call Desiderius king.

162. No other source reports these details, and they are probably not to be trusted.

163. Desiderius actually defended Pavia from the start. Charles suspended his siege to go to Rome at Easter in 774, returned, and accepted Desiderius's submission. The failed marriage had little, if anything, to do with all of this.

164. Some believe that this figure stands behind the literary character Ogier the Dane.

very much accustomed to the affairs and equipment of the incomparable Charles. "When you see," he said, "a grain field bristling with iron, and the Rivers Po and Ticino gushing over the walls of the city and flowing black with iron, then you can hope to see Charles." He had not yet finished speaking these words when a wind arose from the west, or perhaps the North Wind, like a dark cloud that turned the brightness of day into the horror of night. With the emperor[165] approaching step by step, a new day dawned that was darker than any night for those shut up in the city, on account of the splendor of his arms. And then iron Charles himself came into view, helmeted in iron, armed with iron gloves, his iron chest and broad shoulders safe in an iron breastplate. An iron spear raised on high filled his left hand and his right hand always gripped his unconquered sword. To mount more easily, some were accustomed to leave their thighs without armor, but Charles went about with small iron plates. What shall I say about his greaves? As with the whole army's, they were always made of iron. His shield revealed nothing but iron. His horse also shone with the spirit and color of iron. All those who went in front of him, everybody to the side, and all those who followed him alike imitated the whole of his gear as closely as possible. Iron filled the fields and open spaces. The rays of the sun were beaten back by this battle line of iron. Honor was borne to hard iron by harder men. The horror of the dungeon was as nothing next to the splendor of the iron. "O, the iron; alas, the iron": the bewildered wail of the citizens sounded forth. The firmness of the walls and of the young men was set to shaking by the iron; the counsel of the elders perished before the iron. Attentive and truth telling, the observer Otker, when he had seen with one quick look the things I, stammering[166] and toothless, have attempted to explain, not as I ought to have done but by a long, drawn-out path, said to Desiderius, "Look! There you have exactly what you have been looking for so hard." And on saying this, he fell down senseless. The residents of the city, either on account of madness or some hope of resisting, did not wish to receive Charles on that same day. Charles, the most ingenious of all, said to his men, "Today let us do something memorable so that we cannot be blamed for spending this day in idleness. If they do not open up to us promptly, let's hurry and build a little oratory in which we can attend to divine services." When he finished speaking, one man after another ran off to get lime and stones, others gathered wood and paints, and they brought

165. Charles was not yet emperor.
166. *Balbus:* "the Stammerer" was Notker's familiar nickname.

them to the skilled workers who were always in his company. Beginning at the fourth hour of the day, they built before the twelfth such a basilica, with walls and roof, paneled ceilings and paintings—they had help from a band of recruits and regular soldiers—that anyone who saw it would not have believed it possible to build in less than a whole year. On the next day, he conquered the city easily and began to take it over by his own effort alone and without shedding blood.[167] Some of the citizens wished to open the gates to him; others wished, in vain, to hold out or, as I ought to say, to shut themselves up. I leave it to those who hang around Your Highness not for love but only in the hope of gain to finish the story. Then moving on to other matters, the most religious Charles came to the city of Friuli, which the pretentious seem to call Forum of Julius.[168] It so happened that the bishop of the city at that time, or, as I should say in the modern fashion, the patriarch, was speeding to the last moments of his life. Most religious, Charles was hurrying to visit him so that he could name his own successor. The patriarch piously drew a final sigh from the depths of his being and said, "Lord, I leave that bishopric which I have held for so long without any benefit or spiritual advantage to the judgment of God and your disposition so that, when I am dead, I do not add to the heap of sins that I have piled up while alive and wind up condemned by the inescapable and incorruptible judge." Wise as always, Charles accepted this and judged him a not unworthy equal to the ancient fathers.

Charles, the most energetic of all the energetic Franks, was staying in that region for a little while and was appointing a worthy successor to the bishop, who had meanwhile died, when after the celebration of Mass on a feast day he said to his men, "So that we don't become idle layabouts in our leisure, let's go hunting and see if we can catch anything. Each of us will go in the same clothes we are now wearing." It was a cloudy day and cold. Charles himself was wearing a ram's pelt, which did not cost much more than the cloak of Saint Martin, which covered his chest and left his arms bare, so that he would win divine approval when offering a sacrifice to God. The others, since it was a feast day and they had just come from Pavia, to which city the Venetians had recently brought all the riches of the lands across the sea, strutted about in pheasant skins decked out with silk; others boasted the neck, back, and hind feathers of peacocks that had just come into new plumage; still others were tricked out in little cloths in Tyrian purple or lemon yellow, others in

167. In fact it was about ten months before Pavia surrendered, albeit without much of a battle.
168. In fact, Forum Iulii was Friuli's Roman name.

good pelts, and a few in ermine. After rushing along rapidly, they were slashed by the branches of trees, thorns, and nettles, or soaked with rain, and came home fouled with the blood of wild animals and stinking of skins. Astute as ever, Charles said, "None of us should take off our pelts before we go to bed, so that they can dry off better on us." In accord with this command and now more concerned about their bodies than their clothing, they sought out the hearth to warm themselves. But soon he called them back and kept them in his service until late in the night, and then he let them go back to their lodgings. When they began to take off their exceptionally fine pelts and even finer linens, the cracking of their wrinkled and shrunken garments made sounds that could be heard from far away like the breaking of dry branches. They groaned and sighed and complained that they had lost so much money in one day. Then they got an order from the emperor that they were to present themselves to him the next morning in those same pelts. When they did this, they did not strut about in their clothes, for they were all horrified at their stained and stinking rags. Charles was busily engaged and said to his chamber servant, "Rub that pelt between your hands and bring it to me to look at." It was brought over whole and white. Taking it in his hands and showing it to all those standing around, he pronounced these words: "O stupidest of mortals, which hide is more precious and useful, this one of mine, bought for one solidus, or those of yours, bought not only for many pounds but even for many talents?" They turned their faces to the ground, for they could not bear his terrible glare.

Your most religious father imitated that example not once only but throughout his life, such that no one who seemed worthy of his attention or instruction would ever presume to wear anything when the army was on the march against the enemy except his soldier's weapons and wool or linen garments. And if anyone beneath him in rank who was unaware of this rule decked himself out in silk, gold, or silver and happened to bump into him, he got dressed down with words like these and went away a better, even wiser, man: "O, you, twice blinded by gold, or you by silver, or you by all that scarlet. You wretched, unfortunate fellow, it is not enough for you that you might die in battle? Must you also hand over to the enemy those things with which it would be better for you to redeem your soul than to see them decorate the idols of the gentiles?" From the beginning of his life to his seventieth year the unconquered Louis rejoiced in iron, so much so that he made a spectacle before the envoys of the Normans. I will tell you about this, but you know it better than I do.

(18) When the individual kings of the Northmen sent him gold and silver as a token of their devotion, and their swords to mark their eternal subjection and submission, the king ordered that the money be thrown on the floor, be viewed by everyone with contempt, and be trodden underfoot like dirt. He ordered the swords to be brought to him on his high throne, however, so he could test them for himself. At that point the envoys were fearful that some suspicion of mischief might arise against them, and they presented the swords to the emperor in the way that servants hand knives to their lords, that is, by the tip. He took one of them by the hilt and tried to bend one end back to touch the other, but it broke between his hands, which were stronger than the iron. Then one of the envoys drew his own sword from its sheath and offered it in the obsequious manner of servants. "Lord," he said, "as I believe, this sword will be found as tough and as flexible as your ever-victorious right hand could wish." Caesar accepted it, and he was truly caesar, as Isaiah had prophesied: "Look to the rock from which you were hewn."[169] Alone of all the people of Germany, by God's craftsmanship, he rose in skill and spirit to the level of the ancients. Holding the hilt of the sword he bent back the tip like a twig and then let it slowly return to its original shape. The envoys gaped at each other in amazement and muttered, "O, if only gold seemed so vile to our princes, and iron so precious."

(19) Because some discussion of the Northmen has come up, I will explain from a few developments in your grandfather's time how much they think of faith and baptism. As after the death of the great warrior David the neighboring peoples who had long been held in subjection by his powerful hand paid tribute to his peaceful son Solomon, so on account of fear they had paid tribute to the most august emperor Charles, and then that savage people got used to honoring his son Louis with the same respect. The most religious emperor on one occasion took pity on the envoys of the Normans and asked them if they wished to receive the Christian religion, and he received the answer that they were always, everywhere, and in all respects ready to obey.[170] He ordered them to be baptized in His name, of whom the highly learned Augustine said, "If there were no Trinity, the Truth would not have said: 'Go, teach all nations, baptizing them in the name of the Father, and of the Son, and of the Holy Spirit.'"[171] They were adopted by the nobles of the palace almost like children and received from caesar's chamber a white robe,

169. Isaiah 51:1
170. Cf. Ermoldus, pages 173–83.
171. Augustine, *On the Trinity*, 15.28; Matthew 28:19.

and from their godparents costly Frankish garb, arms, and other adornments. When more and more of them had been doing this year after year for a long time, they showed up on Easter Saturday not because of Christ but for earthly advantage, not as envoys but as very devoted vassals in obedience to the emperor. On one occasion as many as fifty of them arrived. The emperor asked them if it was their wish to be baptized, and he ordered that holy water be poured without delay upon those who answered affirmatively. Then, because there were not enough linen garments ready, he ordered short shirts to be cut up and sewed together like wraps or patched together like tunics. When one of these was put on one of their elders and he had looked closely at it with great curiosity, no little indignation welled up in his mind, and he said to the emperor, "I have already been washed here twenty times and dressed in the finest and whitest garments, but, look, this bag is suited to swineherds, not to soldiers. And except that I would be embarrassed by my nakedness, having been deprived of my clothes and given no new ones by you, I would abandon your wrap and your Christ." Christ's enemies assign little weight to what Christ's apostle said: "All of you who have been baptized into Christ have been clothed with Christ"[172] and also "We who were baptized in Christ Jesus were baptized into his death,"[173] and especially what pertains closely to those who despise the faith and offend against the sacraments: "They are crucifying the Son of God again for themselves and holding him up to contempt."[174] If only this were seen to be true among the gentiles and not, as is often found, among those who bear the name of Christ!

(20) There is still something to be said about the kindness of the first Louis, and then we will go back to Charles. Louis was a most unperturbed emperor. Since he was free from all attacks of enemies, he applied himself fully to the works of religion, to prayer and alms, to hearing cases and settling them justly. In the latter activity he was experienced by both intelligence and practice, such that when a certain man who looked rather like Ahitophel and who was held to be an angel by everyone tried to fool him, he gave this kind of response, with a kind enough look and a gentle voice, albeit with a somewhat disturbed spirit: "O wonderfully wise Anselm, if it is proper that I should dare to say so, you are not walking along the right path." From that day forward he was held by everyone to be a person who did not tell the truth.

172. Galatians 3:27.
173. Romans 6:3.
174. Hebrews 6:6.

(21) The most merciful Louis was so dedicated to alms that he chose not only to have them distributed in his own sight but even to be given by himself. What is more, when he was absent, he arranged the cases of poor people so that one of them who seemed in every way physically weaker yet more spirited than the others would decide by himself what was to be done about their offenses, to make good on thefts, to settle just retributions for personal injuries or wounds, and also, in the case of more serious offenses, the cutting-off of limbs, decapitations, and hangings. He put dukes, subordinates of counts, hundredmen and their subordinates, in place, but the poor man fulfilled his assigned task with energy. This most merciful augustus venerated the Lord Christ in all those poor people and never ceased to give them food and clothing. He did this especially on that day when Christ took off his mortal body and prepared to put on his incorruptible one. On that day he also gave gifts individually to all those who served in the palace or worked in the royal court. He ordered that sword belts or leggings and the most expensive clothes to be found in the whole empire be given to the more noble among them. Frisian cloaks in every color were given to those of lower rank. Next, linen garments or wool ones or knives were given to the grooms, bakers, and cooks, just as each one had need. And when finally no one lacked anything,[175] according to the acts and words of the apostles, there was great thanksgiving among all. The ragged poor, now joyfully cleaned up, lifted their voices to heaven—"May the Lord have mercy on blessed Louis"—through the broad courtyard and small enclosures, which the Romans usually call porticoes, of Aachen. The soldiers who could do so embraced the emperor's feet, others worshipped him from a distance, as caesar was passing by on the way to the church. One of the jesters shouted out jokingly, "Happy are you, Louis, who has clothed so many on one day. By Christ, no one in Europe today has clothed more except Atto."[176] So the emperor asked him how he had been able to clothe more, but the mime, taking delight in attracting the emperor's attention, said with a cackle, "Today he has given away more new clothes." His disposition sweet, the emperor, with unperturbed expression, saw that this was a silly joke, and entered the church with humble devotion; he behaved so reverently that he seemed to be holding the Lord Jesus Christ right before his eyes.

(22) Louis always went to the baths every Saturday, not because he had to but because it gave him an opportunity for generosity. Everything that he

175. Acts 4:32–35.
176. This person is unattested, and the point of the story is obscure.

took off, except his sword and belt, he used to give to the attendants. His generosity extended right down to the least of them, so that he ordered all his clothing to be given to the glazier Stracholf, a servant of St. Gall, who was serving him at that moment. When some wandering vassals among the soldiers learned about this, they set an ambush for him beside the road and tried to rob him. He said to them, "What are you doing using force on the emperor's glazier?" They answered, "We allow you to keep your office. . . ."[177]

177. All manuscripts break off at this point.

INTRODUCTION

The author of the elegiac poem *In Honor of Louis, the Most Christian Caesar Augustus,* as well as two verse epistles to Pippin II of Aquitaine, Ermoldus Nigellus, is almost a complete mystery. Everything that can be known about him with any certainty emerges from his writings. In the first of his verse epistles he speaks of the region of Angoulême, watered by the river Charente, as his "homeland." Even educated guesses about the dates of his birth and death are impossible. He was evidently a member of Pippin's court—twice in the poem he asks to be returned there from his exile in Strasbourg. Presumably, therefore, he was Aquitainian by birth. His name may well be Frankish, but that fact is of little help in identifying him. His nickname may mean something like "swarthy little fellow," but that is not very helpful. It is always assumed that he was a cleric, and it seems more likely that he was a secular priest than a monk. He accompanied Pippin on a campaign in Brittany in 824 and says, self-deprecatingly, that no one came to any harm on his account. Pippin told him to attend to his books because war did not suit him. Shortly after his military misadventures, he was exiled by Louis to Strasbourg and placed under the supervision of Archbishop Bernold. In book 4 of his poem, Ermoldus twice admits to some culpability but does not name his offense. In the second of his verse epistles, Ermoldus praises Louis and holds him up to Pippin as a fine example. He then insists that this is all he has ever said about Louis and not what some malicious people, enflamed by envy, have accused him of saying. Perhaps his real or alleged offense was to have expressed to Pippin some criticism of his father. His confinement in Strasbourg seems to have been quite mild; he could move about freely, surely visited Ingelheim, and may have been with the court in 826 when Louis received King Harald Klak of Denmark.

There is no way to know if Ermoldus's plea for release was successful. Some scholars have assumed that he benefited from the disturbances of 830 by gaining his freedom. This is possible; no more. The Astronomer mentions an Ermold who was sent by Louis to Pippin in 834, and documents testify to an Ermold who was chancellor to Pippin in 838. There is too little evidence to say with any confidence that this man, or these men, can be identified with the poet.[1]

Since Ermoldus has no biography, interpretations of his poem depend on the text itself and on a few points that emerge from the verse epistles. The poem can be dated reasonably precisely. Book 4 treats in detail the visit of Harald to Louis's court in June of 826 and also mentions George of Venice, who appeared there as well, promising to build an organ. The last book was therefore written during or after the summer of 826.[2] It is impossible to say when Ermoldus began to compose his verses; presumably the whole work was a product of Ermoldus's exile, and this punishment must have been imposed on him after November of 824, when the Breton campaign ended. The poem must have been completed before the assembly in February of 828 that, among other things, sacked Counts Hugh of Tours and Matfrid of Orléans. Both of these men are mentioned repeatedly and positively in the poem. It is perhaps worth noting that the first verse epistle preceded the poem, whereas the second one followed shortly after it.[3]

Ermoldus was the first medieval author to produce a Latin epic on a secular theme and, incidentally, the first to make Christian struggles with Muslims a central theme.[4] He did not use epic's conventional meter, dactylic hexameter. Instead, he wrote in elegiac distichs, perhaps as an homage to the Roman poet Ovid, who employed that meter in his own poems written from exile. Mentioning Ovid brings up the question of Ermoldus's culture. He certainly knew Ovid, as well as Virgil, Juvencus, and Sedulius among Roman poets, and also the sixth-century Venantius Fortunatus.[5] He knew the Anglo-Saxon

---

1. Schaller, "Ermoldus"; Berschin, "Biographien Ludwigs des Frommen," 220–23; Brunhölzl, "Ermold le Noir"; Godman, *Poets and Emperors*, 106–30; Löwe, "Biographien," 329–32; Raby, *Secular Latin Poetry*, 1:221–24; Faral, introduction to *Poème sur Louis le Pieux*, v–xii; Manitius, "Ermoldus Nigellus."

2. For corroboration, see *Royal Frankish Annals*, anno 826, trans. Scholz, 119–20.

3. Godman, "Louis the Pious and His Poets," 255.

4. Ebenbauer, *Carmen Historicum*, 1:101.

5. Ranieri, "I modelli formali," has traced more than five hundred instances where Ermoldus borrowed from earlier poets texts ranging from a few words to whole lines. See also Schaller, "Ermoldus,"

Aldhelm and also the poets of Charles's court, Alcuin, Angilbert, and Theodulf. His debt to Theodulf is so great that it has led one scholar to suggest that
he might have been his pupil.[6] He knew, too, the *Paderborn Epic,* a work in
four books treating the encounter of Charles and Pope Leo III at Paderborn
in 799; only the third book of this work is extant. The hunt scene in book 4
of the poem, in particular, may be based on this source.[7] Ermoldus alludes
to events in Roman history but not in ways that suggest he was familiar with
particular Roman historians. Neither the Bible nor the church fathers figure
prominently in the poem. It is difficult to pin down Ermoldus's sources. It has
long been assumed that he depended in places on some sort of annalistic work.
He had good court connections and probably witnessed a great deal himself.
On the whole, Ermoldus's culture appears to have been well within the typical
Carolingian spectrum.

Only a few comments are necessary about Ermoldus's poetry, because the
following translation renders his verse into prose. His style has been fairly, if
somewhat one-sidedly, criticized. He is indeed verbose, and the reader of this
translation will spot many places where Ermoldus uses many words instead of
the few that a more skillful writer would have employed. He has a penchant
for singsong phrases: *dante tonante, miserante tonante, dante creante,* for example. The work is panegyrical, so a certain amount of exaggeration and flattery
is only to be expected. Indeed, it is not easy to categorize the work. Is it history, epic poetry, or panegyric? Did Ermoldus consciously blur the boundaries between these genres? He occasionally coins new words, uses classical
words with new meanings, and alters the spelling of certain words. Usually he
alters traditional orthography for metrical reasons—to add or delete a sylla-
ble or to change the length of a vowel. Ermoldus is obsessively fond of direct
discourse. He invents one speech after another. While it would be hazardous
to assume that these speeches reflect what was actually said on particular occasions, it is important to see them as key sites for interpretation and analysis
on Ermoldus's part, and therefore on the part of his readers. In other words,
it is often in these speeches that Ermoldus indicates what he is really writing about, and reveals his interests, principles, and prejudices. Ermoldus was

col. 2161; Berschin, "Biographien Ludwigs des Frommen," 222–23; Ebenbauer, *Carmen Historicum,*
1:113–15; Faral, introduction to *Poème sur Louis le Pieux,* x–xi, xv–xvii.

   6. Schaller, "Ermoldus," col. 2161.

   7. Ibid.; Berschin, "Biographien Ludwigs des Frommen," 222–23; Godman, "Louis the Pious and
His Poets," 258–59.

fond of describing the countryside and landscape. This might be a matter of personal preference, or it might be something he learned from reading Roman poets.[8]

Ermoldus has not fared well with modern scholars.[9] He is dismissed as a poor historian and a mediocre poet. His contemporaries took little notice of him. It is just possible that Walahfrid Strabo, in a poem he composed at court in 829, took a rather nasty dig at Ermoldus. Walahfrid, a touchy "young man in a hurry," was complaining about sycophants and critics. At one point he refers to legs soiled with "little black crap" (*stercus nigellus*), possibly referring to Ermoldus or his poem.[10] Supposing that the poem would have arrived at court in 827 or very early 828, Walahfrid would certainly have seen it. One mid-ninth-century hagiographical work, a verse life of Leudegar, makes some use of the poem.[11] It survives in only two manuscripts, one from the tenth century and one from the fifteenth.

In fact, posterity's judgment has been a little unfair. Ermoldus was a competent poet, and some sections of his poem are well crafted, beautiful, and moving. Although he could not sustain high art, he could achieve it on occasion. Before criticizing Ermoldus as a historian, it is important to remember that he was first of all a poet. As he says twice near the beginning of the work, he carefully chose certain of Louis's deeds for recounting. He never intended to try to tell everything. Although Ermoldus provides many names and some details that appear nowhere else, much of what he says can be corroborated by means of other sources. His chronology is generally correct. His approach is not annalistic; he does not narrate one thing after another. In each of his books, as the reader will see in more detail below, he presents one major event and a series of lesser, sometimes related, sometimes unrelated, developments. There is in fact a sturdy structure undergirding the poem. Ermoldus omits much, but not because of either ignorance or incompetence. Instead, he subordinates

---

8. Schaller, "Ermoldus," col. 2161; Berschin, "Biographien Ludwigs des Frommen," 222–23; Brunhölzl, "Ermold le Noir," 146; Godman, *Poetry of the Carolingian Renaissance,* 45–46; Raby, *Secular Latin Poetry,* 1:222; Faral, introduction to *Poème sur Louis le Pieux,* xvii–xviii, xxi, xxi–xxvii (generally harsh in tone).

9. See the fair characterizations in Ebenbauer, *Carmen Historicum,* 1:148–49.

10. Michael Herren, "The 'De imagine Tetrici' of Walahfrid Strabo: Edition and Translation," *Journal of Medieval Latin* 1 (1991): 118–39, and idem, "Walahfrid Strabo's De imagine Tetrici: An Interpretation," in *Latin Culture and Medieval Germanic Europe,* ed. Richard North and Tette Hofstra, Germania Latina 1 (Groningen, 1992), 25–41.

11. *Vita Beati Leudegarii Martyris,* ed. Ludwig Traube, MGH, PLAC, 3 (Berlin, 1896).

his material to his structures and themes. The reader must appreciate these in order to make sense of the work as either poetry or history.[12]

Consider first Ermoldus's structure.[13] Book 1 centers on the siege of Barcelona in 801. Book 2 centers on Louis's assumption of the imperial title in 813 and the confirmation of that title by Pope Stephen IV at Reims in 816. Book 3 centers on the Breton campaign of 818. Book 4, finally, centers on the mission to the North and the festivities surrounding the submission and baptism of Harald Klak of Denmark. Note the pattern: war then peace; secular endeavors then religious ones. This is precisely how Ermoldus announces his intentions early in the work. The first and last letters of the thirty-five lines of the poem's exordium form a double acrostic reading "Ermoldus sings of the arms of Caesar Louis." Toward the end of this opening section, however, Ermoldus addresses "Pious King Louis," who is "distinguished in the teachings of Christ." Early in book 1 Ermoldus supplies a fanciful etymology of Louis's name that sounds the themes of war and peace, arms and faith. Book 1 proper begins: "Louis, Caesar, you surpass celebrated rulers in wealth and arms, and even more in the love of God." Book 2 opens: "And then, with God's grace, the Franks enjoyed peace everywhere." Book 3 returns to a military focus: "By the gift of highest God, caesar's arms kept on increasing." Book 4 commences this way: "The cares of the pious king extended in every direction, and the faith of the Franks grew right up to the sky." Periodically, within each book, Ermoldus recapitulates his organizational points. On many occasions—but not all—his apparent digressions serve to buttress his overarching structure. For example, in book 1, which is primarily about the war in Spain, Ermoldus pauses to discuss the founding of the monastery of Conques. Once again the reader is reminded of war and peace, arms and faith. Similarly, again in book 1, Ermoldus artfully balances a prophecy about Louis's ascendancy with an account of the satisfied reaction of Charles to the booty and prisoners that Louis dispatched from Spain.[14] Putting all this a little differently, one might say that whereas the poet never loses sight of Louis, it is precisely this focus on Louis that holds the work together, that is its central organizing principle.[15]

12. By far the most sensitive appreciations of Ermoldus's verse and achievement are Godman's: "Louis the Pious and His Poets," 253–71, and *Poets and Emperors*, 106–30.

13. Most fully discussed by Ebenbauer, *Carmen Historicum*, 1:113–33.

14. Godman, "Louis and His Poets," 258–61, 263–64; idem, *Poets and Emperors*, 123; Ebenbauer, *Carmen Historicum*, 1:104.

15. Brunhölzl, "Ermold le Noir," 146.

Einhard extracted from Suetonius a model that called for treating deeds in war and deeds in peace, albeit he modified that model to suit his own purposes. Notker almost certainly deliberately modified that model so as to treat religious deeds and then secular ones. I would not care to suggest that Ermoldus knew either Einhard's *Life* or Suetonius, or that Notker knew Ermoldus's poem, but it is intriguing to note how the three authors built somewhat different structures on relatively common foundations. Ermoldus's poem, taken alongside the works by Einhard and Notker, may hint at some of the ways in which the ancient traditions of biography and panegyric had been internalized by Carolingian writers regardless of which specific ancient texts they had read.[16]

In fundamental respects, Ermoldus's structure serves to support his themes. Two of these seem central to me. First is Louis's piety. Louis "the Pious" is familiar to all students of Carolingian history. It is not so clear, however, when he became "Pious." It may well have been late in the ninth century or even in the tenth, and the point of the nickname, as of other Carolingian nicknames, may have been more to differentiate *this* Louis from other ones than to characterize Louis.[17] Thus Ermoldus's "pious" Louis should not be taken for granted. Moreover, given that Ermoldus was composing his poem for Louis, it is reasonable that he expected Louis and members of his court to recognize the Louis presented in the poem. Louis's piety must not be reduced to a kind of hyperreligiosity. Instead, Ermoldus's characterization of Louis says something about his own ideas of the perfect Christian ruler. In the speeches at Aachen in 813, at Reims in 816, and at Ingelheim in 826, Ermoldus works out his conception of ideal Christian rulership. The ideal ruler must be a man of God and a man of war. If he is truly a man of God, then God will favor his military endeavors, and the ruler will protect his borders and secure peace for the inhabitants of his realm. Peace is more than the absence of war, however. Louis sent out *missi*, for example, to inquire into injustice and oppression.

In addition to being a man of God and man of war, a king must rule. This brings me to a second theme: counsel.[18] Ermoldus highlights this important issue early in the poem when he reports—invents?—the deliberations surrounding Louis's designation as king of Aquitaine. Again and again in his poem Ermoldus mentions individuals or groups who advised the king, or else he alludes to the presence of groups whom we may take to be advisers. This

16. Latowsky, "Foreign Embassies and Roman Universality."
17. Schieffer, "Ludwig 'der Fromme'"; Depreux, "La *pietas*," 204–6.
18. Depreux, "La *pietas*," 212–14.

emphasis on counsel, and on its acceptance and implementation, is another aspect of Ermoldus's vision of the proper polity. That is, while the ruler must be both a man of God and a man of war, the ruler and the ruled must also stand in a harmonious relationship to each other. Einhard, writing at about the same time as Ermoldus, shared this view. Far from portraying Charles as a despot, Einhard depicted him as an attentive Frankish leader. Notker, too, stressed the desirability of seeking noble advice and consent. By contrast, Thegan, the author of the next text in this volume, criticized Louis precisely for listening to his advisers more than was fitting. It is possible that there was some degree of disagreement about this subject in the 820s and 830s.

Ermoldus also makes some sharp topical observations. Three examples will suffice to alert the reader. Near the end of book 4 he remarks on a "demented" person who dares to call into question the efficacy of the relics of the saints. This can only be a reference to Bishop Claudius of Turin, who was condemned in the mid-820s for a variety of heterodox positions including iconoclasm, a denial of the cult of the saints, and a critique of papal authority.[19] Also in book 4 Ermoldus bends over backward to bathe Empress Judith and her son Charles in a favorable light. Ermoldus was unquestionably trimming his sails to the prevailing political winds. Finally, also in book 4, Ermoldus provides a remarkable description of a set of paintings in the palace at Ingelheim. Some have questioned whether these pictures actually existed or were pure literary invention.[20] I think they were real. Be that as it may, Ermoldus uses his description of these pictures to incorporate the Franks of Louis's day into universal history, to align the Franks with the great figures of biblical and classical history.[21] No other Carolingian author did this quite so explicitly or impressively.

ESSENTIAL READING

Ermold le Noir. *Poème sur Louis le Pieux et épîtres au roi Pépin.* Edited by Edmond Faral. Les classiques de l'histoire de France au Moyen Âge 14. Paris, 1932. (I have translated from this edition. The other standard edition is edited by Ernst Dümmler in MGH, PLAC, 2:1–91.)

19. Thomas F. X. Noble, *Images, Iconoclasm, and the Carolingians* (Philadelphia, 2009), 287–94.
20. Lawrence Nees, *A Tainted Mantle: Hercules and the Classical Tradition at the Carolingian Court* (Philadelphia, 1991), 270–76; Walter Lammers, "Ein karolingisches Bildprogramm in der Aula Regia von Ingelheim," in *Festschrift für Hermann Heimpel,* Veröffentlichungen des Max-Planck-Instituts für Geschichte 36.3 (Göttingen, 1972), 227–89.
21. Godman, *Poetry of the Carolingian Renaissance,* 46; Ebenbauer, *Carmen Historicum,* 1:137.

Collateral Sources

(Each of the other texts translated in this volume is relevant to a greater or lesser degree to a reading of Ermoldus.)

Ardo. *The Life of Saint Benedict, Abbot of Aniane and of Inde.* Translated by Allen Cabaniss, revised by Thomas F. X. Noble. In *Soldiers of Christ: Saints and Saints Lives from Late Antiquity and the Early Middle Ages,* edited by Thomas F. X. Noble and Thomas Head, 213–54. University Park, 1995.

Carolingian Chronicles: Royal Frankish Annals and Nithard's Histories. Translated by Bernhard Walter Scholz. Ann Arbor, 1970.

The Lives of the Ninth-Century Popes (Liber Pontificalis). Translated, with an introduction and commentary, by Raymond Davis. Translated Texts for Historians 20. Liverpool, 1995.

"The Time of Louis the Pious (814–840)." Chap. 3 in *Carolingian Civilization: A Reader,* 2nd ed., edited by Paul Edward Dutton, 155–294. Peterborough, Ont., 2004.

Scholarship on Ermoldus

Berschin, Walter. "Biographien Ludwigs des Frommen." In *Biographie und Epochenstil im lateinischen Mittelalter,* vol. 3, Quellen und Untersuchungen zur lateinischen Philologie des Mittelalters 10:220–23. Stuttgart, 1991.

Brunhölzl, Franz. "Ermold le Noir." In *Histoire de la littérature latine du Moyen Âge,* translated by Henri Rochais, vol. 1, pt. 2, 144–48. Turnhout, 1991.

Depreux, Philippe. "La *pietas* comme principe de gouvernement d'après le *Poème sur Louis le Pieux* d'Ermold le Noir." In *The Community, the Family, and the Saint: Patterns of Power in Early Medieval Europe,* edited by Joyce Hill and Mary Swan, International Medieval Research 4:201–24. Leeds, 1998.

―――. "Poètes et historiens au temps de l'empereur Louis le Pieux." *Le Moyen Âge* 99 (1993): 311–32.

Ebenbauer, Alfred. *Carmen Historicum: Untersuchungen zur historischen Dichtung im karolingischen Europa,* 1:101–49. Vienna, 1978.

Godman, Peter. "Louis the Pious and His Poets." *Frühmittelalterliche Studien* 19 (1985): 239–89.

―――. *Poetry of the Carolingian Renaissance.* London, 1985.

―――. *Poets and Emperors: Frankish Politics and Carolingian Poetry.* Oxford, 1987.

Latowsky, Anne. "Foreign Embassies and Roman Universality in Einhard's *Life of Charlemagne.*" *Florilegium* 22 (2005): 25–57.

Löwe, Heinz. "Biographien Ludwigs des Frommen." In Wilhelm Wattenbach and Wilhelm Levison, *Deutschlands Geschichtsquellen im Mittelalter: Vorzeit und Karolinger,* 3:329–38. Weimar, 1957.

Manitius, Max. "Ermoldus Nigellus." In *Geschichte der lateinischen Literatur des Mittelalters,* 1:552–57. Munich, 1911.

Raby, F. J. E. *A History of Secular Latin Poetry in the Middle Ages,* 1:221–24. Oxford, 1934.

Ranieri, Isabella. "I modelli formali del 'Carmen in honorem Hludowici Caesaris' di Ermoldo Nigello." *Acme: Annali della Facoltà di filosofia e lettere dell'Università degli studi di Milano* 36 (1983): 161–214.

———. "La tecnica versificatoria nel 'Carmen in honorem Hludowici Caesaris' di Ermoldo Nigello e la tradizione dattilica latina." *Studi medievali,* 3rd ser., 25 (1984): 93–114.

Schaller, Dieter. "Ermoldus Nigellus." In *Lexikon des Mittelalters,* vol. 3, cols. 2160–61. Munich, 1999.

Schieffer, Rudolf. "Ludwig 'der Fromme': Zur Entstehung eines karolingischen Herrscherbeinamens." *Frühmittelalterliche Studien* 16 (1982): 58–73.

IN HONOR OF LOUIS, THE MOST CHRISTIAN CAESAR AUGUSTUS, BY ERMOLDUS NIGELLUS, AN EXILE

Ermoldus's Elegy

May Holy Mary be with me as I start.

Creator,[1] Ruler of the World and also its patron, redeemer, and author; You who gleam in the heavenly citadel of the Father; You who open the sky's realms to worthy warriors; You, O Christ, who draw back before the court of eternal light those once shut up in the netherworld because of Eve's mistake; and You, David, the Psalmist, who sings with a prophetic voice, holy prophet who long ago in a wonderful telling set forth the future's teachings—help this little rustic to speak of the deeds of great caesar by singing a small poem in the fashion that is required. Now, I do not call on the nymphs[2] here as the wise men of old used to do foolishly, nor do I call on the Muses,[3] nor shall I set my path for the portal of Phoebus as if to win some help from kind Apollo.[4] When those who used to do so were deceived by an empty talent, their hearts were crushed by the horrid and loathsome Behemoth. I seek instead the gateway of

---

1. As noted in my introduction, the first and last letters of the first thirty-five lines of the poem form a double acrostic that reads: "Ermoldus cecenit Hludoici Caesaris arma" (Ermoldus sings of the arms of Caesar Louis). Here Ermoldus is surely evoking the opening of Virgil's *Aeneid:* "Arma virumque cano" (I sing of arms and the man). Such literary conceits were commonplace at the Carolingian court. There has been some controversy over *Hludoici* in the acrostic because one would have expected *Hlodowici* (or *Hludovici*). The absence of a *w* or *v* may indicate that a line has dropped out. But the dedicatory verses read perfectly well without another line.

2. Female goddesses, usually imagined as young and inhabiting natural sites.

3. Goddesses who inspired poets and other artists.

4. Phoebus is another name for Apollo, the god of, among other things, prophecy, poetry, and music.

the starry light so that the true sun of justice may deign to concede gifts upon my prayer. Indeed, I am not asking for myself that with my verses I should run through with my little lyre all the deeds when even great masters would not be able to hold Caesar's attention. But I shall set out to celebrate in song this and that. Look with favor on my songs, Christ, and on the one calling upon You, so that by their help the prince might now show mercy and lighten the burden of my exile, he who lofty in his hall lifts up the downtrodden, spares the offenders, and, as if he were the sun, spreads bright light everywhere. Exalted prince, especially you who hold the scepter of Christ the King, Pious King Louis, indeed caesar famous for the deserved gift of piety, distinguished in the teachings of Christ, receive gladly the gifts that Nigellus brings you, a bold little fellow who tries to match your deeds with his song. May the love of the eternal king always remain in your breast, O Caesar, so that, after you have lifted up your fallen servant, heaven-ruling Christ may raise you to his realm.

Book 1

Louis, Caesar, you surpass celebrated rulers in wealth and arms, and even more in the love of God. I hope I am as ready as I can be to speak the praises of the kind prince; may the Almighty, who can surely do so, accord me the means. I am going to try to describe the deeds of the warlike caesar, which the world rightly recounts with faithful devotion. Perhaps it would have been wiser to stress the origins of my problems and to lament the wicked deeds of my own transgression, for I am an ignorant little fellow; I don't know the dwelling of the Muse; nor am I able to produce measured verses with skill. May the king's mercy comfort me in my hesitation, the one who prefers vows to gifts. Exile compels us to do what we can, I confess, and lacking gifts, I offer what I have.

I am not going to run through each and every deed; it is pointless; it cannot be done; and I have not the wit to do it. If Virgil, Ovid, Cato, Horace, Lucan, Homer, Tullius and Macer, Cicero, or Plato, Sedulius and for that matter Prudentius and Juvencus, even Fortunatus and Prosper himself,[5] were

5. The list of writers ranges from the familiar to the obscure. Ermoldus may be showing off, or he may be subconsciously revealing the school authors he and his contemporaries would have shared. Those on the list that might occasion some questions are Cato, listed here as the presumed author of the *Distichs of Cato*, a collection of verses, usually in four books and probably composed in the third century A.D., containing lots of potted wisdom and guidance; Tullius and Cicero, two names for the same person—it is not clear why Ermoldus lists them as if identifying two people; Aemilius Macer, a poet, friend of Virgil and Ovid; Sedulius, a Christian poet in the early fifth century who wrote

scarcely able to set down everything in their famous writings and to increase
their celebrity with songs, then how do I dare to equal them when as a sailor
I have entered the mighty sea in a rough and leaky boat with a single oar? May
the right hand that kept faithful Peter from perishing in the rising waters and
that drew him into the bark also save wretched me from tumbling into these
waves, and may it bring me to your port, O Best Caesar.

Now let my song of the deeds of Louis go forth, and let him read in our
pages about just a few of the many.

In the time of the Franks, when the scepter of Charles flourished and all the
world celebrated him honorably as father, when a loud report of Francia spread
everywhere and its name became famous in the world, then wise Charles
divided the standards of rule among his offspring, with a chorus of noble
counselors advising him. Indeed, he ceded Francia to his like-named son for
his portion, in case he might be his father's successor. He assigned the kingdom of Italy to his beloved Pippin. But to you, Louis, he gave the Aquitainian kingdom. A report of this equitable division spread throughout the world,
and Louis, exulting, sought his designated kingdom.

That his parents named him so was the stuff of prodigy, for he would be
distinguished in war, powerful, and pious. For he was called Louis (*Hludowicus*), from the noun *ludus,* and the name counsels subjects to enjoy (*ludere*)
the fruits of peace.[6] If anyone wishing to know the name's meaning prefers
to interpret the name as a Frankish word, then of course *Hluto* rings out
"famous" and *Wicgch* means "Mars";[7] hence, it is obvious how his name has
been put together.

Exalted already as a boy, he was filled by the Holy Spirit, yet added to his
rank by war and faith. He swiftly endowed the leaders of the clergy with gifts,
and he restored to holy churches their former benefactions. Having put everything in order, he breathed new life into his subject kingdom, ruling the
people by law and with the riches of his piety.

Paschale Carmen (*Easter Song*), a verse paraphrase of the Gospels; Aurelius Clemens Prudentius, ca.
348–post-405, a superb Christian poet perhaps best known for his *Psychomachia;* Venantius Fortunatus, ca. 530–ca. 610, a prolific poet who was born near Venice but made a career in Merovingian Gaul;
and Prosper Tiro, ca. 390–ca. 463, an Aquitainian monk and theologian among whose many writings
was a lengthy poem on grace.

6. The etymology is flattering to Louis, perhaps, but bogus. *Ludus* means simply a game, an enter-
tainment. Here, by extension, it appears to stretch to enjoyment.

7. The Roman god of war.

The pious ruler tamed the rabid Basques with a teacher's skill, and he brought forth sheep from fierce wolves. And then, roused, he turned his arms against the Spanish, and he himself forced them far from his borders. I know only a little about how many heights he traversed or how many fortifications he subjected to his command, with God giving strength to his arms, but if they were known, my dull pen could not get them all down. But I shall begin to sing what recent news has brought to my uncomprehending ears; the rest I leave to the wise.

So then, there was a city hostile to the forces of the Franks, rather pledged to alliance with the Moors, that the ancient Latins called Barcelona and that was long ago civilized in the Roman fashion.[8] This place was always a haven for Moorish bandits and was usually packed full of armed men. Whoever was passing secretly to or from Spain stopped here in complete safety. Those bands used to pillage our harvests all the time, and that city rejoiced in the spoils they brought back. For a long time many leaders had tried to besiege that city with various strategies—it was enough to have tried—for each one plied what skill he could, in arms or cleverness, but the city's eagerness for battle kept the attackers far away. The city was protected by the mass of its famous walls, built long ago of extremely hard stone. When June leads the whitening harvest toward the sky and the mature grain is ready to be cut with the scythe, the Frank hastens with his mules through the fields and farms and, cutting down the soil's teeming gifts, empties the fields; or when it was time to take the sweet wines of Bacchus[9] from the vineyard, nothing was left to their work. It was just like autumn, when a thick throng of thrushes or of various other birds, whose diet includes the grape, flies through the vineyards seizing and carrying away the grapes and the lovely fruit perishes in their claws and beaks. The wretched vintner mounts a high place and sadly clangs his cymbals or artfully raises his voice on high, but it is not easy for him to stop the work as the thick column of attackers gathers together and snatches up the feast. It is no different when the Franks show up right when the fruit is ready and carry away the gifts of the countryside. But not even these hardships could break the tough Moors, nor various schemes, nor frequent attacks by leaders. And hardly had the Frankish birds hauled off so many gifts than a

8. Cf. Astronomer, cc. 5–10. The events Ermoldus describes here began in 797 and extended some years into the future. Ermoldus has just said that he was not very well informed. That is possible. It is also possible that he has compressed things for literary effect.

9. Often associated with Dionysius, the god of drink and of frenzy and celebration.

swift sailor sent them supplies by sea. For a long time these things went back and forth, and it was said that each side carried harsh attacks against the other.

In the spring, when the countryside warms and grows green again, and winter flees, chased away by the starry sun, and the dawning new year brings back the vanished odors and recent growths flower in the new soil, kings stir and think anew about the customary rights of their kingdoms; each one heads for his frontiers, to guard them. No less, the seed of Charles summoned the assembly of the Franks, according to ancient custom, the well-known forces, that is, the select among the people, the heads of the realm, by whose counsels affairs were going to be organized.[10] The prime men came swiftly, obeying willingly, each one followed by his own huge band. Those who had been summoned sat down, and the king mounted the ancestral throne; outside, the rest of the forces prepared fitting gifts.

As they began speaking, the son of Charles went first and offered these heartfelt words: "Greathearted nobles, worthy of recognition for the performance of your duty, whom Charles set at the frontiers of our homeland, the Almighty has conceded to us the summit of honor so that we might bear due aid to the people. The time of year has returned when peoples menace peoples and each one in turn rushes forth with the arms of Mars. All these things are well enough known to you, but not to us. Tell us your advice; where should we make our campaign?" Thus far the king. Then Lupus Sannio responded. He was a prince of the Basques who took the lead among his own people. Supported by Charles's rearing, he surpassed his ancestors in intelligence and faith.[11] "It is for you to make plans and us to obey, to drink in the plan that flows from your mouth. If in the end the matter falls to us, then for my part, I avow, there will be peace and quiet."

Then Duke William of Toulouse[12] bent his knee, kissed the king's feet, and spoke: "O light of the Franks, king and father, distinguished in arms, you who surpass your ancestors in merits and skill, ruler, you join together the highest virtue and great wisdom, flowing like a stream from the will of your father. If I am worthy, king, attend to my plan; and in your piety, favor my entreaties.

10. Cf. Astronomer, c. 13; the year is 803. Other sources give the initiative to Charlemagne.

11. Several Basque leaders named Lupus appear in the sources from the 760s to the 820s. It is difficult to identify this Lupus precisely. Apparently he spent some time at the court of Charles as a boy, like other Frankish and foreign noble youths.

12. A distant relative of Charles, who made him duke of Toulouse. He aided Louis in the siege of Barcelona in 801 and retired to his monastic foundation of Gellone in 806. His son, Bernard of Septimania, became a major figure in the 820s and 830s.

There is a really foul people, named after Sarah,[13] who habitually devastate our lands. They are brave, trusting to the horse no less than to their skill with weapons. They are very well known to me, as I am to them. I have often taken note of their fortifications, camps, locations, and the rest. I can lead you by a sheltered path. There is also an especially wicked city over in the frontier region, the cause of so many evils, which remains allied to them. Should it be seized by God's grace, with you undertaking the work, there will be peace and quiet for your people. Head there, king; take along the gifts of Mars; and William will be your guide, O kind one."

The king smiled, embraced his companion, exchanged a kiss, and addressed his friends with these words: "Our thanks to you, good duke, and the thanks of our father, Charles. You will always have honor equal to your deserts. What you just related has long lodged concern deep in my breast; hearing about it again just now pleased me. I am attending to your advice, as you ask, and to your entreaties; believe me, Frank, I will arrive very soon. I have one thing to say; I am compelled to speak, William, so listen as intently as possible to my words. If the Lord permits life to remain to me, as I suppose, and this journey of mine prospers, and I can see your walls, steely Barcelona, you who have rejoiced in so many wars against my people, I swear on both our heads (in speaking these words he perhaps laid his head on the shoulder of Count William) that either the unholy crowd of Moors will stand over against me waging battle to protect themselves and their people or else you, Barcelona, like it or not, you will order the forbidden gates thrown open, and you will seek my laws." After he said this, the nobles murmured one thing or another and then gave his saintly feet little kisses. Then the king urgently summoned his well-loved Bigo[14] and rang sweet words in his ears: "Go quickly, Bigo; tell the troops our decision and keep our words in your heart. When Titan, the first star [i.e., the sun] arises in Virgo and his sister [i.e., the moon] journeys to her proper place, then our army will be before that same city, drawn up in a battle line, shouting and brandishing arms." The experienced Bigo acted right away on the utterance of his dear leader. He departed, and went back swiftly, bearing the celebrated orders.

---

13. Isidore of Seville, *Etymologies*, 9.2.6, 57, says that the name "Saracen" is a corruption of Sarah, Abraham's wife, whose slave Hagar bore Ishmael, whom other stories make the ancestor of the Arabs. Cf. Genesis 16.1–4.

14. Husband of Louis's daughter Alpaïs, he was count of Toulouse and then, by late 814, count of Paris; he died in 816. His death is reported on page 153 below.

Meanwhile the pious king, aflame with the love of Christ, was supplying monks with numerous holy and worthy foundations, for it was said countless communities were established under his authority for the service of God.[15] I ask that whoever wishes to know about this go to Aquitaine, for our little book sings of only one of them. There is a place distinguished in devotion and religion to which the previous king himself had given the name Conques.[16] It used to be fit only for wild beasts and songbirds and was unknown to men on account of its wildness. But now it sparkles with a troop of brother monks whose fame reaches out wider than the sky. This cell too was built by the gift of the pious king; he founded it and cherished it in its affairs and rounds of prayer. It sits in a great valley surrounded by a pleasant river and has vines, fruit trees, and various delicacies. The king gave it a path cut through the rocks with heavy, sweaty labor, which made the place accessible. It used to be told that it was a brother named Datus who, they say, was the first to inhabit the place. Here also, while he was keeping his paternal dwellings from the enemy and looking after his mother, who shared his house, a multitude of Moors suddenly laid waste the Rouergue region in an immeasurable swarming tumult.[17] They say that Datus's mother was captured with the extremely valuable booty, all the spoils of the house. After the enemy departed, each fugitive struggled to see his own house and to return to his familiar hearth. Datus, when he learned that his own mother and house had been despoiled, turned these different burdens over in his heart. Right away he decked out his horse, armed himself no less, gathered up his associates, and readied himself to go in pursuit. By chance there was a fort defended by a palisade or a wall to which the retreating Moors returned with their spoils.[18] Here quickly the allies, Datus, and the local people assembled eagerly and got ready to break the enclosures. And just as a hawk drops from the clouds, snatches a bird in its sharp claws, and retreats to its familiar lairs while the other birds croak, filling the air with their raucous voices as they call after and follow the bird fruitlessly—he sitting safe and sound, stripping and tearing his prey, and cutting it into as many pieces as pleases him—not otherwise behaved the Moors; holding a palisade as well as booty, they did not fear the attacks, the darts, or the threats of Datus. Then,

15. Cf. Astronomer, c. 19.

16. Conques was founded in the late eighth century. Louis visited the place at some point around 800/801. He took it under his protection, donated land, and imposed the Rule of Saint Benedict in 819.

17. This probably happened ca. 793.

18. Perhaps Carcassonne.

from the top of the wall, one of them accosted the young man, spewing evil words in a mocking voice: "Wise Datus, tell us, I beg you, what prompts you and your companions to harass our walls? If indeed you would like to give me that horse on which you are sitting and on which you parade about armed to the teeth, then your mother will come out to you safe and sound along with the rest of the booty. If not, then your mother is going to die before your eyes." Datus gave back an awful reply, horrible to relate: "Kill my mother! It matters little to me. For I would never deign to give you this horse that you demand; you wretch, it would be a scandal for you to take its reins." Without delay the cruel Moor stood Datus's mother on the wall and slaughtered her before her son. They say that with his first cut he sliced off her breasts and then, having beheaded her, said, "Behold your mother." Miserable Datus ground his teeth at his mother's death, raged here and there, and groaned. He could not see any way forward, and he had not the strength or skill to avenge his mother. Sad and completely at a loss, he departed.

Having lost everything, he took up better arms; he soon became a pious resident of the desert. He was tougher now than he had been at the death of his mother, and he remained stronger under your yoke, O Christ. For a long time he did everything all by himself because he had refrained from every worldly distraction. A report about all of this reached the pious king, and he soon summoned the servant of God to his residence. Equals in religion, the king and the servant of God spent a whole day in equal conversation. Then the king and Datus laid the first foundations for Conques; they prepared a future camp for monks.[19] Where recently a great troop of beasts lay down to sleep, now cornfields give thanks to God.[20]

Meanwhile,[21] the king's nobles and ranks of ordinary people, having been summoned, followed orders willingly. Bands of Franks assembled from every corner and formed a thick crown around the walls of the city. With an impressive column Charles's son appeared in front of all the others, and he convened his leaders for the destruction of the city.[22] For his part, Prince William

---

19. *Monachis castra futura* seems to me to set off *Forte castrum fuit,* that is, Carcassonne, above.

20. In a document of 819 Louis took Conques under his protection and donated to it nine churches. The document also names Medrald as the abbot and says that Datus (there Dado) had returned to his hermitage at Grandvabre.

21. Above, Ermoldus digressed to tell of one monastery among many. Now he returns to the siege of Barcelona.

22. Cf. Astronomer, c. 13, whose account differs significantly.

set up his tents, as did Heribert,[23] Liutard,[24] and Bigo,[25] as well as Bero,[26] Sannio,[27] Libulf,[28] and Isembard,[29] as well as many others whom it would take too long to name. The young men camped all over the field: the Frank, the Gascon, the Goth, the troop of Aquitainians. Applause rose to heaven, the sky resounded with noise; a cry went up in the city. Everyone was afraid and weeping.

While all this was happening, Barcelona, the evening star returned, and the enemy took possession of all your wealth. And right away, when men saw bright dawn, the counts, summoned, sought out the royal tent. Each one sat down promptly in his rank on the grass, and paying strict attention, they asked for some royal instruction. Then the offspring of wise Charles spoke as follows: "Take this advice to heart, nobles. If this people loved God and pleased Christ with the anointing of holy baptism, there would have to have been peace between us, and peace would have persisted, for we would have been united in the worship of God. But it remains a despicable people, rejects our salvation, and follows the commands of demons. Thus the piety of almighty God, who has been merciful to us, is going to hand over that people to our service. Let's go right now; let's hasten immediately to the walls and towers, O Franks, and may your old strength revive your spirits."

Just as the howl of the wind at Aeolus's[30] summons flies through the countryside and the forests, breaks every restraint, knocks down houses, and makes the fields and woods tremble; just as the bird, used to the sunshine, can scarcely hold on with its talons; just as the miserable sailor who suddenly loses his oar and sail is dragged across the flowing waves of the sea by the loosened cloth; not otherwise did the whole army of the Franks, on the order, go back and forth, again and again, aiming to destroy the city. Some people ran into the

---

23. A murky figure who never appears in the sources with a title. He participated in the sieges of Tortosa and Huesca (cf. Astronomer, cc. 16–17). Given his place here, he may have been a count.

24. He also participated in the siege of Tortosa (Astronomer, c. 16). In the summer of 801, at Toulouse, he was made count of Fezensac (Astronomer, c. 13).

25. See page 000 and note 14 above.

26. Or Bera: a Visigoth, he was named count of Barcelona by Charles after the siege. He was active on the frontier from 801 to at least 810 (Astronomer, cc. 14–16).

27. See page 131 above.

28. He appears here for the first time and remained active under Louis until at least 828. He was probably a count.

29. He appears here for the first time, and then again in the siege of Tortosa (Astronomer, cc. 14, 15). He was probably a count.

30. In Greek mythology Aeolus ruled the winds and kept them locked in a cave.

woods, and occasionally the blows of an ax rang out. Pines fell, tall poplars were cut down. Ladders were built over here; rows of stakes were laid out over there. Here weapons were borne quickly; there stones were gathered. Arrows fell densely, and even iron spears; the battering ram crashed against the doors, and the catapult launched repeatedly. No less did a thick band of Moors rushing along the battlements prepare to hold the fort. The leader of the city, who ruled it with immense skill, was a Moor named Zado.[31] He ran to the walls, surrounded by a distressed entourage. "What is this new racket, men?" he asked. One of his companions replied to the question with unwelcome words, describing everything in harsh terms: "That is not Bero, the prince of the Goths, in the midst of the battle, the one whom our lances have frequently driven away. That is Louis, the distinguished offspring of Charles; he himself is organizing the leaders and bearing arms. If Cordoba does not promptly come to the aid of us wretched men, then we and the populace and this dreaded city are going to fall." Turning this sad report over in his breast, he looked from the tower and saw that weapons were not far away. "Come on, then, comrades, let's hold the walls from the enemy. Cordoba may yet send us help. There is a lot on my mind that distresses and disturbs me, O people, and I, thunderstruck like you, am ready to tell you. That is a remarkable people you see laying siege to our walls; they are powerful and well armed, tough and quick. Behold, I am going to tell you right now that awful news, but whether I am silent or I speak, it is not going to be pleasant. Whoever has joined in battle with them has, whether they like it or not, wound up in servitude. They subjected to their authority the empire of Romulus's[32] successors, who had once built this city. They bear arms all the time, and their youth are trained for war; the young men do the heavy work, while the old direct things on account of experience. Hearing the very name of the Franks makes me tremble, for the name 'Frank' derives from their ferocity. What more can I say in my sadness, citizens? Alas, it is enough that I know these things; I take no pleasure in reciting them. Let us fortify the walls with a strong guard, the gates with strong and wise guardians."

In the meantime, the young men, in a tightly packed band, were wearing down the gates with a ram; everywhere the sounds of battle rang out. The walled enclosure shook right down to the cut stone. Spears fell thickly and

---

31. Zado had submitted himself to Charles in 797 but then rebelled in 799. He appears in Astronomer, cc. 10, 13.

32. Romulus and his brother, Remus, were the legendary founders of Rome.

carried off the wretches. Then the Moor Durzaz cried out from the top of a tower, speaking these derisive words in a booming voice: "O cruel people, spread throughout the world, why are you attacking our holy forts, why are you stirring up our pious people? Do you think you can overturn so suddenly these buildings that the labor of the Romans took a thousand years to build? Go away fierce Frank! Get out of our sight! It is not easy to look at you, and your commands are not pleasing." Hildebert[33] did not trade words with him but grabbed his bow and stood opposite the noisy talker. Holding his curved bow, he drew it, nearly doubled it, and let fly an arrow that struck his black head, and the killing shaft fixed in his bawling throat. Falling, he accidentally slipped off the high walls, and as he died, he soiled the Franks with his black blood. The Franks raised cries with a joyful heart. Meanwhile, weeping overtook the wretched Moors. Various Franks sent different Moors to the underworld: William killed Habirudar, and Liutard, Uriz. A lance took Zabirizum, and a sharp blade, Uzacum. A stone got Colizan; a swift shaft, Gozan. The Franks were unable to fight close-in, so they fired missiles and slings. The clever Zado had ordered his men not to trust in a battle or to wish to leave the camp on foot. So things went back and forth for twenty days, with varying outcomes.[34] No machine was able to break the doorposts, nor could the enemy find any opportunity for an ambush. Once the struggle had begun, the war did not cease, and the walled enclosure was ground down by repeated blows.

Meanwhile the brilliant offspring of mighty Charles went forth bearing a scepter in his hand and surrounded by a band. He was urging on the leaders, rightly urging on the troops, and in his father's fashion he called them to the weapons of Mars. "Believe right now, young men; believe right now, all you nobles; and let my words stay in your heart. With the Lord's help I am determined not to see my ancestral realm and my kingdom before this city and its people are conquered by both war and hunger; may it quickly fall as a suppliant under my authority." Yet again, someone tossed words into the sky—keeping safe on the wall, he proffered silly words: "Frank, are you crazy? Why are you attacking our fortifications? This city will not be taken by any cleverness. We have plenty to eat; meat and sweet gifts remain in the city, but you are desperately hungry." William, in turn, exchanged words, raising his voice with

33. This is the only time this man is mentioned in the sources.

34. Astronomer, c. 13, says six weeks. It is not so much that Ermoldus is in error as that he focuses on one aspect of the siege.

disdain: "I plead with you, pompous Moor, take these bitter words to heart. They are not going to please you, but I think they are true all the same. Do you see this spotted and colored horse that I am riding right up to your walls from a long way off? It will die and our teeth will chew up this foul food before our band will depart from your well-guarded walls. We never give up a battle once begun." The Moor struck his black breast with his black fists, and the wretch dug his nails into his black face. He fell on his face, and struck to the heart, he shook with fear. The miserable, shaking man lifted his voice to the sky. His companions deserted the walls, marveling in great amazement at the Franks and their tough words.

Zado, raging, ran through the huge crowd, saying, "Why are you fleeing, citizens? What road will you take?" "Zado, the Franks gave you the response that pleases them well enough. Pay attention to what they just said. They will eat their own horses shamefully before they will ever desert your fort." "O wretched citizens, I foretold this long ago, when waging war was in prospect. Now, give me advice; tell me what plan seems practical to you, so that I can do something." "Everywhere you see the walls crumbling and your people dying from the cutting iron. Cordoba sends you none of the promised aid. The distress of war is everywhere, along with hunger and thirst. What is there left to do but send envoys to seek peace with the Franks. Let them go promptly." In a rage Zado tore his clothes, tousled his black hair, and raked his eyes. He replied, again and again calling out "Cordoba," and for a long time shouted and wept in an unholy voice: "O swift Moors, why does your confidence fail? Comrades, show me now your customary strength! I ask one thing if any concern remains for me at all; I will be overjoyed at this one gift. I myself have seen from the wall a place where the dense camp thins a bit; there are only a few little tents over there. I can safely launch an attack on them. Perhaps, comrades, I can pass through there to seek the help we need. I only want you to hold the gates with all your effort. Do not be afraid, brothers, until I get back. Let no misfortune compel you to let go of the citadel, and I urge you not to go outside to fight."

Giving his men many further commands, he departed from the city, and lurking about in secret advance, he was moving past the triumphant army. He was traveling through the welcome silence of the night when his unfortunate horse started up an endless whinnying. At that sound the guardians alerted the camp's forces to the horse's sounds, and they were soon following him. Zado left the path in fright, turned his horse, and threw himself straight away into the thick band of troops. He took no delight in seeing these despised troops right in front of him, and the poor fellow had no idea how he might escape. He was quickly captured. Quite rightly was he overcome, and without delay he was led by the bridle, trembling, to the king's tent. A report took flight, proclaimed that the king had been captured, and stirred up the whole city with terror. Mothers, fathers, and youths groaned in mourning; here a little boy, there a little girl, wept. No less a sound reverberated in the camp of the Franks, and the whole people shook with joy.

Meanwhile, with dark night ending, sweet Aurora announced the new day. The Franks sought out the royal position. Then Charles's offspring, at peace with himself, spoke up and offered kind words to his followers: "Zado wanted to run down to the people of Spain to ask for help, for arms and soldiers, but he was captured against his will. He is bound, unarmed, in front of our door here; he cannot flee right before our eyes. William, put him where he can see his walls, and have him order them to open their gates to us right away." Without delay Zado was led along, bound by a tether, and still far away from the walls, he raised his hand deceptively, for before he had departed he had warned his comrades: "I do not know whether good fortune or ill will fall to me, but if by chance I am caught by Frankish troops, then I beg you, as I said, to hold the fort." Then, extending his hand, he called out to his friends: "Open the gates that you have so long defended, comrades!" But he was cleverly turning his fingers down and sticking his nails into his palms; thus his act was for show, because this sign meant that the fort was to be held and that he had called out "Open" by constraint. William, figuring out what was happening, shook him and hit him, *his* act hardly being for show. Grinding his teeth, he turned things over in his heart. The Moor amazed him, and even more his ingeniousness. "Believe me when I tell you, Zado, that this would be your last day if the love and fear of the king did not restrain me." Meanwhile, Zado was held under guard by the Frank, while his weeping people were preparing to hold on to the fort.

After another month had elapsed, the king and the Franks together were still seeking the city that had been denied them. Engines sounded repeatedly, and everywhere the walls shook; Mars raged, before whom of course there was no equal. Countless arrows fell, and missiles came back, wearying the men with their force. The king took it as his job to rally the leaders. The wretched Moors did not dare to climb up on the high walls, and they did not wish to view the camp from the tower.

It is just as when a flock of waterfowl settle down, trembling, in a small stream that they trust but little, and the eagle drops from the high sky and circles for a long time around the birds he has found. Some birds poke their heads to the bottom and then raise them up in the air. Others lie down in the weeds or else get themselves stuck in the mud. But the eagle rides above them on his wings, vexes the trembling birds, and if one of them pops his head up, he snatches it. It was no different when fear, death, and swords pursued the terrified Moors who were flying about the city.

Then the pious king himself set his arm for throwing a spear and let it fly swiftly into the enemy city. The spear flew through the wind toward the city and grandly fixed itself in the stone wall. At this sign the Moors were struck with utter terror, admiring the spear and even more the one who threw it. What could they do? Their king was gone, and they had no heart for fighting. The swords had already carried away the Moors' chiefs. Finally, completely overcome by war and hunger, they desired with one will to hand over the fort. The gates were opened, and everything inside lay exposed. The conquered city came into the king's service. Everything the victorious Franks had hoped for was spread out in the city immediately, and without delay they took up rule over the enemy. These things happened on Holy Saturday, when the city was opened to the Franks for the first time. On the next day, the feast [of Easter],[35] King Louis came down into the city in joyous celebration and paid his vows to God. He purified the places where they had paid cult to demons, and gave reverent thanks to Christ.[36] Then the city was remitted to guardians, while the victorious king and his people went home, giving thanks to God.

Meanwhile, a long train of Moorish booty was taken to Charles, spoils and gifts from their leaders: weapons and breastplates, clothing and plumed helmets, a caparisoned warhorse with its golden bridle. Zado, quaking, certainly did not want to see the Franks again, but he went along taking tiny steps. Clever Bigo rushed ahead of the column and was the first to reach Charles's hall and quickly spread a report of recent events to the whole gathering. His exultant news soon reached the emperor's ears. Summoned, Bigo came forward and kissed the emperor's feet and, on order, spoke as follows: "Behold,

---

35. The chronology is very difficult to establish. Various sources place these events in 801. This text has said that the Franks fought for twenty days without success and then redoubled their efforts. Apparently the city fell after two months. Easter was on April 4 in 801, so the siege presumably began in February.

36. The Franks did not recognize Islam as a legitimate and monotheistic faith. Hence, they dismissed it as demon worship, as the equivalent of paganism.

your son Louis the Pious sends these gifts to his pious father, to the August Charles, gifts that he as the victor won for himself from the Moors with his sword and shield and blows. He also sends you the king of the city that he took by force of arms. Zado stands here before the eyes of caesar. The city that once conquered many Franks now lies beaten in battle and seeks your royal commands."

Then Caesar Charles, lifting his eyes and hands toward heaven, spoke serenely: "May the immense grace of almighty God attend my beloved son, and may my blessing rest with him too. What thanks can I give my worthy offspring for such gifts, what thanks to God for his own blessings? O most eminent son, whom I have always loved, I keep close in my heart what the patriarch told me." The story is told that the good patriarch Paulinus once came on the king's order to the holy palace.[37] On a certain day when he was sitting in the beloved church and, inspired by Christ, began singing a song, it happened that Charles,[38] the renowned offspring of his father, came to pray with a huge band of his nobles. Hurrying, Charles proceeded to that altar where the sacred priest was officiating. Paulinus asked with some agitation who he was. A servant leaned over and answered. When he realized that this was the first son of the king, he stopped singing. Charles continued on his way. A little later the hero Pippin arrived.[39] He was a great-hearted youth, accompanied by a troop. Paulinus right away roused that same servant and asked him who this was. Once again he told him the truth. The bishop, when he learned his name and realized he was a king, promptly bowed his head. Pippin moved swiftly by. Finally, Louis came, and quickly embracing the altar as a suppliant, he prostrated himself. Louis tearfully prayed for a long time, asking Christ, heaven's king, to help him. On seeing this, the patriarch got up from his seat, eager to address a holy man of such piety. Previously, when Charles and Pippin passed by, he kept his seat and did not say a word to anybody. At that point Louis stretched out his body in reverence before the prophet.[40] Behold, Paulinus raised up the pious king and, after singing a hymn, said various things to him. "Go," he said, "to Charles on account of your piety. Good-bye." When

37. Paulinus (ca. 726–802) was patriarch of Aquileia and regularly consulted by Charles on ecclesiastical and theological issues. The *Life of Alcuin*, c. 15, attributes this prophecy to Alcuin himself. The *fama est* suggests that Ermoldus got the story indirectly.

38. Son of Hildegard, died 811.

39. Son of Hildegard, died 810. He was king of Italy, nominally from 781.

40. Granted that Ermoldus needed a two-syllable word for the meter, it is interesting that he used *vatem*, which can mean "poet" or "seer."

the prophet was able to speak to Charles, he told him everything in order: "If God ordains that there is to be a king of the Franks from your seed, this one will be fitting to sit in your seat." On learning these things, Charles shared them with a few of his intimates, men he trusted and who pleased him. Then he called back Bigo and asked once more to hear in all detail how that distinguished city had been conquered, by what artifice King Zado had been captured and brought before him, and what leaders Louis himself had bested in that harsh battle. Good Bigo talked on and told the whole truth while pious caesar took in his words with respect. Joyful caesar gave him the cup from which he usually drank, and Bigo gulped down a draught of wine. In a twinkling, he endowed his servant with presents and various honors, and also sent great gifts to his son. Bigo departed, weighed down with praises and gifts, and went gladly to his own king.

So, let the exile return happy to the kingdom of powerful Pippin.[41] May almighty God confer this, and mighty caesar himself. Meanwhile, may my little book end on this joyful note, and may it go to join its three brothers.

Book 2

And then, with God's grace, the Franks enjoyed peace everywhere, war and God himself having struck down their adversaries. So the old caesar Charles, esteemed throughout the world, called a new assembly at his palace. Sitting on his golden throne and surrounded by his chosen counts, he spoke from on high: "Hear me, O nobles, you who depend on our support, for I believe that what I am going to say will be acknowledged as the truth. When I was young and strong in body, I was concerned to pass my time in feats of strength and war, and I declare that neither through indolence nor shameful fear did any enemy people bring attacks on our borders. Now, however, my passion is dulled and hard old age weakens me, flowing white hair presses on my pale neck, and my warrior's right hand, once renowned throughout the world, now hangs quivering on account of my cold blood. The first children born to me have died; they did their work well and now lie buried in the earth.[42] Nevertheless, you see that the one who seemed stronger and more pleasing to the

41. Son of Louis the Pious and Irmingard (d. 818); born between 795 and 806 (possibly in 797); died 838; king of Aquitaine from 814 to 838. Ermoldus seems to have served him in some capacity.

42. In addition to his sons Pippin, who died in 810, and Charles, who died in 811, Rotrude, his oldest daughter, had died in 810. Cf. Einhard, c. 19, and Thegan, c. 5.

Lord still remains to me. Christ has not deserted you, Franks, for he has still preserved from our offspring the pleasing child. This child took unbroken delight in heeding my orders, and he has enhanced my authority. For the love of God, he has always renewed the rights of churches and bettered the kingdom assigned to him. You saw what he once sent after his destruction of the Moors: a king, weapons, prisoners, and great trophies as well. Franks, give me your advice, from your faithful hearts, and we will act on it right away."

At that time Einhard was particularly cherished by Charles. He was wise by nature and esteemed for his goodness. He fell before Charles, kissed his well-loved feet, and, wise in counsel, was the first to speak: "O Caesar, famous in the heavens, on land and sea, you who give the imperial name[43] to your people, I cannot add anything to your counsels, nor has Christ given it to any mortal to do so. I urge that whatever God in His mercy has laid upon your heart you carry out without delay. Dear one, you have one son of surpassing virtue, the one who, for his merits, is capable of holding your realms. We all—the greater and the lesser, and the ordinary people too—desire him; the church wants him; Christ Himself favors him. After your sad funeral, this one will have the ability to maintain the rights of your empire by arms and skill and faith."[44] Joyful caesar agreed, prayed to Christ, and right away sent for his son. At that time, good Louis, as I have already said, held in exultation the kingdom of the Aquitainians.

Let me come right to the point: he came forthwith to his father's palace. The clergy of Aachen rejoiced, the people too, the nobles, and Charles. Charles began all over again, and both related and explained, word by word, to his beloved son: "Son, you whom God has left to me as a consolation, you are dear to God, to your father, and to your subjects. You can see yourself that I am a weak old man, declining fast, and that the time for my death is approaching. My top concerns involve the government of my kingdom, which God himself assigned to me, even though I did not deserve it. Trust me, it is neither preference nor some mental lapse that prompts me to speak to you, but the love of piety. I was born in Francia. Christ accorded me honor; Christ gave me my father's kingdom. I have held on to this kingdom; indeed I expanded

43. *Caesareum nomen* here but *nomen imperatoris* in Thegan, c. 6.
44. Ermoldus alone assigns Einhard this leading role in settling Charles's succession. The key point to bear in mind is that whereas Charles the Younger had died childless, Pippin left a son, Bernard, whose rule in Italy would prove problematic for Louis. Astronomer, c. 5, and Thegan, c. 6, put the assembly later, after Charles had summoned Louis.

what I received; and I have been both shepherd for the Christians and guardian for the flock. I was first among the Franks to take the name of caesar, and I gave this 'Romulean' name to the Franks."[45] Thus he spoke, and he placed a golden crown with jewels, the token of empire, on his son's head. "Receive, son, with Christ Himself conferring it, my crown, and receive with it the symbol of empire too.[46] May the One who confers upon you the height of honor also grant you the power to please Him." Then the father and son, standing before all joyfully because of this gift, enjoyed an immense banquet, with thanks to God. O festive day, much to be remembered through the years. Frankish land, you have two emperors! Francia applauds freely, and golden Rome too. Other kingdoms look in awe at your empire. Then Charles urged many things upon his dear son, especially that he should love Christ and cherish the church. Embracing him, he covered him with kisses, gave him permission to return home, and bid him farewell.

Not much later, full of age and years, caesar died and went to join his ancestors. A suitable funeral was prepared, and his body was committed to a sepulchre in his own basilica, which he had built in Aachen.[47] At the same time, a message was sent to inform Louis about his father's death. It was Rampo[48] who promptly made ready for this journey; he flew day and night, crossed vast lands, and finally arrived where Louis was to be found.[49] There is a place across the Loire, fertile and comfortable, surrounded on one side by forests and on the other side by fields; its center is refreshed by a calmly bubbling stream; fishing is handy and game is abundant. Triumphant Louis built his outstanding palace there. You want to know the place? Its name is Thedwat, friend.[50] Here Louis saw to his pious duties on behalf of his subject people,

45. *Romuleum nomen.* He refers to Romulus, legendary founder and namesake of Rome. The point is to make the Franks equal to the Romans.

46. Cf. Thegan, c. 6, and Astronomer, c. 20. Thegan insists that there were two crowns, while the Astronomer is vague. Ermoldus and the Astronomer agree that Charles crowned Louis, but Thegan says Charles instructed Louis to crown himself. The language here may be purely poetic or ideologically significant. Just above, Ermoldus writes *pignus imperii,* which I have rendered neutrally as "token of empire." In these lines he uses *imperii decus,* which I have rendered "symbol of empire." Faral translates the latter phrase as "la dignité impériale." Thegan, the Astronomer, and Ermoldus all struggle with political terminology, but I do not think Ermoldus rises to that level of abstraction here.

47. Cf. Einhard, c. 31. See the fanciful account in Notker, 1.28.

48. A somewhat shadowy character who became count of Gerona after 817 and is last attested in 822.

49. Cf. Astronomer, c. 21.

50. Modern Doué. It was one of the four palaces used by Louis in an annual rotation: Astronomer, c. 7.

ruling the people and clergy with piety. When Rampo arrived there unexpectedly, he stirred up the whole palace with his news about the sad death of pious Charles. The good king heard these words like a rumor and right away was saddened; he wept and shed tears for his father. Among the hesitant ministers Bigo came forth—for it was his custom to see his lord in the morning—and urged him to dry his cheeks and stop his weeping. "You have other business to attend to now," he said. "As you know in your heart, Prince, these things happen; this fate binds humans. All of us, I say, will proceed to that end eventually, and there is no one who can escape it. Let us all rise and hurry to the dear church, for the time has come to sing our vows to God." At length, after listening to his companion, Louis arose and urged everyone to offer prayers to God with him. That night was passed with psalms and hymns, and when day arrived, masses were sung.

Then, when the third day[51] broke with a clear sky and the bright hair of Phoebus shone brilliantly in the world, crowds of Franks aroused from the kingdoms rushed forth, and all the people, rejoicing, came out to meet the king. A friendly troop ran out straight away, Charles's nobles and the first men of the kingdom, and the priests. The roads were packed and the houses were filled up; they could not all get in, so some climbed onto the roofs. Rivers could not hold back the bold men, nor scary forests, nor winter's ice, nor days of rain. Those who could not go by boat contented themselves with swimming in an effort to be the first across the river Loire. O how many people without a boat did you see jumping from high rocks into the river! The people of Orléans laughed to see them swimming and called from a high tower, "Head for the shore, men." Everyone had one desire, one wish: they sought to see the face of the king. They all flowed together, and the pious king received them with an abundance of goodwill, each in his rank. Triumphant caesar soon entered the city of Orléans, where you abide, O standard of the cross,[52] and you too, Saint Aignan;[53] and joyful Eburt,[54] who first built this citadel, and also Maximin[55] and even Avitus,[56] you gleam brilliantly. From there they went

51. Astronomer, c. 21, says the fifth day.

52. This implies the cathedral. Astronomer, c. 21, says Archbishop Theodulf was uncertain whether to wait for Louis or to go out to meet him.

53. An early bishop of Orléans who died in 453. His remains lay in the monastery dedicated to him, St.-Aignan.

54. Another early bishop, who died in 391.

55. Saint Mesmin, the second abbot of Micy, who died in 520 and gave his name to the monastery of St.-Mesmin near Orléans.

56. An abbot of St.-Mesmin who died in 527.

with all possible speed to see Paris, where the martyr Stephen holds the high ground,[57] and where your body, holiest Germanus,[58] is venerated, and also where Geneviève,[59] a virgin dedicated to God, shines. Irmino[60] offered his praises. You often asked for them, and on your arrival, with God's help, you received them. Nor did the martyr Dionysius[61] escape your excellency, for you visited him to request his aid.[62] From there they recommenced their journey, passed through the kingdoms of the Franks, and after a peaceful progress, the king entered Aachen.

Come on, Camena,[63] let God be stirred by humble prayers to confer eloquence on me. How shall I begin, when everyone agrees that everything he does, right from the man's first kind deeds, sparkles?

Having put the boundaries of the kingdom in order and settled the frontiers of the empire as well, he forthwith generously distributed the treasure he inherited, to redeem his father and assure the rest of his soul. Whatever the force of his ancestors and Charles himself had amassed, he distributed to the poor and to the holy churches. He gave away golden vases, clothes, and many cloths too. He gathered full talents of pure silver and handed out riches of all kinds, weapons; and to relieve the poor, he distributed gifts far beyond counting.[64] O happy Charles, who left the world such an heir, one who took pains to set his father on the path to heaven. He ordered the prisons to be opened and released those who were being held. As a pious gesture he recalled men from exile. He did amazing things, which must be told, whence his fame now stands above the stars. Without delay he chose *missi,* whom he sent throughout the world, men whose lives were sound and whose faith was full, who would not be distracted by gifts, or by the hard flatteries of the powerful, or by favor, or by

---

57. Stephen, the protomartyr (Acts 6:8–7:60), was allegedly buried in Paris at the spot of the church of St.-Etienne du Mont, which is situated at the highest point on the left bank of the Seine.

58. Bishop of Paris who lived from ca. 496 to 576.

59. Geneviève (or Genovefa), ca. 422–ca. 500.

60. Abbot of St.-Germain, post-794–after 823.

61. Saint Denis, eventually the patron saint of France, lived ca. 250. Allegedly he was one of seven bishops sent to convert Gaul, became bishop of Paris, and suffered a martyr's death. Later legends held that he had been sent to Paris by Pope Clement ca. 90. Still other legends identified him with Dionysius the Areopagite, whose conversion by Saint Paul is mentioned in Acts 17:34, and attributed to him the Pseudo-Dionysian writings.

62. The supposed remains of Dionysius were transferred in 626 by King Dagobert to St.-Denis, his new foundation north of Paris.

63. The Camenae were water goddesses often treated as Muses—inspirers of poets.

64. Cf. Einhard, c. 33, and Astronomer, cc. 20 and 22, where it is clear that Louis did no more than execute his father's will.

clever corruption. They went swiftly through the broad realms of the Franks, doing justice and giving judgments[65] and releasing from servitude those whom his father, or people in his father's time, had oppressed by bribery or by fraud.[66] O how many and what kinds of men whom harsh justice and the law of money and the price of power had pressed down did he, powerful himself, free and restore to the dignity of freedom. Caesar did all this for the love of his father. He confirmed charters with his own hands so that those who sought to maintain their rights might do so for all time. His warrior father, when he was building up the kingdoms by arms, was intent and focused on war, but then abuses grew up everywhere like thick weeds, but you, Louis, cut them down right away. How many works of the serpent were destroyed throughout the world! How many gifts fell to the Christian people! The world, rejoicing, sings these deeds, and they echo far and wide. They resound more among the people than the poet can sing with his art. His distinguished teaching grows throughout the world: he orders, arms, and nourishes the empire he inherited.

Then Louis ordered his patron, to whom the joyful world gave the name Stephen,[67] to come from the Roman see.[68] The holy man complied with love, obeyed the welcome orders, and hurried eagerly to see the kingdoms of the Franks. Joyful caesar waited for him in the city of Reims, where he had already ordered the meeting to take place. Various envoys went back and forth in orderly fashion bearing the gentle vows of pope and emperor. One messenger rushed ahead, picking up the pace, and reported enthusiastically the arrival of the Roman pontiff. Then Louis took charge and arranged, prepared, and arrayed the clergy, people, and senate, placing some on his right and some on his left, organizing those who would go out in front and those who would follow behind. The crowds of clergy held the right side in a long column, singing psalms as they looked upon their father in religion. On the other side stood the chosen nobles and the first among the magnates. The people in general brought up the rear. And there was caesar in the middle, shining with gems and gold. His clothing glittered, but his piety sparkled even more. The two men finally met from their different sides, one strong in his rank, the other powerful in his goodness. As soon as one caught sight of the other, the pious

---

65. Cf. 1 Kings 10:9 (= 3 Kings 10:9 Vulgate).

66. Faral translates *munere sive dolo* as "de l'argent et de la force."

67. Stephen IV, 816–17.

68. These events took place between August and October 816. Cf. Thegan, c. 17, and Astronomer, c. 26. These accounts supply different details and disagree on some points.

men rushed to the embrace. The wise king bent his knee and adored the pope three times or four, in God's honor, or Saint Peter's. Then Stephen humbly raised him from the ground with his consecrated hands and eagerly kissed him. The king and the pious priest kissed each other, now on the eyes, now on the lips, now on the head, the breast, the neck. Then, having joined their hands and entwined their fingers, caesar entered the city with Stephen. First they went to the church, lifting prayers to God on high, giving thanks and prayers in song. They quickly sought the hall and sat down to a great banquet. Servants gave them water for their hands. They enjoyed a suitable meal, tasted the gifts of Bacchus, and engaged aloud in pious conversation. "O holy priest, shepherd of the Roman flock, you who in the apostolic office feed the flock of Peter,[69] what reason brings you," thus caesar began, "to this land of the Franks? Tell me."[70] The pope spoke, looking at the king with a keen countenance, calm, at peace with himself: "What once brought the Queen of Sheba—the love of wisdom—through various lands, across seas and snows, that is what has brought me to your citadel, Caesar, you who so well prepare for me a Solomonic feast.[71] Your fame, O prince, reached me long ago, how much aid you bring, like a father, to the people of God and how much your teaching is renowned throughout the world, and how you exceed your ancestors in skill and faith. Absolutely nothing could break my will to view your accomplishments for myself. No word could tell me so much about your kind deeds as I have seen with my own eyes. I am going to tell you again the words which that queen spoke to Solomon when she saw the king, his servants, his formal garb, his cupbearers, and his various homes:[72] 'Happy the household, happy the servants who stand and see your glorious deeds. Blessed is he who reverently drinks in your teaching. Happy are the people and the kingdom as well. May God on high be adored with complete love, for he has given you, father, such great learning. May it please Him that He has given you the paternal throne to keep, for He loves you and sets you above His people.' With these words the Queen of Sheba addressed mighty Solomon, and with them I have dared to come to you as a suppliant. But you are more capable, you are stronger at heart, than Solomon, for he held to a shadow, whereas you love the truth. He was immensely wise, but he gave in to love; you live chastely, for the love

69. An allusion to John 21:15–17, where Jesus tells Peter to feed his sheep.
70. Note that Ermoldus has just said that Louis ordered the pope to come.
71. An allusion to 1 Kings 10:1–13 (= 3 Kings 10:1–13 Vulgate).
72. What follows is, perhaps for metrical reasons, a loose paraphrase of 1 Kings 10:8–9.

of God. He governed only Israel, but you, in your piety, hold the kingdoms of Europe in your sway. Let us all urge God with our abundant prayers that he keep you for his people for many years."

With these words and others, and more still, the holy man addressed the gentle king, and caesar himself spoke to the pope. Full cups made their way around, Bacchus touched their willing hearts, and all the people shook with gladness. When the banquet was finished, they rose, left the table, and caesar went with Stephen to their private rooms. They gave that night to concerns and various important matters; sleep eluded them. When morning broke, caesar summoned Stephen and the nobles of his senate, and they received the royal command with pleasure. Clothed in a toga, caesar ascended his throne. He had a great deal on his mind and was ready to begin. He placed the pope on a golden chair at his side, and the nobles took seats, each one according to his rank. Pious caesar spoke first, sounding out these golden words to the pope, to his attendants, and to his subjects: "Listen to what I have to say nobles, and you too, most holy pontiff, receive this good advice all at once and in a spirit of unity. Behold, almighty God in His mercy has given me my father's kingdoms and every mark of honor as well. Merciful Christ has given me all this not for my merits, as I believe, but in my father's honor. I beg you, my faithful men, and you, excellent priest, duly to bring me abundant counsel. Bring me your assistance, you servants, and you too, holy priest, who will serve with me in our government. May my clergy and people, the pauper and the powerful alike, be able to continue in their ancestral rights, with my help. May the holy rule of the fathers regulate the life of the clergy, and may the venerable law of our fathers bring our people together. May the order of monks increase in the teachings of Benedict; may it seek by the character of its life the holy and heavenly pasture. May the rich apply the law, and may the poor be held by it without regard to the rank or status of persons. Let there be no situation where foul deeds can be redeemed by money, and let corrupting gifts be banished far away. If we rightly feed the tender flock that the Lord has given to me, and to you too, beloved pastor, if we correct the wicked and reward the just, and if we make the people follow their ancestral laws, then God on high will take mercy on us and on the people who follow us, vouchsafe us the kingdom of heaven, maintain our honor in the present, and keep the attacks of enemies far away. Let us be an example for the clergy and a standard for the people; let both of us teach justice to our people. God so loved his people Israel that they passed with dry feet through the sea, and God gave them manna for food when they had passed so many years in the desert, and gave them wild birds to eat.[73] God was their protection, their sword and shield on the journey, and He led them to the promised land. When Israel kept to the precepts of God and His teaching, it loved justice and gave just judgments, and as long as it loved God Himself with a pious love and did not follow foreign customs but only the holy words of God, His power cast down foreign peoples before it; He gave it every advantage and took away all that was harmful. O happy is the people that follows the commands of God. Rejoicing, it will attain the kingdom of heaven. As soon as it indulged unwisely in an abundance of wealth, it lost justice and every good thing too. For it soon deserted God and worshipped vain idols and right away and rightly suffered so many misfortunes. But the heavenly father corrected it with various plagues and blows, taught it, and restored its former rights. And when, in its misery, the afflicted Israel wished again to be mindful of God, the holy and merciful God took it back right away. This people alone knew God, heeded His words at least a little, and worshipped Him. For the rest of the peoples kept the commands of the serpent; ignoring the creator, they followed the words of demons. Alas, Satan ruled over three-quarters of the world and subjugated the human race in his kingdom. For then the priests and Jerusalem's kings completely abandoned God's laws and holy sacrifices. Still the Holy Father took mercy and sent the world the saving Word that He might save us. In His mercy He washed the world with His own blood, provided clear teachings, and taught justice. In His power, He broke the gates of Hell, rescued His chosen ones, and stripped demons of their weapons. Then the victor rose to heaven and gave us the name of Christians to keep. Whoever now wishes to have the name of Christian must struggle to make the journey to where the Lord has gone. Nevertheless, through God's gift, the whole world now overflows with throngs of Christians and the faith of the church and there is no need for the Lord's servants to be slaughtered in his name, since the name of Christ resounds everywhere in the world and the troop of unbelievers, who reject the teaching of the Lord, flee, driven away by the Christian spear. Even though dark death took away the fathers of the church and our ancestors, God's court holds them now. If we cannot follow them in death now, we can strive to imitate them in purity of heart, in justice, and in faith. Let every man love his brother, whom he sees, as John instructs,[74] so that he can seek Christ in his mind. For Christ said to

73. Exodus 14:15–16, 16:4–12.
74. 1 John 2:10–11.

Peter, 'Simon, do you love me or not?' Three times Peter said to him, 'You know that I love you.' 'If you love me,' Christ said, 'I urge you to feed my sheep with an abundance of devotion.'[75] You are a holy priest; I am the king of Christians. Let us serve our people in dogma, law, and faith."

Then caesar added a few more words beyond these, which the holy priest accepted with devotion: "If your rights persist, you who bear responsibility for Peter's government, and if in the role that has been assigned to you, you feed his flock . . . ;[76] if otherwise, I warn you most seriously, let me know: I will right away act on your words eagerly. As my ancestors served Peter's honor, so I will serve it, prelate, for the love of God."

At that point he summoned his beloved Helisachar[77] and spoke to him respectfully: "Listen, go right away and inscribe in reliable charters these things that I wish to stand firm forever.[78] I resolve, throughout the kingdom subject to our government, likewise throughout the empire that God has given me, that the property of the church of Peter and of his eternal see shall always flourish for the honor of God; we wish that this church, sustained by the merit of its pastors, as it has previously held the highest dignity, may continue to hold it; may Peter's honor grow in our time just as it grew in the time of my father, Charles. But let me add, prelate, no more than was said already, the one who sits on Peter's summit should love justice. That is the reason, holy one, why I have asked you to come; O blessed man, be a powerful helper to me."

Then the holy man, extending his hands and eyes to heaven, offered his prayer by uttering these words to God: "O almighty God, You who have created all governments, and Christ Your son, and the Holy Spirit too; and you, Peter, who stand as the magnificent bearer of the keys of heaven, may you draw the people to your heavenly kingdom in your net;[79] and you, heaven dwellers, whose bodies Rome now keeps and worthily honors with continuous offices:[80] I pray that you keep this king for ever and ever as the leader of his people

75. John 21:15–17 (somewhat altered by Ermoldus).

76. Something is missing here, although there is no gap in the text.

77. Helisachar was a priest, Louis's confidant, director of Louis's chancery in Aquitaine, and, from 814 to 819, Louis's first archchancellor. He died sometime before 840, still close to Louis and influential. See Astronomer, c. 41.

78. No such charters are extant, but this reference appears to apply to the *Pactum Ludovicianum*, a detailed statement of the lands whose possession by the popes the Franks guaranteed and a summary statement of papal and imperial rights in those lands. The surviving version of this document dates from 817, when the pact referenced here was repeated between Louis and Pope Paschal I (817–24).

79. Peter was a fisherman.

80. He refers to the Divine Office, the clergy's daily rounds of prayer.

and the adornment of the kingdom and church. He exceeds the customs of his ancestors in knowledge, war, and faith; he both looks out for the church and rules the empire; he endows the see of Peter with the highest honor; he is both father and spiritual leader, sustainer and protector of his people." Having said this, Stephen immediately took Louis in friendly embrace, joyful for the respect shown him and the gift to Peter. He began again and, admonishing everyone, gave the command to be silent; one pious man spoke kind words to another: "Rome transmits to you, Caesar, the gifts of Peter, worthy gifts for a worthy man, a suitable mark of honor." Then he ordered a crown with gems and gold to be brought forth, one that had previously belonged to Caesar Constantine.[81] He took it in his hands, spoke the words of blessing, and holding the brilliant crown, he prayed, lifting his eyes to heaven: "You who govern the rule of kings and the ages of the world, You who decreed that Rome would stand at the world's head, hear my prayers, I beg. May Christ turn a kind ear; grant my prayers, faithful King, I plead. May Andrew, Peter and Paul, John and Mary, the fruitful mother of holy God, lend help. Keep this emperor Louis for a long time; keep every sadness far away. Give him every good fortune and, what is more, I ask, drive afflictions away. May he be both happy and powerful for a long time." After the pope said these things, he immediately turned to Louis and touched the top of his holy head with his hand: "May almighty God, who increased the seed of Abraham, grant that you see children, whence you will be called grandfather; may He grant you offspring, may He double and triple your descendants, so that a rich harvest may grow from your seed, and may they rule the Franks and potent Rome as long as the name of Christian is heard in the world." Louis was anointed, hymns were sung from the Mass, and the pope placed the crown on caesar's head.[82] "Peter, rejoicing, gives you this gift, O most gentle one, because you allow him to enjoy his rights." Next he looked at the empress, Louis's wife Irmingard,[83] embraced her and held her tight, and, after regarding her for a long time, placed a crown on her sweet head and blessed her:[84] "Hail, God's beloved woman! May

81. Thegan, c. 17, also says that Stephen brought a crown from Rome, but surely the reference to Constantine can only carry symbolic and ideological significance.

82. Thegan, c. 17, also mentions anointing. Astronomer, c. 26, appears to mention anointing as well. Moreover, the Astronomer indicates that the "blessing" and crowning occurred during Mass, which may explain Ermoldus's *hymnis ex ordine dictis,* which I have not translated as "from the ordo," because we have no solid evidence that a particular coronation ordo was used in 816.

83. Thegan, c. 4, and Astronomer, c. 8, tell us much of what we know about Irmingard.

84. Apparently, then, Irmingard was not anointed. Of Louis, Ermoldus says *unguine suffuso,* whereas of Irmingard he says merely *benedixit.* However, *benedixit* is the word the Astronomer uses for Louis.

your life be long and your good health extended for many years. May you always be your husband's beloved in marriage." The prelate gathered together many additional gifts, gold and clothing, which he had been given in Rome. He gave the gifts to augustus, augusta, to their charming offspring, and to each member of the household according to his rank. Wise caesar paid him abundant thanks and promptly ordered Stephen to be weighed down with gifts. He gave him a pair of polished goblets with gems and gold, with which this holy man might drink a draught of Bacchus. He assembled horses with magnificent bodies—the kind the Frankish lands customarily produced. Golden gifts were brought forward; silver vases followed; red cloaks and white linens as well. How can I remember so many things? For he received a hundred times more gifts than he had brought from fortified Rome. Thus far for the holy man; but caesar, so filled with goodness, gave, in his piety, appropriate gifts to the pope's attendants: colored cloaks, quite good for covering the body, fashioned in the fine Frankish style.[85] He gave them various horses of such splendid bearing that men could scarcely mount them. Endowed with all this, the holy man and his joyful attendants got ready to go back to Rome, with permission to leave. Envoys selected by honor were sent to accompany holy Stephen back to his realms. Pious caesar himself went back to Compiègne, joyful, and accompanied by his wife and children.

Faithful Bigo[86] died; the king was told of his end. His departure was painful to his lord. Out of love for their father, Caesar divided Bigo's wealth and shared his offices among his children.

Then a popular story spread through the wide world that the pious emperor wished to renew his realms. Select members of the clergy and renowned followers whose way of life was both known and pleasing to him he appointed to go through the cities of the kingdom and the monasteries and fortified places, fulfilling all his propitious commands. "Go," he said, "attendants who depend on our support or on that of my father Charles, who taught good doctrine, insist urgently that our commands be fulfilled in every respect, and receive my words with a pious disposition. What needs to be done will be quite difficult for you but, I believe, good and fitting for the Christian people. Look, with God's help and the constant work of our ancestors, the frontiers of our kingdoms have remained inviolate, and the fame of the Franks has driven away our malicious enemies. We have lived in happiness and holy peace. But because

---

85. Cf. Notker, 1.34, on Frankish cloaks.
86. See page 132 and note 14 above.

we have no need to rush off to battle, we consider it proper to give our subjects suitable rules. In the first place, I shall look into the leadership and reputation of the church through which my ancestors bore their name to the stars. For it is much on my mind that I recently sent envoys into the world to rule the people with piety.[87] Now, this time, O envoys, hurry through my empire—in orderly fashion, of course—and pay particular attention to specific things: Examine the canonical flock, both men and women, who live in holy fortresses. How do they live? Dress? What is the state of their learning and bearing? How do they practice their religion? What works of piety do they perform? Does harmony join the flock to the pastor? Does the flock love the pastor, and the pastor, the flock? Do the prelates provide walls, houses, food and drink, and clothing, in the right time and place? (For they cannot properly accomplish their divine service in the right way unless the faithful devotion of their fathers provides these things.) Next, think about the church's resources: Is there enough land, and is it reasonably fertile? Memorize by heart everything you discover,[88] and report all to me most carefully—that will please me. Who lives well and maintains the teachings of the ancient fathers, who not so well, and who—heaven forbid—not at all? I will just give you these few words of instruction; it will be well for you to look into many more things." Caesar also commanded envoys to be chosen from the monastic order who would hearken to his demands. He sent them once again through the sacred monastic citadels, and he asked them to inquire about how the holy life was going.

There was a man named Benedict who deserved the name,[89] for he was a man who bore many men to heaven.[90] He first came to the king's attention in the land of the Goths, and I ought to say a little about his life. He stood quite rightly before the flock of Aniane, pastor and abbot, an agreeable leader for his troop. When the king's nourishing affection swelled his sacred heart with thoughts of how he might improve the order and life of monks, he was there as helper, standard, example, and teacher. Thanks to his work, the holy fortresses are now pleasing to God. A beautiful will reigned in his sacred conduct; he was as holy as it is allowed man to be. He was sweet, beloved, agreeable,

87. These are the *missi* he already mentioned, pages 146–47.
88. Note that Louis did not ask for written reports. Scholars have long debated the place of written documents in Carolingian government.
89. It means "blessed."
90. Despite the significance that historians attribute to Benedict of Aniane, Louis's biographers accord him relatively little attention. Astronomer, c. 28, mentions him briefly, and Thegan overlooks him. Perhaps because he was himself an Aquitainian, Ermoldus knew and said more about Benedict than the others. A life of Benedict by Ardo is extant.

calm, temperate: the Rule was fixed in his holy breast. He benefited not only his monks but everyone; like a father, he did everything for everybody. That's why pious caesar loved him so and took him with him to the Frankish realms. The king sent Benedict's disciples through the monasteries to be an example and standard for the brothers,[91] and he ordered them to change for the better whatever they could; what they could not change, they were to report to him in detail and in writing.[92] Meanwhile the pious king and Benedict, the priest himself, discussed intimately their God-loved responsibility. First of all, the emperor addressed him, as usual, with gentle words born from pious affection: "I think you know, Benedict, how concerned I have been about this order since I first learned about it. Therefore, for the love of God, I would like to endow a little sanctuary not far from our seat.[93] This wish lies upon my heart, believe you me, for three reasons, and I want to tell you about them. You see how the burden of empire presses on my heart with all its weight; preserving rights is an immense job. Perhaps I could rest there once in a while and bear my prayers and pleas privately to God. The second reason is that, as you yourself have said, the present situation is disagreeable to you because a monk should not mix himself up too much in civil affairs or participate too freely in palace concerns. There you could take thought for the brothers' affairs, care for guests with fond attention, and, having renewed yourself once again, visit our seat strictly to serve as an advocate for the brothers. And here is the third reason: For us and for our subjects, this place would be of great value because of Aachen. If I should die suddenly, my remains would be buried in this place, and those who changed their lives would take up there Christ's work and willingly accept the plan we have agreed upon."

On hearing this, the holy man fell at his friend's feet and praised God and caesar's faith. "O great man," he said, "I have always known your will in these matters—may God, who gives every good thing, confirm it." The place was called Inde by those who built it a while ago, taking its name from the stream that flows before its gates. It is about three miles from the royal hall, which is called Aachen, as is now so widely known. It was once a favorite haunt of horned stags, good for bears and wild cows and wild goats. But Louis acted to clear the region of beasts and skillfully turned it into a place pleasing to God.

91. Astronomer, c. 28, says the visiting monks inspected houses of monks and nuns.

92. Note here the reference to writing, perhaps because a higher standard of literacy could be assumed among monks.

93. The monastery was founded in 817 or 818.

He built it satisfactorily, endowed it richly, and here, holy Benedict, your Rule is in full vigor. For Benedict was the father of this house, and Louis was present too, at once as caesar and abbot. He stayed here often and came frequently to see the sheepfold; he took care of the expenses and supplied big gifts.

Stop your song, Camena. Behold! This little book, happily concluded, may run to join its brother.

Book 3

By the gift of highest God, caesar's arms kept on increasing, and all people enjoyed peace strengthened by faith. Through the effort of great Louis, the fame of the Franks flew across all the seas and reached heaven itself. By ancient custom, Louis ordered select commanders to come from the farthest frontiers of the kingdoms. Everyone obeyed orders, came together in an assembly, and reported appropriately on their regions.[94] Among them was the noble Lambert, of Frankish stock; he came flying in swiftly from his territory.[95] He had charge of those lands which an enemy people had once seized by attacks across the sea with their fast boats.

These people, whom we call in the Frankish tongue Bretons, came from Britain, from the end of the world. Lacking land and pelted by wind and rain, they seized fields but paid tribute from the start. Of course, in the time when the waves drove these people here, the Gauls lived there. Because they had been baptized and anointed with oil, it seemed acceptable for them to spread out and farm the fields. Since they were left in peace, they quickly turned to awful wars and got ready to make themselves master of their new land. They exchanged lances for rent, battle for fields, and bombast for goodwill. The Frankish kingdoms were reverberating with one victory after another over peoples who seemed to be more dangerous. Consequently, this situation was neglected for many years, and that people grew more numerous and filled up the land. Finally, no longer satisfied with being foreigners, these people, in their arrogance, attacked the realms of the Franks. Unfortunate, ignorant, and quarrelsome, these people hoped to defeat the busy Franks.[96]

94. No other source mentions this particular assembly.

95. He was the count of the Breton March, essentially the triangle of land marked out by Rennes, Nantes, and Vannes.

96. Franks and Bretons had skirmished at their border repeatedly from the sixth century, and there had been significant Frankish campaigns in 753, 786, 799, and 811, which serve as background to the events of 818 and after, which are narrated here.

As I said, caesar, following ancestral custom, addressed Lambert, asking him to give a full report. "How does that people worship God in cult and faith? What high regard for God and the church is to be found there? What affection is there among the people? What justice, peace, respect for the king, works of piety? What is more, what safety is there for our frontiers? I want you to tell me everything, Frank, in order."

Lambert kissed caesar, knelt, and answered faithfully: "That people," he said, "dishonest and pompous, have been in rebellion right up to now, and lacking in goodwill. Untrustworthy, they keep only the Christian name, for their deeds and worship and belief are way off the mark. They take no thought for orphans, widows, or churches. A man will lie down with his sister; one brother will rape another brother's wife; everyone lives incestuously with everyone else; wickedness abounds. They live in briar patches and sleep in the woods and rejoice to live by theft in the manner of beasts. The force of justice claims no hall for itself with them, and the proper kinds of judgment escape them. They do have a king, whose name is Murman, if it is right to call 'king' someone who does not rule anyone. They have very often taken the path to our lands, but they do not go back to theirs unharmed."

That is what Lambert said. Distinguished, pacific, pious caesar said something like this to him: "It is a tough thing that you have told me about, Lambert, and unpleasant to relate, how that foreign people is welcome[97] to inhabit my land, only to be driven by arrogance to unprovoked attacks on my people. It is fitting and proper that I repay this deed with war and that the sea, by means of which they got here, not provide any help. To that same king let a messenger be sent who can well and quickly carry our words to him. Since that king has been anointed with holy baptism, it is right that we warn him first."

He summoned Witchar,[98] a good and wise man, and reasonable too, who by chance was already present. "Go quickly, Witchar; bear our demands— about which there must be no doubt—to the tyrant. I'll lay them out in order for you. He cultivates a wide swath of my fields where he and all his people, after wandering about as exiles, were carried by the sea. Now he declines to pay tribute and is even tempted to fight; he threatens the Franks and makes

97. The word here is "gratis," which could well mean "free" in the sense of "without rent" or "without tribute." But just above, Ermoldus has told us that the Bretons did, or were supposed to, pay rent/tribute. Later sources say that the Bretons were required to pay fifty pounds of silver per year and that in 818 they refused to pay it.

98. An abbot whose monastery is unknown but which, in view of what is related below, was probably situated in western Neustria.

ready his arms. After I received my father's realms and the imperial crown—by God's gift and the people's request—I put up with him to a degree, glossing over whether he wanted to be faithful and whether he wished to follow our laws. Now his malicious mind wavers more and more, and having brandished arms, he denies any intention of making abominable war. Now the time has come! Let this poor fellow stop deceiving himself and his people. Let him seek out the Franks and ask for peace. If he will not comply, come back with all speed and tell me everything." Thus spoke pious caesar.

Witchar got ready to go right away on horseback and carry out these mild commands. The king was already known to him, his home and his haunts too, because through caesar's gift Abbot Witchar possessed estates right along his border. Murman lives in a place with woods on one side and a nice stream on the other, situated amid hedges, trenches, and a swamp. Inside was a grand house that shone with the splendor of weapons whenever it happened to be filled with different soldiers. Murman always particularly liked this place; it was in a good spot and afforded him a certain security. Speedy Witchar got there quickly and asked to be allowed to speak with the king. Murman, when he learned that an envoy of kind Caesar Louis had arrived, was momentarily flustered as he tried to figure out how things would turn out. Affecting confidence, he removed the look of fear from his face. Feigning happiness, he right away ordered his companions to be happy too. Then he invited Witchar into his house.

"Hail, Murman," said Witchar. "I bring you greetings from mighty, pacific, and pious caesar." Receptive, Murman immediately responded in kind and gave him a kiss. "Hail to you, too, Witchar. For the pacific augustus I wish health and long life, and may he rule his empire for many years." Soon they sat down, ordered their attendants to depart, and took turns speaking. Witchar spoke first and explained his orders. Murman listened with mixed feelings. "Louis, the world's caesar, the glory of the Franks, the crown of Christians, first in peace and faith, yet second to none in war, distinguished in learning and in the works of piety, has sent me to you. You cultivate a wide swath of his fields where you and all your people, after wandering about as exiles, were carried by the sea. Now you decline to pay tribute and are even tempted to fight; you threaten the Franks and make ready your arms. Now the time has come! You poor fellow, you must stop deceiving yourself and your people. Go there and ask for peace. I bring these words of caesar's from our side, but for love of you, I will add a few more. If you will now, by your own will, comply with the king's commands, as he just advised you in his kindness, and if you want to keep lasting peace with the Franks, as is right, and as you and your people really need to do, then go quickly and accept the mild laws of the pious king. Don't give him what is yours but, rather, what you owe him. Think about your country, your people, I beg you; think about everything, your children and your wife. You cherish empty things, and you do not observe proper teachings. Still, he may send you back to your own land, and he might give you even greater gifts. You may be the great ruler of a great land, and you may have numerous troops and a soldier's honor. Nations and peoples may come to your aid. But when the Rutulians, swift Camilla, and the whole Latin cohort of Italy came to Turnus,[99] they still could not defeat Aeneas. If Odysseus,[100] Pyrrhus,[101] or hard Achilles,[102] or Pompey[103] and the forces he raised for war against his father-in-law[104] were on your side, it still would not make sense for you to venture war against the Franks, whose lands you inhabit and hold by their indulgence. For when anyone contests them in battle, he himself and his people pay a price. The Frankish people are second to none in strength; they conquer through God's love, and they prevail through faith. They always love peace, and they take up arms grudgingly; but once they take them up, no one had better come near them. Anyone who seeks their trust and protection lives in peace and calm. Get on with it! Stop delaying! And don't let your hostile mind go roaming all over the place and bring destruction upon you."

Murman had stood for a long time looking at the ground and keeping his mouth taut, tapping the soil with his staff. When Witchar's smooth talk and carefully delivered threats began to overcome his reservations, Murman's wicked wife came out of her bedroom and, with her venomous mind, embraced him in her pompous way. She kissed his knees, his neck, his beard, his mouth, his

99. In Virgil's *Aeneid* Turnus is the king of Ardea and the Rutulians. He has been Lavinia's favored suitor, but on Juno's prompting, her father betroths her to Aeneas. With the help of the Volscian Camilla, Turnus stirs up the Latins against the Trojans. Camilla is first mentioned in *Aeneid* 7.803–17 and appears again in 11.539–828. Aeneas's struggles with Turnus, Camilla, and the Latins occupy much of books 9–12.

100. The hero of Homer's *Odyssey.*

101. King of Epirus who fought two wars with Rome in the third century B.C. Having won battles at great cost, he gave his name to the term "Pyrrhic victory."

102. The hero of Homer's *Iliad.*

103. Lived from 106 to 48 B.C.: key Roman politician in the last years of the Republic who was first an ally then an enemy of Julius Caesar.

104. Julius Caesar, 100–44 B.C.

hands. She went round and round him, touched him with her practiced art, and looked for an opportunity to give him her insidious advice. The miserable king received her, embraced her with his arm, and gave vent to her wishes, for his wife's actions pleased him. The cursed woman pressed close to his ear and whispered for a long time. She turned the good sense and then the will of her husband. It was just like when, in winter in the forest, a group of shepherds quickly throws cut wood into the fire: This one hurries to bring suitable materials, that one carries dried straw for kindling, and another one blows on the fire. The pile thus tended will give off flames and touch the lofty stars; the shepherds warm their frigid limbs. Then suddenly, amid thunder, rain and snow crash down and the whole forest resounds. Against its will, the fire yields to the inundation: whence heat had come, now smoke rises. Not a bit otherwise did this deadly woman smother Witchar's words fixed in her good husband's breast. And so disdaining that same gloomy messenger, she raised her eyes to heaven and asked, in her clever way, "O king and crown of the eminent Breton people, whose right arm elevates the name of your ancestors to the heavens, how does such a woman come to be a guest in your fortress?" She said, "And does she speak of peace or war?"[105] Smiling, Murman put together words like these: "This envoy was sent to me by the Franks. Whether he brings peace or war, that is men's business. Woman, tend to your proper duties." When Witchar heard this argument, he spoke up right away: "Murman," he said, "give me the decision that you wish me to take to the king. The time has come for me to report back." This one, turning over sad cares in his breast, said, "I'd like to think about this overnight."

Sleep overcame the peasants in the fields, yet soon the sun's horses dragged Aurora on high. Abbot Witchar hurried to Murman's door at the break of day and demanded a response. The foolish man was entombed in drink and sleep; although present, he could barely open his eyes. Drunk and belching, he just managed to let words escape his lips that would never do him any good in the future. "Go, rush to your king, and tell him this. I do not farm his fields, and I do not desire his laws. He has the Franks. Murman rightly governs the Bretons. He won't pay rent or tribute. If the Franks start a war, I will fight back immediately. My right hand is adept at war."

Witchar replied: "My ancestors always used to tell a story, which now seems to me quite right, that you people were fickle and constantly driven to change

---

105. Murman's wife affects to regard Witchar as a woman, presumably because he is clean shaven and wearing a dresslike monk's robe.

your minds. A single woman could soften a man's mind, change his plans by her whispering. Thus," he said, "do the teachings of King Solomon testify, which the church often reads and takes to heart: 'Take the wood out of the fire and immediately the flame weakens; banish whispering and all quarrels cease.'[106] But since you do not wish to obey our gentle persuasions, I'll have to be your prophet and tell you the truth. As soon as Francia hears the words of your abominable response, then men's shields by the thousands will rush against you, you'll be completely surrounded by Frankish spears, your fields will be filled up with a multitude of soldiers. They will haul you and your people back to Francia as captives, or else you will be thrown on the thirsty sand to suffer wretched death all alone, and the cheering victor will possess your weapons. Don't let your forests or roiling swamps deceive you because your house is fenced by a forest and wall."

Raising himself from his throne, the raging Breton Murman responded: "I have a thousand wagons full of spears with which I can meet them in full fury. My shields are colored—yours are white—and I have a lot of them. There is no fear of war here." The two men exchanged these speeches; they were not of one mind.

Bearing this answer, Witchar left in a hurry, and announced these disgusting words to his pious king. At that point, Louis raised a muster from the kingdoms of the Franks and commanded everyone to prepare his arms right away. There is a city to which the old Gauls gave the name Vannes, set on the edge of the sea where the river Loire discharges violently and spreads along the shore.[107] The place was rich in fish and salt. An irksome troop of Bretons had often brought destruction to this city and carried away, as usual, war's prizes. Therefore, caesar ordered the Franks and their subjects to assemble there, and he headed there himself. The first to arrive were the Franks, properly speaking; accustomed to war, they had their weapons at the ready. Thousands of Swabians came from across the white waters of the Rhine, grouped into hundreds. A band of Saxons equipped with their big quivers came along with an allied troop of Thuringians. Burgundy sent an immense group of young men and increased the number of the Franks by joining with them. I just give up trying to tell of the peoples, indeed the huge tribes, of Europe whose incomprehensible number cannot be grasped. Caesar made a safe progress

106. Proverbs 26:20.
107. Vannes is, in fact, about forty miles from the mouth of the Loire. Although Ermoldus took part in a campaign in Brittany in 824 (page 173 below), his activity was in the region of Rennes.

through his own realms right up to Paris, where, rejoicing, he approached and visited your residence, lofty martyr Denis, where you, mighty abbot Hilduin, prepared gifts for him.[108] From there he went on to your eminent home, Germanus, and that of the martyr Stephen, and yours too, Geneviève.[109] He visited the region of Orléans at a leisurely pace, the pious one first entering Vitry-aux-Loges, where you, Matfrid,[110] readied the most beautiful accommodation for him; you gave him gifts both great and pleasing. Moving on smartly from there, he soon arrived at the city we just mentioned, where he tried to fortify himself with the protection of the cross.[111] Behold, most blessed Bishop Jonas,[112] you came to meet him; dutifully, yet willingly, you paid him his just deserts. Then he visited again your citadel, Aignan, asking you to lend him help.[113] Then, Durandus,[114] you went rushing back and forth and offered to give back to him the gifts that he had given to you. Then he went to Tours, to see the shrines of heavenly Martin and of the pious martyr Maurice.[115] Come on, let's get on with it! The time is coming, Master Fridugis;[116] it is urgent; you are going to greet caesar's arrival with peals of joy, and you will offer great gifts; gentle Martin is praying that God will let him have a safe journey. Caesar then entered the city of Angers in full celebration: Saint Aubin,

---

108. Documentary sources show that Louis was still at Aachen on June 30 and that he was in Orléans on July 27. Hilduin was the abbot of St.-Denis, just outside Paris, so Louis must have been there in early July.

109. See notes 58–60 above.

110. Count of Orléans (815–28), he figures more prominently in the narrations of Thegan and the Astronomer because of his role in the political struggles of the Frankish world between 828 and 834. Because those events happened after Ermoldus had finished his poem, it contains no hint of retrospective condemnation.

111. Presumably in the church of St.-Croix.

112. Bishop of Orléans (818–44), prolific author, and one of the most influential members of the Frankish clergy in the 820s.

113. The church of St.-Aignan; Saint Aignan was the fifth-century bishop of Orléans who saved the city from Attila the Hun.

114. Abbot of St.-Aignan, otherwise obscure, unless he is identical with the Durandus who officially witnessed at least 118 of Louis's diplomas.

115. Legendary leader of the "Theban Legion" (from the Thebaïd in Egypt), a supposedly wholly Christian legion in Diocletian's (r. 284–305) army. The soldiers refused to sacrifice to the emperor Maximian and were slaughtered at St. Maurice-en-Valais. One of the main churches in Tours was dedicated to Maurice, as were churches all over Gaul.

116. An Anglo-Saxon and pupil of Alcuin, Fridugis was named abbot of Tours after Alcuin's death in 804; he is attested in 808. He was a signatory to Charlemagne's will: Einhard, c. 33. In 819 Louis named him archchancellor in succession to Helisachar. At that time he was also made abbot of St.-Bertin. He retired in 832 and died the next year. His handling of monastic properties engendered controversies.

he sought your body with respect;[117] dear Helisachar[118] came out to meet him with joy in his heart and zealously added to his bountiful supplies. Finally, caesar himself marched into the city of Nantes; he sought out every shrine with prayer and petitions. Lambert, you finally received him for whom you had so hoped, and you gave the king important supplies. Caesar, you asked him to march against the detestable Bretons, and he deigned to lend you his help. Other groups were there too, of counts and powerful men; I cannot count them or enumerate their equipment. At last, eminent caesar approached Vannes, prepared for battle in the customary way, and drew up his commanders.

Meanwhile Murman, the haughty Breton, busied himself in preparing arms and a plan. At the same time, caesar, prompted yet again by the love arising from his accustomed piety, sent a messenger who could lay bare the whole situation. "Ask," he said, "O miserable man, what madness twists you, or what are you contriving, or what compels you to get ready for war? Has he forgotten the faith he swore, or the right hand he has often given to the Franks, or the service he paid to Charles?[119] Where is he rushing off to? Does he wish in his madness to betray himself, and even his children, and make them all exiles? How sad that he should perish faithless when, by God's gift, his people and ours share one faith. It can stop right here, if he is willing. Let him do what our command urged upon him; let him take hold of my restraints; let him bind himself to the Christian community in peace and faith. For the love of God, let this poor wretch leave aside his demonic weapons. If he refuses, I will act against my wishes, but I will make mighty and fearful war on him."

The messenger went, and returned promptly. As ordered, he recited the king's excellent words, rebuked, and pleaded. But that wretched man was dedicated to deadly iniquity, did not know how to keep faith, and slinked away from the pious commands. His mind made up, he spewed even more bitter words, carrying in his flaming breast the speech of his arrogant wife. He wanted war, summoned all the Bretons to battle, set traps, and prepared deceptions. Meanwhile Caesar heard the reply of the pompous Breton and ordered it recited to the Franks. The soldiers were outraged at his words, and since

117. The monastery of St.-Aubin in Angers was erected in the sixth century over the tomb of Aubin, bishop of Angers, 529–50.

118. Abbot of St.-Aubin and still archchancellor until 819.

119. This is almost certainly sheer invention. Remember that, above, the talk was only of rents or tributes paid in exchange for permission to settle on the king's land. Now the text shifts to fidelity and the exchange of hands. Ermoldus is, in effect, having Louis claim that Murman was a recalcitrant vassal.

they had been ready for war for a long time, they broke camp and the horn let out its terrible sound. Yet the pious emperor placed excellent watchmen over the others and commanded them, in God's love, "Protect churches, men; don't touch consecrated buildings; for the love of God, let there be peace for the churches." Trumpets were heard throughout the countryside, the woods echoed them back, and the blasts of the horns pulsated throughout the fields.

And so it began. Everywhere the forests provided the people with hidden escapes; the fields were full of Frankish soldiery. The Bretons went looking for the victuals they had placed in swamps and ditches and cleverly laid up in furrows of soil. Poor wretches, men and boys, herds too, were captured; nothing was concealed, no trickery hidden. There was no safety in a ditch, or secure hiding places for men in the underbrush; there was a Frank everywhere destroying valuables. They favored churches, just as caesar told them to, but the rest of the buildings went up in roaring flames. In the end, no one was confident to meet the Franks in the open fields; you haughty Breton, you fled from battle. Men occasionally appeared among the bushes, happily hidden in the woods, and gave battle only with a shout. Like a leaf that falls from the oak tree on the coming of frost, like the rains in autumn and the showers on a warm day, so too did the poor Bretons fill up the swamps and marshes like slaughtered beasts. Furtive attacks popped up along the narrow paths, but those shut up in their houses gave no fight at all. Already, Murman, your lands have been crisscrossed everywhere, your concealed refuges and your vaunted house laid open. Meanwhile, Murman, standing in a brushy valley, passionately spurred his horse and brandished his vaunted weapons. He tried to cheer up his men, and he spoke from the depths of his heart, haranguing thus for a long time: "You, my wife, my children, my companions, don't be afraid; guard your homes and your thatched huts. I am ready to go out there accompanied by just a few men, so that I can look over the battle line more safely. I believe that I'll come back on my horse loaded with booty and weighed down with spoils." He armed his horse and himself and his faithful companions; he took spears in both hands. He mounted his horse swiftly, held the reins, and spurred it sharply; he spun the four-footed beast around several times, and reared up before the doors. After his fashion, he ordered a drink brought to him in a huge vessel, took it, and drank. In the midst of all his servants he embraced his wife and children and in his cheerful way gave them long kisses. Then, shaking his spear repeatedly in his hands, he spoke: "Wife, pay close attention to what I am going to say to you. Beloved, these lances that you see," he said, "your joyful Murman is sitting on his horse and holding them in his hands; if they keep faith with me today, you will see me come home with them stained with Frankish blood. I believe, beloved, that Murman's right hand is not going forth in vain. Farewell, dear wife, and good-bye."

He had no sooner said this than he threw himself speedily into the forest's clearings; the foolish man was drunk when he went looking for you, Louis. He urged his comrades to arms with burning heart. Everyone, thrilled to get on with it, rushed forth impassioned by Mars. "You see, my young men, the Frankish army is destroying all our fields and carrying off our men and all our flocks. O strength of our fatherland, O former fame of our noble ancestors; now, alas, a vain memory shames us. You can see our wretched people hiding in the woods; they don't dare to take the field armed against the enemy. Good faith is safe nowhere. Where now are the promises given for a year with right hands?[120] Now no one dares to go out and meet the Franks. They are taking over far and wide; well pleased, they rage about and carry off the rich resources of the Bretons, built up over such a long time. If an opportunity presents itself and I can see the king, then maybe I can let him have this iron spear; I would certainly give him this iron gift for tribute. I will charge right at him without thinking of myself. I would give my life very gladly for the praise of the fatherland and the safety of our country."

One of his followers, a comrade in arms, responded to him, speaking the truth but hardly what he wanted to hear: "O king, empty words fall from your sad heart; it would be better to keep silent than to speak out that way. I see thousands of Franks holding the flat lands; countless, they rush through the deep haunts of the forest. Their eminent king is surrounded by various soldiers. Safe himself, he travels safely through your lands. Good grief! That's a people spread to the four corners of the world; they have subjected everyone to their commands. If it would please you, Murman, take off in pursuit of the isolated ones you can see going about, but don't think that you are going to get to the king." He turned his head and spoke up this way: "What you say is very true, but not pleasing at all." Suffering in mind, his eyes did not lack tears, nor his heart, grief. But soon he threw himself swiftly against the enemy, struck them in the back, and slashed their broad chests with his sword. Now here, now there, he raged with the weapons already prepared; acting in his ancestral fashion, he retreated and then wheeled around. A band of swineherds

---

120. It is not clear whether Ermoldus means that Bretons habitually swore allegiance annually or that they had sworn allegiance for one year for the present campaign.

fell before Murman's furious blow and lay everywhere, a wretched shepherd too. Like a ravenous she-bear who had lost her cubs, he roared back and forth through the fields and woods.

There was a certain Frank named Coslus, not of the first rank or of a noble line. He was a Frank all the same, and if he was little known up to then, afterward his right hand gave his name renown. Busy Murman saw him at distance and, trusting in his horse, got ready right away to attack him violently. But Coslus was no less confident in his trusty weapons and sought out Murman at the gallop; both were fierce indeed. Using harsh words, Murman began with a challenge: "Frank, I am going to give you my gifts right now. These presents have been kept in reserve for you for a long time already, and after you receive them, you'll remember me." While saying this, he shook his spear and then hurled it from a long way off. Coslus was attentive and deflected it with his shield. Now Coslus was superior in weapons and spirit and, exulting, spoke these words of his own: "Pompous Breton, I've had the gifts of your right hand. Now it is only fitting that you receive those which a Frank is holding." He spurred his horse and roused it to ride right up to Murman. There was no more time for fighting with throwing spears; the time had come for a Frankish lance. Murman's head and limbs were protected by armor, but the Frank attacked him skillfully. He knocked him to the ground and ran him through with his lance. In despair and despite, Murman's body hugged the soil. Coslus dismounted and cut off his head with his sword. Driven away so, his life escaped with a groan. A companion of Murman's struck down Coslus from behind. Alas, Coslus, a victor but careless, you perished! But then Coslus's squire, devoted to his lord, stabbed the fierce enemy in the side. In his agony he ran through that boy. Each one died from the other's wound. These four had fought proudly on Mars's field; victor and vanquished shared the same fate.[121]

Meanwhile, back in the camp, a rumor gradually filled the gentle breezes, announcing the most recent events: arrogant Murman had met his violent end. His head was brought into the camp. A crowd of Franks gathered from everywhere, anxious to look and well pleased. The head, cut off at the base of the neck with a sword, was stained with blood and without honor. They ordered Witchar to appear, and they asked him to say whether the story was true or false; they asked, and he himself was to decide. He immediately washed the head and combed its hair, and knew the answer right way. "Believe me,

---

121. No more than this is known about Coslus. Astronomer, c. 30, makes him the guardian of the baggage train and does not mention the squire.

all of you, this is Murman's head," he said. "That neck is very well known to me." In his piety, pious caesar took pity and ordered the body to be buried in the usual way. The bodies of the Franks were likewise committed to the grave, reverently, and accompanied by hymns.

Like thunder, another report rushed through the Bretons wandering around in the woods. "Dark fate has snatched away the king. Alas! Miserable comrades, let's go in a hurry. The right thing to do now is to seek out benevolent caesar's orders while we are still alive. Our Murman has died, struck by a Frankish lance. He believed too much in his wife's words." Thus compelled, the Bretons sought the royal yoke, the children and whole family of Murman having already come. Louis received the Breton oath with joy. He gave law, and he gave faith; peace and quiet were given in return. The victor gave the grandest thanks to God, and he joined the long-lost realms to his empire. Filled with joy, caesar departed from there, having left behind a few men, and with God's help he sought his own hardy lands.[122]

Meanwhile the envoys that kind caesar had sent into the world long ago, so that the church's honor would increase, came back from everywhere bearing the reports they had prepared, having fulfilled the pious ruler's commands and having completed their tasks in detail.[123] They returned, as great caesar had commanded them, after visiting countless cities, all the monastic settlements, and, Benedict, your communities of canons. Here is their report: "We have seen many things adorned and accomplished, with God's blessing, and your faithful and pious work, by deeds and examples; the whole cult is running properly along the right path. It is a gift of God. In a few places, owing to neglect in conduct and performance, the Divine Office is functioning less well. We ordered each one to carry out resolutely in his own rank the weight of your words. We gave them instructions according to your regulations, so that each one could tread that path of law, or else, because it was necessary for both sexes, we presented in the cities and monasteries the book that your authority had excerpted from the teaching of the fathers and completed fully, saying 'Read these things, men.'[124] The shepherd takes it to heart calmly; the zealous flock reads it right through and cherishes it always. Young men and old,

---

122. Cf. Thegan, c. 25, who also reports that Irmingard died.

123. Cf. Astronomer, c. 32. The envoys, dispatched in September 817, returned in the winter of 818–19.

124. It is difficult to ascertain exactly what this "book" actually was. Perhaps this is a reference to the book pertaining to canons and canonesses described by the Astronomer, c. 28.

masters too, found there what they should hold and teach and take to heart. And, caesar, let us add this: Since the coming of Christ, when the church first began to spread in the world—we are telling the truth here!—the church has not grown in respect or faith in the time of any king as it grows now in your times, through God's mercy, for the love of God and His honor. Your right hand banishes all evildoers and protects your pious servants. Your official efforts teach what your ancestors taught, and you yourself work assiduously to make your people love these things. You are terrifying to the wicked, pious and gentle to the kind, and the world flourishes bountifully in your merits." Caesar promptly gave them heartfelt thanks and enriched them with generous gifts as well.

There was an ancient custom among the Franks, which persists, and as long as it does, it will be an honor and crown for the people. When anyone declines to maintain his lasting fidelity to the king through guile, money, or trickery, or if a wicked person seeks to bring some attack against the king or his children or his rule, contrary to the oath that he swore, then, if a brother Frank appears and denounces him, it is fitting and proper for them both to fight it out in the presence of the king, the Franks, and the whole senate.[125] This kind of criminality is particularly hateful in Francia.

Now, there was once a man called Bero, extremely rich and even more powerful, who discharged his duties for a long time in Barcelona, which he held on Charles's gift.[126] Another man laid a charge against him. The name his homeland gave him was Sanilo. They were both Goths. He appeared before the king and, in the presence of the people and the senate, recited a damning accusation; Bero denied everything. They rushed forward side by side, fell at the king's feet, and pleaded with him to give them Roman spears. Bero spoke first: "Caesar, for the love of piety, I beg you, permit me to refute these accusations, and permit me to do so in our way, that is, on horseback and bearing weapons." He asked several times. Caesar said, "It will be up to the Franks to make the decision; that's right and proper. So we command." When the Franks' decision was given according to ancient custom, they readied their weapons and waited restlessly for the fight to begin. For the love of God, caesar spoke a few words to them, on account of his piety, telling them the whole truth:

125. Cf. Astronomer, c. 46, and Thegan, c. 38, pertaining to Bernard of Septimania's attempt via combat to purge himself of a charge of treason.
126. Cf. Astronomer, c. 13, who says that Louis left Bero in charge of Barcelona after the Frankish siege.

"If one of you will confess to me right now to be answerable for this charge, I will be merciful and grant the mistake, and I will remit the entire debt of the offense, overwhelmed as I am by God's love. Take my word for it, it is better to yield to my promptings than to fight the fierce battles of pernicious Mars." But they immediately pleaded again and again, "We are happy to fight! We are ready to fight!"

Wise caesar instructed them to obey the laws of the Franks, and they gladly did so without delay. There is a noted place near the royal hall, which is called Aachen and whose fame is immense, girded by a stone wall and surrounded by an earthen rampart, situated in the woods, where the recent growth is flowering. A bubbling stream slowly meanders through it. Different birds and beasts live there. When it pleased the king, he would very often go out there with a few companions intent on hunting. He would skewer the fat bodies of bucks with his sword or strike down does and she-goats or, when ice stiffened the ground in wintertime, set his clawed falcons against birds. Thus Bero, and Sanilo too, came there anxiously. The men were sitting on great warhorses. They wore shields over their backs and held spears in their hands. They were waiting for the king to give the signal from the citadel. On the king's order, a troop of his own royal men followed them, also bearing shields, so that if one of them should strike his opponent with a sword, they could grab him, in the pious custom, and drag him from death's bite. As usual, Gundold[127] prepared a typical litter and ordered it to be brought forward as he normally did. On the signal from the throne, they rushed into battle in a quite new way that was previously unknown to the Franks. Indeed, they threw their spears, and then they tried to stir up a fight with sword's blows, in their way. Now, Bero spurred his horse, turned him around, and fled swiftly across the broad field. The other one imitated him and finally dropped his reins and struck him with his sword. Bero admitted that he was guilty. Strong young men gathered around and bound Bero; heeding caesar's warning, they snatched him from death. Gundold was amazed and sent the litter back empty to his house, whence it had come. Caesar gave Bero his life and safety and, taking pity on him, let him keep his own wealth.[128] O, what great piety! It forgives offenses and permits the guilty to enjoy life and wealth. Faithful as I am, I ask, and I ask again, that this same piety send me back to pious Pippin.

127. This is the only time he appears in the sources, but it may be significant that Ermoldus describes his role in this duel as "usual."

128. Cf. Astronomer, c. 33, who says Bero was banished to Rouen.

And now, Benedict, you have run the race to the end; you have kept the faith, as Paul said.[129] Now living joyfully in heaven's palace, you have followed your namesake whom you had imitated here on earth. Behold, this third little book ends in your name so that you, kind one, will be mindful of your Ermoldus.

Book 4

The cares of the pious king extended in every direction, and the faith of the Franks grew right up to the sky. Nations and peoples flowed together from everywhere to see caesar's Christian faith.

But there was a nation from whom the cunning serpent concealed God and revealed the ancient error. For a long time they maintained wicked pagan practices, worshipping empty idols instead of their creator. Neptune was a god, and Jupiter assumed Christ's place; they paid him all sacred honors.[130] This people were called Danes from ancient times and are called by that name still. They are also named Northmen by the Franks; they are fast, agile, and well armed. This very people are well and widely known. They inhabit the sea and seek out wealth by ship. They are handsome, distinguished in both look and stature. One story says the Frankish nation derives from them. Conquered by God's love and taking pity on his ancestral people, caesar tried to enlighten them with God; it grieved him for a long time that so many people of that nation and such great herds of the Lord might perish with no one having attempted to teach them. He made a plan to look for someone he might send there to gain the Lord's long-lost treasures. Ebbo, the archbishop of Reims, was sent to do this work with the intention of making them believe in God.[131] For Louis had nurtured him as a boy and formed him well in the liberal arts.[132] Caesar spoke to him, and his words gleamed. He spoke at length, and gave pious orders to his servant:[133] "Go, holy man, and in the first place speak

129. 2 Timothy 4:7. Benedict died February 11, 821.

130. Ermoldus is probably being "literary" here, although the Romans did, by *interpretatio Romana*, attempt to identify the gods of foreign peoples with their own.

131. Ebbo (ca. 775–851), archbishop of Reims from 816 to 835 and from 840 to 841, was sent on this mission in 822–23. He figures prominently in both Thegan and the Astronomer as one of the rebels against Louis in the 830s. Thegan, c. 44, is especially venomous in his assessment of Ebbo.

132. The story is that Louis and Ebbo shared a wet nurse and became friends.

133. Several aspects of Louis's speech appear to paraphrase the Bible, but it may also be that Ermoldus is making use of a verse life of Christ written ca. 330 by Caius Vettius Aquilinus Juvencus. Juvencus took Virgil as his literary model and drew his material mainly from Matthew.

gently to this fierce people this way: There is a God in heaven, creator of the world and of everything that the land, sea, and sky holds. He created the first man, our ancestor, and placed him over the beautiful valleys of paradise, which he might enjoy with pleasure for ever and ever, for then, by God's gift, he knew nothing of evil. But because he sinned, he fell, and as a result, by the deceits of the demon, the whole race of his descendants fell too. A seed grew and filled the forests and fields, not worshipping God, but idols. Finally a flood buried them in rushing waters except for those few whom the holy ark saved from the waters. From that tiny seed grew a multitude, and a certain one worshipped its God. Other groups, infected by various poisons, sought crooked paths and worshipped dreadful idols. Taking pity once again, God, who reigns in heaven, sent His son, the sharer in His kingdom, to earth. He joined mortal man to His honor, and he freed man from that original sin. Although He, with His Father, had the power to save the world, He wished to die on earth to show His love. Fastened to a cross, He gave Himself over to death that He might grant His blessed kingdom to those who followed Him. He sits at the right hand of His Father, joined in His service, and He calls to His servants, 'Come, I will give you a kingdom.'[134] He orders the elect to assemble all the sheep and give them the holy gifts of the rite of baptism. Not otherwise can anyone rise to the heavenly palace, unless he does what the Son of God commands; that is, having abandoned the dark cult of demons, let him right away receive the sacred gifts of baptism. Ebbo, assiduously summon that nation to this faith; this is our faith; the church loves it. It is right to let go of empty things. Alas, it is a crime for man, whose strength is in reason, to serve metal images. How do Jupiter or Neptune, or whatever gods they follow, or metal statues made by their own hands, help them? The poor Danes worship empty things. They pray to deaf and dumb beings, and they offer to demons the gifts that are owed to God. Our God is not pleased by the blood of beasts; holy Himself, He prefers the blessed prayers of men. Time enough has been allowed to impious error; the time has come to abandon illicit practices. Day's end is calling out to them now; there still remains a share for them in the vineyard of the Lord. And so our gentle pace must stop while sweet light still permits man to seek God, lest dark night fall, seize the idle wretches, and cast them into the flaming furnace. You, holy Ebbo, although you have already read through the Bible, receive the testaments of the new and old teaching. First of all, draw

---

134. A rather free paraphrase of Matthew 25:34: "The king will say to those on his right: 'Come. You have my Father's blessing! Inherit the kingdom prepared for you from the creation of the world.'"

sweet cups from this holy source, so that those who empty them will come to love God's true teachings. Then, when the time comes, start them on harder lessons so that they will be able to learn [what falsehoods][135] they have worshipped up to now. From our realm go quickly to king Harald and relate our words to him. We are compelled to offer him these instructions from our love of God and the teachings of our faith. Let him take our words to heart if he is disposed to obey our benevolent counsels. For pity's sake, we insist that he right away abandon his ancestral error and give his pious prayers to Holy Christ. And we think it most urgent that he offer himself to God, whose creature he is, who created him. Away with nefarious monsters, let awful Jupiter vanish, let him abandon Neptune and love the church. I hope he will accept the gifts of salvation from the holy font and bear the cross of Christ on his forehead. Let him believe on my word that they do not have to yield their realms to me, for I seek only to enlighten one of God's creatures. If he wishes, let him come right now to our palace, let him be washed clean in God's true font. More than washed, he will be delighted with feasts and weapons, and on returning to his own realms, he can live in God's love. True faith and of course the divine commands of the Thunderer remind us to talk about these things, which I wish to see accomplished." Then he ordered Ebbo to be given a huge gift. "Go; may God be with you," the emperor said.

While these things were going on, a messenger came, in the way to which we have become accustomed, bearing distressing news from the region of rebellious Brittany, to wit, that they had broken the pledge and also the trust that caesar had recently concluded with them.[136] Having summoned his people and duly readied his arms, caesar, exulting, hurriedly prepared to go there. All Francia rushed together, nations and subject peoples came; even you, Pippin, got ready to come from your area. Louis divided the whole people into three parts, gave each one a leader, and arrayed the nobles. He committed one part of the battle to his like-named son and associated Matfrid with him, likewise many thousand men. Mighty Hugh[137] and Helisachar were joined to King Pippin, along with troops beyond number. Triumphant caesar kept the middle

135. There is a gap in this line. Faral offers three suggested reconstructions, and I have selected Muratori's *falsa quae*, which scans and makes sense.

136. Under a leader named Wihomarc, the Bretons had rebelled in 822 against the settlement imposed on them in 818. That rebellion was suppressed by Frankish counts stationed in the Breton March. In 824, then, Wihomarc rose up again. Neither Thegan nor the Astronomer report these events, but the *Royal Frankish Annals* do.

137. Count of Tours, father-in-law of Lothar, sacked in 828, and a rebel in the 830s.

column for himself. Fierce and wise, he directed the order of battle. Lambert took the lead in one column, and Matfrid in another.[138] You, Louis, though a boy, shared in your father's battle. Pippin's own men and a mixed troop of Franks carried the attack forward and spread destruction everywhere to the glory of their people. Under caesar's direction, the Franks marched along broad roads, so that the Breton realms, crossed this way and that, lay open. I myself bore a shield on my shoulder and sword at my side, but no one came to any hardship because I did so. When Pippin saw this, he laughed, marveled, and said: "Lay down your arms, brother; it's better to stick to your writing." Then they marched right through the fields, woods, and shimmering swamps. The people were cut down; every herd perished. Miserable captives were led away, and they died by the sword. Finally, those who were left sought out caesar's army, and caesar set the very best leaders over them as guards. Even had they wished to do so, they no longer had the capacity to make war. So, as a victor, pious caesar went home from there, and soon all the victorious Franks went home too.

Holy Ebbo spent a long time traveling around the northern realms, discharging his duties brilliantly, suitably, in God's name. Already, Harald, the prelate visited your palace and filled your heart with the message of Christ. He, at God's prompting, also began to believe the king's words, and he himself spoke before his people. "Go to your king," he said, "tell him this: I put trust in your words, holy man, to the extent that action follows them. I would like to see the kingdom of the Franks, Caesar's faith and arms and banquets, this crown of Christians, and the worship of God, whom every power serves, as you say, and whose sweet faith stands firm. Then, if your Christ, whom you discuss in your teaching, grants my prayer, I will act on it right away. Until I can see the temples of your God, our gods, at whose altars we have offered sacrifice, will be retained. If that God of yours should exceed ours in honor and can give greater gifts to one who prays to Him, that would be a reason to let ours go, and I would happily obey Christ and throw our metal statues into the fiery furnace." He ordered presents to be brought forth, and he gave the holy man such gifts as the land of the Danes is able to possess.

Ebbo came back rejoicing, burning in anticipation of future gains. He reported to the king extremely welcome news, how Harald, the excellent ruler of the Danes, would seek to receive God's holy waters. Pious caesar gave great

138. This is a little hard to follow. It seems that Matfrid led the column with young Louis, whereas Lambert led the one including Pippin, Hugh, and Helisachar.

thanks to the Lord, the Father of all, who has given every good thing, and he ordered everyone under the law of the empire immediately to pray to God with all their might, so that Christ, who saved the whole world by His blood, might redeem the Danes too from the evil host.[139] The pious one, at peace with himself, took the path to Ingelheim to spend the winter with his wife and children.

There is a place located near the fast-moving Rhine, adorned with different crops and riches, where one discovers a large palace supported on one hundred columns. Built by a band of masters and craftsmen, it has various passageways and many kinds of roofs, a thousand entries and exits, and a thousand rooms.[140] The church of the highest God was erected from the quarry, and it had bronze doorposts and little golden portals. The glorious deeds of God and of a long line of memorable men may be read there again and again in distinguished paintings.[141] The left side tells how in the beginning God put the new men in you, paradise, to live, and how a wicked serpent tempted the untutored heart of Eve with evil, and she, her husband, and then he himself took the food; how when the Lord came, they covered themselves with fig leaves, and how, for their sins, they had to cultivate the soil; how one brother struck down another in envy because of their first offering, not with a sword, but with his own miserable hands. Then one encounters the first lessons in numerous subsequent pictures laid out in order: How the flood rightly covered the whole world and killed the whole human race except for a few on whom God took mercy and protected in the ark, and the work of the crow or the dove. Then Abram and his offspring are depicted, and the deeds of Joseph and his brothers, and of pharaoh; how Moses freed the people from bondage in Egypt; how Egypt perished and Israel escaped; and how the law, by God's gift, was inscribed on two tablets; how water came from a rock and food came from birds; how the long-promised Holy Land was restored when Joshua arose as a good leader for the people; and then the outstanding group of prophets and kings were painted, along with the great deeds they accomplished; and

139. Ermoldus has somewhat compressed things here. Ebbo spent several months in Denmark in 823. During the winter of 823–24, Harald came to Frankfurt, but, as Ermoldus reports in detail below, Harald's baptism took place in 826.

140. Einhard, c. 17, says that Charles built "an impressive palace" at Ingelheim, but does not say exactly when he did so. The *Royal Frankish Annals* mention stays at Ingelheim in 774 and 787; the latter date is probably closer to the time of construction. Ingelheim became an important residence for Louis, often in the summer.

141. Frescoes are meant, of which nothing survives. Scholars have debated whether the following account of these pictures is a valid description or sheer literary invention.

the achievement of David and the deeds of mighty Solomon and the temple he built with God's aid; and then the leaders of the people, how many there were and what they did, the high priests and the nobles.

The right side portrays the mortal deeds of Christ, His gifts to the earth after being sent by His Father. How the angel came down and spoke to Mary, and how Mary said, "Behold the handmaid of the Lord." How Christ was born, as the prophets had known long before, and how God was wrapped in rags; how the shepherds soon received the holy commands of almighty God, and how the wise men deserved to see God; how Herod raged, believing that God would supplant him, and how he struck down the boys, sending them to their deaths; how Joseph fled to Egypt and took the boy-child there, and how the child grew, and how He was raised; how He who had come to save all by his blood, those long since perishing, wished to be baptized; how Christ endured so many fasts in the way of man; how He skillfully confounded His tempter; how He soon taught divine precepts throughout the world, and how, holy, He restored their former health to the sick, and how, even more, He restored the dead to life; how He bore arms against demons and drove them away; how, betrayed by a cruel disciple and a hard people, He Himself, although God, wished to die like a man; how, on rising from the dead, He appeared to His own companions, and how He ascended again into heaven and rules from on high. God's hall is filled with these pictures, all achieved at the skilled hand of the artist.

The royal residence is everywhere resplendent with sculptures[142] and cleverly tells the greatest deeds of men. They tell the deeds of Cyrus[143] and of the times of Ninus,[144] many kinds of battles and tough actions.[145] Here you will see how the fury of the king raged against a river to avenge the death of his beloved horse. And then how the boasting wretch seized the lands of a woman[146] and then got his head put in a blood-filled goatskin. Nor are the wicked deeds of horrid Phalaris[147] passed over in silence, or how he savaged his people by

142. The Carolingian period did not know significant freestanding or bas-relief sculpture. In the previous passage Ermoldus used the words *pictura* and *pingo,* so it is hard to take literally his words "regia namque domus late persculpta nitescit" (line 2126).

143. Persian emperor, ca. 557–530 B.C.

144. In Greek mythology, the legendary founder of the Assyrian city of Nineveh.

145. This and the next several stories appear to derive from Orosius (Christian historian who wrote *Seven Books of History Against the Pagans* in the early fifth century as a secular pendant to Augustine's *City of God*). Art works could, of course, have been created based on Orosius's narration.

146. Tomyris, queen of the Massagetai.

147. Tyrant of Acragas in Sicily (ca. 570–ca. 549), whose name was in antiquity a byword for cruelty.

his cruel art; how a certain Pyrillus, an artisan in bronze and gold, joined up with that miserable wretch and quickly built a big bull out of bronze in honor of Phalaris, so that the cruel man could shove victims inside; pretty soon, however, the tyrant shut Pyrillus up in the bull's belly, such that art rendered death to the artist by his own craft. How Romulus and Remus laid Rome's foundations, and how the impious one struck down his brother; how Hannibal continually pursued unjust wars, and how he lost his life; and also how Alexander subjected the world to himself by war; and how the little band of Romans grew right up to the sky.

The wall on the other side gloried in ancestral deeds and in the pious faith of more recent times. The amazing deeds of the Franks are joined to those of the caesars of the great seat of Rome: How Constantine[148] departed, dismissed Rome from his affections, and built Constantinople for himself. Happy Theodosius[149] is depicted there with his own deeds added to their distinguished accomplishments. Here the first Charles is painted, master of the Frisians in war, and the grand deeds of his warriors along with him. Here, Pippin,[150] you shine, giving laws to Aquitaine and joining them to your kingdom with the aid of Mars. And the face of wise Charles appears clearly, his head bearing he crown of his ancestral line. Here the Saxons stand opposite, contemplating battle, but he brings it on, dominates, and subjects them to his law.

That place sparkles with portrayals of these deeds and of others too. They feed the sight and delight those who look at them. It is there that pious caesar gives law to his subjects and duly treats in his customary way the ongoing needs of his kingdom.

Behold! A hundred ships came sailing down the Rhine, their fixed sails tied and gleaming; they were full of Danes, and of gifts too.[151] The first ship carried King Harald. He was seeking you, Louis. This reward was due to you, who make the honor of the church grow so well. Then they approached the bank and came into port. Pious caesar watched all this from a high vantage point, and out of respect he ordered Matfrid, with a group of young men, to hurry

148. Lived from 272/73 to 337; Roman emperor (306–37) who prevailed in a civil war, legalized Christianity, patronized the church, began the construction of Constantinople in 324, and dedicated the new city (actually the rebuilt Greek city of Byzantium) May 11, 330.

149. Lived from 346 to 395; Roman emperor (379–95) who passed legislation that effectively made Catholic Christianity the state religion of the Roman Empire.

150. Pippin III (r. 751–68), Charles's father, who campaigned in Aquitaine throughout the 760s.

151. Cf. Thegan, c. 33; Astronomer, c. 40; *Royal Frankish Annals,* anno 826. Notker, 2.19, has a rather fanciful account of these events.

and meet the men. He sent many horses caparisoned in purple to bring those newly arrived to his residence. Riding a Frankish horse, Harald approached; his wife and his household were getting ready to come too. Caesar came down joyfully from his eminent hall to meet him and, having arranged the details, laid on a banquet. Harald, bowing before the great king, spoke first: "Great Caesar, I will begin to tell what it is that brings me to your palace, me, indeed, my household, and my whole people; if your power should order it, I will tell caesar right away. For a long time I have followed the laws of my ancestors, and I maintain them right up to now after the custom of my people. I have always paid reverence to my gods and goddesses, so that their favor would keep my inherited realms, people, fields, and hearths, so that they would banish famine, forcefully take away all ills, and give every blessing to their people. Your holy man Ebbo came to the lands of the Northmen a while back, preaching and proving differently. For he said the creator of heaven and earth and the sea is the true God to whom every honor is due, that he created the first two people from warm clay, whence the human race spread throughout the world. That highest God sent His son into the world, and from His side flowed blood and water that washed the suffering world clean from every offense and opened the heavenly realms to the reborn. That son of God is called Jesus Christ, and His anointing now blesses every believer. Unless a person confesses that He is God and receives the gifts of baptism, he will rush against his will to the depths of Tartarus, where he will be joined to the demons. But whoever wishes to rise to heaven, where every good thing is to be found and all evil is absent, must confess Him to be true God and true man, must purify his body in the holy font, washing his limbs three times in the saving water in the name of the Father and of the Son and of the Holy Spirit. This God is one even though His names are three. Their glory was equal, is now, and ever shall be. Your bishop says that other things, which we have made with our hands, are empty metal idols and nothing at all. Loving caesar, your most holy bishop warrants with his own mouth that this is your faith. Made anew by his example and honorable words, I believe in the true God, and I reject statues made by hand. Therefore, I have hastened by boat to your kingdom so that I can be joined in your faith."

Caesar answered: "Harald, my friend, what you have asked for I will give you gladly, and I will give thanks to God because you have, by God's mercy, cut off your long-standing submission to Celidrus[152] when you finally learned

---

152. A water snake, apparently a metonym for beasts and demons.

to draw near to the Christian faith." Then caesar commanded, "Look, every-one, hurry, get ready, it is fitting to prepare the gifts of baptism; it will be well for them to wear the white garments of new Christians; bring fonts, chrism, and water too."

With everything in good order and readiness and the sacred rites prepared, caesar and Harald entered the church.[153] Caesar reverently received Harald from the font and garbed him in a white vestment with his own hands. Beautiful Empress Judith raised Harald's queen from the holy font and clothed her as well. Caesar Lothar, the son of gentle Louis, received Harald's son from the water. The nobles raised and clothed the king's retainers, and the ordinary people lifted many others from the font. O great Louis, what multitudes you give to God; what sweet scent rises to Christ on account of your action![154] These winnings will remain safe and sound for you for a long time, Prince, for you have snatched them from the wolf's maw and made them God's own. Harald, garbed in white and reborn in heart, went down to the white place of his eminent father. High caesar gave him superb gifts, products of Frankish workmanship: a woven cloak, studded with gems, dyed purple, and bordered all the way around in gold; caesar gave him a fine sword that he had worn at his side, along with its sword belt and golden straps; golden chains were fixed to both his arms; a golden belt with gems circled his thighs; his head was solemnly endowed with a wonderful crown; golden laced boots covered his feet; a golden wrap shone on his wide back; his hands were adorned with white gloves. At the same time, Judith gave fitting gifts to his wife, pleasing and distinguished: that is, a tunic stiff with gold and jewels, made as if by the art of Minerva[155] herself; a golden circlet with gems all around crowned her head; a grand necklace covered her upper breast; a sinuous gold necklace went around her neck; her arms held women's bracelets; a girdle made from gold and gems covered her strong thighs; and a golden cape covered her back. No less did Lothar lovingly adorn Harald's son with golden clothes. The remaining troops were supplied with Frankish clothes, which caesar gave them out of affection.

In the meantime, holy preparations for Mass were readied, and the signal was given for men to attend the highest rites. The church shone with a

153. The *Royal Frankish Annals* and the Astronomer, c. 40, state that Harald's baptism took place at St. Alban's in Mainz. Other sources, Thegan, c. 33, for example, place the events in Ingelheim. Ermoldus does not really say where.

154. Paraphrase of 2 Corinthians 2:15.

155. The goddess of handicrafts.

glittering array of clergy; the agreeable house flourished with the marvelous arrangements. The corps of priests gathered on Clement's[156] instructions, and the pious deacons sparkled in good order. Theuto led the choir of singing clergy, and Adhallvitus was there bearing his baton;[157] when he struck it, those present made a path of honor for caesar and the nobles, their wives and children. Triumphant caesar, always conscientious in holy rites, passed through the broad entry into the hall. Majestic, he gleamed with gold and gems. Leaning on his attendants, he moved forward joyfully. Hilduin held his right hand; Helisachar, his left; Gerung[158] walked in front of him, bearing the staff as usual and guiding the king's path. Pious Lothar and Harald in his toga followed them, shining in their attire. The handsome boy Charles walked happily in front of his father, glorious in gold, gaily clapping his feet on the marble floor. Judith proceeded too, decked out in her regalia, resplendent in her amazing finery. Two nobles of elevated station, Matfrid and Hugh, walked with her and paid reverence to the distinguished lady's regal status; they both shone in their golden clothes. Immediately after came Harald's wife, delighting in the pious queen's gifts. Then came Fridugis, followed by a group of smart pupils, brilliant white in their clothes and faith. The rest of the youth came next, lined up in good order and wearing clothes caesar had given them. Caesar, when he reached the church at a dignified pace, petitioned the Lord in his usual way.

Soon Theuto's horn gave the signal clearly, which the clergy and then the choir picked up. Harald was dumbstruck; so was his wife and all the nobles and their companions at such a grand display of divine worship. They marveled at the clergy, at the church, at the priests, and at the holy service. They especially marveled at the great king's wealth, and they saw so many things happen promptly at his command. Tell me, distinguished Harald, I beg you, what do you now love more, the king's faith or your statues? Put those metal contraptions in silver and gold into the furnace, and there will be honor for you and your people. If one happens to be iron, perhaps it will be useful for cultivating a field; order them to be made into plows. A plow working the earth will bring you more benefit than that god ever provided you by its skill. This is the true God, whom caesar himself and the Franks worship with fitting prayers; love Him, leave Jupiter behind. Make black pots and dark cauldrons

156. An Irishman who served under Charles and Louis as head of the palace school; he was Lothar's tutor.

157. Neither of these men can be identified.

158. Chief of the palace ushers from at least 822 and influential in court activities in the mid-820s.

out of Jupiter; let them love the fire just as he does. Make yourself a nice water jug out of Neptune, for as a pitcher he will always have the honor of water.

Meanwhile, the stewards ardently prepared a rich feast with different kinds of food and many types of wine. Here Peter, the head baker, and there Gunzo, the master chef, worked fast to prepare the tables in the customary way. They set white napkins of snowy wool and then put food on dishes hard as marble. One looked after the baked goods, and the other tended to the meat. You can see golden vessels near each dish. Young Otho worked no less hard, commanding the cupbearers and preparing the strong gifts of pure Bacchus.[159]

On the reverent conclusion of the grace-giving worship from which he had come, golden caesar readied his departure; his wife and children, golden as well, and the whole crowd, and finally the clergy in their white vestments. The pious ruler walked at a stately pace into the palace, where the imperial banquet had been prepared for him. Joyfully Louis reclined[160] at the table and ordered beautiful Judith to his side; she kissed his knee. Louis ordered Caesar Lothar and Harald, his guest, to take seats on a cushion. The Danes marveled at the banquet. They marveled at caesar's arms, at his attendants, and at the distinguished young men.[161] That was rightly a joyful day for the Franks and the reborn Danes, one afterward to be remembered.

As the sun was coming to signal the next day, the stars were yielding the sky, and the sun began to warm the earth, caesar and the Franks got ready to go hunting, as usual; caesar invited Harald to accompany him. Not far away in the bubbling Rhine there is an island[162] where new grasses flourish along with shady groves. Many different kinds of wild beasts could be found there, lying about lazily in the broad forest. Bands of hunters filled the place as well with their great packs of hounds. Caesar, mounted on a swift horse, rushed into the fields. Wito, bearing his quiver, rode beside him. Numerous groups of young men, and of boys too,[163] came flooding forth, among whom swift Lothar rode up on horseback. The Danes too, and Louis's guest Harald, were happy to be there and watched all this eagerly. Louis's gorgeous wife, Judith, clothed

159. If Otho is the same as the Odo mentioned in a document of 826, then he was *buticularius,* butler. Ermoldus calls him *Otho puer,* which is odd for a major officer of the court. Hence I translate "young" to avoid the implications of "servant," another possible meaning of *puer.*

160. A classicizing anachronism, since the Franks sat at table.

161. A reference, it seems, to the *pueri regis*—the "king's boys"—sons of noblemen who spent some time at court.

162. This may be the island where Louis would die in 840: Astronomer, c. 62.

163. See note 161 above.

and coiffed stunningly, mounted her horse; the highest nobles and a troop of magnates rode before and after the noble lady in honor of the pious king. The whole wood resounded with the constant barking of the dogs, here the cries of men, there the blasts of horns. The animals were flushed out and fled through the sharp underbrush. Neither flight nor woods nor water afforded them any protection. Here a little doe fell among the stags; there a boar with fangs was run through by a spear. Happy caesar bagged many beasts; he struck them down with his own hand. Swift Lothar, in the full flower of youth, killed many bears himself. Other groups of men killed many animals of different kinds in the meadows.

It happened that a little deer, chased by dogs, fled the hunters through the undergrowth in the woods and went jumping through a thicket. Behold, putting its hope in its feet, it went right through the spot where a mighty band and Empress Judith were waiting; the boy Charles[164] was with them. Flight was of no help. Its end was near. When little Charles saw it, he wanted to follow it like his parents and asked for a fast horse. He asked insistently for weapons and a quiver of swift arrows. He wanted to go in pursuit, just like his father. He pleaded and pleaded, but his lovely mother forbade him to go, unwilling to yield to his plea. But neither his guardian nor his mother could break his will, and just like a boy, the youngster rushed ahead on foot. Other young men went out and seized the fleeing little beast and promptly brought it back to the boy. He picked up weapons suited to his tender years and struck the animal's quivering hide. It was a boyish achievement this time, but more would follow, and he would go forth marked by his father's strength and adorned with his grandfather's name. It was like shining Apollo walking through the heights of Delos and bringing great joy to his mother, Leto.

Now the eminent father, caesar, and the rest of the boys, weighed down from the hunt, were getting ready to go home. But in the middle of the forest Judith had skillfully constructed a verdant shelter. She covered it with thatch and boxwood cuttings, tied it together with little strips of cloth, and covered it with linen sheets. And she prepared a seat for the pious king in the field's green grass and laid out a feast. Caesar and his beautiful wife washed their hands and reclined together on a golden cushion. Handsome Lothar and Harald, the well-loved guest, also reclined at the table on the pious king's command. The remaining youths took places in the grass and rested their tired bodies under

---

164. Charles "the Bald" (823–877), Judith's son and the half-brother of Lothar, Pippin, and Louis the German. On his father's death he became king of the West Frankish Kingdom.

the shady trees. The young men soon brought the roasted meat of the beasts; an array of game joined the imperial banquet. Hunger fled before the feast, and they raised cups to their mouths, driving away thirst by the sweet wine. Good Bacchus made their brave hearts joyful, and joyfully they returned to the palace. When they got to the palace, they warmed their hearts with wine and went to the evening Office. When the Office was completed as usual, worthily and reverently, they went from here back to the palace. Behold, a band of youths, showing off the game from the hunt, rushed about anxious to catch the king's eye. They carried a thousand huge deers' antlers and the hides and heads of bears too, and they traipsed around with the carcasses of countless boars; the little boys brought goats and does as their tribute. The pious ruler shared the bounty among all his attendants in his normal way, and the great part fell to the clergy.

Meanwhile, as Harald, the guest, saw such things, many different ideas turned over in his heart. It amazed him to see the royal laws and rule and faith and the duty to God that marched to Louis's command. Finally he swept away his uncertainty and took hold of a plan that God Himself gave him. Full of confidence, he approached the king, fell at his feet, and spoke to him thus: "Best caesar, worshipper of God, rector of your people, whom Almighty God has given you, gentle one, I see that you are distinguished, patient, brave, and pious, armed yet merciful, all by God's gift. The richest of all, yet generous to those in need, you are pleasant and peaceful to your subjects. I see every stream of virtue entrusted to you, caesar, and your heart is drenched with a starry dew. Warned by your persuasion, I am putting my neck in the yoke of Christ, which pulls one out of the eternal flames, draws me and my house away from evil error, and fills the heart in the true font. What is more, delighted by gifts and various weapons, my heart is filled with God, and my body abounds in wealth. Who would do such things, give such gifts to an unworthy people, if he were not inflamed by the love of Christ? I now believe that you are the chief of all good men, that you rightly hold the crown of the Christians' empire. Let all idols fall from me for the name of Christ, and all powers for your name. Let the potent glory of ancient times yield, while your empire, God's gift, flourishes. Perhaps someone could be your equal in generosity and arms, still you exceed all others in the love of God. But what am I doing now? Why do my words hold me back? Why do I wish to carry on with this little speech?" Then folding his hands, he handed himself to the king and, beyond that, his kingdom, which he held by right, with himself. "Caesar," he said, "receive me and my subject kingdom, and I willingly enter your service." Caesar took his honorable hands in his own, and the Danish realms were joined to the pious Frankish ones.[165] Right away triumphant caesar, in the old Frankish custom, gave him a horse and, as was his practice, arms too. The brilliant feast day rose again anew, Franks and Danes resplendent in their celebration. Meanwhile caesar gave Harald, now his faithful man, rich gifts for his loyalty. He gave him lands near his frontier, a wine-growing region bountiful in many ways. On top of this, mighty caesar gave him all the vessels he would need for divine worship, the vestments for each holy rank, priests, and catholic books. Taking pity, he also sent there willing monks who could bring his people to the pious realms of heaven. How many gifts he gave him to keep, and what kinds they were, conquers wit and exceeds verse.

So the sailors who knew the signs of the sea loaded the vessels with gifts and regal foods. The breezes were calling their sails; the winds told them not to delay; the dreaded signs of winter admonished them. Finally, when the ships were stabilized and the sails were set, Harald received permission to enter his boat in honor. The king's son and nephew kept watch with the guardians in the palace and learned to observe Frankish laws. Harald, loaded down with riches and various weapons, went back to his own kingdom through the churning sea.

Louis, you gave this gain to almighty God and also joined distinguished realms to your own. Kingdoms that your father's arms were unable to take by any contest offer themselves to you willingly. You, father, take in hand everything that neither Roman power nor Frankish law had held.

And even an organ, which Francia had never built, whence the Greek kingdom boasted so much, and which was the only reason, caesar, Constantinople thought itself superior to you, is now found in the palace at Aachen. Perhaps it will be a sign that they are bending their necks to the Franks, that their particular glory has been taken away.[166] Rejoice, Francia! It is only right. Give pious thanks to Louis, by whose virtue you receive such gifts. May Almighty God, creator of heaven and earth, grant that His name will resound throughout the world for ages.

165. In fact, Harald had sworn homage already in 814: Astronomer, c. 24.
166. The *Royal Frankish Annals*, anno 826, report that George, a priest from Venice, appeared at Mainz offering to build an organ "in the Greek style." The *Royal Frankish Annals*, anno 757, also report that Constantine V sent an organ to Pippin III. It was still at Aachen in the early ninth century. See also Astronomer, c. 40.

While I was singing this song, I was held under guard in Strasbourg, aware of and answerable for my own offense, in a place where a church dedicated to the Virgin Mary shines and where her praises are rightly and reverently observed. Often, indeed, the heavenly host is said to visit this seat, and the choir of angels love it. Many marvels are reported. Help me, Thalia,[167] to tell a few, if the holy Virgin favors you. It is said that the guardian of the church was once a man named Theutram, a man worthy of his name.[168] He kept watch alone day and night before the altar of the Virgin and often prayed to God, so that, counting on heaven's gift, the holy man merited to see the angels regularly. On a certain night, after the psalms and hymns had been completed, when he wished to rest his tired limbs, he suddenly saw the church filled with a brilliant light like the burning sun on a fine day. He rose from his bed to discover the reason why such a light beamed in that sweet house. It happened that wings like an eagle's covered the altar, but no bird like this was ever created on earth. Its beak was golden, its claws more precious than jewels, its wings the color of the sky, and light itself sparkled in its eyes. The priest was struck dumb, and he could not keep the bird in his gaze. The bird amazed him, its wings too, and especially the light, and its whole body as well. He sat there for along time until the cock's voice rang out three times, summoning the brothers to the morning Office. Then the bird rose, and, marvelous to believe, the window opposite opened on its own and let him fly outside. Right when the bird flew away to heaven, the light itself dimmed. It seemed to have been sent from God.

On another occasion the same teacher had a vision, which a group of brothers told me about. As usual, he was singing his psalms in the above-mentioned place before the altar, passing the night seeking God in prayer. With him were pupils keeping the night watch and closely observing the time. Behold, suddenly thunder clashed and the winds blew and the strong roof of the church shook vehemently. The pupils fell to the ground and, terrified, prostrated themselves in the nave, their minds having fled in terror. The fearless priest raised his hands to the stars and wanted to know what that noise meant. He soon saw the roof of that sacred building open, and he saw three distinguished men entering, shrouded in light and vested in white, their bodies whiter than snow, their heads than milk. The third one, in the middle, was older and stepped forward supported by the other two, advancing piously. When their

167. The muse of comedy.
168. Ermoldus does not explain the name. It seems to mean something like "godly."

feet touched the ground, they approached the Virgin's altar reverently and sang their prayers. Walking along like men, they sought the other altars, sang aloud, and offered their prayers in proper order. The right side of the building rejoices in the gifts of Paul; the left upholds the name of Peter: here the great teacher, there the bearer of heaven's keys. Between the two shone the glorious mother of God. Michael and the cross claimed the center of the nave; the joyful rear is resplendent with John's anointing. These heaven dwellers addressed prayers from earth to those whose souls they had often seen in heaven before God. What foolish person could be so demented as to think that the bodies of the holy fathers are not to be venerated when God is rightly venerated in his beloved servants to whom we raise our prayers on high?[169] For Peter is not God, but I believe that prayer to Peter can free me from punishment for my offense. Now, while the men were passing through the church of Mary, the roof above was still open and exposed. Once they had finished their prayers, they returned to the starry sky, and the roof closed up and took its normal place.

When the holy man saw this, he got up and looked for his companions, who, senseless for a long time, were lying on the ground. "Get up, fellows," he said; "what could possibly make you sleep when you should be keeping watch?" Shaking with sobs, they could hardly get out a word, and claimed to be ignorant of what had just happened. He spoke urgently, "Let the hour and the time be noted; perhaps there is a further message for us in all this. I believe that it was a prophet and priest endowed with great honor whom the angelic chorus took back to heaven." How marvelous to believe! Holy Boniface, whom the priest saw, died at that moment, while he was trying to break the hardened hearts of the Frisians with the teaching of Christ and show them a path to the kingdom of heaven.[170] Alas, this deadly people killed its best healer and with their blow prepared the kingdom for him. While he was on his way to heaven with his two companions, he wished to see your church, Virgin

169. A topical reference: Bishop Claudius of Turin (d. after 827), a noted biblical scholar, had launched an iconoclastic campaign in his diocese in the 820s, denying the cult of the cross and the value of relics and of prayers to the saints. In 825 several Frankish bishops gathered in Paris to study, and affirm, traditional Frankish teaching on religious images: they existed for commemoration and decoration; they could not be either destroyed or worshipped. Louis directed Bishops Jonas of Orléans and Dungal of Pavia to write treatises against Claudius.

170. Boniface (born Winfrith) was an Anglo-Saxon born in Wessex ca. 675 and killed by Frisian bandits in 754. He preached and taught in central Germany for more than three decades, visited Rome three times, and played a key role in facilitating Franco-papal relations. He founded the great monastery of Fulda and was archbishop of Mainz. Boniface had no known connection with Strasbourg.

Mary. Great is your strength in heaven and your power on earth, you who brought forth the father of the world. Help me, unworthy though I am; release me from exile, you at whose doors I often worship. And if the passing glory of the present age eludes me, then with you as my guide, Holy Virgin, I will seek heaven.

Ermoldus, a poor and needy exile, gives you this work, Caesar, rudely played on a croaking flute. Lacking in gifts, I bring a few songs to a powerful man; lacking wealth, I offer a book of verses. May Christ, who moves and adorns the hearts of kings with His touch, who turns those hearts in whatever direction pleases Him, who especially fills up your heart with flourishing virtues and allows it to overflow with piety, grant that you look more closely at our case, Eminent King, and lend a benevolent ear. Perhaps you will be able to grasp from truthful words that I am less guilty of the crime imputed to me. Believe me, I do not hold myself innocent of the offense that got me exiled. But I plead that the immense piety that relaxes debts be mindful of my exile.

You also, beautiful Judith, worthy spouse, who rightly hold the heights of empire with him, bring help to one who has fallen, console a suffering wretch, raise up a fallen man, open the doors of the prison, so that through a very long life the Lord Almighty may exalt you, save you, enrich you, honor you, and love you.

Thegan, The Deeds of Emperor Louis

INTRODUCTION

Thegan,[1] like the other biographers of Louis the Pious and unlike the biographers of Charlemagne, is a shadowy figure. His name is not a common one but does appear occasionally in the Moselle–Middle Rhine–Fulda region. He was surely born before 800. It is possible that he was educated at Lorsch, and if so, he might have written documents for the monastery in 798.[2] He became chor bishop[3] of Trier under Archbishop Hetti (814–47). Walahfrid Strabo addressed two poems to him in 825, when he was already chor bishop.[4] Given Walahfrid's penchant for self-promotion, his dispatch of poems to Thegan suggests that he may have been a person of some consequence (albeit the poems themselves do not tell us much). Additionally, he was provost of St. Cassius and St. Florentius in Bonn, in the archdiocese of Cologne, which suggests that he had fairly wide-ranging connections. In 844 he was present at the translation of the relics of Saints Chrysanthus and Daria to the monastery of Münstereifel. In about 836 he wrote a letter to Count Hatto, possibly a relative, whose seat is unknown.[5] Thegan signed a document for Saints Cassius and Florentius in 848, but in 853 a new person signed as provost. A necrology from St. Maximin in Trier dates Thegan's death to March 20. Presumably be died sometime between 849 and 853.[6]

1. He is called in some sources Degan, Theganbertus, and Theigenbertus.
2. He had some sort of connection with Abbot Adalung (cc. 30, 42), and Lorsch is the only monastery mentioned in the text.
3. A chor bishop was basically an auxiliary bishop who shared the work of an ordinary bishop who presided over a large diocese.
4. MGH, PLAC, 2, ed. Dümmler, nos. 2 and 3, pp. 351–53.
5. MGH, Epp. Karolini Aevi, 3, ed. Dümmler, 337.
6. For basic biographical details, see Eggert, "Thegan." For more details, see Tremp, *Studien,* 4–18, and idem, introduction to *Gesta Hludowici imperatoris,* 1–5.

Thegan neither dedicated nor addressed his work to anyone in particular. There is no evidence that anyone commissioned it. Nowhere in the work does Thegan signal his identity explicitly. Walahfrid Strabo, in his prologue, identifies Thegan as the author of "this little work." Notker certainly knew this work, but otherwise its influence is hard to trace. Thegan might have known Louis the Pious personally,[7] but there is no evidence that he ever held a court office, communicated with members of the court, or played a role in the maelstrom of Frankish politics. The work survives in seventeen manuscripts, none earlier than the eleventh century. Typically the work circulated in collections of historical works, often alongside Einhard. It is from Thegan's pages alone, therefore, that the reader can form a sense of what kind of work this is and why Thegan wrote it.

Getting a sense of the nature and intent of the work requires a look at its sources, structure, style, and content. Let us begin with sources. Thegan certainly knew Einhard's *Life of Charles the Emperor*. He may have had it on his desk, or he may have been working from memory.[8] Be that as it may, Einhard's imprint is unmistakable—up to a point. Through chapter 19 Thegan to a limited degree imitates Einhard's thematic approach. From chapter 21, however, Thegan does exactly what Einhard does not do: he narrates events in strictly chronological fashion. Walahfrid was quite right to say that Thegan wrote "in the fashion of the annals." Chapter 19 itself, Thegan's description of Louis, clearly mirrors Einhard's chapters 22 to 26. A comparison of the two depictions displays two very different imperial images. Einhard's classicizing Charles is "uncomfortably human," whereas Thegan's Louis is an ideal Christian ruler. Each ruler is depicted as moderate at table, but whereas Charles is rather stoic, Louis is virtually monastic. Charles is genial, "cheerful," as Einhard puts it. Louis "never showed his white teeth in laughter." In his geniality, as well as in his concern for the "very old barbarian songs," Charles is very much the Frank. Louis comes off as a late antique or even Byzantine ruler. For Einhard, laughter, feasting, drinking, and old songs were "central images of secularity."[9] Thegan rotates this picture 180 degrees. In connection with the ancient songs, it is interesting to reflect on whether Thegan knew the anonymous (to us) biography of Alcuin written in the 820s. There he would have read that the young Alcuin, too, loved the old poetry but abandoned it in his

7. The surmise of Tremp, *Studien*, 46.
8. Hageneier, *Jenseits der Topik*, 165–67.
9. Innes, "Politics of Humour," 137–47 (the quotations are on 138 and 147).

maturity.[10] Einhard, of course, says that Alcuin was Charlemagne's teacher and adviser. Was Thegan saying that Charles was a reluctant pupil? One might also instructively compare the way the two authors describe Charlemagne's death. Einhard's account (cc. 30, 31) is simple, elegant, dispassionate. Charles took ill, fasted, lingered, received the Eucharist, died, and was buried amid much weeping. Thegan (c. 7) either had additional sources or else embroidered Einhard's account. He depicts Charles correcting texts of the Bible before fever gripped him after his bath. After seven days of torments he asked Hildebald to give him Communion. Then he made the sign of the cross, extended his hands and arms, and quoted Christ's last words on the cross. He then died and was buried. In addition to supplying more details, Thegan pointedly Christianizes the scene.[11]

As Walahfrid says, Thegan wrote in an annalistic style. Whether he used the Moissac annals, the Royal Frankish Annals, or the so-called Annals of St. Bertin, it seems clear that both his details and his basic structural approach owe something to the year-by-year approach of the annalistic sources. Walahfrid was right to say that Thegan wrote *gesta* (deeds), not *vita* (life). The Bible is also a key source for Thegan, in several respects. He cites the Bible often (which Einhard does not do), he portrays Louis as a biblical/Christian king, and his style is manifestly biblical. Oral informants may also have contributed to Thegan's *Deeds*. If, as some think, he was a nobleman from the Rhine region, he may well have had connections to major "players" in the politics of Louis's reign. As a chor bishop, he would have had regular meetings with his ecclesiastical superiors. He might have attended the annual assemblies of the Franks. A circle of abbots from St.-Vaast, Lorsch, Weissenburg, and Prüm may have provided information. No fact or detail can be confidently attributed to such oral sources, but Thegan's readers should keep an open mind to the possibility.[12]

The structure of Thegan's work calls for only a few comments.[13] Whereas Einhard begins by ridiculing the late Merovingians and then seats the Carolingians in power, Thegan opens with the eternal reign of Christ and the earthly

10. *Vita Alcuini*, 16, MGH, SS, 15.1, p. 193. It is to be noted, however, that the *vita* says that as a youth Alcuin "had read the lies of the ancient philosophers and of Virgil." See also Hageneier, *Jenseits der Topik*, 173–75, and Innes, "Politics of Humour," 145–46.

11. Innes, "Politics of Humour," 137–38; Hageneier, *Jenseits der Topik*, 162–80.

12. Tremp, *Studien*, 44–55, and idem, introduction to *Gesta Hludowici imperatoris*, 7–12.

13. Löwe, "Thegan," 332–34; Berschin, "Biographien Ludwigs des Frommen," 223–27; Tremp, *Studien*, 63–83; idem, introduction to *Gesta Hludowici imperatoris*, 12–19; Rosamond McKitterick and Matthew Innes, "The Writing of History," in *Carolingian Culture: Emulation and Innovation*, ed. Rosamond McKitterick (Cambridge, 1994), 209; Hageneier, *Jenseits der Topik*, 136–37, 154–55.

rule of the Carolingians as the descendants of Saint Arnulf. He then continues, in annalistic fashion, as noted, to the year 835. Perhaps as a member of
the ecclesiastical and secular elite of the central Rhineland, Thegan regarded
that year's settlement of the acute political disturbances of the years 833 and
834 a fitting conclusion. He probably began composing his text as early as
835. Given that he reports about the plague that struck Lothar's partisans in
Italy in 836 (c. 55), that he does not mention the death of his friend Abbot
Adalung of St.-Vaast and Lorsch in 837, and that his hopes for Louis the German would have been dashed by the latter's rebellion in 838, it seems safe to
conclude that the work was composed between late 835 and early 838, or perhaps late 837. By eschewing Einhard's thematic approach for a strictly chronological and narrative framework, Thegan may have been implicitly rejecting
his predecessor's model. That is, Thegan constructs Louis's image by means
of narrative, by a straightforward account of what happened, of what Louis
did in particular circumstances. Nevertheless, in two instances, Thegan does
interrupt his narrative flow to pause and insert "Einhardian" interludes. The
first interruption occurs in chapters 18, 19, and 20, where Thegan describes
Louis's coronation in Reims in 816 by Pope Stephen IV, offers his description
of Louis himself, and proffers his critique of parvenus and bad advisers. These
chapters put on display a divinely and properly instituted emperor and the
dangers such an emperor might encounter. The second interruption falls into
two separate parts. In chapter 44 Thegan presents his blistering critique of
Archbishop Ebbo of Reims, and in chapter 50 he returns to the topic of slaves
mastering their masters. These two chapters constitute a pendant to the three
that form the first interruption of the narrative flow. To the extent that Thegan's structure reveals his meaning, then, the reader must attend carefully to
the one-thing-after-another narration while keeping in mind the more general
issues raised in the two interruptions.

Thegan's style was gently criticized by Walahfrid and has found no cham-
pions since.[14] Walahfrid comments on Thegan's lack of elegance and his "clumsiness" (*rusticitas*). Walahfrid attempts to excuse Thegan on the grounds that
he was so busy with preaching and pastoral work that he had little time for
the niceties of a stylish composition. The criticisms are fair, but it should
be noted that Thegan's Latin, while substantially less polished than that of all
the other authors gathered into this volume, is not really too far outside of

14. Berschin, "Biographien Ludwigs des Frommen," 226–27; Tremp, *Studien*, 83–90; idem, introduction to *Gesta Hludowici imperatoris*, 21–22; Hageneier, *Jenseits der Topik*, 150–51, 155–61.

the standard of the majority of Carolingian writers. Thegan's style is simple, paratactic. His vocabulary is limited. His syntax is uncomplicated, although occasionally his Latin gets away from him, leaving his meaning ambiguous if not downright unclear. The attentive reader will notice a few constantly re-peated words and phrases that a more accomplished writer would have varied. The "interlude" sections just mentioned, however, are intriguing. These are more gracefully written, more rhetorically sophisticated, and more forceful by far than any other sections of the text. It would appear that Thegan did have it in him to write in an agreeable and impressive style.

Thegan's writing reveals little that is distinctive about his education. He cites no fewer than twenty-eight biblical passages, and his whole work is con-structed by means of biblical terms and concepts. He mentions explicitly only three early Christian texts: Augustine's *City of God* (c. 19), *The Apostolic Canons* (c. 20), and Gregory's *Pastoral Rule* (c. 20). Thegan quotes two passages from Virgil (cc. 44, 52), one from the *Aeneid* and one from the *Eclogues*. In his screed against Ebbo, Thegan mentions several classical authors, but not in such a way as to indicate that he was familiar with them. On the whole, his work is edifying. For the most part he avoids abstractions and sweeping generaliza-tions. That said, his annalistic portrayal of both Louis and his enemies con-veys a sense of a ruler imbued with classical and Christian virtues struggling against the world's vices. The work thus shares something with the "Mirrors for Princes" genre.[15] Several Carolingian authors wrote *Specula Principum* (Mirrors for Princes) treatises that set forth the virtues that a truly Christian ruler should embrace, live, and embody. Nevertheless, in Thegan's *Deeds* it is always Louis himself who is front and center, whereas in a Mirror it is the virtues themselves that are on parade.

Finally, then, the content of the work: What is Thegan saying? Why did he write the *Deeds*? Some of Thegan's arguments and perspectives are palpa-ble. Others are more subtle and can be understood only if one knows a good deal about the issues that motivated various people during Louis's reign. For example, Thegan despised Ebbo. Louis made his "milk brother" (they shared a wet nurse) archbishop of Reims only to be betrayed by him. Thegan re-sented this betrayal deeply. What is more, Thegan possessed a characteristic aristocratic disdain for lowborn persons who had risen above their natural station. These points are pretty obvious. Less obvious to the nonspecialist is

---

15. Hageneier, *Jenseits der Topik,* 183.

the fact that Ebbo had taken the lead in trying to diminish the office of chor bishop by confining it to priestly duties and stripping it of all administrative, episcopal, responsibilities.[16]

Thegan liked Lothar no more than he did Ebbo. He believed Lothar was unworthy of his father and of the imperial succession to which he had been designated. Thegan placed all his hopes in Louis the German. It is quite possible that one major motivation for the *Deeds* was to effect a reconciliation between the two Louis; note that Thegan regularly calls Louis the German "like named" (*aequivocus*). Perhaps it was Thegan's favorable impression of Louis the German that led Notker to make use of the text. Thegan disliked people who gave bad or self-serving advice. His chief specimen of this kind of person is "Hugh the Timid," that is, Lothar's father-in-law, Count Hugh of Tours.

Thegan's portrait of Louis is a positive and admiring one. By saying (c. 20) that Louis did everything well except that he listened to his advisers more than was fitting, Thegan distances Louis from some of the troubles of his reign. At the same time, Thegan frankly admits that the succession scheme of 817 angered Louis's sons, that Louis mistreated Bernard, and that the plan to carve out an inheritance for Charles the Bald proved troublesome. In other words, Thegan does not whitewash Louis.

In the end, Thegan seems to have tried to understand why things turned out so badly.[17] From his opening lines, Thegan puts the events of Louis's reign into the context of salvation history. His overarching aim is to see the will of God in the ordinary events of the Carolingian world. Thegan's account is relentlessly spiritual but rarely ecclesiastical. That is, he neglects the great reform councils on which modern historians have lavished much attention. His reportage is never naive. Instead, it seeks to delineate the moral qualities necessary to the achievement of the divinely constituted imperial mission. Louis appears as a hypostatized guarantor of the universal Christian order. Moral failings all around, some of them Louis's own, bring divine displeasure and punishment. Louis's image is monastic and ministerial.[18] He bears awesome

16. Tremp, *Studien,* 70–76.

17. In general, see Tremp, *Studien,* 69–79; idem, introduction to *Gesta Hludowici imperatoris,* 15–18; Berschin, "Biographien Ludwigs des Frommen," 224–25; Innes, "Politics of Humour," 133–36; Hageneier, *Jenseits der Topik,* 155–61.

18. Thomas F. X. Noble, "The Monastic Ideal as a Model for Empire: The Case of Louis the Pious," *Revue bénédictine* 86 (1976): 235–50; Mayke de Jong, "Power and Humility in Carolingian Society: The Public Penance of Louis the Pious," *Early Medieval Europe* 1 (1992): 29–52; Innes, "Politics of Humour," 144.

responsibilities on behalf of the Christian people. The reader is left to decide whether Louis bears them well or badly.

I have translated Walahfrid's prologue as well as his chapter titles, which he listed immediately after the prologue. I have instead placed them at the head of each chapter. The reader should bear in mind that these materials help us to understand how Thegan's text was understood shortly after its composition, but do not bring us closer to the author.

ESSENTIAL READING

Thegan. *Gesta Hludowici imperatoris.* Edited by Ernst Tremp. MGH, Scriptores rerum Germanicarum in usum scholarum separatim editi 64. Hannover, 1995.

Collateral Sources

(Ermoldus Nigellus and the Astronomer are crucial companions to this text.)

Ardo. *The Life of Saint Benedict, Abbot of Aniane and of Inde.* Translated by Allen Cabaniss, revised by Thomas F. X. Noble. In *Soldiers of Christ: Saints and Saints Lives from Late Antiquity and the Early Middle Ages,* edited by Thomas F. X. Noble and Thomas Head, 213–54. University Park, 1995.

Carolingian Chronicles: Royal Frankish Annals and Nithard's Histories. Translated by Bernhard Walter Scholz. Ann Arbor, 1970.

Charlemagne's Courtier: The Complete Einhard. Edited and translated by Paul Edward Dutton. Peterborough, Ont., 1998.

Charlemagne's Cousins: Contemporary Lives of Adalhard and Wala. Translated, with an introduction, by Allen Cabaniss. Syracuse, 1967.

The Lives of the Ninth-Century Popes (Liber Pontificalis). Translated, with an introduction and commentary, by Raymond Davis. Translated Texts for Historians 20. Liverpool, 1995.

"The Time of Louis the Pious (814–840)." Chap. 3 in *Carolingian Civilization: A Reader,* 2nd ed., edited by Paul Edward Dutton, 155–294. Peterborough, Ont., 2004.

Scholarship on Thegan

Berschin, Walter. "Biographien Ludwigs des Frommen." In *Biographie und Epochenstil im lateinischen Mittelalter,* vol. 3, Quellen und Untersuchungen zur lateinischen Philologie des Mittelalters 10:223–27. Stuttgart, 1991.

Eggert, Wolfgang. "Thegan." In *Lexikon des Mittelalters,* vol. 8, cols. 613–14. Munich, 1999.

Hageneier, Lars. *Jenseits der Topik: Die karolingische Herrscherbiographie,* Historische Studien 483:129–86. Husum, 2004.

Innes, Matthew. "'He Never Even Allowed His White Teeth to Be Bared in Laughter': The Politics of Humor in the Carolingian Renaissance." In *Humour, History, and Politics in Late Antiquity and the Early Middle Ages,* edited by Guy Halsall, 131–56. Cambridge, 2002.

Löwe, Heinz. "Thegan." In Wilhelm Wattenbach and Wilhelm Levison, *Deutschlands Geschichtsquellen im Mittelalter: Vorzeit und Karolinger,* 3:332–35. Weimar, 1957.

Manitius, Max. "Die Biographien Ludwigs des Frommen." In *Geschichte der lateinischen Literatur des Mittelalters,* 1:653–55. Munich, 1911.

Tremp, Ernst. *Studien zu den Gesta Hludowici imperatoris des Trierer Chorbischofs Thegan.* MGH, Schriften 32. Hannover, 1988.

———. Introduction to *Gesta Hludowici imperatoris,* by Thegan, MGH, Scriptores rerum Germanicarum in usum scholarum separatim editi 64. Hannover, 1995.

THE DEEDS OF EMPEROR LOUIS

Thegan

The Prologue of Walahfrid Strabo

Thegan, a Frank and chor bishop of Trier, composed this little work in the fashion of the annals. It is short, to be sure, and inclines more to truth than to elegance. Some of his remarks may seem too effusive and passionate in expression, because as a noble and perceptive man he could not be silent when grief drove him to speak of the calumny of vile persons. At the same time, the love of justice and of its promoter, the most Christian emperor, was rather exaggerated by the ardor of natural zeal. Thus his work is pleasing on account of his goodwill, and we should not worry too much about a certain amount of clumsiness. Indeed, we know that he was well read and much occupied with preaching and pastoral work and that he could preach the core of the Scriptures, not their surface. I, Strabo, have inserted some divisions and chapter headings into this little work because I want to hear and promote regularly the deeds and praises of Emperor Louis of holy memory and so that those who wish to know may find the individual titles easily.

(1) *A List of the Kings of the Frankish People from the Blessed Arnulf Right Down to Charles the Great, and His Consecration.*

Our Lord Jesus Christ reigns forever. In the year of His incarnation 813, which is the forty-fifth year of the reign of the glorious and orthodox emperor Charles, of that very Charles who, as we learn from ancestral tradition and as many histories testify, descended from Christ's bishop Saint Arnulf.[1] Saint Arnulf, a duke when he was a young man, begot Duke Ansegis. Duke Ansegis begot Pippin the Elder, also a duke.[2] Duke Pippin the Elder begot Charles the Elder, likewise a duke. Duke Charles the Elder begot Pippin, whom Stephen, the Roman pontiff, consecrated and anointed as king.[3] King Pippin begot Charles, whom the Roman pontiff Leo consecrated and anointed as emperor in the church where the most blessed body of Peter, the prince of the apostles, lies, on the day of the birth of our Lord Jesus Christ.[4]

(2) *Concerning Queen Hildegard and Her Three Sons.*

When he was a young man, the above-mentioned emperor took to wife a girl named Hildegard from a very noble family of the Swabians. She was related to Duke Godfred of the Alemans.[5] Godfred begot Duke Huoching; Huoching begot Nebi, who indeed begot Imma, who actually bore the most blessed queen Hildegard. After the above-mentioned emperor married her, he begot three sons by her. One of them was called Charles after his father, the second was Pippin, who was king of Italy, and the third, who was king of Aquitaine, was called Louis. Their father lived with them happily for a long time and brought them up usefully in the liberal arts and in worldly laws.[6]

1. Arnulf was critically important in Frankish politics in the first decades of the seventh century. He was bishop of Metz from 614 to 629. He retired as a recluse near the convent of Remiremont and died around 640. It was only at the end of the eighth century that sources with close connections to the Carolingian court began to claim Arnulf as an ancestor of Charlemagne.

2. Thegan was probably using Paul the Deacon's late eighth-century *History of the Bishops of Metz*, local traditions, and perhaps a genealogy of the Carolingian family. Still, he is imprecise. Arnulf's son Ansegisel married Begga, the daughter of Pippin I (sometimes called "of Landen"), who was mayor of the palace in Austrasia (the northeastern portion of the Frankish kingdom), the first member of his family to hold this office. Pippin died in about 640. Pippin II ("of Herstal") was the son of Ansegisel and Begga. He was also mayor of the palace and died in 714. Charles ("Martel"), his son, succeeded as mayor. On Charles's death, in 741, he divided his mayoral office between his two sons Pippin (III, or "the Short") and Carloman. Compare Einhard's presentation of this family history.

3. In July 754 at St.-Denis. The pope had come to Francia to seek aid against the Lombards.

4. December 25, 800.

5. The Franks long claimed lordship over the Alemans. Godfred declared independence in the time of Pippin II, and for three generations Pippin, Charles Martel, and Charles's sons warred against the Alemans. In 746 at Cannstadt several Aleman leaders were murdered by the Franks, and the area passed under Carolingian control. Some scholars suggest that Carloman's remorse over this event led to his decision in 747 to become a monk. Neither Einhard nor Thegan mentions that Hildegard's father came from a distinguished Frankish family, the Gerolds. Charles's marriage to Hildegard was certainly intended to promote peaceful relations between two peoples who were old enemies.

6. Only Charles really remained at court with his father. Pippin and Louis were made kings of Italy and Aquitaine respectively in 781 and rarely saw their father after that date. Note that Thegan here ignores Charlemagne's other children; but see c. 6 below.

(3) *Concerning Louis, the Youngest, and His Goodness, with Examples from the Ancients.*

That one who was born the youngest always learned from his infancy to fear and love God, and whatever he had of his own he used to distribute to the poor in the name of the Lord. For he was the best of his sons, just as, since the beginning of the world, the younger brother so often precedes the older brother in merit. This was proclaimed for the first time, among the sons of the first parent of the human race, concerning Abel, whom the Lord called just in His Gospel. Abraham had two sons, but the younger became better than the older. Isaac had two sons, but the younger was chosen. Jesse had many sons, but the youngest, who was shepherd of the flocks, was on God's command elected and anointed as king in order to lead the kingdom for all of Israel. Christ, who had formerly been promised, deigned to become man from his seed.[7] But it would be verbose to go on telling such stories.

(4) *Concerning Queen Irmingard and the Sons She Bore.*

So Louis, after he came of age, married a daughter of the very noble duke Ingram, who was a nephew of the holy bishop Chrodegang.[8] The name of the virgin I just mentioned was Irmingard, and with the advice and consent of his father, [Louis] made her queen. He had three sons by her while his father was still alive. One of them was called Lothar, another Pippin, and the third, like himself, Louis.[9]

(5) *The Death of Pippin and Charles, Sons of Emperor Charles.*

The great emperor Charles ruled well and usefully, and he loved his kingdom. In the forty-second year of his reign his son Pippin died, in the thirty-third year of his life. In the next year Charles died, the firstborn son of the above-mentioned Queen Hildegard. Only Louis remained to assume the rule of the kingdom.

(6) *How Emperor Charles, with the Consent of the Franks, Committed the Highest Authority in the Realm to Louis.*

When the above-mentioned emperor understood that the day of his death was approaching—for he was very old—he summoned his son Louis to himself, along with his whole army, bishops, abbots, dukes, counts, and minor

---

7. The same trope is employed by Ermoldus, page 129. Thegan returns to it below, c. 57.

8. Thegan provides few details about one of the most distinguished families in the empire. The family was rooted in the Hesbaye region of what is now eastern Belgium. They were neighbors of the Carolingians. Chrodegang was bishop of Metz from 742 to 766 and one of the principal ecclesiastical advisers of Pippin III. Another relative, Rupert, was bishop of Salzburg in Bavaria. Another relative, Count Cancor, founded the important monastery of Lorsch. Note how Thegan, in his accounts of Charles's and Louis's marriages, lays great stress on familial attachments.

9. Lothar was born in 795, Pippin in about 797, and Louis in 806.

officials.[10] He held a general assembly with them peacefully and honorably at the palace at Aachen, urging them to be faithful to his son and asking everyone, from the greatest to the least, if it was agreeable to them that he give his dignity,[11] that is, the imperial office, to his son Louis. They all responded joyfully that this was the counsel of God in this affair. That done, on the next Sunday he put on his regalia, placed a crown on his head, and processed forth decked out and adorned with such distinction as befitted him. He reached the church that he himself had built from the ground up and approached the altar that had been built in a higher place than the other altars and was dedicated in honor of our Lord Jesus Christ. He ordered that a golden crown, different from the one he was wearing, be placed on that altar. After he and his son had prayed for a long time, he spoke to his son in the presence of the whole multitude of his bishops and magnates. First of all, he urged him to love and fear almighty God, to keep his commands in every way, to lead the churches of God, and to defend them from wicked men. He instructed him always to show unfailing mercy to his younger sisters and brothers and to his nephews and all his relatives. Then he told him to honor priests like fathers, to love the people like sons, to drive haughty and wicked men onto the path of salvation, to comfort monks, and to be a father to the poor. He instructed him to appoint faithful and God-fearing officers who would detest bribes. He was urged to dismiss no one from his office without due judgment and to show himself blameless at all times before God and the whole people. After speaking these and many other words to his son, in front of the crowd, he asked him if he wished to obey his instructions. He responded that he would willingly obey and that, with God's help, he would keep every precept that his father had given him. Then his father ordered him to pick up with his own hands the crown that was on the altar and to place it on his own head, as a remembrance of all the precepts that his father had given him. So he fulfilled his father's command. After this was done, they heard a solemn Mass and went back to the palace. The son steadied his father both coming and going and did so as long as he was with him. A few days later, his father honored him with magnificent and countless gifts and dismissed him to return to Aquitaine. Before they parted, they embraced and kissed and began to weep on account of the joy of their love. He went back to Aquitaine, and the lord emperor retained the kingdom and his title honorably, as was fitting.

10. Compare the accounts of these events in Einhard, c. 30; Astronomer, c. 20; and Ermoldus, pages 142–44.

11. Like Einhard, Thegan often speaks of the *nomen imperatoris*.

(7) *What the Emperor Charles Did in His Last Days, and His Death and Burial.*

After they parted, the lord emperor undertook to do nothing, except to give himself to prayers and alms and to correct books. Right before he died, he had, with the help of Greeks and Syrians, excellently corrected the four Gospels of Christ, which are denoted with the names of Matthew, Mark, Luke, and John.[12]

In the next year, the forty-sixth of his reign,[13] in January, a fever gripped the emperor after his bath. Since he was growing feebler day by day—he was not eating or drinking anything, but he took a little water to refresh his body—on the seventh day, after he had begun to suffer so terribly, he ordered his most trusted bishop Hildebald[14] to come and to give him the Sacrament of the Lord's body and blood to strengthen him for his passing.[15] After this had been done, he suffered in his illness that day and the following night. The next day, as dawn was breaking, knowing what was going to happen, he extended his right hand with the strength he had left and made the sign of the cross on his brow and then signed himself again on his breast and over his whole body. Finally, drawing his feet together and extending his arms and hands over his body, he closed his eyes and slowly sang this verse from the Psalms: "Into your hands, Lord, I commend my spirit."[16] Immediately after this, "in a good old age and full of days,"[17] he died in peace. On that same day, his body was buried in the church that he himself had built in the palace at Aachen, in the seventy-second year of his life, the seventh indiction.[18]

(8) *How Louis, on Succeeding to His Father, Divided His Father's Bequests.*

After the death of the most glorious emperor Charles, his son Louis set out from the region of Aquitaine, arrived at the palace at Aachen, and received

---

12. Charlemagne's adviser Alcuin made editorial corrections to a text of the Bible, and Theodulf of Orléans actually prepared a new edition of the Bible. Nothing is known about the biblical scholarship mentioned here.

13. Note the chronological confusion: Einhard, c. 30, says "forty-seventh year."

14. Charles's archchaplain, or head of the palace clergy. He was archbishop of Cologne, and Charles secured permission from both Hadrian I and Leo III to keep Hildebald with him at the palace. He continued to serve under Louis until his death, in 818. In Einhard, c. 33, he appears as a signatory to Charles's will.

15. Much of this account probably derives from Einhard, but a few details here must have come from someone else, perhaps an eyewitness.

16. Psalm 31:6 (= 30:6 Vulgate); cf. Luke 23:46.

17. Genesis 25:8.

18. Thegan, like Einhard, says that Charles died in the seventy-second year of his life. This statement puts Charles's birth in 742, whereas recent scholarship places it in 748. See also note 13 above.

without any opposition all the kingdoms that God had handed to his father. This was in the year of the Lord's incarnation 814 and the first year of his reign after his father. He took up residence in this palace, and right away, with the greatest haste, he demanded that he be shown all his father's treasures in gold, silver, and precious gems and all the furnishings. He gave his sisters their legal share, and whatever was left he gave away for the soul of his father. He sent the greatest part of the treasure to Rome in the time of Pope Leo, and whatever still remained, he distributed all of it to priests and the poor, foreign visitors, widows, and orphans. He kept for himself only one silver table that was triple in form, like three shields joined together as one. He kept it for himself out of love for his father, but even so, he compensated for it with another valuable item that he donated on behalf of his father.

(9) *He Received and Dismissed Various Envoys, Especially from the Greeks.*

Later, envoys came to him from all the kingdoms and provinces and from foreign nations, indeed from everyone who had been under his father's authority, announcing that they would keep peace and faith with him, and without pressure they offered their obedience freely. The envoys of the Greeks along with Bishop Amalar of Trier were among those who came. Amalar was the envoy of Charles of good memory to the prince of Constantinople, whose name I do not remember.[19] When they arrived, they found the lord Louis sitting on his father's throne, just as the Lord ordained. He received them graciously, accepted their gifts politely, and held intimate discussions with them from time to time while they were with him. After a few days, he honored them with rich gifts and let them go home. He sent his own envoys ahead of them to prepare anything they needed for their work while they were in his kingdom.

(10) *How He Confirmed the Decrees of His Ancestors.*

In that same year, he ordered the renewal of all the charters[20] that had been issued in the times of his ancestors for God's churches. He confirmed them with his own hand by a signature.[21]

19. In writing *ad principem Constantinopolitanum,* Thegan continues the Carolingian reserve with respect to the exclusive legitimacy of the emperors at Byzantium. The Franks had been negotiating for the recognition of their own imperial title. In Frankish and Byzantine sources, each party tends to call the other by a variety of names.

20. The Latin is *praecepta,* which could have a variety of meanings. From other evidence we know that at least immunity privileges were confirmed and reissued with royal protection.

21. He may have traced out his monogram, but twice below (cc. 13, 19), Thegan says that Louis signed with his signature. Charlemagne, as Einhard says, could not write, but it is possible that Louis could.

(11) *A Legation of the Beneventans Promised Their Tribute.*

Meanwhile, envoys of the Beneventans came, handing over the whole land of Benevento into his power and promising to pay every year many thousands of gold coins.[22] This they have continued to do right up to today.

(12) *Bernard, the Son of Pippin, Submitted Himself to His Uncle.*

At the same time, Bernard, the son of his brother Pippin, arrived, submitted himself to him as a vassal, and took an oath of fidelity to him. The lord Louis received him willingly and honored him with great and worthy gifts. He then let him go back safe and sound to Italy.

(13) *How He Sent Envoys Throughout His Realm to Learn About and Correct Whatever Needed Emendation.*

At that same time, the prince sent his envoys throughout all his realms to inquire and investigate whether any injustice had been inflicted on anyone. If anyone could be found who wished to say so and who could prove it with very reliable witnesses, he instructed such a person to come into his presence immediately with his witnesses. Those who went out to investigate found a numberless multitude of oppressed people whose ancestral lands had been seized or whose liberty had been taken away because evil officials, counts and their subordinates, had discharged their duties badly. The prince ordered all these deeds, which had been committed at the hands of wicked officials in the days of his ancestors, to be undone. He restored patrimonies to the oppressed, freed those unjustly cast into servitude, and ordered that documents be drawn up for everyone. He signed them himself with his own signature. It took a long time for him to accomplish this.

(14) *While Holding an Assembly in Saxony, He Received and Dismissed Envoys of the Danes and of Bernard.*

In the next year of his reign,[23] he held his general assembly in Saxony. He accomplished many good things there, and a legation of Danes came to him seeking peace. All the surrounding pagan peoples came to him. Even the above-mentioned Bernard came to him there, and once again he let him go back to Italy. The lord Louis, after he had confirmed the boundaries of his realm in those regions, went back to his seat at the Aachen palace and passed the winter there.

---

22. Apparently this was, after the change of rulers, a confirmation of the treaty concluded in 812, which required the annual payment of seven thousand solidi. The mention of gold coins is unusual at this date.

23. In early July 815.

(15) *He Sent an Army Against the Slavs and Conquered Them.*

In the next year, he sent his army against the Slavs, who lived to the east.[24] He beat them badly and paraded his victories as God's gift. After this, everyone went back to his own home.

(16) *How Pope Stephen Succeeded to Leo, Came into Francia, and Met the King at Reims.*

In that same year, the Roman pope Leo died and Stephen succeeded him.[25] Immediately after he became pope, he ordered the whole Roman people to promise fidelity to Louis with an oath.[26] He sent his envoys to the prince, telling him that he very much wished to see him in any place that would be acceptable to him. On hearing this, Louis was filled with great excitement and began to rejoice.[27] Right away he ordered his *missi*[28] to meet the holy pontiff with the greatest festivity and to provide for all his needs. The lord Louis set out after his *missi* to meet the pontiff. Encountering each other in a great field near Reims, each dismounted, and the prince bodily prostrated himself on the ground three times at the feet of the holy pontiff. When he got up for the third time, he saluted the pontiff with these words: "Blessed is he who comes in the name of the Lord. The Lord is God, and His light has shone upon us."[29] The pontiff responded, "Blessed be the Lord our God, who permits our eyes to see the second King David."[30] Embracing and kissing in peace, they went to the church.[31] After they had prayed for a long time, the pontiff arose and, at the top of his voice, with his clergy, sang for him the royal lauds.[32]

(17) *How the Same Pontiff Consecrated Him Emperor and They Honored Each Other with Mutual Gifts.*

Afterward the pontiff honored him with many great gifts, and also Queen Irmingard and all his magnates and officers. On the next Sunday, in the

24. The Sorbs.

25. Leo III (795–816), Stephen IV (816–17).

26. This was the first change in the papacy since Charlemagne's imperial coronation. Popes had in the past signaled their election to the Byzantine emperors, but Charles had not demanded this token of recognition. Leo's pontificate had ended amid intense political strife in Rome, so Stephen may have been trying to reassure Louis.

27. Compare the different accounts of these events in Astronomer, c. 26, and Ermoldus, pages 147–58.

28. Up to this point Thegan has used relatively neutral words like *legati,* which I have translated as "envoys." Here he shifts to *missi,* implying perhaps something more formal and official, *missi dominici* being a regular element of the Frankish institutional structure.

29. Psalm 118:26–27 (= 117:26–27 Vulgate).

30. This paraphrases 1 Kings 1:48 (= 3 Kings 1:48 Vulgate).

31. Presumably to the monastery of St.-Rémi, outside the walls of the city.

32. The *laudes regiae* was a litany of praise and prayer that began taking shape in Franco-papal encounters in the eighth century.

church,[33] before solemn Mass and in the presence of the clergy and the whole people, he consecrated and anointed him emperor and placed upon his head a gold crown that he had brought with him. It was amazingly beautiful and adorned with the most precious gems. He also called Queen Irmingard *Augusta,* and put a gold crown on her head. As long as the most blessed pontiff was there, they held daily meetings concerning the needs of the holy church of God. After the lord emperor honored him with great and countless gifts, three times or more what he had himself received, for such was always his custom—"it is better to give than to receive"[34]—he dismissed him to return to Rome with his envoys, whom he instructed to serve him honorably throughout his journey.

(18) *On the Death of Stephen, Paschal Succeeded.*

Not many days after the pope returned to Rome, he died. Afterward, God revealed through several miracles that he was a living and true follower of God. Pope Paschal succeeded him.[35]

(19) *On the Customs of the Pious Emperor, His Daily Practice, and His Manifold Praises.*

Then the lord emperor went home to his seat at the palace of Aachen. He grew from day to day in holy virtues, which it would be prolix to enumerate. He was of modest height, with large, clear eyes, a bright face, a long, straight nose, lips that were neither too thick nor too thin, a strong chest, broad shoulders, and such strong arms that no one could rival him in shooting a bow or throwing a spear,[36] long hands, straight fingers, long but graceful legs, big feet, and a manly voice. He was very well educated in the Greek and Latin languages, but while he understood Greek better than he could speak it, Latin came to him like his native tongue. He knew very well the spiritual, moral, and anagogical meanings of all the Scriptures.[37] He despised the pagan songs

33. The cathedral of Reims.
34. Acts 20:35.
35. Paschal I, 817–24.
36. Cf. Ermoldus page 120.
37. Various methods of scriptural interpretation arose in Christian antiquity and, through the influence of the church fathers, persisted into the Middle Ages. The topic is fraught with difficulties because authors did not always use the same words in the same ways. The "spiritual" sense of scripture could mean the deeply hidden connotations that could only be discovered by learned, and sometimes fantastic, allegorizing. On occasion, the spiritual sense included the "typological," which held that most of the New Testament was foreshadowed in the Old. The "moral" sense was immediately practical: What does the Bible teach you to do? How are you supposed to act? The "anagogical" sense of biblical passages interpreted them as foreshadowing the life to come in heaven. A fourth sense, the "literal," was a close reading of the actual words on the page and required a sound knowledge of languages, history, and so forth.

that he had learned as a youth, and he wished neither to read nor to hear nor to learn them.[38] He was strong in his limbs, nimble and active, slow to anger, and quick to forgive.[39] He went to church every single morning to pray, and bending his knees, he humbly touched his forehead on the pavement and prayed for a long time, sometimes tearfully. He was always adorned with every good quality. He was so generous—no one has ever heard of such a thing in ancient books or in modern times—that he gave, in perpetuity, royal estates that had belonged to his father, grandfather, and great-grandfather to his faithful men,[40] and prepared documents that he confirmed with his signet ring and with his own signature. He did this over a long period of time. He was temperate in food and drink and inconspicuous in his dress. He never strutted about in golden clothing except alone on the highest feast days, as his ancestors used to do. Even on those days he put on nothing more than a shirt and breeches woven and fringed with gold and drawn up with a golden sword belt, a shining gold sword, golden greaves, and a chlamys woven with gold thread. He wore a golden crown on his head and held a golden staff in his hand. He never raised his voice in laughter, not even when on the highest feasts musicians, jesters, mimes, flautists, and zither players proceeded before his table in his presence to entertain the people. The people used to laugh heartily in his presence, but he never showed his white teeth in laughter. Every day, before he ate, he dispensed generous alms to the poor, and wherever he was, he always set up poorhouses. In the month of August, when the deer are fattest, he went hunting and kept at it until it was time for the boars.

(20) *Concerning the Inappropriate Promotion of Unsuited Men to Ecclesiastical Offices, and Their Vices.*

He did everything wisely and carefully, and did nothing rashly, except that he trusted his advisers more than he should have. This happened because he

---

38. Cf. Einhard, c. 29, who says that Charles collected these songs.

39. Cf. Psalms 86:5, 86:15, 103:8, 145:8 (= 85:5, 85:15, 102:8, 144:8 Vulgate), where, however, the Lord is slow to anger and full of kindness.

40. Thegan's word here and elsewhere is *fideles*. Generally, this word pertains to a large group of men who swore fidelity to the king/emperor; Charlemagne required such oaths of allegiance in 793 and again in 802. Such fidelity did not imply a reciprocal relationship and essentially required that "faithful" men avoid harming the king's interests. There was a smaller group, probably not more than a few hundred men at any given time, who were the king's vassals and fulfilled specific responsibilities in connection with vassalic status; for example, many served as counts. Sometimes these vassals received material considerations along with their vassal status. These considerations usually appear in the sources as benefices or fiefs, but such considerations rarely represented more than a small fraction of the material and social resources of the vassals, who normally were important men to start with.

was busy with psalm singing and zealous in reading, and also because of something else that did not start with him. For there had long been an awful custom of making the highest bishops out of the lowest servants, and he did not put an end to it, even though it is the greatest evil for the Christian people.[41] This can be read in the history of the kings concerning Jeroboam, the son of Nadab, who was a slave of King Solomon and after him held the rulership over the ten tribes of Israel. The Scriptures say of him: "Jeroboam did not give up his evil ways after this event, but again made priests for the high places from among the common people. Whoever desired it was consecrated and became a priest of the high places. This was a sin on the part of the house of Jeroboam for which it was cut off and destroyed from the earth."[42]

After men like this seize the reins of government, they are never again so calm and tame as before, and they right away begin to be wrathful, quarrelsome, slanderous, stubborn, harmful, willful, immodest, and threatening to all their subjects. Through this kind of behavior, they wish to be feared and praised by everyone. They strive to lift their wicked kin from the due yoke of servitude and make them free. Then they educate some of them in the liberal arts, marry others to noblewomen, and force the sons of nobles to accept their daughters in marriage. No one can live with them in harmony except those alone who enter into such marriages with them. The rest, indeed, pass their days in the greatest sorrow, groaning and weeping. The relatives of these people, if they have gained a little learning, mock and despise the old nobles. They are puffed up, changeable, willful, lewd, and immodest. Little good abides in any of them.

After they have tossed aside holy reverence for their Lord, they do not wish to know anything about the canonical writing that is called the "Teaching of the Apostles." For this says and teaches: "If a bishop has poor relatives, let him give to them as if to the poor so that the property of the church shall not perish."[43] They do not want to hear the book of Pope Saint Gregory entitled *Pastoral*.[44] No one can believe how they behave except those alone who suffer this evil without any interruption. If their relatives have got a little learning, they are pushed into holy orders, which is an immense danger for those giving

41. See c. 44 below.

42. 1 Kings 13:33–34 (= 3 Kings 13:33–34 Vulgate).

43. *Canones apostolorum*, c. 38. Thegan's point is that bishops should only dispense alms from church revenues and not give away actual church properties.

44. Gregory I (590–604), *Regula Pastoralis*, ca. 591. The *Pastoral Rule* was tremendously influential in the Carolingian period and beyond.

and receiving them. If they have become rather learned, the multitude of their crimes nevertheless overwhelms their learning. It often happens that because of the crimes of his relatives the pastor in the church has to overlook some serious offenses and does not dare to invoke canonical justice. That holy ministry is often wholly despised by some people because it is exercised by such ministers. May almighty God, with his kings and princes, deign from this moment forward to eradicate and snuff out this most vile custom, so that it shall no longer exist among the Christian people. Amen.

(21) *The Father Named Lothar Emperor.*

The emperor [in 817] designated his son Lothar to receive, after his death, all the kingdoms that God had given to him at his father's hand and to hold his father's dignity and empire. The other sons were angered by this.[45]

(22) *The Conspiracy of Bernard Against the Emperor Was Discovered and Overcome.*

In that very same year Bernard, the son of Pippin by a concubine, incited by evil men—indeed, he had wicked advisers on every side—rose up against his cousin and wished to expel him from the kingdom.[46] When the lord emperor heard this, he departed from the palace at Aachen and went to the city of Chalon-sur-Saône. Bernard and his wicked advisers met him there, and they commended themselves.[47] The emperor celebrated Christmas there. He then went home to his seat at Aachen, and after Easter he held a great assembly of his people to investigate all the foul plots of infidelity in this affair. Quite a few were found to have fallen in with this sedition, both Franks and Lombards, and they were all sentenced to death, except the bishops, who were deposed after they confessed. They were Anselm of Milan,[48] Wolfold of

45. In the *Ordinatio Imperii* (July 817) Louis assigned kingdoms to his sons Pippin and Louis, while making Lothar sole heir to the imperial title. Pippin was given Aquitaine and Gascony plus small portions of western Septimania and southwestern Burgundy. Louis was assigned Bavaria with the Slavic lands to the east. Lothar eventually received special responsibility for Italy. Louis, born in 806, was too young to be sent to Bavaria right away. This succession plan, and attempts to modify it, eventually caused intense disagreements, but not yet in 817.

46. This is an exaggeration. Bernard was omitted from the *Ordinatio Imperii,* and he probably wanted no more than a secure title to Italy, which was not itself mentioned in the *Ordinatio.* Perhaps, too, he wanted reassurance that his heirs could succeed him. Note that in chapter 6 above, Louis promised his father to look out for his nephew. The *Royal Frankish Annals,* anno 817, say that Bernard closed the Alpine passes and took up the fidelity of the Italians. This suggests that Bernard was seceding from the empire more than trying to expel Louis from it.

47. The language suggests that they swore fidelity (again?), which ought to have put an end to the affair. The sedition must have persisted through the winter of 817–18, or else Louis learned a good deal more by Easter of 818 than he had known in the autumn of 817.

48. Archbishop of Milan, 813/14–818, died in 822.

Cremona,[49] and Theodulf of Orléans.[50] The emperor did not wish to execute the capital judgment that had been handed down for the others. But his
advisers[51] deprived Bernard of his sight and likewise his instigators Eggideo,[52]
Reginhard,[53] and Reginhar,[54] who was a son of a daughter of Hardrad,[55] that
most faithless duke in Austrasia who long ago wished to rise up against the
lord Charles and to diminish his kingdom and who was himself assigned the
same punishment that his grandson and his collaborators received.

(23) *The Emperor's Regret at the Death of Bernard.*

Bernard died on the third day after he was blinded. When the emperor
heard this, he wept with great sorrow for a long time, and he confessed in the
presence of all his bishops,[56] and on their judgment he did penance for this
reason alone: he did not prevent his advisers from executing this disfigure-
ment. As a result, he gave a great deal to the poor for the cleansing of his soul.

(24) *The Emperor Forced His Brothers to Enter the Religious Life.*

At the same time, he ordered that his brothers be tonsured to diminish
discord, and commanded that they be educated in the liberal arts. Later he set
them up honorably, giving Drogo a bishopric and Hugo monasteries and
convents.[57]

(25) *Murman the Breton Was Killed and Irmingard Died.*

Then [in 818] the lord emperor went to the region of Brittany with his army.
Their duke, Murman, was killed there, and that whole land subjected to his
authority. On returning from there, he found his wife, Irmingard, suffering
from a fever. A few days later she died in peace.[58]

49. Bishop of Cremona, 816–18.

50. Bishop of Orléans, 798–818, died in 820/21. His implication in this rebellion may owe more
to court intrigue in Francia than to any real participation in Bernard's activities. Theodulf was a great
biblical scholar, gifted theologian, and accomplished poet. He was a Goth, probably Septimanian, not
Iberian, who came to Charles's court ca. 790.

51. Nithard assigns responsibility to Count Bertmund of Lyon.

52. Count of Camerina, attested 811–14.

53. Probably a Frank, judging from his name. He was Bernard's chamberlain—a key adviser and
treasurer. Nothing else is known about him.

54. Possibly Louis's former count of the palace in Aquitaine.

55. Einhard, c. 20, tells of this rebellion but does not name Hardrad.

56. Thegan compresses his account here: Louis's public penance took place at the annual assembly at Attigny in 822 (see c. 29 below). Cf. Astronomer, c. 35.

57. Louis tonsured and dismissed his three half brothers (Theoderic is not mentioned here) and
then reconciled with them in 821. Drogo became bishop of Metz in 823; Hugo, abbot of St.-Quentin
and St.-Bertin. Drogo was a key adviser, and Hugo was Louis's chancellor.

58. For more details, see Ermoldus, pages 156–68, and Astronomer, cc. 29–30.

(26) *Judith Was Made Queen.*

In the following year [819], he married the daughter of his duke Welf, who came from the noblest family of the Bavarians. The virgin's name was Judith, and her mother, whose name was Heilwig, came from the noblest family of the Saxons. He made her queen. She was very pretty. In the same year, he held his general assembly at a royal estate at Ingelheim.

(27) *An Army Was Sent Against Liudewit.*

In the following year [820], he sent his army against the eastern Slavs. Their leader was called Liudewit, and they put him to flight and wasted his land. Then they came home.

(28) *How Lothar Came to Receive Irmingard as His Wife.*

In the next year [821], he held his general assembly, and there his son Lothar, the firstborn of Irmingard, married a daughter of Count Hugh, who descended from the family of a certain duke named Etico[59] and was cowardly above all men. For his household servants used to sing tales about him to the effect that he sometimes did not dare to step outside. Even then the infidelity that the son would show to the father was already imminent, owing to the urging of his father-in-law and of many other evil men. Then Lothar went back to Worms with his wife.

(29) *Lothar Was Sent into Italy.*

In the next year [822], he held his general assembly at the palace of Attigny. From there he sent his son Lothar and his wife, Irmingard, to Italy. The lord emperor departed from there and went to Frankfurt, where he celebrated Christmas.

(30) *Pope Paschal Purged Himself of Charges in the Presence of the Emperor's Envoys; on His Death, Eugenius Succeeded as Pope.*

Afterward [in 823] he sent his envoys, Adalung,[60] the venerable abbot and priest, and Hunfrid, the duke of Rhaetia,[61] to Rome on account of a certain accusation that the Roman people had launched against the Roman pontiff Paschal. They said he had murdered several men. The pontiff, along with thirty-four bishops and five deacons, purged himself by oath in the Lateran Palace, in the presence of the envoys and the Roman people. Immediately after these envoys departed, the pope died. The Roman people did not wish him to be buried in the church of blessed Peter the Apostle. Then

59. Or Adalric, a seventh-century duke in Alsace.
60. Abbot of Lorsch (804–37) and St.-Vaast (808–33).
61. Count of Rhaetia (806–23) or else his son Hunfrid II.

Eugenius[62] succeeded him and ordered that his body be buried in the place that he had built while he was alive.[63]

(31) *The Emperor Returned and Devastated Brittany.*

In the next year [824], the emperor went yet again to Brittany and struck that whole land with a great blow on account of its infidelity.[64]

(32) *He Received and Dismissed Envoys of the Bulgars.*

In the next year [825], he was at the palace at Aachen with a great army, and legates from the Bulgars came bearing gifts. He received them kindly and let them go home.

(33) *Harald the Northman Became Christian, Along with His Men.*

In the next year [826], he was at the royal palace at Ingelheim, and Harald of the Danes came to him. The lord emperor raised him from the holy font of baptism, and the lady empress Judith raised his wife from the font.[65] Then the lord emperor gave a large part of Frisia to him, adorned him with worthy gifts, and dismissed him in peace, accompanied by his own envoys.[66]

(34) *An Army Was Sent Against the Saracens.*

In the following year [827], he sent his army against the Saracens.[67] In the next year [828], he departed from Ingelheim after his general assembly and went to Commercy.[68]

(35) *The Emperor Gave Alemannia and Rhaetia to His Son Charles.*

In the next year [829], he went to Worms, and there he gave to his son Charles, who was born of Judith Augusta, the land of Alemannia and Rhaetia and a certain part of Burgundy.[69] He did this in the presence of his sons Lothar and Louis. Henceforth, they were outraged, along with their brother Pippin.

(36) *How Pippin and His Treacherous Nobles Attacked His Father, and Judith and Her Brother Were Dishonored.*

In the next year [830], the lord emperor departed from the palace at Aachen and went to Compiègne. His son Pippin met him there along with his father's

---

62. Pope, 824–27.

63. Paschal constructed at least two oratories—small chapels, in effect—inside St. Peter's. He moved papal remains from the catacombs to both of them and was himself buried in one.

64. Cf. Ermoldus, pages 172–73; Astronomer, c. 35.

65. Probably in St. Alban's at Mainz. Ermoldus, pages 176–83, treats this encounter at great length. Cf. Astronomer, c. 40 and Notker's fanciful account, 2.19.

66. Politics in Denmark had become complicated, and Louis was supporting Harald in an attempt to secure some influence. Harald was actually a fugitive. Louis did not give him a large part of Frisia but instead an estate at Rustringen for material support. Among the envoys sent back with Harald was the famous missionary Anskar.

67. A campaign in the Spanish March.

68. A town on the Meuse. Louis probably went hunting.

69. Charles was born in 823.

chief magnates, the archchaplain Hilduin[70] and Bishop Jesse of Amiens,[71] Hugh and Matfrid,[72] Abbot Helisachar,[73] Gotefrid,[74] and many other faithless ones.[75] They wished to deprive the lord emperor of his rule, but his beloved, like-named son stopped them. The wicked ones raised many complaints against him, which it would be foul to tell or to believe. They said that Queen Judith had been ravished by a certain Duke Bernard, who was of the royal family and the godson of the lord emperor, but they were lying in all respects.[76] They seized Queen Judith, veiled her, and sent her to a monastery, tonsured her brothers Conrad and Rudolf, and sent them into a monastery.

(37) *By What Right the Emperor Overcame His Enemies and Accepted the Queen.*

In that same year,[77] the lord emperor went to the fortress of Nijmegen, which is situated on a river called the Waal. A multitude of men from all his kingdoms came to him. Among them were the adversaries we just mentioned. The lord emperor overcame them, divided them from one another, and received their obedience. His son Lothar promised fidelity with an oath to the effect that he would never again commit such acts. Jesse was deposed there by a just judgment of the bishops. His like-named son[78] was there, the one who had shown himself in all his efforts to be his father's supporter. Then the lord emperor went to his seat at Aachen, and his wife came there to meet him.[79] He received her honorably on the order of the Roman pontiff Gregory[80] and on the just judgment of other bishops.

(38) *Where Bernard Purged Himself of Charges.*

In the following year [831], the emperor was in his palace at Thionville with his sons Lothar and Louis, and Duke Bernard came and purged himself

70. Abbot of St.-Denis and archchaplain, 819–30.

71. Bishop of Amiens, 799–830, 833–36.

72. Count Hugh of Tours was Lothar's father-in-law. Matfrid was count of Orléans and seems to have become prominent after the deposition of Archbishop Theodulf in 818.

73. One of Louis's key advisers while he was king of Aquitaine. Abbot of St.-Aubin in Angers and of Jumièges, possibly of St.-Maximin in Trier and St.-Riquier. Louis's chancellor in 814–19.

74. Perhaps a count in Alemannia.

75. Astronomer, cc. 43–45, provides a more detailed account.

76. Bernard of Septimania had served ably in the campaign in the Spanish March (c. 34 above), whereas notable counts, such as Hugh and Matfrid, had been dilatory. As a reward, Louis named Bernard his chamberlain. Bernard himself was the son of Count William of Toulouse, and his grandmother was a daughter of Charles Martel.

77. In October 830. Thegan glosses over the summer's intense political machinations.

78. For some reason Thegan, almost without exception, refers to Louis as *equivocus filius* instead of naming him.

79. This took place in February 831. Strictly speaking, this throws off by a year the chronology of the next several chapters.

80. Gregory IV (827–44).

of the above-mentioned disgrace when no one could be found who dared to lay the charge against him by force of arms.[81]

(39) *The First Rebellion of Louis Against His Father, Which Was Mended by Reconciliation.*

In the next year [832], it was heard that his like-named son, scheming with Lothar, wished to march against his father. He went as far as the monastery of St. Nazarius[82] and stayed there for a little while, until his father went to Mainz, raised an army, and came after him. His son went home and waited for his father, wishing to defend himself. His father, however, ordered him to meet him on the way. His father received him kindly; they had a harmonious meeting and, after a few days, parted in great affection. The son stayed at his home, and the father went back to Francia.

(40) *Lothar Wished to Prove Himself Innocent of That Scheme of Rebellion.*

When he got to the palace at Frankfurt, his son Lothar came and asked his father to permit him to purge himself because it was neither on his will nor on his urging that his brother had made some trouble for his father. Whether this is true is known to many.

(41) *How Pippin, Having Been Ordered by His Father to Go to Francia, Took Flight Again.*

While the king was staying there, he heard that his son Pippin desired to make sedition against his father. Stirred up, he went to Limoges to meet him and ordered his son, with his wife and children, to come into Francia. When he first heard of his father's command, he started to go to the palace at Doué, but then he turned around and went back to Aquitaine. The emperor went from there back to his seat at Aachen. From there, he went on to Worms before the holy time of Lent.

(42) *What Happened on the Field of Lies.*

After Easter [833], he heard that his sons again wished to come to him, and not peacefully.[83] He gathered his army and went to meet them in a great field that lies between Strasbourg and Basel. The place where the fidelity of many was snuffed out is today called the Field of Lies. His sons, with the Roman pope Gregory, proceeded to meet him, and no matter what they demanded of their father, he yielded nothing to them. After a few days, the emperor and the pope had a meeting. They did not talk long, but the pope honored him

81. A reference to trial by combat.
82. At Lorsch.
83. Astronomer, cc. 48–53, provides a more detailed account.

at the start with great and countless gifts. After each went back to his own tent, the emperor sent regal gifts to the pontiff through Adalung, the venerable abbot and priest. All the while a good many were plotting to abandon the emperor and to go over to his sons, first of all those who had previously offended him, and then the rest followed them. That same night the largest part left him and, abandoning their tents, went over to his sons. On the next morning the few who remained went to the emperor, and he instructed them, saying: "Go," he said, "to my sons. I do not wish that anyone should lose life or limb on my account." And so they, shedding tears, withdrew from him. They had already separated his wife from him, confirming by oath that they wished her neither death nor harm. They immediately sent her to Italy, to the city of Tortona, but they did not keep her there long. Afterward they seized their father and led him away with his men. After they had done this, they separated. Pippin went back to Aquitaine and Louis to Bavaria.

(43) *How the Pious Emperor Bore Accusations, Especially at Compiègne.*

Lothar took his father with him to the palace at Compiègne, and there, along with bishops and some others, he goaded him harshly. They ordered him to go to a monastery and to spend the rest of his days there. But he refused and did not consent to their wish. All the bishops importuned him, especially those whom he had lifted up from the vilest servile condition, along with those who had been elevated to this exalted rank from barbarian peoples.

(44) *The Scolding of Ebbo and His Ilk.*

Then the bishops chose one shameless and very cruel man, Ebbo, the bishop of Reims, who descended from generations of slaves, to batter him savagely with the fabrications of the others. Unheard-of things were said, unheard-of things were done; they reproached him every day. They took his sword from his side, and on the judgment of slaves, they garbed him as a penitent. Thus was fulfilled the last word of the prophet Jeremiah, who said: "Slaves lord it over us."[84] O, how you have repaid him! He made you free, not noble, which is impossible. After he clothed you with freedom, purple, and a pallium, you dressed him as a penitent. He drew you up, wretch that you are, to the episcopal dignity, but you wanted to expel him from the throne of his fathers by a false judgment. O cruel man, why didn't you understand the teaching of the Lord: "A slave is not above his master"?[85] Why do you hate the

84. Lamentations 5:8.
85. Matthew 10:24.

apostolic teaching of the one who "was caught up to the third heaven,"[86] so that he could learn among the angels what he should command men to do? This is indeed what he taught: "Let everyone be subject to higher authorities, for there is no power except from God."[87] And again, he said something else: "Fear God, honor the king. Slaves accept the authority of your masters with all deference, not only those who are kind and gentle but also those who are harsh. For this indeed is grace."[88] You, however, have neither feared God nor honored the king. If everyone can win the grace of God by doing such things, then assuredly one will earn God's wrath by despising them. O cruel man, who was your adviser or your guide? Was it not that one who "is king over all the sons of pride,"[89] who said to God his creator, "I will give you all these things if you will fall down and worship me"?[90] O Lord Jesus Christ, where was your angel who on one night easily destroyed all the firstborn of Egypt, or that one who in the camp of the Assyrians on one awful night in the reign of Sennacherib destroyed 185,000 of the wicked ones, as the prophet Isaiah testifies?[91] Or the one who struck down Herod the Younger while he was speaking, so that he "immediately began to teem with worms"?[92] And you, earth, who held him up at that time, why didn't you open your mouth and devour him as you once did to Dathan and Abiron?[93] You have not understood your triple law, which says, "Fodder and a stick and burdens for a donkey; bread and discipline and work for a slave."[94] The prophet Zechariah was speaking to you when he said: "You shall not live, for you have spoken lies in the name of the Lord."[95] God has revealed your wickedness,[96] and He has saved his kingdom and glory. On account of greed and dishonesty, you have lost yourself by your great impiety. Away with you now; may you live in disgrace all the days of your life! You fell into the abyss of greed and falsity, so may your dishonor grow from day to day, just as a little number grows into a big one through the skill of the mathematician. O cruel man, your canonical

---

86. 2 Corinthians 12:2. Thegan refers to Saint Paul.
87. Romans 13:1.
88. A rough paraphrase of 1 Peter 2:17–19.
89. Job 41:34 (= 41:25 Vulgate).
90. Matthew 4:9.
91. Isaiah 37:36.
92. Acts 16:20, concerning Herod I Agrippa (10 B.C.–A.D. 44); cf. 2 Maccabees 9:8–10, concerning Antiochus IV Epiphanes (r. 175–164 B.C.).
93. Cf. Numbers 16:1–33.
94. Sirach 33:25 (= Ecclesiasticus Vulgate).
95. Zechariah 13:3.
96. Cf. Sirach 14:7 (= Ecclesiasticus Vulgate).

judgment has not yet been carried out. But it is necessary for it to be completed to make your disgrace greater. Your ancestors were goatherds, not advisers to princes. You, with the judgment of others, deposed Jesse from the priesthood, but now you have recalled him to his former rank. Either then or now you showed false judgment. You imitated the one of whom the poet sang in the sixth book of the *Aeneid:*

> Theseus forever
> Sits in dejection; Phlegyas, accursed,
> Cries through the halls forever: *being warned,*
> *Learn justice; reverence the Gods!* The man
> Who sold his country is here in hell;
> The man who altered laws for money. . . .[97]

What more can I tell you? Even if I had an iron tongue and bronze lips,[98] I could neither explain nor count your iniquities in all respects. But if there were someone who wished to lay bare all your crimes in poetic song, perhaps he might surpass the seer of Smyrna,[99] ancient Homer, or Mincian[100] Virgil, and Ovid too. But the trial of the most pious prince, which he endured at the hands of utterly wicked men, is thought to have been no more than a proof of his goodness. Indeed, he was as patient as blessed Job. But there was a big difference between the persecutors of each man. One reads in the book of holy Tobias that those who taunted blessed Job were kings, while those who particularly harassed him were his and his ancestors' legal slaves.

(45) *Louis's Envoys Were Sent to Lothar on Behalf of Their Father.*

Afterward, they led the most pious prince from Compiègne to the palace at Aachen. After he heard this, his like-named son departed from Bavaria, driven by great grief at his father's suffering. When he got to the palace at Frankfurt, he immediately sent his legates, Gozbald,[101] the abbot and priest, and Morhard,[102] the palatine count, asking, even demanding, that his father be accorded a more humane treatment. His brother Lothar did not receive the

---

97. Rolfe Humphries, trans., *The Aeneid of Virgil* (New York, 1951), 165 (= *Aeneid,* 6.618–22).

98. Virgil again, *Aeneid,* 6.625–27.

99. Perhaps an obscure reference to Lucan, *Pharsalia,* 9.984. Homer was reputed to be of Smyrnean origin.

100. Pertaining to the Mincio River. Virgil was from Mantua, on the Mincio.

101. Abbot of Niederaltaich, 825–55, bishop of Würzburg from 842, and Louis's archchaplain, 830–33.

102. Nothing more is known about him. As count of the palace he was the chief judicial officer.

message kindly. After these envoys returned, he immediately sent others to his father, but they were prevented from seeing him.

(46) *Their Colloquy at Mainz.*

Later Lothar set out from the palace at Aachen, went to Mainz to meet his brother, and they had an unbalanced meeting for this reason: all those whom Lothar had with him were, wrongly, his father's enemies, while those whom Louis had with him were faithful to his father and to himself. Lothar departed from there and went back to Aachen, where he celebrated Christmas, with his father still locked up.

(47) *Louis's Envoys Came to His Father.*

After the holy day of Epiphany,[103] Louis again sent envoys to his father, the venerable abbot and priest Grimald,[104] and the most noble and faithful duke Gebhard.[105] When they arrived at Aachen, Lothar agreed to let them speak to his father in the presence of spies, one of whom was called Bishop Otgar,[106] and the other the faithless Righard.[107] When the envoys came into the prince's sight, they humbly prostrated themselves at his feet and afterward offered greetings from his like-named son. But they did not want to say anything confidential to him, on account of the spies who were present, but signaling by gestures, they made him understand that his namesake had not agreed to his father's punishment.

(48) *How the Emperor Was Freed from Lothar and Ebbo Was Captured.*

After these envoys had departed, Lothar immediately compelled his father to go with him again to Compiègne. He consented to his son and went with him. On hearing this, his like-named son assembled a multitude and followed them. When he got pretty close to them, Lothar let his father go and departed from him with his wicked advisers. His like-named son went to him, received him honorably, took him back again to his seat at Aachen, and, on God's command, restored him to his kingdom and to his rightful place. They celebrated Easter there together. When he heard this, Ebbo immediately fled. But he was caught, bound, and led into the presence of the prince, who handed him into custody.[108]

---

103. January 6, 834.

104. Abbot of Weissenburg, 833–38/39, abbot of St. Gall from 841, chancellor of Louis the German, 833–37/40, and his archchaplain, 848/54–70.

105. He was based in the Lahngau and was an ancestor of the Conradiner family.

106. Archbishop of Mainz, 826–47.

107. Apparently the *ostiarius*—ceremonial doorkeeper—at Louis's palace. Called faithless (*perfidus*) because he changed sides in 833.

108. He was sent to the monastery of Fulda, whose abbot, Hrabanus Maurus, was loyal to Louis.

(49) *Concerning the Forgiveness and Patience of the Pious Emperor.*

In that same year [834], the twenty-first of his reign, he pardoned all those who had been compelled to abandon him. This was neither burdensome nor distasteful to him, this most pious of emperors, since he had previously spared his enemies, fulfilling that gospel precept that says: "Forgive, and it shall be forgiven you."[109] The one who established this teaching prepares for him a good and grand reward: "For the Lord disciplines those whom he loves, and chastises every son whom he accepts."[110] And whoever does not willingly receive the Lord's corrections cannot become his son.

(50) *Concerning the Need to Avoid and Suppress Ignoble Counselors.*

But this must at all costs be avoided, so that it will not happen again: let not slaves be counselors, for if they can—and they will try hard to do this— they will oppress the nobles, and they will strive to put their own vile kindred in their place. This is not suited to his holy dignity,[111] and it happened rarely in the times of his father of holy memory that anyone of that sort rose up to an honored position. The greatest self-discipline taught him not to give an opening to arrogance. There is a great need to follow this example now. When this mildest of princes was in his trial, those very men to whom he had shown every kindness were harsh to him. How they treat their subordinates, there is no need to ask.

(51) *The Recall of Empress Judith from Italy.*

After the emperor had gotten the upper hand, he sent his faithful envoys to Italy to bring back his much maligned wife. When they got there, they received her honorably and led her back with joy and gladness into the presence of the prince, who was at that time in the palace at Aachen.

(52) *Lothar's Deeds at Chalon.*

Lothar meanwhile was residing in the city of Chalon-sur-Saône, where he committed many evils, despoiling the churches of God and making martyrs of his father's faithful men wherever he could catch them, excepting only his envoys. What is more, he ordered the nun named Gerberga, who was Duke Bernard's sister,[112] to be shut up in a wine barrel and thrown into the river Arar.[113] The poet sung of this: "Either the Parthian shall drink of the Arar or

---

109. Luke 6:37.
110. Hebrews 12:6.
111. That is, to the dignity of the imperial office.
112. Astronomer, c. 52, says she was drowned as a witch.
113. That is, the Saône.

the German of the Tigris."[114] Mistreating her there for a long time, until she died, on the judgment of the wives of his impious advisers, he fulfilled the words of the prophetic psalmist: "With the holy, you will be holy, and with the perverse, you will be perverted."[115]

(53) *The Father's Admonition to Lothar Sent Through Envoys.*

After this, the emperor sent him his envoys, the venerable abbot Markward[116] with some of his other faithful men, with hortatory letters warning him in the first place to be mindful of almighty God and his commands, to turn away from his evil path, and to understand what a harsh punishment there is for one who scorns God and his teachings. For among other precepts, God says: "Honor your father and mother" and "Whoever speaks evil of his father or mother shall be put to death."[117] He set forth this teaching neither through prophets nor apostles, but almighty God himself ordered it to be written down and observed. And how serious it is to neglect this teaching, he showed later in the Book of Deuteronomy when he said: "If someone has a stubborn and rebellious son who will not obey his father and mother, who does not heed them when they discipline him, then his father and his mother shall take hold of him and bring him out to the elders of his town at the gate of that place. They shall say to the elders of this town, 'This son of ours is stubborn and rebellious. He will not obey us. He is a glutton and a drunkard.' Then all the men of the town shall stone him to death. So you shall purge the evil from your midst; and all Israel will hear, and be afraid."[118]

(54) *How Lothar Agreed to Come Back to His Father.*

After Lothar spoke with these envoys, whose message he received gravely and bitterly, he made threatening promises that have not yet been fulfilled, nor will they be. They turned around and left him and went to the emperor, telling him everything that they had heard and seen. His father, saddened at this, collected a substantial force and went after him where he heard that he was. His sons came to meet him, Pippin from the West and his like-named from the East, each with a great multitude, to assist their father. They hastened toward Orléans. Lothar was nearby with his wicked betrayers of whom we spoke above. He did not wish to give in to his father's pleadings, and on a certain night, he put some distance between them as if he were fleeing. Then

114. Virgil, *Eclogues,* 1.63. Notker, 2.9, cites this same aphorism, albeit in a different context.
115. Psalm 17:26–27.
116. Abbot of Prüm, 828–53.
117. Exodus 20:12 and 21:17.
118. Deuteronomy 21:18–21 (NRSV trans.).

the emperor sent his envoys after him: Badurad, the bishop of Saxony,[119] Gebhard, the most noble and faithful duke,[120] and Berengar, his wise kinsman.[121]
When they reached him, the above-mentioned bishop immediately instructed
him on the ordinance of almighty God and all his saints to separate himself
from the company of his wicked tempters, so that the emperor's faithful men
could indicate whether it was God's will that their discord would persist or
not. After the message of the above-named bishop, the dukes came forward
and did what they had been commanded to do. He asked them right away to
step outside for a little while and then called them back in and asked them
urgently to give him advice concerning all his actions. They instructed him,
with the rest of his advisers, to depend on his father's mercy and promised
them peace. Indeed, he promised to come with his men. The envoys went
back to the prince and told him what had happened.

(55) *By What Agreements They Parted from Each Other, and the Punishments
for the Treacherous.*

Lothar followed them to where his father the emperor was sitting in his
tent, which was placed in a very high spot on the broad field where his whole
army could observe him. His sons and his faithful men stood beside him.
When Lothar arrived, he fell at his father's feet, and after him his father-in-
law, Hugh the Timid, and then Matfrid and all the others who were foremost
in that villainy. After they rose from the ground, they confessed that they
had erred badly. Then Lothar swore fidelity to his father, said that he wished
to obey all his commands, and agreed to go to Italy and to stay there and not
to leave except on his father's orders. Then the others swore as well. Then the
most pious prince gave them his pardon, if they would keep this oath. He let
them keep their patrimonies and everything else that they had except whatever he himself had given them with his own hand. They separated at that
point, and Lothar headed for Italy with his evil associates, and immediately
Matfrid, who was the particular instigator of all their evils, died, as did not a
few of the others. The rest were struck with a fever.

(56) *Ebbo Was Degraded from the Episcopal Rank.*

The emperor departed, went to the palace at Thionville, and spent the
whole winter there. After Christmas, in the next year [835], he held a great

---

119. Bishop of Paderborn, 815–62.
120. See c. 47 above.
121. Count of Toulouse and brother of the powerful duke Eberhard of Friuli, who married Louis's
daughter Gisela.

assembly of people. That rotten rustic Ebbo came there, but the other bishops did not dare to act decisively against him, for fear that he might become their betrayer. Therefore they persuaded him to agree that he could scarcely retain the episcopal ministry. He did so and was unconditionally dismissed. But there was still a need to put this matter right, because it is better to execute the just judgment of the holy fathers against him than to show false piety under the pretense of religion.

(57) *Envoys of the Emperor Were Sent to Lothar from Lyon.*

In that same year, the emperor went to the region of Lyon, where his sons Pippin and the like-named one came to meet him. The latter son was still the very image of those we talked about earlier who were born younger.[122] The emperor sat with his sons while his envoys went to Italy, to Lothar, and then turned around and came back to him. Then the emperor turned around and went to his seat at Aachen. Pippin went back to Aquitaine, and his like-named son headed back to the eastern regions.

(58) *The Death of Berengar and the End of This Little Book.*

In that very same year, the wise and faithful duke Berengar died on a journey. The emperor and his sons mourned him for a long time. This is year twenty-two [835] of the reign of the most pious lord emperor Louis. May He, who is blessed for all ages, deign to keep and to protect him for a long time, while he toils in this world, and, after his days are done, agree to lead him into the company of all his saints. Amen.

---

122. See c. 3 above. But Louis the German was in open rebellion against his father in 838.

INTRODUCTION

"The Astronomer" is the conventional moniker applied to the anonymous author of this *Life of Emperor Louis*. For at least two centuries serious scholars have tried unsuccessfully to identify the Astronomer. I consider speculation pointless. The nickname is attributable in part to the author's comment that he was expert in astronomical matters (c. 58). In 837 Louis asked this author for advice on what a comet—now known to have been Halley's Comet—might portend. In part, too, the author reveals a general interest in celestial phenomena.[1] Whoever he was, the Astronomer was well informed and well connected. In his prologue he says that he was involved in courtly affairs. He was interested in the details of ecclesiastical life and reform to a greater degree than any of the other biographers collected in this volume. Scholars have therefore identified him as a member of the palace chapel. His work also testifies to monastic interests and sensibilities, so it is possible that he was a monk, although, if he were a monk, it is difficult to understand just how he was continuously involved in palace affairs. He betrays a persistently aristocratic outlook. Common people are ignorant, tools easily manipulated by the mighty. The Astronomer was particularly knowledgeable about affairs in the South and Southwest, in Aquitaine and Gascony. He disliked Basques and believed that Aquitainians were fickle and needed Frankish guidance and supervision. Consequently, historians do not necessarily take his interest in the southern regions of the empire to point to his own origin there. Often he has been seen as a member of the Frankish elite who accompanied Louis when he was king of Aquitaine. At the same time, the author once appears to cite

---

1. Cc. 21, 31, 37, 41, 42, 58, 59, 62.

an antiphon from the Mozarabic liturgy, and he speaks well of Theodulf. These facts have led some to speculate that he might have been a Septimanian Goth, an origin that would at once explain his familiarity with the South and his distaste for Basques and Aquitainians. The Astronomer is relatively skimpy in relating details pertaining to northern and eastern regions, and he speaks of Germany as lying "beyond the Rhine," which surely testifies to a West Frankish perspective.[2] Perhaps it is not so strange that the author did not identify himself. Neither Einhard nor Thegan did so in their biographies, and thus they would remain as anonymous as the Astronomer were it not for Walahfrid Strabo, who, in the prologue he prepared for each text, took some care to identify the author.

It is not too difficult to ascertain when the Astronomer wrote his *Life*. He describes Louis's deathbed scene movingly and in detail. Louis died June 20, 840. Obviously, the *Life* postdates that precise date. Most historians have believed that the Astronomer wrote the *Life* in the winter of 840–41. In his account of the year 839 (c. 60) the Astronomer describes how Louis made his son Lothar sole imperial heir and also guardian of Charles the Bald and his rights. In May of 841 Charles and Louis the German allied against Lothar and fought the bloody battle of Fontenoy. The Astronomer could hardly have placed his hopes in the settlement of 839 after the devastating outcome of Fontenoy.[3]

The Astronomer's sources are for the most part straightforward. He knew, used, adapted, and evaded Einhard's *Life of Charles*.[4] I will have more to say about this below, but for now it suffices to draw attention to the opening sections of both works. Each begins in earnest with the demise of Carloman, turns back to the wars in Aquitaine, and then jumps forward to the ill-fated trans-Pyrenean campaign of 778 (i.e., 771–769–778). This cannot be coincidence. The Astronomer admired Einhard and called him "the wisest man of his time" (c. 41). Nevertheless, the Astronomer consciously rejected much in Einhard's approach and outlook. He tells his readers that he added to the "account" (*relatione*) of the monk Adhemar through the point when Louis

2. In general on the Astronomer, see Tenberken, *Die Vita Hludowici Pii*, 1–10; Heyse, "Astronomer"; Brunhölzl, *Histoire*, vol. 1, pt. 2, pp. 148–49; Berschin, "Biographien Ludwigs des Frommen," 228–30; Tremp, introduction to *Vita Hludowici imperatoris*, 53–63.

3. Tremp, introduction to *Vita Hludowici imperatoris*, 66–68; Tenberken, *Die Vita Hludowici Pii*, 42–44.

4. Tremp, "introduction to *Vita Hludowici imperatoris*, 75–81; Tenberken, *Die Vita Hludowici Pii*, 11–13.

became emperor. This Adhemar may very well have been the Count Adhemar who appears frequently in the early sections of the text (esp. cc. 12–15). Perhaps Adhemar was like other powerful magnates from the South who, after successful secular careers, became monks. In any event, the *Relatio* does not survive, and there is no way to determine what use the Astronomer made of it.[5] From 814 to 823 (cc. 23–43) the Astronomer followed the *Royal Frankish Annals*, a quasi-official history kept in the very palace where the Astronomer may have served. But the Astronomer was no slavish imitator. He made several kinds of changes as he adapted his source. He both added and dropped annalistic material. He moved the focus squarely onto Louis himself. And he made stylistic changes. One example may serve for many. For the year 816 the *Annals* say, "Hieme transacta . . ." (The winter, having run its course . . .), whereas the Astronomer revises this to say, "Postquam imperator hiemis inclementiam serena valetudine et tranquillo transegit successu . . ." (After the emperor spent the harsh winter in restful health and calm success . . .").[6] He declares that he was eyewitness to much and mentions many important, influential people who could have been oral informants. For some years there was lively debate over whether the Astronomer drew some information about the later 830s from Nithard's *Histories* or whether Nithard, in fact, drew upon the Astronomer. Given that the Astronomer wrote in the winter of 840–41 and that Nithard composed his *Histories* between the autumn of 841 and the late winter of 843, it can only be possible for Nithard to have drawn upon the Astronomer. That said, careful textual analysis suggests that the two authors drew on one or more common sources. This discovery points to the fact that the Astronomer did have access to letters, documents, and perhaps treaties.[7] His chronology occasionally got away from him in the period before 814 and again after 829, but on the whole he provides a detailed, reliable, and valuable account.

Given that we know a little about the author, something about when he wrote, and a good deal about his sources, we may ask, what did the Astronomer intend to say, and how did he say it? The second part of this question is easier to answer than the first, so I shall begin there.

5. Tremp, introduction to *Vita Hludowici imperatoris*, 70–75; Tenberken, *Die Vita Hludowici Pii*, 13–16.

6. Tremp, introduction to *Vita Hludowici imperatoris*, 81–86; Tenberken, *Die Vita Hludowici Pii*, 16–22.

7. Tremp, introduction to *Vita Hludowici imperatoris*, 86–91; Tenberken, *Die Vita Hludowici Pii*, 22–25.

The Astronomer's style, basically his Latin, is commendable. It is, to be sure, less classical, supple, and elegant than Einhard's, but it nevertheless compares favorably to the basic standard of Latin composition current in the mid–ninth century. The reader might find it interesting to compare the first sentence of the Astronomer's first chapter with any sentence in Thegan—or, for that matter, in Notker. The Astronomer can write in agreeable and flowing periods; his command of basic principles of subordination is impressive. On occasion he is a bit verbose; his prose has been called cluttered. Yet the appearance of excess may be attributable to the Astronomer's aspiration to come up to the standard of the patristic writers who were familiar to him. He knew and emulated Jerome, Augustine, Gregory, and Isidore. Allusions—probably not quotations—suggest that the Astronomer knew Ambrose, Lactantius, Prudentius, Venantius Fortunatus, Aldhelm, and Bede. Here and there turns of phrase and points of perspective hint that the Astronomer was well acquainted with many classical historical writers. He echoes Virgil and Cicero but seemingly at second hand. The Astronomer represents a textbook case of the achievements of the Carolingian Renaissance.[8]

As noted, the Astronomer knew Einhard's *Life of the Emperor Charles* and admired Einhard himself. Undoubtedly the authors knew each other, given that the Astronomer was probably present at court throughout Louis's reign and Einhard was at court until at least 828 or 829. If Thegan was the first Carolingian writer inspired by Einhard to write biography, then the Astronomer was the second. But he responded to Einhard's inspiration largely by standing the earlier work on its head. Einhard wrote about Charles's "life, character, and accomplishments," whereas the Astronomer wrote about Louis's "life and deeds." At a first glance, the two accounts would seem to be parallel. In fact, however, the Astronomer's *Life* is very different in both structural and conceptual terms. Einhard's account is thematic, whereas the Astronomer's is strictly chronological. In addition to structural differences there are conceptual differences between the two texts. Einhard pauses to describe Charles physically and morally, and Thegan does so with Louis. The Astronomer never does so. More like Thegan than Einhard, however, the Astronomer constructs his portrait of Louis by means of narration pure and simple. The Astronomer's Louis emerges from what he did and from how he reacted to what happened around

8. Manitius, "Die Biographien Ludwigs des Frommen," 655–57; Tenberken, *Die Vita Hludowici Pii*, 44–49; Berschin, "Biographien Ludwigs des Frommen," 230–34; Tremp, introduction to *Vita Hludowici imperatoris*, 112–14.

him. What is more, Einhard says that Charles was scarcely imitable by the men of later times, whereas the Astronomer insists that Louis's deeds are worth recounting because sensible men can both learn from and emulate good deeds, intentions, and aspirations. For Einhard, Charles is a king of the Franks. He only mentions the imperial title in connection with the—to him at least—controversial coronation in Rome and then in two "added" sections, the testament and the epitaph. For the Astronomer, Louis is always the emperor. Einhard's utterly secular Charles is a blend of the classical and the Germanic heroes. He is marked by "greatness of spirit" (*magnanimitas*) and "boldness" (*animositas*). The Astronomer's Louis is "beloved of God" (*Deo amabilis*) and "orthodox" (*orthodoxus*). Einhard says nothing about Charles's church reforms, while the Astronomer treats Louis's policies and reforms in lavish detail (with the sole exception of the reform councils of 829).[9]

It would, however, be incorrect to say that the Astronomer set out simply to reverse Einhard's imperial portrait, as if literary, or ideological, image making were all that was at stake. In fact, the Astronomer, as an involved, informed member of Louis's court, reflects the views of the new Carolingian generation. In his prologue the Astronomer signals that Louis exemplified the four cardinal virtues: prudence, justice, temperance, and fortitude (although he uses "wisdom," "justice," "moderation," and "courage").[10] Still, the Astronomer introduces these classical, Stoic virtues by means of a citation of the biblical Book of Wisdom (8:7) and insists that he does so on divine authority. In addition, the Astronomer characterizes Louis in terms of the monastic virtues of obedience, humility, and self-control.[11] He treats Louis's handling of, or reaction to, one event after another in terms of one or another of these virtues. If Einhard's Charles was to be admired with a kind of awestruck reverence and admiration, the Astronomer's Louis was to be emulated. In some ways the Astronomer's *Life* was true to its subject—as the Astronomer saw things—and also a mirror for future princes, who could find in its pages concrete examples of how to be and of how to behave. The Astronomer's *Life* is at once real and ideal.

9. Löwe, "Biographien," 336–38; Tenberken, *Die Vita Hludowici Pii*, 39–42; Tremp, introduction to *Vita Hludowici imperatoris*, 98–103; Hageneier, *Jenseits der Topik*, 256–60.

10. Siemes, *Beiträge zum literarischen Bild Kaiser Ludwigs*, 67–93, particularly emphasizes this aspect of the Astronomer's work.

11. Tremp, introduction to *Vita Hludowici imperatoris*, 99–107; Tenberken, *Die Vita Hludowici Pii*, 32–37.

The Astronomer is deeply sympathetic to Louis. That is clear. But he is not so partisan as to whitewash his hero. He says that Louis's one great fault was that he was too merciful, or perhaps indulgent (prologue). Unlike Thegan, for example, who says Louis failed only in listening too much to the wrong people, the Astronomer locates Louis's one great flaw in the emperor's own character. He also speaks candidly about Louis's failures. In doing so, he is strikingly different from Einhard, who overlooks, glosses over, or explains away Charles's shortcomings. The Astronomer skillfully presents a Louis who is both a superhuman ideal and an authentic, flawed human being.

The Astronomer does not leave his portrayal of Louis at the level of abstract reflections on ruler virtues. He makes at least two points, addresses two concerns, that are both political and ideological. One the one hand, he is desperately concerned with peace, order, concord, and harmony. Louis stands for each of these essential qualities, while his sons and their bad advisers threaten all of them. Moreover, on at least two occasions (cc. 30, 48), the Astronomer shifts blame from worldly actors to Satan. An ideal ruler, properly emulated, will effect peace, order, and the rest. Alas, even such a ruler will occasionally confront unbeatable diabolical forces. On the other hand, the Astronomer is keenly interested in the imperial succession and in the—to him—legitimate interests of Charles the Bald. The Astronomer is measured in his criticism of Lothar during the awful events of 833–34 but otherwise sees in him the only lawful, legitimate hope for the preservation of the unitary Christian empire. Charles, the Astronomer believed, had a right to a territorial share in the imperial succession even if Louis's attempts to provide such a share for Charles provoked a good part of the troubles of the 830s. Some scholars believe that Lothar might have commissioned the *Life,* and no internal evidence contradicts this belief.[12] It is worth asking whether the Astronomer was responding to Thegan's championing of Louis the German.

Bearing in mind that secular biography was an innovative genre when the Astronomer wrote, one can still see that he tried to do something new. He effected an artful blend of Einhard's thematic *vita* and Thegan's chronological *gesta.* Embedded in the Astronomer's account are several themes, ranging from the moral to the political, which his narrative repeatedly brings to the

---

12. Löwe, "Biographien," 337–38; Siemes, *Beiträge zum literarischen Bild Kaiser Ludwigs,* 23, 29–30; Tenberken, *Die Vita Hludowici Pii,* 39–42; Rosamond McKitterick and Matthew Innes, "The Writing of History," in *Carolingian Culture: Emulation and Innovation,* ed. Rosamond McKitterick (Cambridge, 1994), 209–10; Tremp, introduction to *Vita Hludowici imperatoris,* 104–7.

surface. Einhard implicitly rejected the hagiographical model most familiarly represented by Sulpicius Severus's *Life of Martin*. The Astronomer embraced and adapted that model. Martin practiced the imitation of Christ so as to save his soul, and those who might read his life should similarly imitate and, so, similarly save. The Astronomer, by contrast, portrays an ideal Christian ruler who imitated Christ, to be sure, but who did so not merely to save his own soul but also to save the souls of the Christian people entrusted to his rule.[13]

It was probably at the court of Charles the Bald that the *Life of Emperor Louis* first found a welcome reception. The work survives in twenty-two manuscripts written between the middle of the tenth century and some point in the seventeenth. Most of the manuscripts are West Frankish or French. Generally, the Astronomer's *Life*—the longest of all the Carolingian biographies, it should be noted—was bundled in historical collections, usually containing also Thegan, Einhard, and the *Royal Frankish Annals*. There is no way to know what the Astronomer's text looked like. The familiar modern division into sixty-four chapters dates only from the eighteenth century.[14]

ESSENTIAL READING

Astronomus. *Vita Hludowici imperatoris.* Edited by Ernst Tremp. MGH, Scriptores rerum Germanicarum in usum scholarum separatim editi 64. Hannover, 1995.

Collateral Sources

Ardo. *The Life of Saint Benedict, Abbot of Aniane and of Inde.* Translated by Allen Cabaniss, revised by Thomas F. X. Noble. In *Soldiers of Christ: Saints and Saints Lives from Late Antiquity and the Early Middle Ages,* edited by Thomas F. X. Noble and Thomas Head, 213–54. University Park, 1995.
Carolingian Chronicles: Royal Frankish Annals and Nithard's Histories. Translated by Bernhard Walter Scholz. Ann Arbor, 1972.
Charlemagne's Courtier: The Complete Einhard. Edited and translated by Paul Edward Dutton. Peterborough, Ont., 1998.
Charlemagne's Cousins: Contemporary Lives of Adalhard and Wala. Translated, with an introduction, by Allen Cabaniss. Syracuse, 1967.

13. Löwe, "Biographien," 338; Siemes, *Beiträge zum literarischen Bild Kaiser Ludwigs,* 23; Tenberken, *Die Vita Hludowici Pii,* 37–39; Tremp, introduction to *Vita Hludowici imperatoris,* 100, 103; Hageneier, *Jenseits der Topik,* 259–60.
14. Tremp, *Die Überlieferung.* Tenberken, *Die Vita Hludowici Pii,* 61–65, has some keen insights but is less sound than Tremp on the manuscripts.

The Lives of the Ninth-Century Popes (Liber Pontificalis). Translated, with an introduction and commentary, by Raymond Davis. Translated Texts for Historians 20. Liverpool, 1995.

"The Time of Louis the Pious (814–840)." Chap. 3 in *Carolingian Civilization: A Reader,* 2nd ed., edited by Paul Edward Dutton, 155–294. Peterborough, Ont., 2004.

SCHOLARSHIP ON THE ASTRONOMER

Berschin, Walter. "Biographien Ludwigs des Frommen." In *Biographie und Epochenstil im lateinischen Mittelalter,* vol. 3, Quellen und Untersuchungen zur lateinischen Philologie des Mittelalters 10:227–37. Stuttgart, 1991.

Brunhölzl, Franz. *Histoire de la littérature latine du Moyen Âge,* translated by Henri Rochais, vol. 1, pt. 2, pp. 148–49. Turnhout, 1991.

Cabaniss, Allen. *Son of Charlemagne: A Contemporary Life of Louis the Pious.* Syracuse, 1961.

Hageneier, Lars. *Jenseits des Topik: Die karolingische Herrscherbiographie.* Historische Studien 483. Husum, 2004.

Heyse, E. "Astronomer." In *Lexikon des Mittelalters,* vol. 1, col. 1153. Munich, 1999.

Löwe, Heinz. "Biographien Ludwigs des Frommen." In Wilhelm Wattenbach and Wilhelm Levison, *Deutschlands Geschichtsquellen im Mittelalter: Vorzeit und Karolinger,* 3:329–38. Weimar, 1957.

Manitius, Max. "Die Biographien Ludwigs des Frommen." In *Geschichte der lateinischen Literatur des Mittelalters,* 1:655–57. Munich, 1911.

Siemes, Helena. *Beiträge zum literarischen Bild Kaiser Ludwigs des Frommen in der Karolingerzeit.* Freiburg, 1966.

Tenberken, Wolfgang. *Die Vita Hludowici Pii auctore Astronomo.* Rottweil, 1982.

Tremp, Ernst. Introduction to *Vita Hludowici imperatoris,* by Astronomus, MGH, Scriptores rerum Germanicarum in usum scholarum separatim editi 64:53–152. Hannover, 1995.

———. *Die Überlieferung der Vita Hludowici imperatoris des Astronomus.* MGH, Studien und Texte 1. Hannover, 1991.

THE LIFE OF EMPEROR LOUIS

The Astronomer

Prologue

When the good or bad deeds of the ancients, especially of princes, are drawn back into memory, a twofold advantage is conferred upon those who read about them: the one serves to benefit and edify them, and the other to warn them. The foremost men stand on the heights like watchtowers and therefore cannot hide, so the more widely their fame is disseminated, the more broadly it is understood. To the extent that many are attracted by their good, then, they boast of emulating the most distinguished men. The records of our ancestors prove that this is so, for those who wrote them were zealous to instruct posterity by their narration of how each prince traveled the journey of mortals.

In imitating their zeal, although in a less learned style, we do not wish to be careless with the present or begrudging to the future, so we present the deeds and life of the orthodox emperor Louis, whom God loved. For I confess and I say, without vainly seeking praise, that the skill of great writers surrenders to such themes, and I say nothing of my own, for it is tiny. Indeed, we learn on the authority of God's word that holy wisdom teaches moderation and wisdom, justice and courage, and that nothing is more useful in the life of men.[1] He clung so fully to their company that you did not know which one to admire more in him. For what is more moderate than his moderation, which by another name is called frugality or temperance? He so practiced it that the very ancient proverb that is celebrated right up to heaven was most familiar to him, the one that says, "Nothing too much."[2] He took delight in that wisdom, which he learned on the authority of Scripture, which says, "Behold, the fear of the Lord, that is wisdom."[3] Moreover, he loved justice with such devotion that there are witnesses who know with what zeal he burned, that every order of men should fulfill the duties of his order and that each man should love God above all things and love his neighbor as himself. He had made courage such a part of himself that, although he was struck by so many evils and wounded by so many injuries, both public and private, with God guarding him no burden of injury could break his invincible heart. The envious

1. Cf. Wisdom 8:7. The four "cardinal virtues" were popularized by the Stoics, who believed that cultivating them would lead to happiness, or at least to a contented resignation. Christian writers were for a long time loath to cite these virtues explicitly despite their appearance in this one scriptural passage. Several writers (Ambrosius Autpertus, Alcuin, Paulinus of Aquileia, Jonas of Orléans, and Hincmar of Reims) in the Carolingian period produced treatises on the virtues and vices, and these treatises were meant to provide commonsense spiritual guidance for laymen. Often these books set the three Christian virtues—Faith, Hope, and Love—alongside the cardinal virtues as remedies for the seven "deadly" sins (pride, greed, lust, envy, gluttony, anger, and sloth). The cardinal virtues, in other words, were thoroughly Christianized by the ninth century.

2. Another interesting Christianization of classical values: The phrase here is *ne quid nimis*, the exact equivalent of the older Greek μηδὲν ἄγαν. The phrase also appears in the Rule of Saint Benedict, c. 64.

3. Job 28:28.

could find only one fault to which he had succumbed: he was too merciful.[4] With the apostle, however, we ought to say this: "Forgive him this fault."[5] But whether these things are true or not, whoever peruses this account will be able to find out.

What I have written, up to the time when he became emperor, I have added to the account of the most noble and devoted monk Adhemar,[6] who was his contemporary and was raised with him. For later events, since I participated in courtly affairs, I have written down what I was able to see or to learn.

(1) When Charles, the most famous of kings, whom one must not rank behind any man of his time, assumed the sole governance of the people and kingdom of the Franks after the death of his father and the unfortunate demise of his brother Carloman, he believed that he would win himself an unshakable confirmation of his salvation and prosperity if, in supporting the peace and concord of the church, he could bind peaceful people skillfully into a fraternal union, strike down rebels with just severity, bring hope to those oppressed by the pagans, and even somehow lead those enemies of the Christian name to the recognition and confession of the truth. Therefore he dedicated the beginning of his reign to these efforts and committed to Christ whatever needed to be guarded and strengthened, and later, with God's help, he settled the affairs of Francia as he judged fitting and useful, and then headed for Aquitaine, which was scheming to go to war again under the leadership of a certain tyrant, Hunald, who was at that very moment rushing headlong into war.[7] This very same Hunald was driven by fear of Charles to leave Aquitaine, and having fled, he saved his life by hiding and wandering around.

(2) With these things accomplished, and after settling both public and private affairs as far as he could, he left the most pious and noble queen Hildegard, who was pregnant with twin offspring, at the royal estate whose name is Chasseneuil and crossed the Garonne River, the boundary between the

---

4. Cf. Thegan, c. 20, who says that Louis's one fault was that he had too much confidence in his advisers.

5. Cf. 2 Corinthians 12:13: "Forgive me [Paul] this injustice."

6. Nothing is known about this person or his account of Louis. He *might* be the person mentioned in cc. 12–15 below.

7. Hunald II, who succeeded to his father, Waifar, against whom Pippin III had warred throughout the 760s. This campaign took place in 769, when Carloman was still alive and refused to help his brother.

Aquitainians and Gascons, the latter of whose lands he had long before taken under his authority when Prince Lupus surrendered himself and his holdings.[8] Having accomplished there whatever opportunity and usefulness dictated, he decided to contest the difficulty of the Pyrenees mountains, go to Spain, and with Christ's aid bring help to the church, which was laboring under the extremely harsh yoke of the Saracens. These mountains almost touch heaven with their summits, terrify with the sharpness of their peaks, turn everything dark with the denseness of their forests, and nearly prevent the passage not only of an army but even of a few men with the narrowness of their passageways, or rather mere paths. But with Christ's help he made a successful crossing. For the king's vast spirit, ennobled by God, was not to be troubled more than Pompey's or less active than Hannibal's, who with great exhaustion and loss to themselves and to their men had once struggled to overcome the adversity of this place.[9] But if it is permitted to say so, the happy outcome of this successful crossing was spoiled by faithless, uncertain, and changeable fortune. For although they accomplished what they could in Spain, and made a successful return journey, misfortune met them when some soldiers at the very end of the line of march were slaughtered on that same mountain. Because who they were is widely known, I refrain from naming them.[10]

(3) When the king returned, he discovered that his wife had brought forth twin male offspring, one of whom was snatched away by an untimely death, beginning to die almost before he had begun to live in the light, but the other emerged from his mother's womb in fine shape and was nurtured lavishly through childhood.[11] They were born in the year of the incarnation of our Lord Jesus Christ 778. When it happened that the child who gave promise of a vigorous nature was reborn through the sacrament of baptism, it pleased his father to call him Louis,[12] and he handed over to him the kingdom that he had assigned to him at his birth.

8. Lupus had submitted to Charles in 769, but the Astronomer here jumps forward to 778.

9. In 218 B.C. the Carthaginian general Hannibal crossed the Pyrenees going north on his way to Italy at the beginning of the Second Punic War. In 77 B.C. Pompey crossed the mountains going south as he went to Spain to assist in putting down a rebellion.

10. He refers to Roland, who fell at Roncesvalles. Cf. Einhard, c. 9. This passage is an interesting indicator of the way information circulated orally among the elite. It also shows how the Roland story, which would eventually (ca. 1100) become *The Song of Roland,* was taking shape.

11. It is difficult to see what the Astronomer means by this remark. As he says just below, Louis was sent to Aquitaine at the tender age of three and so was raised away from the court.

12. Hludowicus is a Latinized form of Chlodovech, more familiar as Clovis. Charles was claiming the heritage of the Merovingians for his son—*sons* actually, for the one who died shortly after birth was going to be named Lothar, another famous Merovingian name.

The very wise and perspicacious king knew that a kingdom is just like a body and that it can be struck down by this or by that illness unless its health is guarded by receiving counsel and courage as if from doctors, so he bound the bishops to him [i.e., to Louis] in whatever way he thought appropriate. He set up counts and abbots through all of Aquitaine, and many others too who are commonly called vassals. They were Franks whose wisdom and courage would be able to keep him safe from any cunning or force. He committed the care of the kingdom to them as far as he judged beneficial, likewise the safety of the frontiers and the revenues of the royal country estates. Initially he made Humbert count of Bourges and a little later Sturbius, then Abbo in Poitiers, Widbod in Périgord, and also Iterius in Auvergne, not to mention Bullus in Velay, Chorso in Toulouse, Sigwin in Bordeaux, Haimo in Albi, and Rotgar in Limoges.[13]

(4) With these things duly accomplished, he crossed the Loire with the rest of his forces and went to Lutetia, which by another name is called Paris.[14] After just a little while indeed, the desire welled up in him to see Rome, once mistress of the world,[15] and to approach the thresholds of the prince of the apostles and of the teacher of the nations,[16] and to commend himself and his offspring to them, so that in striving with such allies, to whom power in heaven and on earth was given, he could work for the benefit of his subjects and crush insolence if any treachery should happen to arise. He also thought that it would be of no little benefit to himself if he and his sons received their royal insignia with a priestly blessing from their [the apostles'] vicar. God being favorably disposed, this happened according to his vow, and there his son Louis, still dressed as an infant, received a blessing and a royal crown suited to one who was about to rule from the hand of the venerable high priest Hadrian.[17]

When they had done everything that seemed necessary to do at Rome, King Charles, with his sons and his army, returned peacefully to Francia, and he sent his son Louis, who was going to be king, into Aquitaine. He assigned

13. These people cannot be identified in any detail. Abbo does appear to have been count of Poitiers from 778 to 795. On Chorso, see c. 5 below.

14. There is some scholarly controversy about whether this visit to Paris actually took place. In any case, Louis was made king of Aquitaine, and his brother Pippin king of Italy, in 781, and it was around that time when the decision was taken to go to Rome. The author omits three years.

15. The precise phrase once used by Pope Gregory I (590–604) in one of his homilies on the prophet Ezechiel.

16. Saints Peter and Paul.

17. Pope Hadrian I (772–95); Easter 781.

him Arnold[18] as a mentor, and he set up in orderly and fitting fashion other officers suited to the safeguarding of the boy. He was taken as far as Orléans in his infant's clothing and there was girded with arms appropriate to his age, seated on a horse, and transported into Aquitaine with God's help. While he stayed there for not many years, four actually, the glorious king Charles waged continuous and cruel war again and again against the Saxons.[19] Meanwhile he wanted to prevent the people of Aquitaine from growing insolent on account of his long absence, and to keep his son from learning foreign customs on account of his tender years, for it is difficult to undo things learned at that age, so he sent and summoned his son, who was already riding well, along with his whole military force, leaving behind only marcher lords who could guard the frontiers of the kingdom and prevent all incursions by the enemy, if by chance they should attack. His son Louis obeyed the summons with all his knowledge and ability and went to meet him at Paderborn.[20] He and the other boys his age were dressed in Basque garb, that is, in a round mantle, wide shirtsleeves, baggy trousers, little boots with spurs, and carrying a spear in the hand. His father's will commanded this amusement. He stayed with his father and then went with him to Eresburg, where he stayed until the sun dropped from its high point and the onset of autumn tempered the summer heat. At the very end of that period, he received permission from his father to return and spend the winter in Aquitaine.

(5) At that time[21] Chorso, the duke of Toulouse,[22] was captured by the treachery of a certain Basque by the name of Adelrich,[23] forced to bind himself by oaths, and only then released by him. To avenge this affront, King Louis and the magnates by whose advice the realm[24] of Aquitaine was administered decided to hold a general assembly at a site in Septimania whose name is "Death for the Goths."[25] The Basque was summoned but, conscious of what he had done, declined to appear until an exchange of hostages could take

18. Perhaps a count somewhere in Aquitaine who lived on until 822.

19. From 781 to 784.

20. Summer 785.

21. Perhaps between 787 and 789.

22. Toulouse is sometimes called a county and sometimes a duchy, and so its rulers are designated counts and dukes. It was formally a county; the ducal appellations are probably acknowledgments of the ancient significance and prestige of the city, of the high status of the men who governed there, and of the military significance of the *duces,* the local leaders.

23. Otherwise unattested; his name is Frankish, not Basque.

24. The Astronomer writes *res publica.*

25. Mors-Gothorum, or Mourgoudou, a royal estate.

place. The hostages incurred no risk, and he was given gifts, so he returned ours to us, got his own back, and departed.

In the following summer,[26] on his father's command, King Louis went to Worms in simple estate and not with a full military array. He spent the winter there with him. Meanwhile that Adelrich we just mentioned was ordered to appear before the kings and to state his case. He was heard, and although he wished to purge himself of the charges against him, he could not, so he was condemned and sent into permanent exile. Chorso, on account of whose carelessness such a disgrace had befallen the king and the Franks, was deprived of the duchy of Toulouse, and William[27] was put in his place. He discovered that the Basque people, because they are naturally fickle, were very agitated by this outcome and were raging savagely on account of Adelrich's punishment. In a short time, however, he subjected them both by cunning and by force, and he imposed peace on that people. King Louis in that same year held his general assembly in Toulouse, and while they were there, Abu Taher,[28] the leader of the Saracens, and the rest of the leaders who lived along the frontiers of the kingdom of Aquitaine sent to him envoys who sought peace and presented gifts. On the king's will, these were accepted, and then the envoys went home.

(6) Meanwhile, in the next year, King Louis went to meet the king, his father, at Ingelheim and went from there to Regensburg with him. While he was there, since he had reached the age of adolescence, he was girded with a sword and then, after accompanying his father, who was leading an army against the Avars, as far as Kaumberg, he was ordered to return to Regensburg and to stay there with Queen Fastrada until his father's return.[29] And so he passed the coming winter with her while his father carried on with the expedition he had begun. But when Charles was returning from the Avar campaign, Louis received an order from him to go back to Aquitaine and then to go to Italy with as many forces as he could raise in support of his brother Pippin. Complying, he returned to Aquitaine in the autumn, and having arranged everything that pertained to the safety of the kingdom, he traveled through

26. This occurred in 790.

27. William of Toulouse (or of Gellone), a cousin of Charlemagne's who subsequently retired to the monastery of Gellone in 806. William is mentioned repeatedly in Ermoldus, bk. 1.

28. He was the wali of Huesca; according to the *Royal Frankish Annals* he had given hostages to Charles in 778.

29. Louis had not been raised at court by his mother, so he had never learned the courtly ways of the Carolingians. Probably this is what Fastrada was to teach him. The acculturation of noble boys was an important responsibility of noble women.

the harsh and winding bends of the Mount Cenis pass into Italy and joined his brother to celebrate Christmas at Ravenna. After they had met and joined forces, they headed for the province of Benevento, devastated everything in their path, and took over one castle.

After having spent the winter this way, and while returning together successfully to their father, they heard a report that overshadowed their immense joy. They learned that their natural brother Pippin[30] had planned a rebellion against their common father and that many of the nobles who fell in with this scheme had been caught and crushed. Proceeding rapidly, they came to their father in the region of Bavaria, at a place called Salz, and were received by him most warmly. Louis spent whatever was left of the summer, the fall, and the winter with his father, the king. The royal father was especially concerned that the royal son not lack an honorable upbringing and that the adoption of foreign customs would not in any way dishonor him.

When indeed he was just about to leave his father, he was asked by him why, since he was a king, he was so abstemious in domestic affairs that he could not even permit himself a treat unless he was asked to do so. Charles learned from him that because some of the nobles were so zealous for their private affairs, they turned things around, neglected the public good, and made public property private. He was held to be a lord in name only and rendered lacking in everything. He wanted to confront this problem, but did not want the magnates' affection for his son to suffer a blow. So, in order prudently to recover anything that he had through inexperience given away, Charles sent him his *missi*, Willebert, later archbishop of Rouen,[31] and Count Richard,[32] the supervisor of his estates,[33] instructing them that those estates which had previously served the kingdom needed to be returned to public service. So it was done.

(7) After he had gotten these estates back, the king gave continuous evidence of his wisdom and mercy, and he made his disposition so plain that one could see that these qualities were authentic in him. For he ordained that he would spend each winter in [one of] four places, so that after three years had passed, each one of those places would only have supported him for one

---

30. This is Pippin "the Hunchback." Einhard, c. 20, calls him the son of a concubine, reflecting the family line. Probably Pippin was legitimate, but physically impaired. Notker tells fanciful tales about Pippin, 2.12.

31. Ca. 802–28.

32. The name is so common that this person cannot be securely identified.

33. The Astronomer writes *villarum suarum provisorem*, which is not an official title.

winter. They were the palaces of Doué, Chasseneuil, Angeac, and Ebreuil, and each of these places, when the fourth year had come around, would provide adequate resources for the royal service. With these arrangements most prudently ordained, he forbade that military expenses, commonly called fodder, be met any longer by the common people. Although this measure angered the military men, nevertheless this man of mercy thought about the poverty of those who had to pay, the harshness of those who demanded payment, and the losses suffered by each,[34] and judged it enough to support his men from his own resources rather than expose his men to dangers by permitting them to forage for their supplies. At that time he relaxed, through his generosity, the tribute that burdened the Albigeois,[35] since they had to pay it in wine and grain. At that time he had Meginar with him,[36] who had been sent to him by his father. He was wise and strong and expert in the royal advantage and honor. These actions are said to have been so pleasing to his father, the king, that in imitation he forbade the payment as tribute of military fodder in Francia. Taking great joy in his son's happy progress, he ordered many other things to be corrected by him.

(8) In the next year,[37] the king came to Toulouse and held a general assembly there. He received, gave gifts to, and dismissed in peace the envoys that Alfonso, the prince of Galicia, had sent to him for the purpose of confirming friendship[38] between them. He also received and dismissed the envoys of Bahaluc,[39] the leader of the Saracens who ruled over the mountainous regions on the frontier of Aquitaine, who had come seeking peace and bearing gifts. At that time, fearing that he might be led astray down the many paths of lust and overcome by the natural heat of his body, with the advice of his men, he chose Irmingard as his future queen.[40] She came from a distinguished family, since she was the daughter of Count Ingram.[41] Also in that time he set up an extremely strong defense for the boundaries all around Aquitaine. He

34. That is, the poor had been burdened by providing fodder, and now the elite were burdened by losing the privilege to collect fodder.

35. People from the city and region of Albi.

36. Meginar's name first appears in documents in 794.

37. The assembly took place in 798, but some of the events reported in this chapter occurred earlier.

38. *Amicitia:* but the word has the more formal sense of an alliance.

39. Bahlul Ibn Marzuk, a Saracen rebel who was driven from Saragossa in 797.

40. The union with Irmingard probably took place in 794. By then Louis seems to have had two illegitimate children, Alpais and Arnulf.

41. Cf. Thegan, c. 4.

fortified and repopulated the city of Vich, the fortress of Cardona, Caserras, and other towns that were once deserted, and he instituted Borel[42] as count with suitable forces to guard them.

(9) At the end of winter his father, the king, summoned him to come with as many men as he could to march with him against the Saxons.[43] Not hesitating to go, he came to him at Aachen and set out with him to Friemersheim, where he held a general assembly on the bank of the Rhine. He stayed with his father in Saxony until St. Martin's day.[44] Then he left Saxony with his father and was permitted to return to Aquitaine, a great part of the winter having passed.[45]

(10) In the next year, King Charles sent for him and commanded him to set out with him to Italy, but then he changed his plan and ordered him to stay home. While Charles was going to Rome and receiving the imperial insignia, King Louis stayed put in Toulouse and then marched into Spain. As he was approaching Barcelona, Zado,[46] the duke of that city, met him as though he were already a subject but did not hand over the city. Passing on, Louis arrived suddenly at Lérida, subjected it, and destroyed it. Having destroyed that city and having wasted and burned several others, he proceeded on to Huesca. A military band cut, plundered, and burned its fields, which were full of crops, and whatever was found outside the city was consumed by the fire that was destroying the crops. After finishing this work, and with winter already coming on, he returned home.

(11) With summer's return, the glorious emperor Charles went to Saxony and commanded his son to follow him into that same land and to plan on spending the winter there.[47] He set out in haste, came to Neuss, crossed the Rhine there, and hurried to meet his father. But before he got to him, he encountered a messenger from his father in a place that is called Ostfaloa,[48] with orders that he not wear himself out any longer in marching but rather

42. He was a count from 798/9 to 804. His seat is unknown.

43. There were campaigns in 796 and 799. From the structure of the narrative, it is difficult to determine which one the Astronomer is referring to: 796 follows more naturally upon what has just been said, but 799 fits with what is reported in the next chapter.

44. November 11.

45. This passage is indicative of the problems involved in trying to pin down the Astronomer's chronology. If Charles and Louis left Saxony in early November and then Louis returned to Aquitaine after much of the winter had run its course, then Louis must have stayed with his father, perhaps at Aachen, for two or three months. The matter is of consequence because Louis seems to have spent a lot more time with Charles and his courtiers than one might otherwise think.

46. Zado appears, rather differently, in Ermoldus, pages 136–41.

47. Winter 804–5.

48. Precise place unknown; somewhere in Eastphalia.

pitch camp in a suitable place and wait there for his return. For the entire Saxon people had been conquered, and Emperor Charles, already victorious, was on his way back. When his son met him, he embraced him and kissed him many times, extolled him with praise and many thanks for his effort, repeated again and again how valuable his support was, and pronounced himself fortunate to have such a son. With the long and especially bloody Saxon war brought to a conclusion, a war that, as they say, filled up thirty-three years,[49] King Louis was dismissed by his father, and he gathered up his forces to spend the winter in his own kingdom.

(12) After the end of winter, Emperor Charles found the moment opportune, insofar as he was at rest from foreign wars, to begin making a circuit around those places of his realm that bordered on the sea.[50] When King Louis learned about this, he sent his envoy Adhemar[51] to Rouen to ask him to detour into Aquitaine, to visit the kingdom that he had given him, and to come to the place that is called Chasseneuil. The father received his request honorably and thanked his son, but nevertheless denied his request and commanded Louis to meet him in Tours. When Louis came there, his father received him with immense joy, and Louis followed him on his return to Francia as far as Ver. Louis departed from there and returned to Aquitaine.

(13) In the following summer, Duke Zado of Barcelona was persuaded by a certain friend, as he thought, to advance right up to Narbonne.[52] He was captured there, brought to King Louis, and then led away to his father, Charles. At that same time, King Louis, having gathered the people of his kingdom, was engaged at Toulouse in drawn-out deliberations concerning the things that seemed necessary to do. Burgundio having died, his county of Fézensac was assigned to Liutard.[53] The Basques took this very badly and rushed forth with such impudence that they killed some of his men with the sword and burned others with fire. They were summoned, but at first drew back from coming, then came to try somehow to plead their case, but finally were given suitable punishments for such audacious deeds; some of them were burned by the *lex talionis*.[54]

---

49. A reference to Einhard (c. 7)?
50. Once again the Astronomer's chronology is shaky. These events took place in 800.
51. Possibly the person who supposedly informed the Astronomer about Louis's early years.
52. Probably in the summer of 801.
53. Son of Count Gerhard I of Paris and brother of Louis's later son-in-law Bigo.
54. Literally the "law of the talon" but more familiar in such expressions as "an eye for an eye and a tooth for a tooth."

After these things had happened, in the next season, it seemed to Louis and to his advisers that they ought to go and lay siege to Barcelona.[55] The army was divided into three parts. Louis kept one with himself while he was waiting at Roussillon. The second, under the command of Rastagnus,[56] the count of Gerona, was enjoined to besiege the city. He instructed the third to take up a position beyond the city so that the troops attacking the city would not be unexpectedly overrun by the enemy. The besieged meanwhile sent to Cordoba and demanded help. The king of the Saracens sent an army to help right away. When those who had been sent got to Saragossa, they learned about an army that had been dispatched to block their way. For William was there as the leader,[57] and Adhemar, and strong forces with them. When they heard this, they turned against the Asturians[58] and inflicted an unforeseen slaughter on them but got back an even more serious blow. While they were withdrawing, our men returned to their allies, who were besieging the city and, having joined forces with them, surrounded the city. In permitting no one to enter or to exit, they harassed the city until the inhabitants were forced by the bitterness of hunger to take down the old skins from their doorways and make most unappealing food out of them. Some, preferring death to such a miserable life, jumped headlong off the walls. Others were cheered up by an empty hope, for they thought that the Franks would give up the siege of the city on account of the harshness of winter. But the plan of wiser men cut off their hope. For materials were assembled from everywhere, and they began to build shelters as if they planned to spend the winter there. On seeing this, the inhabitants of the city lost all hope and, thrown into final desperation, betrayed their prince, a relative of Zado by the name of Hamur,[59] whom they had chosen in his place. They handed over themselves and their city after they had received permission to withdraw safely. This is what happened. Our men could see that the city was worn out from the long siege, and they believed that it was just about to be captured or handed over. As was fitting, they devised an honorable plan and summoned the king so that a city of such renown

---

55. Cf. Ermoldus, pages 128–35, who tells this story rather differently.

56. Probably the *vassus dominicus* attested in Narbonne in 782, who at some point became count of Gerona. He is not mentioned again after this campaign.

57. *Willelmus, primus signifer:* This locution means that he marched behind the first standard of battle; that is, he was the leader.

58. The Kingdom of Asturias slowly coalesced in extreme northwestern Spain from a Christian remnant after the Muslim conquest between 711 and 716.

59. An obscure figure who may have ruled Barcelona for a year or two after Zado's capture.

would enhance the king's glorious reputation by actually being taken while he was there. The king right away granted his assent to this honorable suggestion. He therefore met up with his army, which had surrounded the city with a ditch. Barcelona had endured the siege obstinately for six weeks without cease but finally, conquered, fell into the hand of the victor. The city was handed over and opened up, and on the very first day the king set up guards. But he refrained from entering until he could decide how to consecrate this desired and welcome victory to God's name with suitable thanksgiving. On the next day his priests and clergy preceded him and his army through the gate of the city. In majestic solemnity and singing psalms, they processed right to the church of the holy and most victorious Cross, where they gave thanks to God for the victory divinely bestowed upon them.[60]

After this, he left count Bero[61] there to guard the place with a troop of Goths, and he went home to spend the winter. His father, having learned of the danger that appeared to be threatening him from the Saracens, sent Louis's brother Charles to help. When he had reached Lyon, as he was hurrying to help his brother, a messenger from his brother the king arrived and, telling him that the city had been captured, informed him that he need trouble himself no further. Charles turned around from that place and went back to his father.

(14) While Louis was spending the winter in Aquitaine, his father, the king,[62] commanded him to come to his colloquy at Aachen on the feast of the Purification of Holy Mary, the Mother of God.[63] He went to meet him, stayed as long as it pleased Charles, and then went home during Lent.

In the following summer, he set out for Spain with as great a military array as seemed fitting. He passed by Barcelona and went to Tarragona. He seized those he found there, put others to flight, and cut down with military force all the villages, fortifications, and towns right up to Tortosa. A devouring flame consumed them. Meanwhile, in a place called Sancta Columba, he divided his forces into two, leading the greater part himself against Tortosa and directing Isembard,[64] Adhemar, Bero, and Borel with the rest as promptly as possible to higher ground so that they could cross the Ebro River, attack the enemy

---

60. Was this a former church now either abandoned or else turned into a mosque, or had a Christian community retained a place of worship under Muslim rule?

61. See note 26 to Ermoldus's *In Honor of Louis.*

62. The Astronomer is careless about designating Charles as emperor after 800.

63. February 2, probably in 802, judging from the order of events as the Astronomer presents them.

64. See note 29 to Ermoldus's *In Honor of Louis.*

unexpectedly while they were still sitting in their homes, or at least stir up the region and sow disorder. Therefore, while the king was bearing down on Tortosa, the others whom we just mentioned, going by night into the high ground around the Ebro and in the daytime spreading out in the wilds of the forests, were moving ahead right up to the Cinca and the Ebro, which they crossed by swimming. The march took six days, and on the seventh they crossed over. When they had all passed through unharmed, they laid waste the enemy's land on every side and advanced as far as their greatest village, which was called Villa Rubea, from which they hauled off immense booty because the enemy were unprepared and never expected such an attack.

When this had been accomplished, those who had been able to escape the blow sent messengers far and wide. A good-sized force of Saracens and Moors was assembled and planned to meet the enemy in the valley that is called Ualla Ibana. It is the nature of this valley that it stretches out deeply and is surrounded by steep and high mountains. Had not a divine premonition prevented our men from entering, the enemy would have been able to kill them almost effortlessly by throwing stones, or else they would have fallen into the enemy's hands. While they were blocking the way, our men were looking for another route that was more open and broader. The Moors thought that our men were doing this not so much out of concern for their safety as out of fear, and followed along behind them. Our men, however, left their booty behind, bared their faces to the enemy, resisted sharply, and with Christ's help forced them to turn tail. They killed those whom they captured and returned happily to the booty that they had left behind. Finally, after twenty days of this diversion, they returned briskly to the king, having lost very few of their men. King Louis received them joyfully, and the enemy's lands everywhere lying in waste, he returned home.

(15) Later on[65] King Louis prepared yet another expedition for Spain, but his father refused to let him go there himself. For he had at that time ordered that ships be constructed against the incursions of the Northmen in all the rivers that flowed in from the sea. He assigned his son this task for the Rhone, Garonne, and Silida.[66] Nevertheless, he sent him his *missus* Ingobert[67] to take his son's place and to stand in for both of them in leading the army against

---

65. *Sequenti vero tempore* would normally, in the Astronomer's narrative style, mean "in the next season," but the events he relates here seem to have taken place in 808, whereas the preceding account dates to 802.

66. The latter is unidentified. One would have expected the Loire to be mentioned.

67. Perhaps a relative of Queen Irmingard, who was active on Louis's behalf between 817 and 825.

the enemy. While the king was staying in Aquitaine for this reason, his army came to Barcelona by a successful march, and taking counsel among themselves here regarding how they might overcome the enemy by a sneak attack, they decided to do it this way: They built transportable boats and divided each one of them into four parts, since a fourth part of each could be carried by two horses or mules, and having prepared nails and hammers, they could, as soon as they came to the river, easily put them back together again with the pitch, wax, and tow they had also prepared. Once they were built, the greater part of them, with the above-mentioned *missus* Ingobert, headed for Tortosa. But those who had been deputed to the above-mentioned work, Adhemar, to be sure, and Bero and the rest, planning on a journey of three days, for they were without pack saddles, had only the sky for cover, did not make fires, for fear the smoke would give them away, hid themselves by day in the forest and marched as much as they could at night, rebuilt the boats on the fourth day and crossed the river; they let the horses swim across.

This great undertaking gave complete success to their plan, which might have been swiftly overturned. For while Abaidun, the duke of Tortosa,[68] was blocking the banks of the Ebro to keep our men from crossing, and while those, about whom we spoke above, were crossing higher up in the way we discussed, a certain Moor entered the river to bathe and saw horse dung borne along by the river. Having seen it, for these are clever people, he swam out, grabbed the dung, held it to his nose, and shouted: "Look!" he said, "O comrades, I warn you to watch out. This dung is not from a wild ass or from any animal that feeds on pasture grass. To be sure, these are horse droppings that were certainly barley once upon a time and therefore the fodder of horses or mules. So be on the lookout because further up the river, it seems to me, an ambush is being prepared for us." Immediately they directed two of their men to mount horses and look around. Having seen our men, they reported back to Abaidun that it was true. They were driven by fear, and leaving behind as worthless everything they had in their camp, they took flight, and our men took over everything they left behind and enjoyed the hospitality of their tents that night. But Abaidun, having collected a substantial band of the enemy, prepared to meet our men in battle the next morning. Our men trusted in divine help, although they were unequal and much fewer in number, and still compelled the enemy to flee, filled up the path with a great slaughter of those

68. Arabic sources call him the wali of Tortosa.

who were fleeing, and did not stay their hand from the destruction until the day's sun and light began to dim and darkness began to cover the earth, until the light of the stars followed and started to light up the night. When these things had been done, and with Christ's help, they came back to their own men with great joy and riches. The city having been besieged for a long time while this was happening, they marched back home.

(16) And then, in the next year,[69] Louis decided to go back to Tortosa himself, and he took along Heribert,[70] Liutard,[71] Isembard, and a strong troop from Francia. On arriving there, he battered and wore down the city with rams, mangonels,[72] covered sheds,[73] and other torments, so that its citizens abandoned hope, and seeing that Mars had turned against[74] them and that they were beaten, they handed over the keys of the city, which Louis on his return sent to his father with great satisfaction. These events, carried out in such a way, struck great anxiety in the Saracens and Moors, for they feared that a similar fate might be in store for each city. So forty days after he had begun the siege, the king went home from the city and reentered his kingdom.

(17) After the end of the present year,[75] Louis drew up his army and decided to send it against Huesca with his father's *missus* Heribert. When those who had been sent arrived there, they laid siege to the city, and they either captured or put to flight whoever assembled to meet them. But while they were settling in around the city, some of the imprudent and lighthearted young men, behaving with less caution than was smart, went up close to the walls and tried first of all to lash with words and then with missiles those who were defending the battlements. The townsmen were contemptuous of the small number of those who were present, expected the imminent arrival of those [reinforcements] who were not there yet, opened the gates, and sallied forth. There was a battle whose outcome was this: Men were killed on both sides.

---

69. Actually, it seems, 809.

70. See note 23 to Ermoldus's *In Honor of Louis;* perhaps the *missus* of Charlemagne mentioned in c. 17 below.

71. See note 24 to Ermoldus's *In Honor of Louis.*

72. A machine to hurl projectiles. This is the first certain mention of this Byzantine device in a Western source.

73. That is, a sort of mobile roof that protected besiegers from arrows shot or stones thrown from the walls.

74. *Adverso Marte:* The allusion is to Virgil, *Aeneid,* 12.1: "Turnus ut infractos Marte adverso Latinos / defecisse videt." Literally this means that Mars, the god of war, had changed sides. Figuratively it means "the tide had turned."

75. These events appear to fall in 811, after Charlemagne had concluded peace with the emir of Cordoba in 810.

The townsmen retreated into the city, and our men went back to camp to stay there. The siege was therefore prolonged, devastation was wreaked, and after doing whatever seemed possible to the enemy to satisfy their bitter anger, our men returned to the king, who was at that time keenly busy hunting in the forests, for it was the very end of the fall season. On receiving back the men who were returning from the expedition on which they had been dispatched, the king settled down with his men to pass the coming winter in peace.

(18) In the following summer,[76] with his people summoned to a general assembly, Louis related to them a rumor that had reached him that a certain group of Basques who had already accepted his overlordship were now contemplating defection and had risen up in rebellion. The public good demanded that he go to repress their defiance. Everyone honored the king's will with praise, testifying that such behavior was utterly contemptible among subjects and, what is more, should be stopped with the greatest severity. Having drawn up his army and put it into motion as the situation demanded, he arrived at the villa of Dax and ordered those who had been charged with infidelity to come to him. But when they refused to come, he went down to their area and permitted a military squadron to ravage everything of theirs. Finally, when it looked like everything that belonged to them had been destroyed, they came as suppliants, and in the end, having lost all their goods, they were entitled to a pardon in exchange for the huge tribute.

Having then overcome with some difficulty the crossing of the Pyrenean Alps, he descended on Pamplona. He stayed in that area as long as it seemed there were things to arrange that would lead to the public or private good. But when it was time for him to return through those same narrow mountain passes, the Basques tried to use their native and customary manner of deception, but they were detected by cleverness and avoided by a plan of caution and watchfulness. For one of them, who had come forward as a provocation, was caught and hung, and then wives and sons were snatched from almost all the rest, so that our men came through to a place where their deception could bring no damage to the king or the army.

(19) These things having been accomplished, the king and his people returned home with God's favor. Since he began to come of age, but especially at that time, the most pious spirit of the king was roused to divine worship and the exaltation of the church, so that his works proclaimed that he was not

76. That of 812.

only a king but also a priest. For whoever appeared to be a clergyman in all of Aquitaine, before the area was entrusted to him, seemed to be laboring under tyrants and knew better how to apply himself to riding, to military exercises, and to hurling missiles than to divine worship. With teachers having been brought in from everywhere by the king's zeal, he built up more quickly than one would believe the study of reading and singing and also the comprehension of divine and worldly letters.

This outcome was brought about especially by those who for the love of God abandoned all their goods and sought to take a share in the speculative life.[77] For before Aquitaine passed under his rule, the order of people like this had collapsed there. But under him it grew strong again, and he even thought about imitating the memorable example of his grandfather's brother Carloman and striving to reach the summits of the contemplative life.[78] So that such a vow would not be fulfilled, his father laid down a strong objection to it; or rather it was a sign of God's will that a man of such great piety should not wish to shut himself away and think only about his own salvation but instead that the salvation of many should grow through him and under him. Indeed, as is reported, under his authority many monasteries were restored, and monasteries were built from the ground up, especially these: the monastery of St.-Filibert,[79] the monastery of St. Florentius,[80] the monastery of Charroux,[81] the monastery of Conques, the monastery of St.-Maxentius,[82] the monastery of Menat,[83] the monastery of Manglieu,[84] the monastery of Moissac, the monastery of St.-Savinus,[85] the monastery of Massay,[86] the monastery of Noaillé,[87] the monastery of St.-Theotfrid,[88] the monastery of St.-Pascentius,[89] the monastery of Donzère,[90] the monastery of Solignac,[91] the women's convent of

77. A slightly odd formulation, since it is commoner to see the active life compared to the *contemplative* life.
78. Here he writes *theoricae . . . culmina vitae.*
79. Noirmoutier.
80. St.-Florent-le-Vieil.
81. Uncertain, perhaps near Poitiers.
82. Niort.
83. Riom.
84. Clermont-Ferrand.
85. St.-Savin-sur-Gartempe.
86. Bourges.
87. Poitiers.
88. St.-Chaffre-le-Monastier, in Le Puy.
89. St.-Paixent, in Montmorillon.
90. In Montélimar.
91. Near Limoges.

St.-Maria,[92] the women's convent of St.-Radegond,[93] the monastery of Devera,[94] the monastery of Deutera in the district of Toulouse,[95] the monastery of Vadala;[96] in Septimania, the monastery of Aniane, the monastery of Gellone, the monastery of St.-Lawrence,[97] the monastery of St.-Mary that is called "In Rubine,"[98] the monastery of Caunes,[99] and many others that adorned the whole kingdom of Aquitaine like so many lights. Many of the bishops and a large number of laymen imitated his example and restored dilapidated monasteries or tried to start new ones. This is plainly to be seen.

Finally, the public condition of the kingdom of Aquitaine had achieved such happiness that whether the king set forth or stayed in his palace, hardly anyone could be found who could complain that he had suffered some blow to this rights. The king devoted three days of every week to judicial business. On one occasion, Charles had sent his chancellor Archambald[100] and committed to him some orders that had to be taken to his son and the responses that had to be brought back to him. On his return he reported to Louis's father the good order that he had seen, and Charles is said to have exulted and wept on account of his immense excitement. He said to those standing nearby, "O comrades, let us rejoice that we have been overwhelmed by the mature wisdom of this youth." Since Louis had been a faithful servant of the Lord in what was entrusted to him and prudent in expanding the resources he had been given, he was appointed as one having complete authority in his household.[101]

(20) At around the same time, with Pippin, the king of Italy, already dead and his brother Charles having also very recently departed from the realm of human affairs, the hope of ruling everything welled up in Louis. He had already sent Gerricus, his falconer,[102] to consult with his father about certain

92. Notre-Dame de la Règle, in Limoges.
93. Ste.-Radegonde/Ste.-Croix, in Poitiers.
94. Possibly Dèvres, near Bourges.
95. Unknown.
96. Possible S. Salvador de la Valeda, in Berga, near Barcelona.
97. St.-Laurent-de-Vernazoubres, near St. Pons.
98. La Grasse am Orbieu, near Carcassonne.
99. Near Carcassonne.
100. Chancellor from 797 to 812.
101. "Constitutus est potestatem habens in cuncta patrisfamilias domo": the implication being that Charles was no longer going to supervise Louis's "household," meaning his government.
102. The falconer was an influential palace official in Carolingian times and especially so under Louis, who was so fond of hunting. This Gerricus may be the man who witnessed a charter in 794 and also the one whom Louis sent as an envoy to Lyon in 826 or 827 to investigate the situation of the city's Jews. If this is indeed one man, then Gerricus was one of Louis's longest serving associates.

urgent matters, and while Gerricus was waiting in the palace so he would be present to receive the response he was to be given, he was advised by both Franks and Germans that Louis ought to come to his father and attend upon him. It appeared to them, as they said, that since his father was already declining into extreme old age, and since he was bearing most bitterly the unfortunate deaths of his children, then perhaps these things signaled his own rapidly approaching bodily demise. When Gerricus had related this to the king, and the king to his advisers, then it seemed to some, actually to almost all of them, to be a sound plan. But the king was troubled, listened to higher counsel, and delayed so that he would not give his father cause for suspicion. Nevertheless, that very Divinity, for fear and love of Whom he did not wish to act, arranged things more prudently, as it is His way to ennoble those who love Him more sublimely than can be imagined. Furthermore, the king was indulging those seeking peace, the very ones he had been accustomed to wearing out with war, and he marked off a precise period of two years.

Meanwhile Emperor Charles was contemplating his speeding tumble into old age and was afraid that when he was withdrawn from human affairs, he would leave behind in a state of confusion the kingdom that he had with God's help nobly organized. That is, he feared that it might be struck by external attacks or troubled by internal divisions, so he sent to his son and summoned him from Aquitaine. He received him gently when he arrived, and spent the whole summer with him. He instructed him on those matters that he thought needed discussion, for instance, how he ought to live and to rule, how the realm should be organized and, once organized, maintained. He admonished him and finally crowned him with an imperial diadem and informed him that with Christ's help he was going to have the highest power over all. When this affair had been completed, he granted him permission to return home. Louis departed from his father in the month of November and went back to Aquitaine.[103]

As his father drew nearer to death, he began to suffer from frequent and strange troubles. For death, as if by some kind of messengers, was announcing by such signs that its arrival was coming very soon. Finally, with his painful ills combating each other and sapping his strength, the weakness of his condition took its toll. He took to his bed, and in the days and hours when his death was drawing nearer, he distributed his possessions in writing just as

---

103. Cf. the very different accounts of these events in Thegan, c. 6, and Ermoldus, pages 142–44.

he wished. He finished his last day and left an almost unbearable sorrow to the kingdom of the Franks. But indeed Scripture was proved to be truthful in his successor, where it says, to console those who are suffering such trials, "The just man is dead, and yet he is not dead, for he has left behind a son like himself as an heir."[104] The most pious emperor Charles died on the twenty-eighth of January in the year of the incarnation of our Lord Jesus Christ 814. At that time, as if by some presentiment, Emperor Louis had announced to the people a general assembly for the feast of the Purification of Holy Mary, the Mother of God,[105] in a place called Doué.

(21) After his father of holy memory had died, Rampo[106] was sent to him by those who had attended to his burial, that is, by his children,[107] and the foremost men of the palace, so that he would promptly know of Charles's death and not in any way delay his own arrival. When Louis was approaching the city of Orléans, Theodulf,[108] the bishop of the city and a man most learned in every subject, perceived the reason for his coming[109] and anxiously sent a messenger as quickly as possible to the emperor to learn just what he would command him to do, whether to wait for his arrival in the city or to meet him at some point along the way, as he was coming to the city. On brief reflection, Louis understood the reason and ordered Theodulf to come to him. Then Louis received one sad messenger after another with news of the event, and after the fifth day he moved on from that same place, and with as many people as the narrow space of time permitted, he began his journey again. For Wala,[110] who held the highest place with Emperor Charles, was especially feared in case he might be organizing something sinister against the new emperor. But Wala came to him very quickly and with humble submission yielded to Louis's will, commending himself according to the custom of the Franks. After he had come to the emperor, all the Frankish nobles swiftly

104. Paraphrase of Ecclesiasticus 30:4 (NAB Sirach 30:4: "At the father's death he will seem not dead, since he leaves after himself one like himself").

105. February 2.

106. Perhaps the later count of Barcelona-Gerona.

107. Presumably Louis's sisters and half brothers.

108. Cf. Thegan, c. 22 and note 50; see also cc. 26 and 29 below.

109. Namely, Charles's death.

110. Ca. 773–836: Charlemagne's cousin, a son of Bernard, Charles Martel's youngest son and half brother to Charlemagne's father, Pippin. He was count of the palace in the last years of Charles's reign, spent some years in exile (see below), was rehabilitated, became abbot of Corbie (826–31), got involved in the civil wars of the early 830s, and died as abbot of Bobbio in Italy, where he had followed Louis's son Lothar.

imitated him, and a great crowd of them hurried to go and meet him. Finally he arrived at Herstal after a favorable march, and on the thirteenth day since he departed from Aquitaine, he set foot happily in the palace at Aachen. Although he was most mild by nature, he had nevertheless long since made up his mind about the behavior of his sisters in his father's household, by which stain alone his father's house was blemished. He wanted to remedy the offense but also to prevent a new scandal arising like the one that once happened on account of Odilo and Hiltrude.[111] He sent Wala and Warnar,[112] and Lambert[113] too, and even Ingobert,[114] and when they got to Aachen, they took precautions that such things would not happen, and they restrained carefully, until Louis's arrival, a few who were particularly debauched or whose scornful arrogance was treasonous. Some of them got what they had asked for when, as suppliants, they had requested pardon while he was still on his way. At the same time, he gave orders that the people who were staying there should await his own arrival without fear. But indeed Count Warnar, without the knowledge of Wala and Ingobert, but after summoning his nephew Lambert, commanded Odoin,[115] who was already criminally liable, to come to them, as if they were going to seize him and hand Louis over to royal judgment. But he, with his conscience stinging sharply, foresaw the trap. Because he continued to go down the wrong path, even though he himself deserved to be tried, he brought down the ultimate destruction on Warnar. For on coming to him, just as he had been ordered, he killed that very Warnar and rendered Lambert lame for a long time with a wound to his leg. But finally he was himself run through with a sword and killed. When these things had been announced to the emperor, the death of his friend so turned his mind from mercy that a certain Tullius,[116] who had formerly seemed worthy of a pardon by the emperor's mercy, was punished with the loss of his eyes.

111. Hiltrude was a daughter of Charles Martel by his Bavarian wife, Swanahild. She married Odilo, the duke of Bavaria, and they had a son, Grifo, who was a constant and serious threat to Carloman and Pippin until his death in 753. "Official" Carolingian historiography came to regard Hiltrude as a concubine and Grifo as illegitimate. Louis's sisters, as Einhard reports (c. 19), were unmarried but had both lovers and children. Louis's moral sense may have been offended by his sisters' behavior, but as the Astronomer somewhat obliquely admits, Louis wished to avoid rivalry from blood relatives.

112. A member of the influential Widonid family, a count in Aquitaine, and a close associate of Louis's.

113. Count of Nantes and lord of the Breton March.

114. Cf. c. 15 above.

115. Unidentified, but possibly the lover of one of Louis's sisters.

116. Also unidentified. His name, recalling Cicero's, suggests that he might have been one of the court scholars in Charles's time, since many of these had classical or biblical nicknames.

(22) The emperor then came to the palace at Aachen, and received with great favor by his relatives and by many thousands of Franks, he was declared emperor for the second time. He gave sincere thanks for the burial of his father, and he brought solace with fitting consolation to his relatives, who were struck with bitter sadness. And whatever was lacking in his father's rites, he supplied most readily. For after the reading of his father's will, nothing remained of his father's goods that had not been shared out by his plan of division, since nothing had been left unbequeathed by him. But whatever Charles thought should be distributed to churches, he divided among the metropolitans by name, and there were twenty-one shares.[117] Whatever was suitable for royal equipment, he left to a later time.[118] He also decreed what, according to the custom of Christians, should be distributed in common to his sons and grandsons, to his daughters, to his male and female slaves, to his royal servants, and to all the poor. The lord emperor Louis executed the task of fulfilling everything he found written down.

(23) After he had done these things, the emperor ordered the whole crowd of women—it was extremely large—to be excluded from the palace, except for a very few whom he deemed suitable for royal service. Each of his sisters withdrew to the properties they had received from their father; since the distributions had not yet taken place for each of them, they got what they deserved from the emperor and then departed for the properties they had obtained.

Later the emperor received the embassies dispatched to his father but now coming to him. He listened to them diligently, dined them elegantly, and sent them back laden with sumptuous gifts. The most important among them came from the emperor at Constantinople, named Michael,[119] to whom the lord Charles had sent Bishop Amalar of Trier[120] and Abbot Peter[121] of Nonantola for the sake of confirming peace. When they returned, they brought with them the envoys of the above-mentioned Michael, the protospatharius[122] Cristophorus and the deacon Gregory. They had been sent to Charles to reply

117. Possibly a reference to Einhard, c. 33.

118. *Posteriori reliquit aetati:* "to the next generation"? Quite possibly this refers to the royal (and imperial?) regalia.

119. Michael I, 811–13.

120. Often referred to as Amalar of Metz (775/808–850). Archbishop of Trier from 809 to 814, of Lyon from 835 to 838.

121. Abbot from 804 to 821.

122. The protospatharius was not a specific officer at Byzantium. Rather, this was an honorific title that conferred great prestige on its bearer. Presumably the Astronomer knew this and mentions the envoy by title so as to indicate the prestige and seriousness of this legation.

to everything that had been written [to Michael]. The emperor sent them back to Michael's successor, Leo,[123] along with his own envoys, bishop Norbert of Reggio[124] and Count Ricoin of Poitiers,[125] seeking to renew the former friendship and to confirm the treaty.[126]

In the same year, he held a general assembly at Aachen, and he sent from his presence through all parts of his realm faithful and trustworthy men, men who were known to be committed to just law, so that they could correct evils and assign to everyone his due in equal measure. He summoned his nephew Bernard, for a long time already the king of Italy, and when he obediently appeared, Louis sent him back to his own kingdom amply endowed with gifts. He obliged Prince Grimoald of the Beneventans, who did not come in person but sent his envoys, by a treaty and oaths to pay every year seven thousand gold solidi to the public treasury.

(24) In the same year, he sent two of his sons, Lothar and Pippin, to Bavaria and Aquitaine, respectively, but he kept back his third son, Louis, for he was still a boy. At the same time, Harald, to whom the highest authority in the kingdom of the Danes appeared to belong and who had earlier been driven from the kingdom by the sons of Godfred, fled to Emperor Louis and commended himself into his hands after the Frankish custom.[127] The king received him and ordered him to go to Saxony and to wait there for a time, until he could provide aid to help him recover his rulership. At this time too the imperial clemency restored their paternal heritage to the Saxons and Frisians, which they had legally lost under his father on account of treachery.[128] Some attributed this to generosity and some to a lack of foresight, because those peoples, accustomed as they were to natural savagery, ought to have been held sufficiently in restraint that, unbridled, they could not rush headlong into treachery. The emperor, however, thought that he could bind them more effectively to himself if he bestowed desirable benefits upon them, and his hope was not deceived, for after this he always kept those very same peoples in the greatest devotion to himself.

123. Leo V, 813–20. While the envoys were en route, Charles died and Michael I was deposed.

124. Bishop from before 814 to 835. It is not known why he was chosen.

125. Possibly a son-in-law of Charles. He was still count of Poitiers in 835.

126. The key issue was to win from Byzantium recognition of the new Western imperial title.

127. Harald II Klak was the Danish king after 812 (called Heriold by the Astronomer). Godfred had been murdered in 810 (cf. Einhard, c. 14). Ermoldus devotes a good deal of his book 4 to the encounter between Harald and Louis in 826 that resulted in Harald's baptism.

128. That is, Louis repatriated some of these people whom Charles had exiled to various places in Francia. See Einhard, c. 7.

(25) When this year had run its course, it was reported to the emperor that some of the powerful Romans had entered into a vile conspiracy against the apostolic Leo. After they had been captured and convicted, this same apostolic man condemned them to capital punishment, for the law of the Romans permitted this. On hearing about this, however, the emperor took it badly that the first priest of the world should have punished so harshly. So he sent King Bernard of Italy there so that he could review for himself what was true or false in the rumors that were going around. Bernard was to report back to him through Count Gerold.[129] King Bernard himself went to Rome and reported back through the above-mentioned envoy the things he saw there. But soon there followed envoys of this same apostolic Leo, Bishop John of Silva Candida,[130] the nomenclator Theodore,[131] and also Duke Sergius,[132] who sought to purge the apostolic Leo of the crimes of which he had been accused.

The emperor then ordered the Saxon counts and the Abotrits,[133] who had formerly submitted themselves to the lord Charles, to give aid to Harald, so that he could be restored to his own kingdom. Baldric[134] was deputed to carry this message. When they had crossed the Eider River, they entered the land of the Northmen in a place called Sinlendi.[135] Although the sons of Godfred had abundant forces and two hundred ships, they did not wish to come close and give battle. Both forces withdrew, and our men destroyed and burned everything they encountered, and what is more, they received forty hostages from that same people. Having done this, they returned to the emperor in

129. Count of the Ostmark from 811 to 832. A member of a powerful family and a relative of Louis's through his mother.

130. From ancient times the Romans divided Italy administratively into Italia Annonaria (grain-producing Italy) and Italia Suburbicaria (Italy around Rome). The bishop of Silva-Candida, a town lying a little north of the city, was one of the "suburbicarian bishops," who advised the pope and who shared with him liturgical responsibilities in the city. John is known to have served between 815 and 826.

131. The nomenclator was one of the more important officers of the papal government. He was the chief protocol officer. Theodore held this office from at least 813 to 817, when he became primicerius, the head of the notaries and one of the three greatest officers of the church after the pope. He was murdered in 823; see c. 37 below.

132. Under the Byzantine administration, Rome was governed by a *dux Romae*—a duke of Rome. After the popes assumed local rule, dukes appear from time to time in the sources as lay dignitaries, probably charged with military responsibilities—especially as long as the Lombards were a threat—and possibly judicial and police duties. Certainly they were high-status laymen and probably often related to the popes and high papal officials. About Sergius nothing else is known.

133. A Slavic people who lived to the east of the Elbe River and along the southern shore of the Baltic. They allied with Charles in about 789.

134. Possibly the later margrave of Friuli.

135. Apparently not a place-name but a characterization of a "broad region."

a place called Paderborn, where he had gathered all his people in a general assembly.[136] To that same place came the princes of the eastern Slavs and all their most important men.[137]

In that same year, King Abulaz[138] of the Saracens sought a three-year peace from the emperor, which was at first granted but then rejected as useless, and so war was declared on the Saracens.[139] At that time Bishop Norbert and Count Ricoin came back from Constantinople bearing a most welcome pact of alliance between him [the Byzantine emperor] and the Franks. In that same period, when the apostolic Leo was burdened by a serious illness, the Romans, without waiting for any judgment, tried to seize and restore to themselves all the farms that they call *domuscultae* and that had recently been instituted by this same apostolic, complaining that these had been snatched from them against the law.[140] King Bernard put a stop to their undertaking through Duke Winigis of Spoleto[141] and sent a sure report about all these things to the emperor.

(26) After the emperor spent the harsh winter in restful health and calm success, and with the approach of summer's most welcome charms, those who are called the eastern Franks and the counts of the Saxon people were sent by him against the Slavic Sorbs, who were said to have withdrawn from his authority. With Christ's help their attempt was suppressed very quickly and easily. And then the nearer Basques, who live in places close to the ridge of the Pyrenees, slipped away from us completely on account of their ingrained fickleness. The cause of the rebellion was this: the emperor removed from authority over them their count, Sigwin,[142] to punish him for his foul and almost unbearable moral failings. They were nevertheless so overwhelmed by two campaigns that they began tardily to regret their conduct and pleaded mightily to return to submission.

136. July 815.

137. Other sources specify Abotrits, Sorbs, Wilzi, Bohemians, and Moravians.

138. Al-Hakam I, called Abul 'Asi, emir of Cordoba (798–822).

139. The Astronomer is confused here. A three-year truce had been concluded in 812, and when it ran out in 815, the Franks, instead of renewing it, attacked Barcelona.

140. Since the time of Pope Zachary (741–52), popes had been reorganizing clusters of rural farms into compact estates called *domuscultae*. Leo had poor relations with the Roman nobility. Noble land-holdings had often formed the basis for the *domuscultae*, and while nobles were being elected pope, the same families basically maintained control of their lands. Social turmoil, about which there is lit-tle information, surely lies behind this attack on Leo's new *domuscultae*.

141. Duke from 788/89 to 822 and a loyal agent of Frankish power in central Italy.

142. Other sources call him, as well as his successor, Sigwin II, duke of the Basques. Each may also have been count of Bordeaux.

In the midst of these things the death of the lord Leo, the bishop of Rome, which happened on the twenty-fifth of May in the twenty-first year of his episcopate, and the substitution of the deacon Stephen in his place were announced to the emperor.[143] After his consecration he did not hesitate to come to the emperor; after scarcely two full months he hastened with the greatest possible speed to meet him. He even sent a legation on ahead to make satisfaction to the emperor concerning his ordination. The emperor, however, having been warned in advance of his coming, ordered his nephew Bernard to accompany him, and then, as they were approaching, he directed other envoys to lead him forward with suitable respect. He himself decided to await his arrival at Reims. He ordered Hildebald, the archchaplain[144] of the sacred palace, Theodulf, the bishop of Orléans, John of Arles,[145] and a multitude of other ministers of the church to process to meet him, garbed in their priestly vestments. Finally, the emperor processed one mile from the monastery of the holy confessor Remigius and received him most honorably as the vicar of blessed Peter, helped him dismount from his horse, supported him with his own hand on entering the church, with various orders of the church singing out in abundant joy *Te Deum Laudamus*[146] and the rest. When this hymn was finished, the Roman clergy sang to the emperor the appropriate praises,[147] which the lord apostolic concluded with a prayer.

When these things were finished, and after retreating deep into the church, the pope explained the reasons for his coming. They participated together in the blessing of the bread and the wine,[148] and the emperor went back to the city while the lord apostolic stayed there. On the next day, the lord emperor summoned the lord apostolic, prepared a most lavish banquet, and honored him with many gifts. In similar fashion, the emperor was invited by the lord apostolic on the third day and was given many different kinds of gifts. On the

143. Stephen IV (816–17) was consecrated on June 22, a rather long vacancy in the Carolingian period. The word used by the Astronomer, *subrogatio,* is interesting in that one might have expected *electio* or simply *consecratio.* This was the first change in the papal office since Charlemagne's imperial coronation, and it might have been unclear in Rome exactly how papal elections were to proceed and what role, if any, the emperor was going to demand. Perhaps the Astronomer is trying to capture a sense of this uncertainty.

144. The title of *arch*chaplain was actually first used by Hildebald's successor Hilduin.

145. Archbishop of Arles from 811 to 819.

146. "We Praise Thee, O God": The great hymn of praise and thanksgiving possibly composed by Ambrose of Milan in the fourth century.

147. *Laudes imperatori debitas:* Possibly the *Laudes regiae,* a litany in praise of the king that emerged at the Frankish court in the late eighth century; cf. Thegan, cc. 16, 17.

148. A meal or the Eucharist?

next day, which was Sunday,[149] he was crowned with an imperial diadem and signed with a blessing during the celebration of Mass.[150] And finally, when these things had been accomplished, the lord apostolic went back to Rome, having obtained everything he had asked for. The emperor withdrew to Compiègne and there received and listened to the envoys of Abd ar-Rahman,[151] the son of King Abulaz. After staying there for twenty or more days, he went back to Aachen to spend the winter.

(27) The emperor wisely ordered the envoys of the king of the Saracens to go on ahead of him to Aachen, while he himself was on his way there. When they arrived there, they were detained for almost three months, and when his [delayed] arrival had already begun to weary them, they went home with the emperor's permission.[152] While he was staying in that palace, he also received the envoy of Emperor Leo of Constantinople, whose name was Nicephorus. Apart from friendship and alliance, the legation treated the boundaries of the Dalmatians, Romans, and Slavs. But because they [the Slavs] were not present, nor was Cadalo,[153] the prefect of those border regions, and because without them affairs could not be brought into order, Albgar[154] was sent to Dalmatia to pacify and organize the situation, along with Chadalo, the prince of those very same borderlands. In that same year, the sons of Godfred, formerly king of the Northmen, since they were being worn down by Harald, sent envoys to seek peace from the emperor. But this legation was rejected by him as useless and phony, and he gave Harald help against them. On the fifth of February in that year, in the second hour of the night, there was an eclipse of the moon, and a most unusual comet appeared in the sign of Auriga.[155] Pope Stephen finished his last day in the third month after he had come back from Francia, and Paschal[156] succeeded him in the see of the Roman pontificate.

149. Probably October 5, 816. Thus, the first meeting at St.-Rémi took place on Thursday, October 2; Louis's banquet for the pope, on Friday, October 3; and the pope's banquet for Louis, on Saturday, October 4. Other Sundays and sequences of days in October are possible, but the pope was back in Rome by mid-November, and the trip normally took several weeks.

150. It is instructive to compare closely the differing accounts of these proceedings in the Astronomer, Thegan, and Ermoldus.

151. Emir of Cordoba (822–52).

152. The slight confusion in this passage results from the Astronomer's having misread the account in the *Royal Frankish Annals,* which he was following here. That is, the annalist says the Saracen envoys despaired, after having been detained for three months, of their own return, not of Louis's.

153. A member of the powerful Alaholfing family and margrave of Friuli until his death, in 819.

154. A member of one of the greatest families of the empire, the Unruochinger. He served in Alemannia, northern Italy, and Carinthia, and died after 842.

155. Also called the Charioteer, a constellation in the Northern Hemisphere.

156. Pope from 817 to 824.

After his solemn consecration had been completed, he sent the emperor messengers with a letter of apology and many gifts, suggesting that he had not risen to this dignity by his own ambition or will but that he had been elevated to it by the election of the clergy and the acclamation of the people.[157] The leader of this legation was the nomenclator Theodore,[158] who went home after his business was finished and he had obtained what he asked for in connection with confirming the pact of friendship in the manner of his predecessors.[159]

(28) At almost the end of Lent in the same year, on Thursday of the last week, when the memory of the Lord's supper is celebrated, when everything had been finished that the solemnity of so great a day required, the emperor wished to go back from the church to the palace. The lower course of the wooden porticus[160] along which he had to pass, which was worn out by decay and age and rotted by continuous moisture, gave way and collapsed under the feet of the emperor and of those who were with him. Great fear struck his whole palace at the noise of the crash, with everybody fearing that the emperor might have been crushed as a result of that disaster. But he was at this time spared judgment by God, to Whom he was beloved. And although twenty or more of those who were accompanying him fell to the ground and suffered different wounds, he incurred no serious harm except in one place on his lower chest where he was struck by the hilt of his sword, a little scratch on the tip of his ear, and a blow from some piece of wood on his leg near his groin. Aid was administered to him immediately, and on application of the doctors' skill, he was restored to his former health in no time. Indeed, after twenty days he went hunting at Nijmegen.

With that business over and done, the emperor held a general assembly at Aachen[161] in which he declared with all his might how much passion there

157. For the most part, this phrasing is traditional and says no more than that Paschal did not seek the office of pope. But the mention of popular acclamation is intriguing because this old part of the process of electing a pope had been eliminated in an election decree of 769. This is likely yet another echo of the strife of Leo's pontificate.

158. See c. 25 above.

159. The *Royal Frankish Annals* report that Paschal sent two legations, the first being the one mentioned here and the second having had as its charge the renewal of Franco-papal friendship. The second legation also confirmed the *Pactum Ludovicianum,* a detailed inventory of the lands whose possession by the popes the Franks had been guaranteeing and a statement of the respective rights and obligations of the popes and the Franks in those lands. The lands and legal relationships had been the subject of negotiation since the 750s, but the *Pactum* contains the first extant and detailed testimony about them. See also note 78 to Ermoldus's *In Honor of Louis.*

160. A porticus is a roofed and colonnaded passageway. The Franks would have seen many of these in Rome.

161. July 817. Cf. Ermoldus, pages 143–44, on these reforms.

was in his heart for divine worship. Having assembled the bishops and the noblest clergy, he had composed and set out in orderly fashion a book containing the rule of canonical life in which the totality of that whole order was contained, as, upon reflection, he himself acknowledged. He even ordered to be included in it a summation of food, drink, and every necessity so that all those, both men and nuns, who serve Christ in this order, having been freed of needs, might remember to offer free service to the Lord of all. He sent this book to all the cities and monasteries of the canonical order in his empire through the hands of prudent *missi* who were to have it copied down in all the above-mentioned places and who were to demand that the duly owed and specified payments be made. This was cause for great rejoicing in the church and an immortal monument to the most pious emperor and the praise he was owed. In the same way, this very same emperor, whom God so loved, set Abbot Benedict, and with him monks who were of strict observance in every way, the task of going back and forth among all the monasteries and of transmitting to all the monasteries, whether of men or of nuns, a uniform standard for living according to the unchangeable norm of the Rule of Saint Benedict.[162]

This pious emperor also thought that ministers of Christ ought not to be liable to human service, and because many through greed abused ecclesiastical service for their own gain, he decreed that if any of servile status should, on account of knowledge and probity, be elevated to the ministry of the altar, they should first be manumitted by their own masters, whether private or ecclesiastical, and then be placed at the steps of the altar. Wishing that each and every church should have its own income, so that divine worship would not be neglected because of a lack of resources, he included in the abovementioned edict [a provision] that one *mansus*[163] should be assigned to each church with its legitimate endowment, and a male and female slave.

This was the holy emperor's exercise, this was his daily game, this was his sport: seeing to it that the state might shine forth more brilliantly in holy teaching and practice, that he who adorns himself with sublime humility by imitating Christ in humility might rise higher in eminence. Finally, at that time

---

162. On these reforms, cf. Ermoldus, pages 154–56.

163. *Mansus* can have a variety of shades of meaning in Carolingian texts. In principle, one *mansus* was the amount of land necessary to provide a living for one household. In some reasonably well documented regions, *mansi* averaged between twenty-five and forty hectares (one hectare is about 2.4 acres). We read of *mansi* held by single individuals, by more than one generation of a single family, and by two or more unrelated people. Precision is elusive in defining most Carolingian institutional relationships.

belts outfitted with golden bindings and jeweled daggers, refined clothing, and ankles decked out with spurs began to be cast aside and abandoned by the bishops and clerics.[164] For the emperor considered it to be quite monstrous if someone deputed to the ecclesiastical troop should aspire to the ornaments of worldly glory.

(29) The enemy of the human race could not bear the emperor's holy and godly devotion but pursued him everywhere and laid attacks for him by every order of the church. He also began, with every force at his disposal, to oppose the very one who was fighting him and, with as much power and cunning as he had, to wound Christ's bravest warrior through his adherents.[165] With these things already properly ordered, the emperor then, in that same assembly, wished for his firstborn son, Lothar, to be, and to be called, co-emperor,[166] and he sent forth two of his sons, Pippin into Aquitaine and Louis into Bavaria, so that the people might know whose authority they ought to obey.[167] Immediately, a defection of the Abotrits was announced to him. They had come to an understanding with the sons of Godfred and were disturbing Saxony beyond the river Elbe. The emperor sent adequate forces against them, and with God's favor their movement was stopped. He himself went hunting in the forests of the Vosges.

After the hunt had been completed according to the custom of the Franks, he returned to Aachen to pass the winter, and it was announced to him that his nephew King Bernard of Italy, whose cause, namely, that he should be made king of Italy, he himself had advanced with his father, had taken the advice of some wicked, indeed crazy, men to fall away from him. All of the leading men of the cities of the kingdom of Italy fell in with this scheme, and they placed obstacles and guards in every passageway by which Italy could be entered.[168] When he had finally gotten a reliable report, especially through

164. Cf. Notker's barbs directed against immoral bishops (1.5, 11, 14, 20, 23, 24, 25) and also against ones who coveted luxuries (1.16–18).

165. These two sentences seem to telegraph matters that come up later in the text.

166. Co-emperorship was a long-standing Byzantine institution introduced into Francia for the first time at Aachen in 813 and then again here.

167. Louis's succession was regulated by means of the *Ordinatio Imperii*, which was novel in that it gave each of his legitimate sons a royal title and a landed inheritance while reserving the imperial title for one son. The extant text of the *Ordinatio* goes on to specify many aspects of the sons' mutual relations.

168. Note that Bernard and his supporters appear to have blockaded Italy, perhaps fearing that, after the *Ordination Imperii*, Bernard would be supplanted by one of Louis's other sons. The *Ordinatio* did not mention Bernard.

the messengers Bishop Ratold[169] and Suppo,[170] he summoned his troops from everywhere, both from Gaul and from Germany, and with a very large military force he marched as far as Chalon-sur-Saône. But Bernard, when he perceived that he was unequal in strength and not up to the task he had begun, and inasmuch as many of his troops were deserting him every day, gave up hope and went to the emperor. Having laid his arms at Louis's feet and having prostrated himself before him, he admitted that he had behaved badly. His leading men followed his example, laid down their arms, and submitted to Louis's power and judgment. At the first interrogation the conspirators exposed how the rebellion had begun, what sort of a result they had wished to achieve once they had started on their course, and who was complicit in it. The ringleaders of the conspiracy were Eggideo, chief of the royal friends, Reginhar, formerly count of the emperor's palace and a son of count Meginher, and Reginhard, the head of the royal chamber.[171] There were many more, both clergy and laity, who knew about this conspiracy, and this stormy tempest swept up some bishops: Anselm of Milan, Wolfold of Cremona, and even Theodulf of Orléans.

(30) After the leaders of the conspiracy were divulged and placed under guard, the emperor returned to Aachen to spend the winter just as he had announced, and he stayed there until he had celebrated the holy solemnity of Easter. When the celebration of that feast had been concluded, he decided to lay aside the harsher sentence and to subject Bernard and his accomplices in the above-mentioned crime to blinding, although by the law and judgment of the Franks they ought to have undergone capital punishment. Many objected and wished to bring down upon them the full severity of the law. But even though the emperor acted more indulgently, the punishment that had been set aside was actually effected for some of them; for Bernard and Reginher suffered so much at the loss of their eyes that they brought down a bitter death on themselves. Moreover, after the bishops who had been caught up in this monstrosity had been deposed by the rest of the bishops, he banished them to monasteries. He ordered that none of the others should be deprived of life or mutilated by the amputation of their limbs, but according to what their offense seemed to demand, he decreed that some should be exiled and others tonsured.

169. Bishop of Verona, 789/802–40.
170. Count of Brescia; he was also count of the palace and duke of Spoleto from 822 to 824.
171. On these participants, see the notes to Thegan, c. 22. Ermoldus does not name them.

After these things, the impudent disobedience of the Bretons was reported to the emperor. They rose to such heights of insolence that they dared to call one of them king, Murman by name, and they rejected submission in every way. The emperor, for the purpose of avenging their insolence, assembled a military force from all sides and headed for the Breton frontier. He held a general assembly at Vannes,[172] entered the province, and with little time or effort devastated everything until Murman, while he was attacking the baggage train, was killed by a certain keeper of the royal horses named Coslus.[173] All of Brittany was conquered with him, gave up, and surrendered to whatever conditions the emperor might wish to impose; in the end, future servitude. The Bretons gave and he accepted hostages—who they were and how many, he decided—and he organized the whole land according to his will.

(31) With this accomplished, the emperor withdrew from the Breton frontier and went back to Angers, where Queen Irmingard, who had been worn out by a long illness, survived the emperor's return for two days but died on the third day, on the third of October. In that same year there was an eclipse of the sun on the eighth of July.[174] After attending to his wife's burial, the emperor went right back to Aachen, by a route through Rouen and Amiens, to spend the winter. On his way back, he entered the palace at Herstal and was met by envoys of Sigo,[175] the Beneventan duke, who bore as many gifts as possible, and he excused Sigo of any role in the death of his predecessor, Grimoald. Meanwhile, the envoys of other peoples were there too, that is, of the Abotrits, Goduscani, and Timotiani,[176] who had recently renounced an alliance with the Bulgars and associated themselves with us. And the envoys of Liudewit,[177] the commander of lower Pannonia, were there also accusing Cadalo,[178] falsely as it turned out, of being unbearably cruel to them. All these were heard, dealt with, and dismissed, and the emperor moved on to that very palace where he planned to spend the winter. While he was there, King Sclaomir of the

172. In August or September 818.

173. For a much fuller treatment of this encounter, see Ermoldus, page 166. Thegan is briefer, c. 25.

174. According to scientific evidence, the eclipse occurred on the seventh.

175. Duke of Benevento from 817 to 832.

176. The Abotrits here are South Slavs who lived on the north bank of the middle Danube. The Goduscani lived on the Croatian-Dalmatian coast. The Timotiani lived along the Serbian-Bulgarian frontier. These people were pressured by the recent expansion of Bulgaria.

177. A leader of the Croatians who allied himself with the Franks, rebelled in 819, and was murdered in 823 (see c. 36 below).

178. Margrave of Friuli (see c. 27 above).

Abotrits[179] was paraded before him by the Saxon leaders. Since he was accused of defection and could not answer the charge, he was sent into exile, and his kingdom was given to Ceadrag, a son of Thrasco.

(32) At the same time, a certain Basque named Lupus,[180] son of Centulus, rose up in rebellion and challenged Counts Werin[181] of Auvergne and Berengar[182] of Toulouse to battle, but in that effort he lost his brother Garsand along with many others. Although he then took flight and escaped, he was later hauled before the emperor and told to state his case. He was overcome by rational argument and condemned to exile.

In that same winter, the emperor held a general assembly of his people, and he heard reports about his whole realm from the *missi* whom he had sent out to restore what had fallen and to strengthen what was upright in the condition of the church. With holy devotion leading him on, he added whatever he thought was useful, and he left nothing untouched that might possibly contribute to the honor of the holy church of God. Meanwhile certain chapters were added to the laws in those cases where judicial affairs seemed weak, and right up to today they are retained as most indispensable. At that time, on the advice of his men, he began to think about taking a wife again, for many were afraid that he might wish to give up the governance of the realm. But he was finally compelled to accede to their will, and after he looked over the daughters of the nobles who had been brought in from everywhere,[183] he married Judith, the daughter of the most noble count Welf.[184]

In the following summer, his people came to him in the palace of Ingelheim. There he received the messengers from his army that had been sent to suppress the open treachery of Liudewit, but that affair remained more or less unresolved. Indeed, puffed up by arrogance on account of his actions, Liudewit, through his envoys, laid before the emperor certain demands that, if the emperor were prepared to fulfill them, would lead him to return to his former obedience to Louis's commands. But these seemed pointless to him, and so he

---

179. These are the frequently mentioned people who lived along the eastern frontier of Saxony. Sclaomir had murdered Thrasco in 809 or 810 and then, from about 816 or 817, shared rule over the Abotrits with Ceadrag.

180. Possibly a descendant of the Lupus mentioned in c. 2 above.

181. Either a relative of or in fact the often-mentioned count of Mâcon; cf. cc. 44, 49, 51, 52 below.

182. Successor to Bego, who died in October 816.

183. This is the first recorded example in Frankish history of the so-called bride show, a practice supposedly imported from Byzantium. It is quite possible that there was no such thing, in Byzantium or elsewhere. This may be a literary confection.

184. February 819. Cf. Thegan, c. 26.

tossed them aside and did not accept them. Liudewit decided to remain disloyal, and he associated with himself in perfidy whomever he could. Indeed, after the return of the army from the frontiers of Pannonia, and while Liudewit was still in opposition, Duke Cadalo of Friuli succumbed to a fever and lived his last day. Baldric took his place. When he first came into the province and entered the lands of the Carinthians, he put the forces of Liudewit to flight near the river Drava with only a few men. Harrying the rest, he compelled them all to leave his territory. Chased out by Baldric, Liudewit confronted Borna, the duke of Dalmatia, who was camped on the Kupa River. Borna had been deserted because of either the treachery or the fear of the Goduscani—it is not clear which—and he escaped the impending reckoning of accounts safe and sound only by using a force of personal bodyguards. Later on he dealt with those who had deserted him.

Meanwhile Liudewit entered Dalmatia again, in the following winter, and he tried to destroy everything by cutting down with the sword every living thing and by setting fire to every inanimate thing. Since Borna was unable to meet his attack, he looked for a way to harm him by cunning. He did not declare open war on him but harassed him and his army with sneak attacks such that Liudewit was ashamed and sorry that he had undertaken such things. With three thousand of his soldiers killed and many horses and lots of equipment of various kinds destroyed, he was forced by Borna to leave the region. The emperor, who was then at Aachen, heard all these things most joyfully.

Meanwhile the Basques, even disagreeing among themselves in their native plague of sedition, were so cowed in that same year by the emperor's son Pippin that none of them dared to rebel. That is just what his father sent him there for. After these things were done, the emperor dismissed the assembly, gave himself an appropriate time for hunting in the Ardennes, and then went back to Aachen to spend the winter.

(33) In that same palace, with winter coming on, the emperor gathered together an assembly of his people.[185] At that time Borna, who complained bitterly about the attack of Liudewit, received from the emperor substantial forces to help him grind down Liudewit's land. The forces were in the first place divided into three, and they devastated almost all the land under his authority by fire and sword, but Liudewit protected himself by the heights of a certain fortress and would not come forth to fight or to talk. After these forces returned

185. January 820.

home, the people of Carniola and certain of the Carinthians who had gone over to Liudewit surrendered to our duke Baldric. At that assembly Bero, the count of Barcelona, when he was called out by a certain man by the name of Sanilo and accused of infidelity, met with him in battle on horseback according to their own law, since both of them were Goths, and was defeated. But when the law ought to have been turned against him and he should have borne a capital sentence for treason, his life was spared by the emperor's mercy, and he was ordered to go and stay in Rouen.[186] At that time it was announced to the emperor that thirteen pirate ships from the lands of the Northmen had sailed across the sea and planned to attack and lay waste our coasts. When the emperor commanded that lookouts and guards be arrayed against them, they were driven from Flemish soil and from the mouth of the Seine. They turned to Aquitaine, wasted a village named Bouin, and went home having loaded up a great deal of booty.[187]

(34) In this year the lord emperor spent the winter season in Aachen.[188] In that same winter, in February, an assembly was held at Aachen, and three armed bands were dispatched to lay waste the land of Liudewit. The phony peace that appeared to have been concluded with Abulaz, the king of the Saracens, was broken, and war was declared on him. In the same year, on the first of May, the emperor held another assembly at Nijmegen, in which he had the partition of the realm that he had already made among his sons adjusted and confirmed in the presence of all his nobles who were there. He also received, heard, and dismissed the envoys of the apostolic Paschal, Bishop Peter of Civitavecchia,[189] and the nomenclator Leo.[190] Departing from there, he went back to Aachen, and from there through the Vosges to Remiremont and to the vast expanse of the Vosges, where he spent what was left of the summer and about half of the fall. In the midst of these things, Borna lost his life, and the emperor made his nephew Ladasclao his successor. He also then received news of the death of Emperor Leo of Constantinople, who was killed by his domestic servants and especially by Michael. Michael was put in his place with the particular assistance of his accomplices, chiefly the imperial bodyguards.[191]

---

186. Cf. Ermoldus, pages 168–69.

187. Imprecise: These attacks took place in the summer of 820. The North Sea and English Channel were generally too treacherous for winter raiding. Bouin is just south of the mouth of the Loire, opposite the island of Noirmoutier.

188. That is, the winter of 820–21.

189. Ca. 821–36.

190. See c. 37 below.

191. Leo V was murdered December 25, 820, and followed by Michael II (820–29).

In the month of October of that year, an assembly was held at Thionville.[192] There the emperor solemnly joined in marriage Irmingard, the daughter of Count Hugh,[193] to his firstborn son, Lothar. Envoys were also there from the Roman pope, the primicerius Theodore,[194] and Florus,[195] with many different kinds of gifts. Indeed, although the emperor's mercy always sparkled in other admirable ways, in this assembly it became especially clear how much there was of it in his breast. For after he had recalled everyone who had conspired against his life or his realm, he not only granted them life and limb, but he also, as a great mark of generosity, restored their possessions, of which they had been legally deprived. He restored Adalhard,[196] formerly abbot of Corbie but then living in the monastery of St.-Filibert,[197] to his monastery and earlier office. Likewise he summoned his brother Bernhar[198] from the monastery of St. Benedict, reconciled himself with him, and restored him to Corbie with his brother. These things having been completed and other things usefully finished, he sent his son Lothar to spend the winter at Worms, and he himself went back to Aachen.

(35) In the next year, the lord emperor ordered an assembly to come together at a place called Attigny.[199] He called the bishops to council there, and the abbots and clergy, and also the nobles of his realm, in the first place because he was anxious to be reconciled with his brothers whom he had had tonsured against their will,[200] and then with all of those who appeared to have suffered any harm. After this he openly confessed that he himself had erred, and imitating the example of the emperor Theodosius,[201] he accepted a penance of his own volition both for those things and also for the things that he had done to his own nephew Bernard. He also corrected anything of

192. Louis several times held more than one general assembly in a given year. This had been unusual earlier.

193. Cf. Thegan, c. 28, with note 59.

194. See c. 25 above.

195. The *Royal Frankish Annals* call him the *superista,* who was the secular commander of the papal palace and probably the leader of a modest armed bodyguard.

196. A cousin of and key adviser to Charlemagne; after 821 one of Louis's most trusted advisers.

197. Adalhard was abbot of Corbie from 780 to 826. From 817 to 821 he was in exile at St.-Filibert, Noirmoutier, near the mouth of the Loire.

198. Virtually nothing is known about this person. Adalhard's other brother, Wala, was one of the great figures of the age.

199. August 822.

200. Half brothers, actually: Drogo, Hugo, and Theoderich. See Thegan, c. 24.

201. Roman emperor (379–95) who was required by Archbishop Ambrose of Milan to undergo public penance in 390. Thus Louis did not imitate his example.

the sort that he could discover anywhere, whether done by himself or by his father, both by generous almsgiving and by the continuous prayers of Christ's servants, and even by making amends himself. He was concerned to return to God's grace, as if those things which each person had legally suffered had in fact been done through his own cruelty.

At the same time, he sent an army from Italy into Pannonia against Liude-wit. Since he was unable to maintain himself there, he left his own city[202] and went to a certain chieftain of Dalmatia and was admitted to his city. Then, however, he turned the tables on his host, brought him to grief, and subjected the city to his own domination. And although he would neither fight nor talk with our men, nevertheless he sent envoys to say that he had made a mistake and he promised that he would come to the lord emperor. It was announced to the emperor at the same time that the guardians of the Spanish March had crossed the river Segre, penetrated deeply into Spain, and returned in fine fashion with great booty, having devastated and burned all the cities that presented themselves along the way. What is more, those who were keeping watch in the Breton March entered Brittany and laid waste the region with sword and fire on account of the rebellion of a certain Breton whose name was Wiomarc'h. This accomplished, they returned successfully.

When this assembly was finished, the lord emperor sent his son Lothar to Italy with his kinsman the monk Wala, and with Gerung, the *ostiarius*.[203] With their advice he was to put in order, promote, and watch over Italy's public and private affairs. He also decided to send his son Pippin into Aquitaine, but first he joined him in marriage to a daughter of Count Theotbert[204] and then sent him off to rule his assigned regions. With these things taken care of, he spent the autumn hunting in the way of the kings of the Franks, and to pass the winter, he sought out a place across the Rhine whose name is Frankfurt. There he ordered an assembly of the neighboring peoples to come together, of all of those, that is, who lived beyond the Rhine and who obeyed the command of the Franks. He discussed with them everything that appeared to contribute to the public good, while he took thought suitably for the affairs of each. In that same meeting, a legation of the Avars appeared bearing gifts.[205] Envoys

202. According to the *Royal Frankish Annals,* Sisak in Croatia, on the confluence of the Drava and the Sava.
203. Cf. Ermoldus, n. 158.
204. Her name was Ringart. Theotbert was count of Madrie, near Chartres.
205. This is the last historical reference to these people.

of the Northmen seeking to renew and confirm the peace did not fail to show up. He listened to them all and then sent them away appropriately. He wintered in that same place after having prepared the buildings with new works that were worthy and fit for the season.

(36) In that same estate, that is, Frankfurt, after winter had ended, the emperor in May held an assembly of the eastern Franks, the Saxons, and of the other peoples who bordered on them. There he brought to a fitting end a struggle between two brothers who were fiercely contending for the kingship. They were Wilzi[206] by birth, sons of King Liubi, and their names were Milegast and Celeadrag. When their father, Liubi, declared war on the Abotrits, he was killed by them, and the kingdom was conveyed to the firstborn. But when he showed himself to be more sluggish in the administration of the kingdom than the situation demanded, the favor of the people shifted on behalf of the younger son. They came into the emperor's presence on account of this altercation. He investigated, discovered the will of the people, and declared the younger to be chief. The emperor endowed both with ample gifts, bound them by oaths, and dismissed them as friends, both to himself and to each other.

Meanwhile Lothar, the son of the lord emperor, when, as was said above, he was sent to Italy by his father, arranged for advantageous negotiations according to the advice of the men who had been sent with him. Some things he completed and some were still unfinished, and he was thinking about how to respond to his father concerning each thing on his return. He went to Rome for the holy solemnity of Easter on the urgent request of Pope Paschal.[207] He was received by that same pope with a brilliant display, and on that very holy day at St. Peter's he received an imperial crown and the name of augustus. After this, when he had returned to Pavia, he stayed there for a little while on account of weighty demands on himself, and thus he returned to his father in June, telling him what he had accomplished and asking him about what he had left unfinished. To complete what had been less than fully accomplished, Adalhard, the count of the palace, was sent, and Mauring was associated with him.[208]

---

206. A West Slavic people who lived between the Elbe and the Baltic and who were, after 789, usually allied with the Franks. See Einhard, c. 12.

207. April 5, 823.

208. This Adalhard is probably the man who was made duke of Spoleto in 824 and who died later that year. Mauring is probably the count of Brescia (822–24) who succeeded Adalhard as duke of Spoleto but survived his appointment by only a few days.

At just about the same time, Gundulf, the bishop of Metz, died, and all the clergy and people of that city, as if enlivened by a single spirit, asked to be given Drogo, the emperor's brother, as bishop. He was then living honorably as a canon.[209] It was marvelous how the consensus of the emperor, his nobles, and the whole people came together as one, so that everyone desired this and no one could be found who opposed it. So the emperor yielded with great joy to the request of the church and gave them as bishop the one whom they sought. In that same assembly the death of the tyrant Liudewit was announced. He was killed by some trickery. The emperor dissolved this assembly and called for another one at Compiègne in the autumn.

(37) At that same time,[210] the emperor was informed that Theodore, the primicerius of the Holy Roman Church, and Leo, the nomenclator, were blinded and then beheaded in the episcopal residence at the Lateran.[211] Envy had flared up among the murderers, it was said, because those who had been killed had suffered for their loyalty to Lothar. Even the reputation of the pope suffered in this affair because it was alleged that the whole thing had happened with his consent. While the emperor was getting ready to send Abbot Adalung[212] of the monastery of St.-Vaast and Count Hunfrid[213] of Chur to investigate this matter down to the last detail, the envoys of Pope Paschal arrived, namely, Bishop John of Silva Candida[214] and Benedict, the archdeacon of the Holy Roman Church.[215] They countered the accusation with an

---

209. He was also well below the canonical age of thirty for election as a bishop. Canons were members of the clergy, usually but not always serving in a cathedral (i.e., bishop's) church. One effect of Louis's ecclesiastical legislation (c. 28 above) was to make clerics decide whether to be monks or canons. If they chose the former life, they had to follow the Rule of Saint Benedict. If they chose the latter life, they had to follow the Rule for Canons written by Chrodegang of Metz in the 750s.

210. June/July 823.

211. The reference, if it is accurate, is a bit odd. Sources occasionally refer to the Lateran "Palace" and frequently to the "patriarchate" (*patriarchium*). Here, however, the Astronomer says explicitly *in domo episcopali Lateranensi.*

212. Abbot of Lorsch from 804 to 837 and of St.-Vaast from 808 to 833. One of Louis's key advisers. He was also a close associate of Thegan's.

213. Either Hunfrid I (806–23) or Hunfrid II (823/24) of Rhaetia, leaders among the nobility of Alemannia.

214. He appears, in c. 25 above, as one of Leo III's envoys to Louis in 815.

215. Nothing is known about Benedict, but he was clearly an important man. The papal government at this time was divided into branches dealing with administration, worship, and charity. The archdeacon headed the latter. He was also one of the three men who administered the church between the death of one pope and the installation of another (the other two were the archpriest and the primicerius of the notaries).

The Astronomer in this chapter regularly uses the phrase *Sancta Romana Ecclesia,* which was the more or less official name for the papal church in and around Rome. Visitors to Rome today will still see SRE in inscriptions around the city.

explanation and invited the emperor to look into these things. After he had listened to them and dismissed them with a suitable response, he instructed his own designated *missi* to go to Rome, as had already been ordered, and to look into the truth of these dubious affairs. He himself, so it seems, spent some time in a few places and then at the predetermined time, that is the first of November, came to Compiègne.

In that assembly the legates who had been sent to Rome appeared, announcing to him that Pope Paschal and a good many bishops had by oath purged themselves of responsibility for the death of those who had been killed. The pope also said he could not hand over the murderers, and he asserted that those who had been killed had met their fate deservedly. At the time, the envoys sent by the apostolic appeared, telling a similar story. The names of these legates were John, the bishop of Silva Candida, Sergius,[216] the librarian, Quirinus,[217] a subdeacon, and Leo, the master of the soldiers.[218] The emperor, who was most merciful by nature, was unable to pursue any further the cause of the dead, although he very much wished to do so; thus he decided to abandon inquiries of this sort, and he let the Roman envoys go with fitting instructions.

At about that time strange signs and omens stirred up the emperor's spirit, especially an earthquake at the palace of Aachen, weird sounds at night, a certain girl who fasted for twelve months, virtually abstaining from food, frequent and unusual lightning, stones falling with hail, and diseases of people and animals. On account of these remarkable occurrences, the pious emperor urged that frequent fasts and continuous prayers and generous alms be offered through the priestly office to placate God, saying on his own behalf that on account of these prodigies an enormous future catastrophe was in store for the human race.

In that same year, in the month of June, Queen Judith bore him a son, whom it pleased him to name Charles at the time of his baptism.[219] In the same year,[220] Counts Eblus and Asinarius[221] were ordered to cross the heights of the Pyrenees. With great forces they went right up to Pamplona, and having settled their business, they experienced the normal treachery and innate

216. A deacon who was papal librarian from 817 to 829. The librarian had only emerged as a separate officer in the papal government during the time of Pope Hadrian I.

217. In 828/29 he appears as primicerius under Gregory IV; clearly an important, if shadowy, figure.

218. There is no certain information about the troops a pope might have had at his disposal in this period.

219. Born June 13, 823. Lothar was his godfather.

220. Actually in 824.

221. No solid information is available about them.

deceit of the inhabitants of the region when they were returning. They were surrounded by the local people, and after having lost their supplies, they fell into the hands of the enemy. They sent Eblus to the king of the Saracens at Cordoba, but they spared Asinarius because he was a blood relative of theirs.

(38) Meanwhile, when Lothar had arrived at Rome, having been sent there by his father as already mentioned, he was received most willingly and honorably by Pope Eugenius.[222] While he was complaining about what had happened, that is, about why those who were faithful to the emperor and to himself and to the Franks had been cut down by foul murder and why those who survived were ridiculed by the rest and why so many complaints were noised about concerning the Roman bishops and officials, he discovered that the estates of many had been unjustly confiscated by the ignorance or idleness of certain popes or even by the blind and insatiable greed of the officials.[223] Therefore, in returning what had been unjustly taken away, Lothar created immense happiness for the Roman people. It was also decreed that, according to the ancient custom, men would be sent by the emperor to exercise judicial power and to dispense justice equally for all the people for as long as it seemed fitting to the emperor.[224] When the son had returned and made a full report to his father, who loved equity and cherished piety so much, he was filled with great joy because he had fostered a reinstatement of proper devotion.

(39) Later the emperor ordered an assembly to be celebrated by his people in May[225] at Aachen. While it was meeting, a legation from the Bulgarians, who had for a long time lived in Bavaria according to his instructions, was brought in to be heard. They were especially concerned about the boundaries to be observed between the Bulgarians and the Franks after the establishment of peace. Present as well, and promising submission and obedience with many words, were not a few leaders of the Bretons, among whom was Wiomarc'h, who seemed to exceed the others in authority, the very one who had by reckless boldness and stupid audacity gone so far as to provoke the emperor to send an expedition into those regions to suppress his insolence. Therefore, when he

---

222. Eugenius II, 824–27.

223. The economic well-being of Rome depended on agricultural productivity in the city's hinterland. From at least the 760s there is evidence of intense rivalry for control of estates in Rome's environs. See c. 25 above for Leo III's troubles in this regard.

224. Arrangements were more complicated than this. The surviving *Constitutio Romana* spells out in considerable detail the main features of a more carefully defined set of papal and imperial rights and responsibilities in Rome.

225. 825.

said that he regretted his deeds and that he would commit himself loyally to the emperor, he was received mercifully by him in his usual fashion—for he was always accustomed to bestow clemency—and he, along with others of his countrymen, was endowed with gifts. He was allowed to go home. But later, not unmindful of his customary perfidy yet forgetful of all that he had promised and of the good things that he had experienced, he did not miss a chance to complain about his neighbors, the emperor's faithful men, and to harass them with persistent harm. So it happened that, overwhelmed by the men of Lambert, he met the end of all his evils and the term of his life in his own house.

So, having dismissed the envoys of the Bulgarians and of the Bretons, the emperor went off hunting in the wilds of the Vosges, believing that he could do that until the month of August, when he would return to Aachen to hold an assembly, as he had planned. At that time he ordered that the peace which the Northmen were seeking be confirmed in October. After everything had been accomplished that seemed necessary to do or define in that assembly, he himself, with his son Lothar, went to Nijmegen, while young Louis was sent to Bavaria. After completing the autumn hunt, he returned to the palace at Aachen at the beginning of winter.

When the envoys of the Bulgarians returned from that assembly bearing the emperor's letters, their king received what was written with little pleasure, because he had not obtained what he had sought. With a certain irritation he sent back that same messenger and demanded that either a common boundary be established or he would, with whatever force he could muster, see to his own frontiers. But then the rumor spread that the king who had made such demands had lost his kingdom, so the emperor retained the envoy for a bit, until he could send Bertric,[226] the count of the palace, who learned that what was going around was false. Having learned the truth, he dismissed the envoy with the affair still unfinished.

(40) In the same year,[227] the emperor's son Pippin came to his father, who was wintering at Aachen. Before he went home, the emperor carefully instructed him to be ready in case any novelty should arise in Spain and suggested how he might deal with it. On the first of June the emperor came to Ingelheim and an assembly of his people met him there, just as he had instructed. In that same assembly, according to his custom, he recalled, regulated,

226. This is the only time Bertric is mentioned. The count of the palace was always an important adviser to the ruler and chiefly a judicial officer.
227. Actually 826.

and defined many things that were beneficial to the church. He also received, heard, and dismissed legations from the holy Roman see and from the Mount of Olives,[228] sent by Abbot Dominic. Moreover, two dukes, Ceadrag of the Abotrits and Tunglo of the Sorbs, when they were accused and the verdict did not appear clear enough, were chastised and sent home. Harald also came from the lands of the Northmen with his wife and a considerable band of Danes. At St. Alban's at Mainz he, with all of his men, was washed by the waters of holy baptism and was given many gifts by the emperor.[229] The emperor was, however, afraid that because of this deed Harald might be denied residence in his native land, so he gave him a certain county in Frisia whose name was Rüstringen, where he and his people could shelter in safety if it should be necessary to do so.

Meanwhile, when Baldric[230] and Gerold[231] and other guardians of the Pannonian frontiers appeared, Baldric presented to the emperor a certain priest named George, a man of good life, who promised that he could build an organ in the Greek style.[232] The emperor received him gladly and gave thanks because God had accorded to him what was previously unusual in the kingdom of the Franks, and he commended him to Tanculf, who supervised the treasury,[233] ordered him to be paid at public expense, and commanded that he be supplied with whatever was necessary to his work.

In the middle of October in that same year, he ordered an assembly of the German people to gather across the Rhine, in a villa whose name was Salz.[234] While it was in progress, the treachery and defection of Aizo[235] was announced. He had fled from the palace of the lord emperor and gone to the city of Vich. There he was received, overthrew Roda, and inflicted no little harm on those who resisted him. The fortifications he was able to seize he strengthened by introducing garrisons, and he sent his brother to the king of the Saracens, Abd ar-Rahman by name, and received a strong army for use against us. These

228. This was a Frankish monastery near Jerusalem that had communicated with Pope Leo III and Charlemagne in 809 on theological issues.

229. Cf. Ermoldus, pages 173–83; Notker, 2.19.

230. The margrave of Friuli.

231. The count of the Ostmark.

232. Cf. Ermoldus, page 000 and note 166.

233. Tanculf appears in other sources of this period as *camerarius,* or treasurer. The Astronomer calls him *sacrorum scriniorum praelato,* which might imply that he oversaw the writing and record-keeping office in the palace.

234. This assembly actually met at Ingelheim, and after it was concluded, Louis went to Salz.

235. A Goth who had presumably been present at the February assembly.

things indeed stirred up the emperor's spirit and prompted him to revenge, but he thought that nothing should be done too hastily, and he decided to wait and hear the opinion of his counselors concerning what ought to be done in such a situation.

Around the same time, Hilduin,[236] abbot of the monastery of blessed Denis, sent monks to Rome, to Eugenius, the chief priest of the holy Roman see, bearing his petition and asking that the bones of the most blessed martyr Sebastian be sent to him. The lord apostolic made good on his request and sent the relics of this most holy soldier of Christ through the above-mentioned envoys. These were received with the greatest devotion by the previously mentioned man, and he right away placed them, in the portable casket in which they had arrived, next to the body of the blessed Médard.[237] For those who were present at their arrival, God granted such a multitude of miracles that their number was beyond counting. Indeed, their nature would outstrip belief unless those people who are convinced that nothing can oppose the divine command and, to be sure, that "all things are possible to one who believes"[238] heard about them with their own ears.

(41) Meanwhile[239] Aizo was attacking our people who lived in the frontier areas, and he was particularly devastating the region right up to Cerdaña and Vallés; his cruelty went so far that, with supporting troops of Moors and Saracens, he forced some of our men to relinquish the castles and cities that they had held up to then. Many defected from us and associated themselves with them. Among them Willemund,[240] the son of Bero, along with many others, joined in their treason. The lord emperor was moved to suppress them and to strengthen our men, so he decided that an army had to be sent there, and he sent on in advance Abbot Helisachar,[241] Count Hildebrand,[242] and also

236. One of the most important advisers of Louis and influential men in the realm. He became archchaplain in 819 and held this office until 830, when he joined the rebellion against Louis. He was reconciled to Louis in 831 and regained his influence but not his office. He was abbot of several monasteries in addition to St.-Denis, notably St.-Germain-des-Prés and St.-Médard de Soissons.

237. That is, at St.-Médard de Soissons, of which Hilduin was also abbot; December 9, 826. Médard was a bishop of Noyon who died sometime before 561. His remains were transferred to Soissons.

238. Mark 9:22.

239. 827.

240. See c. 33, which says that Bero was deposed in 820.

241. A Goth who was Louis's chancellor from 808 to 819 and then abbot of St.-Aubin d'Angers, Jumièges, and possibly of St.-Riquier and St.-Maximin in Trier. He died before 840. He is mentioned several times by Ermoldus (pages 151, 163, 172, 179) and once by Thegan (c. 36). See note 77 to Ermoldus's *In Honor of Louis.*

242. A count who is attested from 796 to 827 but whose seat is unknown.

Donatus.[243] With them going on ahead, they joined forces with the Goths and Spaniards and resisted their [i.e., Aizo and his forces'] impudence sharply, and with the magnificent count of Barcelona, Bernard,[244] in the lead, their attempts were reduced to nothing. Seeing this, Aizo departed to request crack troops from the Saracens, which he received, under the command of their leader Abu Marvan,[245] and he led them to Saragossa and then further to Barcelona. The emperor, furthermore, sent his son Pippin of Aquitaine against them and, at the same time, sent *missi* of his own, Counts Hugh and Matfrid.[246] They advanced more slowly and haltingly than was fitting, and the Moors profited from the delay as long as possible, such that they devastated the region of Barcelona and Gerona and then returned unharmed to Saragossa. Just before this catastrophe, there appeared in the night sky terrible battle lines reddened with human blood flashing with the color of fire. The emperor learned of these things while he was receiving the annual gifts at Compiègne, and he sent auxiliary forces to guard the above-mentioned march and then announced that until the onset of winter he was going hunting in the forests around Compiègne and Quierzy.

In August of the same year, Pope Eugenius finished his last day, and the deacon Valentine succeeded him. But he scarcely survived a month, and in his place the priest Gregory of the title of St. Mark[247] was elected, but his consecration was put off until the emperor could be consulted. When he had looked into and approved the election of the clergy and people, Gregory was ordained in the place of his predecessor.[248] In September of that same year, legates of Emperor Michael came to Compiègne bearing gifts. They were received nobly, feted lavishly, given generous gifts, and sent home after a successful mission.

243. Perhaps the man used again as a *missus* in Aquitaine in 838 (cf. c. 59 below).

244. Bernard is mentioned repeatedly by Thegan, cc. 36, 38, 52; see note 76 to Thegan's *Deeds*.

245. A relative of the emir of Cordoba.

246. Respectively, counts of Tours and Orléans. Hugh was Lothar's father-in-law. Matfrid profited from and may have engineered the fall of Theodulf in 818.

247. Gregory IV (827–44). There were some twenty-five or more title churches in Rome, each led by a priest who was a member of the pope's clerical entourage and administration. St. Mark's was in the middle of an aristocratic region—Pope Hadrian I had trained there—at the foot of the Capitoline Hill. Gregory adorned this church with a beautiful mosaic, still extant.

248. This is a slightly muddled account of what the *Constitutio Romana* of 824 required. That is, the Carolingians did not claim the right to approve or reject elected candidates for the papacy, as the Byzantines had once done. Rather, they insisted on their right, as papal allies and protectors, to ensure that elections had been lawful and peaceful.

In that year Einhard, the wisest man of his time, aroused by the ardor of holy devotion, sent to Rome for the bodies of Marcellinus and Peter. The pope agreed, and Einhard had them conveyed into Francia and reinterred very honorably, at his personal expense, on his own property. By their merits the Lord has been working many miracles there right up to today.[249]

(42) In February of the following winter,[250] there was a public assembly at Aachen, where, among other things, affairs in the Spanish March, which recently were timorously and shamefully conducted, elicited heated discussion. When these issues were aired and investigated down to the smallest detail, the leaders who had been set in charge by the emperor were discovered to have been responsible for the failure. Having stripped them of their offices, the emperor ordered them to make amends for their faintheartedness. Also, a charge was lodged and investigated against Duke Baldric of Friuli, that on account of his laxity and carelessness the Bulgarians had wasted our land. He was expelled from his duchy, and his power was divided among four of his counts. But, then, the spirit of the emperor was most mild by nature, and he was always eager to request mercy for those who had sinned. And yet it will soon be seen how those who revealed themselves in such affairs abused his mercy and repaid it with cruelty. Events will show how they brought down on him the greatest slaughter of which they were capable in return for the gift of their life. At the same time, Bishop Halitgar of Cambrai[251] and Abbot Ansfrid[252] of the monastery of Nonantola came back from the lands across the sea and told how they had been most kindly received by Emperor Michael.

In the following summer, the emperor held a public assembly in Ingelheim, and envoys of the Roman pope—Quirinus,[253] the primicerius, and Theophylact,[254] the nomenclator—came with many gifts; he received and dismissed them. And when he had arrived in Thionville, he heard the report that the Saracens were about to overrun our frontiers, so he sent his son Lothar to that march and equipped him with numerous strong troops. When, obedient to

---

249. Einhard's fascinating account of this relic translation is extant.

250. 828.

251. Bishop of Cambrai from 817 to 831, he was envisioned as an envoy to Constantinople in 825, probably in connection with Michael's appeal to Louis in late 824 concerning the renewed struggle over religious images in Byzantium. It is not clear whether the embassy recorded here is the same one, extended over some years, or a different one.

252. Abbot of Nonantola from 821 to 838.

253. See c. 37 above.

254. He had a long career in papal service: a notary in 817, nomenclator from 826 to 829, secundicerius (second in command to the primicerius) and datarius (a judge) from 854 to 858.

his father's instructions, he had reached Lyon and was awaiting a messenger from the Spanish area, his brother Pippin came to meet him. While they were staying there, the messenger returned, saying that the Saracens and Moors had moved an extremely large army but had halted their march and at that time were not advancing further against our borders. Having heard these things, Pippin returned to Aquitaine, and Lothar went back successfully to his father.

Meanwhile the sons of Godfred, formerly king of the Danes, expelled Harald from the kingdom. Although the emperor wanted to help Harald, he entered into a peace treaty with the sons of Godfred. Having sent Saxon counts along with Harald himself against them, he instructed them [the counts] to treat with the sons of Godfred so that they might associate themselves with Harald as far as possible and as had previously been the case. Harald, however, was impatient with these delays and, unbeknownst to our men, set fire to some of their [Godfred's sons'] estates and hauled off booty. Thinking this to have been done by our will, they [Godfred's sons] advanced against our men, who were unprepared and suspected nothing. They crossed the river Eider, fell upon our camp, and hauled off whatever they could to their own encampment. But after this happened, knowing the truth of the matter and fearing a just retribution, they made representation, first to those who had borne the brunt of such attacks and then to the emperor. They professed that they had made a mistake, and made suitable satisfaction in recompense according to the emperor's desire so that a solid peace might thereby remain undisturbed.

Count Boniface,[255] whom the emperor had put in charge of the island of Corsica, with his brother Bernard and some others, set sail in a small fleet and, while he was looking for but not finding the pirates who were sailing the sea, landed on the island of Sardinia, where he had friends. There he gathered some experienced sailors and crossed over to Africa, between Utica and Carthage. A multitude of Africans came out to meet him, fought with him five times, were defeated as many times, and lost a large number of their men, for some of our men happened to meet those whom either excessive boldness or unwise levity had compelled to such audacity. Boniface, however, having reassembled his allies, gathered them into ships and went home, leaving behind among the Africans an unprecedented and unheard-of fear.

255. Count of Lucca, first attested in 823 and last in 838. He was always loyal to Louis. See c. 52 below.

In that year there were two eclipses of the moon, on the first of July and the twenty-fifth of December. What is more, a certain grain was brought to the emperor from Gascony, smaller than wheat but not as round as peas,[256] which, they said, had fallen from the sky. The lord emperor spent the winter at Aachen.

(43) When winter was over and the holy days of Lent were being observed, and indeed the venerable solemnity of Easter was approaching, on one terrible night the earth moved with such strength that it threatened to ruin all the buildings. And then followed a violent wind that not only shook the smaller buildings, but its force so disturbed even the palace at Aachen that the lead plates with which the basilica of Holy Mary, Mother of God, was roofed were mostly pulled off. He stayed in that palace on account of many urgent necessities and public benefits, and then he decreed that he would depart from there promptly on the first of July and go to Worms to hold a general assembly of his people in the month of August.[257] A rumor that put it about that the Northmen wished to violate the terms of the agreement and to cross over from their own lands into the regions beyond the Elbe compelled him to change his plan for a little while. But that is not how things really stood, so the emperor arrived according to his plan regarding time and place, and he dealt carefully with those things that seemed to need attention, received the annual gifts, and dismissed his son Lothar to go back to Italy.

In that same assembly he learned about the plots against him of those whose lives he had spared.[258] Their schemes were spreading like cancer and undermining the confidence of many, so he decided to erect a bulwark against them. For he set Bernard, formerly the count of the Spanish march and border regions, over his chamber. This did not stem the seeds of discord but instead increased them. Yet those who were seething with such affliction could not reveal their wounds, inasmuch as they were not supported by any forces that could accomplish what they desired, so they decided to defer their plans to another time. The emperor, however, having done what the present opportunity dictated, crossed the Rhine and sought his estate at Frankfurt, and as long as it seemed all right and the approaching cold of winter allowed, he gave himself up to hunting, and then, around Saint Martin's day,[259] he turned back

256. Probably rice, which Muslims cultivated in Spain, or else millet.
257. The Astronomer neglects to mention an assembly in the winter of 828–29 and the great round of church councils held in the early summer of 829 at Mainz, Paris, Lyon, and Toulouse.
258. These events are treated much more briefly in Thegan, cc. 36–37.
259. November 11.

to Aachen and there observed the feast of Saint Andrew,[260] the birth of the Lord, and the other feasts most joyfully, as was fitting.

(44) Later, around the time of Lent, while the emperor was making a circuit through the places lying close to the sea, the leaders of the wicked faction, able to delay no longer, laid bare their long-concealed grievance. First of all the leaders swore a kind of pact among themselves; then they won over some lesser people to themselves, a part of whom was always greedy for change after the fashion of rapacious dogs and birds who seek to increase their own advantage at someone else's loss. Relying therefore on a multitude and on the assent of many, they went to the emperor's son Pippin, insisting that he was slighted, that Bernard was arrogant, that many were disgusted, and even asserting that Bernard—it is evil to say it—had invaded his father's bed. They also said that Louis was deluded by certain tricks, so that he could neither avenge nor escape all these things. They said that it was only fitting for a good son to bear his father's disgrace with indignation, to remove such ills from his presence, to restore his father's mind and dignity. Not only would a reputation for virtue follow the one who acted this way, but also an enhancement of his earthly realm—arguing this way, they concealed their crime. The young man was swept away by these enticements, and he proceeded with them and many of their troops through Orléans, where they removed Odo[261] and restored Matfrid, and went right on to Verberie.

When the emperor learned just how unyielding the armed and deadly conspiracy against himself, his wife, and Bernard was, he let Bernard protect himself by flight, but he wished his wife to remain in Laon, in the monastery of St.-Marie, while he himself went to Compiègne. Later those who came with Pippin to Verberie sent Werin and Lambert[262] and a great many others to drag Queen Judith out of the monastery and even the basilica[263] and had her brought to themselves. After assailing her for a long time with all kinds of threats, even death, they compelled her to promise that if she were given ample opportunity to speak with the emperor, she would persuade him to lay down his arms, receive the tonsure, and take himself off to a monastery;

---

260. November 30.

261. Probably a relative of Bernard's. He succeeded Matfrid as count, was removed in 830, and died in 834.

262. Counts, respectively, of Mâcon and Nantes.

263. By mentioning both the monastery and the basilica, the Astronomer appears to be saying that the rebels violated Judith's rights of sanctuary, for a church was supposed to be a place of inviolable refuge.

she herself was also to take the veil. The more they desired this, the more easily they believed it would happen. Sending some of their men with her, they
led her to the emperor. When he asked permission to speak more privately
with her, he permitted her to take the veil in order to escape death, but the
emperor demanded more time to think about accepting the tonsure. So great
was the unjust hatred under which the emperor labored, he who has always
been kind to others, that his existence was painful to those who might legally
and justly have lost their lives but who were alive through his gift. When the
queen came back to them, they resisted further evils, but giving in to the
shouting crowd, they ordered her to be taken away and shut up in the monastery of St.-Radegond.[264]

(45) Later, around the month of May, the emperor's son Lothar came from
Italy and met him at Compiègne. As he was on his way, the whole faction hostile to the emperor went over to him. He himself does not seem to have caused
any disgrace to his father at that time, but he did approve what had been
done. Then Heribert, Bernard's brother, was punished by blinding, against the
will of the emperor, and Odo, his cousin, was disarmed and sent into exile.
They were treated as if they were accomplices and promoters of the charge
that was noised about against Bernard and the queen. With all of this going
on, the emperor, now in name only, passed the summer.

When, however, the milder temperatures of autumn approached, those who
judged themselves opposed to the emperor wished to hold a general assembly
somewhere in Francia. The emperor resisted secretly, for he distrusted the
Franks and had more confidence in the Germans. Finally, the opinion of the
emperor, that the people should assemble in Nijmegen, prevailed. Fearing,
however, that the vast number of his opponents would overwhelm the tiny
number of his loyalists, he ordered that each man who was coming to that particular assembly should have only a single retainer. He also instructed Count
Lambert to keep watch on the borders assigned to him, and he directed Abbot
Helisachar to accompany him for the purpose of doing justice. Finally, therefore, the meeting at Nijmegen commenced, and all of Germany came flowing
in to provide help for the emperor. The emperor still wished to diminish the
strength of his adversaries, and he brought a charge against Abbot Hilduin,
asking him why, when he had been ordered to appear with one retainer, he
had showed up with a whole troop. Since he could not deny this charge,

264. In Poitiers.

he was ordered to leave the palace immediately and to go to Paderborn with a very few men and to spend the winter there in a military tent. Abbot Wala was ordered to go back to the monastery of Corbie and to keep to the monastic life there.

When those who had assembled to oppose the emperor saw these things, they, even with reduced forces, turned themselves to a last desperate step. For throughout the night they went over and assembled at the modest quarters of the emperor's son Lothar and urged him either to begin a war or else to withdraw a little, even without the emperor's permission. After they had spent the whole night in these deliberations, the emperor in the morning commanded his son not to believe their common enemies but to come to him as a son to his father. After he got this message, and although he was discouraged by those around him, he came to his father, who did not upbraid him with a bitter assault but corrected him with calm moderation. When he had entered a little way into the royal residence, the crowd began to rage against him [Louis] by diabolical instigation, and the fury might have led to mutual slaughter had not the emperor's prudence intervened. For while they were rushing about against each other in an almost insane fury, the emperor walked into the full view of everyone with his son. After they did this, that whole wild-animal-like commotion quieted down, and after they had heard the emperor's speech, the tumult of the whole people dissipated. Then the emperor instructed that all those leaders of this wicked conspiracy be assigned individual guards. Afterward they were all brought to judgment, and all the judges and the emperor's sons agreed that they ought to face capital punishment for being legally judged guilty of treason. He permitted none of them to be killed but was more forgiving than seemed fitting to many—nevertheless, kindness and mercy were his habits—and he instructed the laymen to be tonsured in suitable places and the clerics to be shut away in appropriate monasteries.

(46) These things having been accomplished, the emperor went to Aachen to spend the winter. However, he always kept his son Lothar with him through that same period. Meanwhile he sent to Aquitaine and recalled his wife and her brothers, Conrad and Rudolf, who had been tonsured long before. Still, he did not deign her worthy of her wifely honor until she had purged herself of the charges in the prescribed legal way. After this had been done, on the feast of Mary's Purification,[265] he granted life to all those who had been condemned

265. February 2, 831.

to death, and he permitted Lothar to go to Italy, Pippin to Aquitaine, and Louis to Bavaria, while he himself solemnly celebrated the Lenten and Easter seasons in that same place.

After the Easter solemnities were completed, the emperor went to Ingelheim. Then, at that time, not unmindful of his usual mercy, which, just as Job said of himself, "grew up with him from the beginning and seems to have emerged with him from his mother's womb,"[266] he summoned those whom he had a while back sent into different areas accordingly as their offenses merited. He restored their personal property, and if they had been tonsured, he conceded to them the right to choose whether they wished to remain in the habit or to return to their former status. From there the emperor crossed over to the region of Remiremont through the Vosges, and there he gave himself over to fishing and hunting as long as he liked, and he sent his son Lothar to Italy.[267]

Later on he ordered his people to convene in a general assembly in the autumn, in the royal estate at Thionville. In that place appeared three envoys of the Saracens who lived beyond the sea, two of them Muslims and one a Christian, bearing vast gifts from their land, different kinds of perfumes and textiles. After they had sought and received peace, they departed. Bernard was there too, after he had saved himself by flight and spent a long time in the Spanish borderlands. He approached the emperor and asked to purge himself in the normal way of the Franks; that is, he wished to meet in armed combat the one who had charged him with a crime. But when the sought-for accuser did not appear, weapons were set aside, and the purgation was accomplished by oaths. The emperor had also commanded his son Pippin to appear at this assembly, but he held back for a while and showed up afterward. The emperor, however, wished to punish him for this disobedience and for his very many moral offenses against him, so he commanded him to stay put, and he kept him with himself at Aachen until Christmas. But Pippin was aggrieved to be kept against his will, took flight, and without his father's knowledge returned to Aquitaine. The emperor, having settled into winter quarters, remained at Aachen.

(47) With the harshness of winter truly over and the spring coming on, the emperor received news that certain movements were stirring in Bavaria. He

266. Job 31:18. Cf. NAB: "Though like a father God has reared me from my youth, guiding me even from my mother's womb."

267. Although hunting was a favorite Carolingian pastime, Louis is the only king said to have gone fishing. See again below, c. 52.

departed swiftly to suppress them and, arriving at Augsburg, calmed the insurgency, [then] went straight home, ordered a public assembly to be held in Orléans, and commanded his son Pippin to appear there. He came, although he did not welcome the invitation. The emperor was reflecting on how the schemes of certain evil men were quickly turning the minds of his sons to baser ends both by threats and by promises. He especially feared Bernard, whose advice, it was said, Pippin was then employing and who was certainly then hanging around in Aquitaine. So he crossed the Loire with his entourage and came to Jouac, a palace situated in the vicinity of Limoges, where the cases of both were fully aired. Bernard, indeed, when he was charged with infidelity, was deprived of his honors, even though his accuser did not wish to present himself at the meeting. He ordered Pippin, so as to correct his bad moral conduct, to be placed in private custody in Trier. He was indeed taken there and treated quite kindly, but he escaped from his guard at night and, until the emperor returned from Aquitaine, wandered about wherever he wished and could do so.

And then indeed the emperor effected a certain division of the realm between his sons Lothar and Charles, which, however, could not be carried out because of emerging hindrances that will have to be discussed. It seemed that the emperor would withdraw from Aquitaine at a suitable moment, but after a little while, that is, around the eleventh of November, he assembled the people, for he wished to find some way to recall his fugitive son Pippin. But with Pippin still at large, a very harsh and inclement winter settled in. First of all there was a deluge of repeated downpours, and then the damp earth was gripped by ice-cold stiffness. This was so disagreeable that the horses' hooves were worn down, and it was rare for anyone to go out on horseback. The army was much afflicted by this unpleasant situation and bore very badly the unforeseen attacks of the Aquitainians, so the emperor decided to come to an estate called Rest, to cross the Loire River there, and to go back to Francia to spend the winter. He did this, albeit in a less dignified fashion than was fitting.

(48) The devil, the enemy of humankind and of peace, never stopped striking the emperor with his attacks, but won over his sons by the tricks of his accomplices, persuading them that their father wanted them to lose everything, and they did not stop to think that he who was so mild to all foreigners could not be cruel to his own. But because "evil communications corrupt good manners"[268] and because even a tiny drop of water that strikes repeatedly

268. 1 Corinthians 15:33.

will wear smooth even a hard stone, it finally came to this, that they made the emperor's sons come together as one with whatever forces they were able to assemble, and they summoned Pope Gregory[269] under the pretext that he alone could and should reconcile the sons to the father. The truth of the matter became clear later.[270]

The emperor, on the other hand, later in May, came to Worms with a strong force and there deliberated for a long time about what he had to do. He dispatched emissaries, Bishop Bernard[271] and the rest, to urge his sons to come back to him, and he discussed with the pope of the Roman see why he was contriving such delays in coming to see him, if he had come in the manner of his predecessors. Then a rumor spread everywhere that was true about other things but asserted that the pope had come from Rome because he wished to ensnare both the emperor and the bishops in bonds of excommunication if they were disobedient to his will or to that of the emperor's sons. Yet this audacious presumption was not enough to win away the emperor's bishops, who said that they in no way wished to withdraw themselves from the pope's authority but that if he had come to excommunicate, he would leave excommunicated, for the authority of the ancient canons held against him.

Finally, however, on the feast of Christ's precursor John,[272] in a place that, on account of what took place there, is known by a perpetually ignominious name—it is called the "Field of Lies"[273]—those who had promised fidelity to the emperor lied. The place where this happened remains a witness to this evil in its very name. When they were arrayed, with their battle lines drawn up not far from each other, and the rush to arms was already thought to be imminent, the arrival of the Roman pope was announced to the emperor. The emperor stood right in that battle line to receive him as he arrived—to be sure, rather less honorably than was normal—telling the pope that he had brought on such a reception for himself by coming to him in such an unusual way. The pope was then led to the emperor's tent. He carefully set forth many assurances, to the effect that he would not have undertaken such a journey except that it was reported that the emperor was struggling in unremitting discord against his sons, and therefore he wished to sow peace among both

269. Gregory IV (827–44).
270. Thegan, cc. 42–48, presents these developments much more briefly.
271. Bernard of Vienne (810–42) or possibly Bernold of Strasbourg (822–ca. 840).
272. June 24, 833.
273. Campus Mentitus, an open field not far from Colmar.

parties. He then listened to the emperor's side and remained with him for a few days. Then, when he had gone back from the emperor to his sons, so that he could fashion a mutual peace, just about all the people, drawn away by gifts or led away by promises or scared away by threats, had flowed like a torrent to the sons and to the people who were with them. Orders had been given that he [i.e., the pope] would never be permitted to go back to the emperor. So many troops were brought there and won away from the emperor—and the defection grew day by day—that on the feast of Saint Paul[274] the common people, fawning upon his sons, threatened to launch an attack against the emperor. The emperor was not strong enough to counter their forces, and he commanded his sons not to turn the mob loose on the environs. They shot back that if he would leave his camp and come to meet them, they would march out to meet him most promptly. And so they met each other, and the emperor admonished his sons, as they were dismounting and approaching him, to be mindful of their promises and to keep to what they had once promised both to him and to his son[275] and to his wife. They gave a suitable response. They embraced, and he followed them to their camp. When they got there, his wife was taken away and led to the tent of Louis.[276] Lothar led him and Charles, who was still a boy, to his own lodgings and assigned Louis, with a very few men, to a tent set aside for this purpose.

After all this, the people having already been bound together by oaths, the brothers divided the empire among themselves in three parts. Louis already having custody of his father's wife, she was again sent into exile, to Tortona, a city in Italy. On seeing such things, Pope Gregory returned to Rome with the greatest sadness, and two of the brothers, Pippin and Louis, returned to Aquitaine and Bavaria. Later Lothar took his father and, having him ride along separately with a few assigned men, treated him as a private person. He reached the estate of Marlenheim and stayed there as long as he wished, took care of what seemed to need attention, dismissed the people but called them to an assembly in Compiègne, and then crossed the Vosges by way of Maurmünster and arrived at Mediomatricum, which is called Metz by its other name. He left there and pressed on to Verdun, then approached the city of Soissons, and ordered his father to be kept there under tight guard in the monastery of

274. June 30.
275. Charles is meant here.
276. Louis the German. He was not only Judith's stepson but, from 827, her brother-in-law, for he had married her sister, Emma.

St.-Médard. Charles was sent to Prüm, but he was not yet tonsured. He himself went hunting until the autumn season, that is, the first of October, and then, as he had decreed, he came to Compiègne, bringing his father with him.

(49) While he was there, a legation arrived from the emperor of Constantinople, Archbishop Mark of Ephesus and the emperor's spatharius.[277] They had been sent to his father, gave Lothar the gifts assigned to him, but kept back the gifts sent to Louis. Although sent to his father, Lothar received the legation as if it had been sent to him, heard them out, and then dismissed them after reporting the almost unheard-of tragedy. In that same assembly, since many were accused of devotion to the father and disloyalty to the son, some met the charges with words alone and some with oaths. The pathetic nature of an affair of this kind and the changeableness of such affairs gripped everyone except those who started it all. The instigators of this unprecedented crime feared that if things turned around, they could not bear what they had done, so they quickly contrived an argument with a few bishops, so it seemed. They said the emperor would be condemned for those things for which he had already done penance, and then, having laid down his arms, do public penance again to make satisfaction to the church in some irrevocable way. But the public law does not find twice against a person who has committed one crime a single time, and our law holds that "not even God judges twice for the same offense."[278] Some disputed this judgment, many assented, but the greater part, as is normal in such cases, consented at least verbally so as not to offend the leaders. So he was condemned, although absent, unheard, unconfessed, and untried, and they compelled him to remove his arms before the body of Saint Médard the Confessor and Saint Sebastian the Martyr and to place them before the altar. They dressed him in penitential garb and took him away under heavy guard to a certain house.

With this business completed, on the feast of Saint Martin,[279] the people, deeply saddened by such deeds, were given leave to go home. Lothar, however, went back to Aachen for the winter, taking his father with him. During the course of this winter season the people of both Francia and Burgundy, and even of Aquitaine and Germany, flocked together and complained with bitter indignation at the emperor's misfortune. And indeed in Francia Count

277. A spatharius was an honorary officer of great prestige.
278. Nahum 1:9.
279. November 11. Note that since the assembly commenced at the beginning of October, it had taken several weeks for Lothar to arrange his father's deposition.

Eggard[280] and Constable William[281] joined to themselves whomever they could with a view to restoring the emperor. Later the Abbot Hugh[282] was sent into Aquitaine by Louis the German and by those who had fled there, namely Bishop Drogo and the rest, for the purpose of winning Pippin to this movement. Then Bernard and Werin[283] won over the people in Burgundy by persuasion, attracted them with promises, bound them with oaths, and joined them into one will.

(50) When the winter was over and spring was already actually showing its rosy face, Lothar took his father, marched through the Hesbaye, and headed for the city of Paris, where he had already instructed all his faithful men to meet him. Count Eggebard[284] and other nobles of that region came out to meet him with the large force they had assembled for the purpose of liberating the emperor. That is how things would have turned out except that the most pious emperor, wishing to avoid danger for the great many and for his own people, turned them from this plan by insistent instruction and pleading. Finally, therefore, everyone got to the monastery of St.-Denis the Martyr.

(51) Pippin indeed departed from Aquitaine with a large force and came right up to the Seine, but had to stop there, since demolished bridges and sunken ships prevented a crossing. Later Counts Werin and Bernard, having assembled a good many allies from Burgundy, arrived at the Marne and then stayed for a few days at the royal estate of Bonneuil and in those fields that lay around it. In part they were held back by the sharpness and unseasonableness of the wind, and in part they paused to assemble their allies. The holy season of Lent was just beginning; it was Thursday of the first week.[285] Envoys were sent by them, Abbot Adrebald[286] and Count Gauzhelm,[287] to the son of the emperor, Lothar, demanding that the emperor [Louis] be released from the bonds of custody and come back with them. If he would yield to their demand, they were prepared to help him with his father, with respect to both

280. A count in the Hesbaye.
281. A count of Blois. The constable (*comes stabuli*) headed the royal stables, was in a sense the court's transport officer, and had other duties in the palace.
282. One of Louis's half brothers; Drogo, another, was bishop of Metz.
283. It is not possible to identify this Bernard. Werin was count of Mâcon and is often mentioned in this text: cc. 32, 44, 49, 51, 52.
284. Surely the same person as the Eggard in c. 49.
285. February 19, 834.
286. Possibly the abbot of Flavigny, but differences in the spelling of this name in various sources make precise identification difficult.
287. Count of Rousillon and brother of Bernard of Septimania.

his safety and the honor that he once held. If otherwise, and if it were necessary, they were going to seek out Louis themselves. They were ready to meet danger, to resist with arms anyone who confronted them, and to let God be the judge. Lothar responded reasonably to this command. No one suffered more in his father's calamity or rejoiced more in his good fortune than he did; nor should they impute to him the crime of withdrawing his allegiance, since they too had abandoned and betrayed him; nor should the brand of Louis's incarceration be burned onto him, since this had been done by episcopal judgment. The above-mentioned legates were sent back with this justification to those who had sent them. Counts Werin and Odo and Abbots Fulco[288] and Hugo were ordered to come to him so they could deliberate on how it might be possible to fulfill their request. The emperor's son Lothar instructed that messengers be sent to him the next day to learn from him the time for the arrival of the above-mentioned men so that they could meet him on the appointed day and discuss the pending case. Then, however, he changed his plan, left his father in the monastery of St.-Denis, and, with those who were being led along by his favor, headed for Burgundy, going as far as Vienne, where he chose to halt.[289]

Those who had remained with the emperor were urging that he had to take up the imperial insignia. But the emperor, since he had been removed from communion with the church in the way already described, and even though he did not wish to acquiesce in that hasty judgment, because the next day was Sunday, wanted to be reconciled in the church of St.-Denis by episcopal ministration and consented to be girded with his arms at the hand of the bishops. In this affair the exaltation of the people rose to such an extent that even the weather, which seemed to have suffered an injury with him, now rejoiced in his restoration; for up to that time such powerful winds and driving rains had settled in that a superabundance of water far beyond the norm rose up and the gales of wind rendered the rivers impassable for boats. The elements seemed somehow to have participated in his absolution, such that the harsh winds soon calmed and the face of heaven returned to its old but long unseen serenity.

(52) The emperor then marched away from that place, but he did not wish to pursue his retreating son, even though many were urging him to do so.

---

288. Abbot of St.-Hilary in Poitiers and Fontanelle (St.-Wandrille) and later of St.-Vaast; archchaplain to Louis the Pious 830–34; administrator of Reims after the deposition of Ebbo.

289. Lothar fled St.-Denis on February 28, so negotiations had been going on for more than a week.

From there he went to Nanteuil and later to the royal estate at Quierzy. He stopped there and waited for his son Pippin and for those who lived beyond the Marne, even for those who had taken flight to his son Louis beyond the Rhine, and indeed for that son Louis himself, who was coming to him. While he was waiting there, in the middle of Lent, even the joy of the day smiled on him, and the singing of the church's Office encouraged him, saying: "Rejoice, Jerusalem, and make joyful the day, all you who love her."[290] A great multitude of his faithful men met him there, sharing happily in the common joy. The emperor received them warmly, and giving thanks for the integrity of their loyalty, he gladly dismissed his son Pippin to go back to Aquitaine, and he permitted the rest to go back happily to the places that were appropriate to them. He himself, however, went to Aachen, and there he received Judith Augusta, who was brought back from Italy by Bishop Ratold[291] and Boniface,[292] and even Pippin;[293] he had already had his son Charles with him for a while. He celebrated the solemnity of Easter there with his usual devotion. After the celebration he applied himself to hunting in the Ardennes, and after the feast of Pentecost he gave himself over to hunting and fishing around Remiremont.

Although the emperor's son Lothar had withdrawn to the area mentioned above, Counts Lambert and Matfrid and a great many others remained in the region of Neustria, which they were trying to hold by means of their own strength. Count Odo and many others who supported the emperor took this very badly, raised arms against them, and tried to drive them from those regions, or at least to join battle with them. But the affair was managed more slowly and watched less cautiously than was fitting, and this caused them no little trouble. For when the enemy overtook them unexpectedly, they, employing much less caution than the situation demanded, showed their bare backs to the onrushing enemy. And right there Odo himself perished along with his brother William and many others; the rest saved themselves by flight. When this encounter was over, those who had been able to prevail did not think it was possible for them to remain there safely, and could not join up with Lothar.

---

290. Isaiah 66:10. The Astronomer quotes the line from the day's liturgy and not directly from the Bible, where one reads: "Rejoice, Jerusalem, and be glad with her, all you who love her."

291. Bishop of Verona; see c. 29 above.

292. Count of Lucca; see c. 42 above. When Lothar's forces entered Italy in 834, Boniface was expelled.

293. Son of King Bernard of Italy, who had been deposed in 818.

They feared that if they stayed there, the emperor would overtake them or he would certainly cut them off if they hastened to join their people. They sent urgently to Lothar to come and help them because they were afraid, surrounded, and a long way from him. When he learned of their danger and of what had happened, he resolved to help them.

At that time Count Werin, with many of his allies, took the fortress of Chalon-sur-Saône, even though it was well fortified, so that if anyone from the eager partisans of their opponents should try anything untoward, it would serve as a refuge and protection for himself and his men. When Lothar learned of this, he was inclined to show up there unexpected, but he could not do so. But he did approach and surround the town, and he put to the torch whatever was lying around it. There was bitter fighting for five days, but finally the city was received in formal surrender. Afterward, however, the situation having reversed itself, the cruel victors, after their fashion, right away devastated the churches with plundering, seized everything of value, and pillaged the common supplies; finally the city was consumed by a fierce fire except for one small basilica that by an amazing miracle could not be burned, even though it was surrounded by furious and lapping flames. It was consecrated to God in honor of blessed George the Martyr. Yet it was not Lothar's will that the city be burned down. After the town was captured, Count Gauzhelm, Count Sanilo, and Madalhelm,[294] a vassal of the emperor, were decapitated, and Gerberga,[295] the daughter of the former count William, was drowned as a witch, all to the shouting of the soldiers.

(53) While these things were taking place, the emperor and his son Louis had reached the city of Langres, where he received a messenger with the news of these events. This made him very sad. His son Lothar meanwhile took to the road from Chalon to Autun, and from there he went to Orléans, and then on into the territory of Le Mans, to an estate whose name is Montaillé. The emperor followed him with his own men, with a large army, and also with his son Louis. When Lothar heard this, and after he had joined forces with his men, he pitched camp at no great distance from his father. He stayed there for four days with envoys running back and forth. On the fourth night, Lothar and all his men quite sensibly began to retreat. His father, the emperor, took

---

294. Madalhelm is otherwise unknown. For the other two, see cc. 33 and 51 above.

295. The sister of Bernard of Septimania. She was apparently the first woman executed as a witch, although amid such partisan politics it is hard to know how seriously to take the accusation. Cf. Thegan, c. 52.

a shortcut, and they both reached the river Loire before the fortress of Blois, at the point where the river Cisse enters the Loire. After they had pitched camps there, Pippin, his son, approached his father with as a great a military entourage as he could muster. Even though unbeaten by the opposing force, Lothar came to his father as a suppliant. Louis upbraided him verbally, bound him and his nobles with such oaths as he wished, and dismissed him to go to Italy, having first secured the narrow passes of the roads crossing to Italy so that no one could pass by without the permission of the custodians. With this accomplished, he went to Orléans with his son Louis, and from there, after having given permission to that son and to others to return to their homes, he himself went to Paris.

At around the time of Martinmas he held a general assembly at the palace of Attigny, where he decided to make amends for all the things that had gone so terribly wrong in both ecclesiastical and public affairs, among which [amends] these were the chief ones: he commanded his son Pippin through Abbot Ermold[296] to restore to churches without delay the ecclesiastical properties that he himself had given to his men or that they had seized on their own; he sent envoys through the cities and monasteries and ordered that the virtually collapsed condition of the church be put back in its former state; likewise he instructed *missi* to go through each county to suppress the cruelty of robbers and thieves, which had risen to unheard-of levels; where they encountered superior strength, they were to join up with the neighboring counts and the men of the bishops because such forces had to be overcome and crushed. They were supposed to report back to him in detail at the next general assembly in Worms, which he said would take place after winter was passed and the tempting grace of spring had arrived.

(54) The emperor spent the greatest part of the winter at Aachen, and then he set out for Thionville before Christmas, which he celebrated in Metz with his brother Drogo. Then, for the feast of the Purification of Saint Mary,[297] he decided to go to Thionville, where the people whom he had instructed to [meet him] arrived. While he was there, he raised serious complaints about some of the bishops in respect of his deposition, but since certain of them had fled to Italy and others, although summoned, did not wish to obey, only Ebbo was there among those who were called. When he was pressed to give

296. Several identifications of this person have been proposed: Ermoldus Nigellus, who appears in this volume; Ermenald, abbot of Aniane (830–38); Hermold, chancellor of Pippin ca. 838.
297. February 2, 835.

an explanation for what had happened, he pleaded that he alone was left to be investigated of all those in whose presence these things had been done. But when some bishops ignored the urgency of the situation and excused themselves with a protestation of innocence, Ebbo, ground down by such arguments, took this poorly and, having sought the advice of some of the bishops, offered some sort of an admission against himself, confirmed that he was unworthy of the priesthood, and agreed to resign irrevocably from it. This he communicated to the bishops and, through them, to the emperor. This done, Agobard, the archbishop of Lyon, who was summoned but declined to come—indeed he was called three times to explain himself—was removed from the leadership of his church. The others, as we said, had fled to Italy.

On the following Sunday,[298] the one preceding the beginning of the holy season of Lent, the lord emperor, the bishops, and his whole people came to an assembly in Metz, and during the celebration of Mass seven archbishops[299] sang seven prayers of reconciliation over him, and all the people who saw this gave great thanks to God for the complete restoration of the emperor. After all this, both the lord emperor and his people went back joyfully to Thionville, and when the first Sunday of Lent arrived, he instructed each one to go to his own home. He, however, spent Lent there, but he celebrated the solemnity of Easter at Metz.[300]

After the solemnity of Easter and the venerable day of Pentecost,[301] he went to the city of Vangiones, which is now called Worms, to hold a general assembly according to his decree. There his son Pippin came to him, and his other son, Louis, did not fail to appear. After his fashion, the emperor would not permit that assembly to be empty of public benefit. He was very keen to examine there what the *missi* whom he had sent into various places had been doing. Because some of the counts were found to be lazy in checking and eliminating robbers, he chastised their sloth with various pronouncements of deserved blame. He admonished his sons and people to love justice, to crush criminals, and to relieve good men of those who oppress them. He threatened that he would hand down even more severe punishments against those who would not obey this warning.

---

298. February 28.
299. Presumably the archbishops of Trier, Mainz, Rouen, Tours, Sens, Arles, and Bourges. Drogo bore the honorary title of archbishop but was not a metropolitan bishop.
300. April 18.
301. June 6.

When he had dismissed the people from that assembly and had determined that the next one would be in Thionville after Easter, he took himself off to Aachen for the winter. He commanded his son Lothar to send his nobles and the rest of his men to that very place so that the cause of mutual reconciliation between them might be explored. Judith Augusta embarked on a plan with the emperor's advisers, because it seemed that the strength of the emperor's body was declining, and if he should happen to die, then there might be danger for her and for Charles. If [only] they could align themselves with one of the brothers; and given that none of the sons of the emperor was as suited to this purpose as Lothar, they urged the emperor to send peacemakers to invite him for this reason. He was always eager for peace, a cherisher of peace, and a lover of unity, and he sought to unite to himself in love not only his sons but even his enemies.

(55) Later, in the assigned estate and at the designated time, many envoys from his son appeared, as he had instructed. Among them, Wala was foremost. The issue discussed above was fully deliberated and brought to a conclusion. The emperor, along with his wife, wished first of all to be reconciled with Wala, and right away and with hearts filled with kindness they put aside any offenses he had committed against them . Through him and the rest of his son's envoys, he told Lothar to come as quickly as he could and that, if he would do this, he would learn that it would be of the greatest advantage to him. They went back and related the situation to Lothar. But the emperor's command could not be brought into effect, because sickness and fever intervened. Wala indeed died, and Lothar was laid up in bed, where he languished for a long time. The emperor, most merciful by nature, when he heard that his son was seized by strength-sapping illness, communicated with him through his most faithful envoys, that is, his brother Hugo and Count Adalgar,[302] for he was most anxious to learn all about his son's distress. In this he imitated blessed David, who, although afflicted by his son in many ways, nevertheless bore his death most bitterly.[303]

But after he recovered from the raging illness, a report reached the emperor to the effect that Lothar had broken the conditions of the oaths sworn long before and that his men were disturbing with the cruelest attacks the great church of St. Peter, which his grandfather Pippin and his father Charles and

302. Possibly a member of the powerful Unrochinger family and later a loyal supporter of Charles the Bald.
303. Absalom; cf. 2 Samuel 19:1.

he himself had taken under their protection. These things really did so embitter his normally mild spirit that he sent *missi*, quite extraordinarily as it seemed, since he hardly gave them enough time to complete such a journey. He sent to Lothar and warned him not to let such things happen, urging him to remember that when he gave him the kingdom of Italy, he also committed the care of the holy Roman Church to him, and in undertaking to defend it against adversaries, he should never permit it to be plundered by his own men. He reminded him of the oaths that he had recently sworn to him, so that in forgetting or making light of them he would not offend God, and that he ought not to be unaware that such acts would not go unpunished. At the same time, he ordered food supplies and suitable resting points to be prepared all along the path that led to Rome, for he said that he himself wished to visit the thresholds of the holy apostles. But he could not do it, because an invasion of the Northmen in Frisia prevented it. While heading off to crush their insolence, he sent *missi* to Lothar, Abbot Fulco, and Count Richard, and also Abbot Adrebald;[304] of these, Fulco and Richard were supposed to bring him Lothar's answer, and Adrebald was to go on to Rome to consult with Pope Gregory about the state of affairs, to let him know the emperor's will, and to report other things as he had been instructed. When Lothar was brought up to date on these matters, as well as on the lands snatched from certain churches that are in Italy, he acknowledged certain things but also answered that he could not prevent others. Fulco and Richard announced all this to the emperor, who was returning to the palace at Frankfurt after the flight of the Northmen. Louis spent the fall there hunting and then moved to Aachen for the winter.

(56) When Adrebald arrived at Rome, as he had been ordered, he found the lord pope Gregory ill, especially with a mild but continuous flow of blood from his nose. He was restored so quickly at the emperor's words and sympathy that he insisted he had almost forgotten his own discomfort. While the *missus* was with him, he looked after him in a most lavish manner, and when he was leaving, he gave him gifts most generously and sent with him two bishops, Peter of Civitavecchia[305] and George, a regionary of the city of Rome and also a bishop.[306] Then Lothar, when he heard that the two above-mentioned

304. On Fulco, see note 288 above; on Adrebald, note 286. Richard cannot be identified.

305. See c. 34 above.

306. Possibly the suburbicarian bishop of Gabii after 826. Regionaries were Roman deacons, so the point here may be that George *was then* a bishop and *had been* a regionary.

bishops were heading for the lord emperor, sent Leo,[307] who was held in very high regard by him, to Bologna, where he stirred up a great terror to keep the bishops from going any further. But Adrebald secretly received from them the letter intended for the emperor and gave it to a certain one of his men, who pretended to be a beggar, to take across the Alps. Later it got to the emperor.

It is awful to say what a mortal disease fell at that time upon the people who followed Lothar. In a short time, from the beginning of September to the feast of Saint Martin, the following nobles departed this life: Jesse, formerly the bishop of Amiens;[308] Elias, the bishop of Troyes;[309] Wala, the abbot of Corbie;[310] Matfrid; Hugh; Lambert;[311] Godfred and his son Godfred; Agimbert, the count of Perthois; and the former master of the royal hunt, Burgarit; Richard escaped the illness but died a little later.[312] These are the people of whose death it was said: Francia is bereaved of its nobility, emptied of its strength like a nerve that has been severed, deprived of its wisdom with all these having passed away. With these snatched away by death at the edge of the double-wounding sword, God shows how healthy, how sober it is, to keep to what is proved to have come from His mouth: "Let not the wise man glory in his wisdom, nor the strong man in his strength, nor the rich man in his riches."[313] Anyone may rightly marvel at the emperor's spirit, at how much moderation with which divine mercy ruled him. For when he got this news, he took no pleasure in it himself, and he did not dismiss the dead as enemies, but he struck his breast with his fist, his eyes filled with tears, and with deep groans he prayed to God to shed His grace upon them.

At this same time the Bretons moved to the attack, but he quieted them down easily because the emperor put his hope in Him of Whom it is most truthfully said: "For Your power is at hand, Lord, when You wish."[314] In those days, around when the Purification of the Ever Virgin Mary is celebrated, a great assembly, but especially of bishops, met at Aachen. In it, although many things necessary to the benefit of the church were discussed, particular attention was devoted to the matter of the injuries Pippin and his men had inflicted

307. Most likely the count of Milan (824–41/44) but active as a Carolingian agent in Italy from at least 801.

308. Deposed in 830.

309. 829–36.

310. Died in August/September 836.

311. Hugh of Tours and Lantbert of Nantes died in 837.

312. In the summer of 839.

313. Jeremiah 9:22 (= 9:23 Vulgate).

314. Wisdom 12:18.

on the churches. On account of this issue, the authority of the emperor and the common warning of the council were set forth so that Pippin and his men would be warned what danger they incurred in respect of ecclesiastical property. Things turned out well: Pippin willingly received the warnings of his pious father and the holy men and appeared obedient. With the seal of his ring he ordered all invaded properties to be returned.

(57) The emperor held his next assembly with his sons Pippin and Louis in the summer, at a place called Stramiacus[315] in the territory of Lyon. Lothar was not present, because of weakness caused by the above-mentioned sickness. In this assembly he had the case of the vacant churches of Lyon and Vienne fully discussed because of their bishops: Agobard had been ordered to appear and explain himself but would not come, and Bernard of Vienne came but then turned around and fled. So this affair remained unresolved on account of the absence of the bishops, as is said. But the case of the Goths was aired there; some of them supported the followers of Bernard, and others were led to favor Berengar, the son of the former count Unruoch. But because Berengar died well before his time, as much power as possible remained with Bernard in Septimania. Envoys were sent there to point out those things that required correction and to put affairs into better order. These things done, and his sons and people having been dismissed, the emperor turned to his autumn hunt, then went back to Aachen for the feast of Saint Martin and spent the winter there. He spent Christmas and the Paschal solemnity there in his normal way that was most familiar to him.

(58) In the middle of the Easter celebration a dire and sad portent, a comet, appeared in the sign of Virgo, in that part of this sign where they bind his cloak under the tail of the Serpent just like the Raven.[316] It did not seek to move toward the east after the fashion of the seven wandering stars,[317] but for twenty-five days—it is marvelous to tell it—it crossed through the signs of that same star, Virgo and then Leo and Cancer and then Gemini, until it finally dropped its fiery mass and abundant brilliance, which it used to spread everywhere, at the head of Taurus and under the feet of the Charioteer. The emperor, who was first of all very keen about such things, when he saw that the comet had stopped, was anxious, before he went to bed, to interrogate

315. Possibly Tramoyes; maybe Crémieu. This assembly met in June 835.
316. This was Halley's Comet, visible from March 22 to April 28, 837. The Serpent and the Raven are also constellations.
317. The then-known planets.

a certain person who had been summoned, namely me, who is writing this and who is believed to have knowledge of these matters,[318] and to ask what it looked like to me. I asked for time so that I could examine the appearance of the star and through this explore the truth of the matter. I said I would the next day announce what I had learned. The emperor thought, and it was true, that I was only trying to buy a little time so that I would not have to report something sad. "Go out on the balcony adjoining this house," he said, "and you will see what seems new to us. For I know I did not see that star last evening, and you did not point it out to me, but I do know that it is a sign of the comet of which we have spoken in the past days. Out with it, then! What does it seem to portend to you?" I said something and then was silent. "There is one thing," he said, "that you have still passed over in silence: this sign is said to mean a great change in the realm, and the death of the prince." When I brought forth the testimony of the prophet, where it says, "Do not fear the signs from heaven which the nations fear,"[319] he, showing only magnanimity and prudence, said: "We ought not to fear anyone except Him who is our creator, and that star. For we cannot praise or marvel enough at the mercy of Him who deigns to warn our worthless selves with such signs, for we are sinners and impenitent. Because this manifestation touches me and everyone else commonly, let us hasten to do everything we can and know how to do, so that we do not find ourselves unworthy of the mercy we have already asked for because our impenitence makes us so."

Having said this, he indulged in a little wine and ordered everyone to do this as well, and he ordered everyone to go home, while he kept vigil almost all night, as is related, and when dawn approached, he offered that night to God with praises and prayers. In the last bit of darkness, he called his court servants, and he ordered alms, as much as possible, to be given to the poor and the servants of God, both monks and canons, and he had solemn masses celebrated by whomever could do so, not so much out of fear for himself as to benefit the church entrusted to him. When all of this had been properly taken care of, just as he ordered, he went hunting in the Ardennes. The hunt yielded to him vastly more than usual, and everything that pleased him at that time turned out to have a happy end.

(59) Meanwhile, on the urging of the augusta and the palace officials, at Aachen the emperor handed a certain part of his empire to his dearly beloved

318. This is the closest the Astronomer comes to identifying himself.
319. Jeremiah 10:2.

son Charles, but because this remained without effect, we will pass over it in silence here.[320] When Charles's brothers heard about this, they took it very badly and arranged a mutual meeting, but saw that they could not do anything to oppose the decision, so they managed to conceal what they had started to do, and easily calmed the distress that seems to have arisen in their father on account of this. The emperor held to his plans throughout the summer and called for a general assembly in the autumn, that is, in the middle of September, at Quierzy. In that place and time his son Pippin came to him from Aquitaine and took part in that assembly. There the lord emperor girded his son Charles with the weapons of an adult man, that is, with a sword; he adorned his head with a royal crown and assigned to him a portion of the kingdom that his like-named ancestor Charles had held, namely Neustria.[321] And so the lord emperor, having put together as firm a bond of goodwill as he could manage between his sons, sent Pippin back to Aquitaine and Charles into the portion of the realm assigned to him. The nobles of the province of Neustria who were present gave their hands to Charles and bound themselves by oath to be faithful, and those who were absent later did the same.

In the same place and time practically all the nobles of Septimania were present complaining about Bernard, the duke in those areas, that his men were abusing both ecclesiastical and private property as they wished and without any respect for God or man. Therefore they asked the emperor to take them under his protection and afterward to send into those same regions *missi* who would have the power and wisdom to dispense justice equally concerning the stolen lands and who would preserve for them their ancestral law.[322] To carry this out, *missi* were sent, following up on their request, and the emperor's choice fell upon Counts Boniface and Donatus[323] and also on Abbot Adrebald of the monastery of Flavigny.[324] With these things properly settled, the emperor departed from there and got on with the autumn hunt in his normal way, and

---

320. A portion of the empire was assigned to Charles at an assembly late in 837, but shortly thereafter Pippin of Aquitaine died and Lothar and Louis the German went into revolt.

321. In 789 Charlemagne had assigned Neustria to his son Charles.

322. As early as 759 Pippin III had permitted the Goths to live by their own law.

323. Boniface of Lucca has been mentioned several times. Donatus is mentioned once, in c. 41 above.

324. This person's identity is not certain. It seems that an Adrebald became abbot of Flavigny only in 839. Perhaps the author means St.-Germer-de-Fly, a small house that belonged to Flavigny. Flavigny and its dependencies had close ties to the royal court, especially to the chancery. The Astronomer may have anticipated Adrebald's promotion.

then took himself off to Aachen for the purpose of spending the winter.[325] In this winter, that is, on the first of January, a terrible comet appeared not long after sundown in the sign of Scorpio. The death of Pippin followed not long after this threatening apparition.[326]

Meanwhile Judith Augusta never forgot that she had already entered into an agreement with the palace officials and other nobles of the kingdom of the Franks and that they had persuaded the emperor to send to his son Lothar *missi* who would invite him to come to his father on this condition: if he were willing to be the patron, helper, tutor, and protector of his brother Charles, he should come to his father, know that he would receive forgiveness for everything he had done wrong, and receive half of the empire, Bavaria excepted. This proposition seemed satisfactory in every way to both Lothar and his men.

(60) As determined, therefore, he came to Worms after the solemnity of Easter.[327] His father received him most eagerly, ordered his men to be looked after sumptuously, and did everything just as he said. Louis granted Lothar a truce of three days for the purpose of dividing his empire with them, and if it should be agreeable, the choice of the portions would remain with the emperor and Charles, or else Lothar might propose to the emperor and Charles the partition to be made. But Lothar and his men committed the division of the realm to the discretion of the lord emperor, claiming that they themselves [Lothar and his men] could never make this division, because of ignorance of the places involved. Therefore the emperor, as it seemed to Lothar's men and to his own, divided his whole empire with balanced judgment, except for Bavaria, which he left to Louis and therefore included in none of the other shares. This done, and having called together his sons and his whole people, each one was given his choice. Lothar chose for himself the part lying to the east of the river Meuse, and he left the West for his brother Charles to have, and so that this would turn out to be the case, he said in the presence of all the people that this was his wish. The emperor rejoiced at these things, and with the whole people applauding, he said that all these arrangements pleased him. But indeed Louis [the German's] feelings bore no small hurt at these deeds. The emperor gave thanks to God for what had happened and warned his sons to be in accord with each other and to look out for each other, and

---

325. Actually, Louis spent the winter of 838–39 in Mainz and Frankfurt on campaign against his son Louis.

326. Pippin actually died December 13.

327. The assembly at Worms began May 30, 839.

urged Lothar to take care of his younger brother as he ought to do, since he should remember that he was his godfather, and Charles should pay due respect to his godfather and older brother. When the emperor, as a true lover of peace, had done these things and had sowed mutual love between each brother and as far as he could between each of their peoples, he happily dismissed Lothar to Italy. Lothar was happy too, enriched with many gifts, endowed with his father's blessing, and warned not to forget in any way the promise he had recently offered him. He spent the solemnities of Christmas and Easter with the greatest festivity.[328]

(61) When Louis heard of his father's plan with respect to his brothers and of his desire to divide the realm between them, he would have nothing to do with it, and he decided to claim for himself whatever of the realm was seen to lie beyond the Rhine. When news of this had been communicated to the emperor, he judged it best to put off a decision until after the completion of the Easter festivities. Once these were finished, he thought there was no reason for any delay in these matters, and with many men he crossed the Rhine and then the Main, came to Tribur, and waited there a little while for the purpose of assembling his forces. Once they were mustered, he marched right to Bodman, and his son came there, to be sure unwillingly, as a suppliant. Louis addressed him angrily, and he [Louis the German] confessed that he had acted badly, and he promised that he would change for the better the things he had done objectionably. But the emperor, employing the friendly kindness that was always his way, forgave his son but rebuked him with harsh words at first, as was fitting, and then more gently with milder remarks, and let him return to his kingdom. On his way back, he crossed the Rhine at the place called Coblenz so that he could enter the Ardennes for his customary hunting.

While he was engaged in that activity, very reliable messengers came affirming—it was true, after all—that some of the Aquitainians were awaiting his decision about how the affairs of the kingdom of Aquitaine should be organized, while others were very angry because they had heard that the kingdom had been conferred upon Charles by his father. While the emperor was deeply distressed by such reports, Ebroin,[329] the most noble bishop of Poitiers, came

328. Louis spent Christmas of 838 at Mainz, Easter of 839 on Lake Constance, Christmas of 839 in Poitiers, and Easter of 840 at Aachen.

329. Extremely well connected and important: bishop of Poitiers from 837/38 to 851/54; chancellor of Pippin I of Aquitaine in 831; archchaplain of Charles the Bald after 839/40; abbot of St.-Germain-des-Prés after 840/41.

to Vlatten and announced that both he and the other leaders of his kingdom
were awaiting the emperor's will and would obey his command. The greatest
part of the magnates were in accord with this plan. The most eminent among
them were the venerable Bishop Ebroin himself, Count Reginhard,[330] Gerard,
also a count and the son-in-law of the late Pippin, and also Rathar, likewise a
count and son-in-law of Pippin.[331] A great many others followed their lead
and could not be separated from them by any plot. But then another part of
the people, the most important of whom was a certain Emenus,[332] followed
the son of the former king Pippin, likewise named Pippin, and wandered
about wherever they could, as is the manner of such people, giving themselves
over to plunder and coercion. The above-mentioned Bishop Ebroin asked
the emperor not to put off any longer dealing with this growing disease, but
to heal such a disagreeable condition in good time through his own arrival,
before such a contagion could infect many more people. The emperor then
sent this bishop back to Aquitaine with many displays of gratitude and commanded his faithful men to do what seemed necessary. He ordered some of
them to meet him in the autumn in Chalon-sur-Saône, and he called for a
general assembly there.

Let no one think that the emperor bore a grudge or that, driven by cruelty, he wished to deprive his grandson of his kingdom, since he knew well
the native custom of that people among whom he had been raised. They were
so inclined to fickleness and other vices that they practically renounced seriousness and stability. So that they could make of Pippin what his father had
been, they chased from the region of Aquitaine almost everyone who had been
sent to watch over it, men just like those who had once been given to Louis
by his father, Charles. After their departure, the most recent tribulations of
the present time make vividly clear the number and type of displays of both
public and private evils and vices that emerged in that kingdom. The most
pious emperor wished for the boy to be brought up piously and reasonably
so that he would not dishonor himself with vices and afterward make himself
incapable of leading or benefiting himself or anyone else. Louis thought about
what is written about a certain man who is said to have excused himself this
way when he did not wish to hand over a kingdom to sons who were still in
tender years: "It is not because I envy them that I forbid honors to those born

330. Probably count of Herbauges, on the lower Loire.
331. Gerard was a count in the Auvergne, and Rathar was count of Limoges.
332. Possibly a count of Poitiers or Angoulême.

of me, but because I know that such honors add hearty nourishment to the high-spiritedness of youths."[333]

And so the emperor, as he had indicated, sought out the city of Chalon-sur-Saône in the autumn and handled both ecclesiastical and public business after his manner. Then he turned himself to the organization of the kingdom of Aquitaine. He moved on from that place with the queen, his son Charles, and a strong force and, after having crossed the Loire, went to Clermont. There he received in kindly fashion, in his usual way, his faithful men who had come to meet him, and he had them commend themselves to his son Charles with the customary oaths. Some refused to attend the obligatory meeting and declined to swear loyalty. Moreover, they wandered about like a troop of robbers and pillaged whatever they could. He ordered them to be captured and subjected to legal investigation.

(62) While he was doing these things, the Christmas holiday came around again, and he celebrated this solemnity with due and accustomed honor at Poitiers. While he was staying there and doing what the public good demanded, a messenger came to him saying that his son Louis, having gathered up some Saxons and Thuringians, had invaded Alemannia. This affair was extremely disagreeable to him. For he was already weighed down by old age, and his lung was more than usually burdened with an abundance of phlegm, which increased in winter, and his chest was heaving, so this messenger added to these ills. His message drove Louis to the point of bitterness, even though he was, almost beyond human nature, mild in his character, generous in his resolution, and prudent in his piety. Increasing infection turned into an abscess, and a deadly ulcer grew more and more in his belly. Still, his unconquered spirit did not give in to anger or, broken, succumb to grief when he learned that the church was thrown into confusion and the people of God were distressed by such an affliction. After he had begun the holy season of Lent with his wife and son Charles, he took himself off to meet this storm and to calm it. He who was accustomed to give this season wholly and solemnly to the singing of psalms, to constant prayers, to the celebration of masses, and to generous alms, such that he scarcely permitted himself one or two days for a bit of riding, now wished to have no day idle, since he aimed to put discord to flight and recall peace. Following the example of the good shepherd, to

---

333. Herod the Great is reported by Flavius Josephus (*The Jewish War*, 1.23) to have said this. The Astronomer would have gotten the quotation from a Latin translation. Louis's concern is intriguing, since Pippin II was about the same age as his son Charles.

be of benefit to the flock committed to him, he did not take refuge from any harm that might befall his own body. Hence there can be no doubt that he received the reward that the great "Prince of Pastors"[334] promised would be given to those who labored.

With the greatest fatigue, and with the ills we just mentioned attacking his strength, he arrived at Aachen just before the most holy solemnity of Easter, which he celebrated there with his customary devotion. This done, he hastened to deal with the business at hand. He crossed the Rhine and headed for Thuringia by a rapid march, for he had learned that Louis was staying there at that time. But Louis was unwilling to stay there any longer, with his father already approaching, and, not confident about the situation, sought safety in flight. Coming back from there, the emperor called for a general assembly in the city of the Vangiones that is now called Worms. Because the affairs of [his son] Louis stood at such a pass, his son Charles and his mother went to Aquitaine, and the emperor sent to his son Lothar in Italy, ordering him to attend that assembly so that he could discuss with him the current situation and other things too.

At that time there was a most unusual disappearance of the sun on the third day of the Greater Litany; darkness so prevailed with the receding of the light that, in truth, it seemed to differ not at all from night.[335] The determined order of the stars was perceived such that no star seemed to suffer from the extinguishing of the sun's light except perhaps the moon, which lay opposite the sun. But as the moon moved gradually to the east, a little horn of light was restored to the sun's western parts, as is the case when it is seen at first or second light. Thus little by little the whole circle got back its total beauty. Although this prodigy is rightly ascribed to nature, nevertheless it was completed with an awful result. For it portended that the great light of mortals, which shone before all like a candelabrum placed in God's house—I am referring to the emperor of most pious memory—would very soon be withdrawn from human affairs, leaving the world in the darkness of tribulation[336] by his departure.

He therefore began to waste away by refusing food, for food and drink made him nauseous, and he was tortured by labored breathing and shaken by

---

334. 1 Peter 5:4.

335. The Greater Litany (*letania maior*) was celebrated on April 25. It did not have a "third day," nor was this eclipse three days after the litany, for it seems to have occurred on May 5, 840.

336. Cf. Isaiah 5:30. Solar eclipses were seen in antiquity as foretelling the deaths of rulers. Einhard, c. 32, speaks this way too.

choking and through all of this robbed of his strength. For when nature is abandoned by its companions, then it must be that the force of life fails. Perceiving this, he ordered that summer campaign quarters be set up for him on a certain island opposite the city of Mainz, and there, his strength having fled, he committed himself to bed.

(63) Who could possibly describe his deep concern for the condition of the church or his sadness at its disruption? Who could tell of the river of tears he shed to hasten the outpouring of divine mercy? He did not so much grieve because he was about to die, but instead trembled because he knew the future and said he was unhappy that the end of his life would come amid such miseries. Venerable bishops and many other servants of God were present to console him. Among these were Hetti, the venerable archbishop of Trier, Otgar, likewise the archbishop of Mainz, and also Drogo, the bishop of Metz and archchaplain of the sacred palace and, what is more, the lord emperor's brother. The closer he knew that Drogo stood to him, the more intimately he listened to him and entrusted himself and his affairs to him. Through him he offered daily the gift of his confession, "the sacrifice of a broken spirit and contrite heart that God will not refuse."[337] Through forty days his only food was the Lord's body, and he praised the justice of God, saying, "You are just, Lord, because I have not even completed the Lenten fast before, so now I am compelled to pay it in full to you."[338]

He commanded his venerable brother Drogo to have the ministers of his chamber appear before him, and he ordered to be described [by them] in detail his personal property, which consisted of the royal finery, that is, crowns and arms, vessels, books, and priestly vestments. He instructed him to hand out, as seemed right to him, something to the churches, to the poor, and finally to his sons Lothar and Charles. He sent Lothar a crown and a sword embellished with gold and gems to keep on the condition that he maintain faith with Charles and Judith and that he agree to and protect the whole share of the kingdom that, as God and the palace nobles witnessed, Louis had given

337. Psalm 51:19 (= 50:19 Vulgate), slightly paraphrased. Perhaps a reference to the prayer of Azariah (Daniel 13:9), which also appeared in the offering prayer of the liturgy.

338. This paraphrase is a good example of the biblical culture of the clergy of the Carolingian world. The Astronomer may have had in mind any or all of several Scriptures: Tobit 3:2, "You are righteous, O Lord, and all your deeds are just"; Psalm 119:137 (= 118:137 Vulgate), "You are just, O Lord, and your ordinance is right"; Jeremiah 12:1, "You would be in the right, O Lord, if I should dispute with you"; Revelation 16:5, "You are just, O holy One, who is and who was, in passing this sentence," and 19:2, "for his judgments are true and just."

to Charles already. With these things properly disposed of, he gave thanks to God because he knew that nothing of his own still remained.

While all this was going on, the venerable bishop Drogo and other pontiffs were giving thanks to God for everything, but especially because they saw that he whom the chorus of virtues had always accompanied was persevering right to the end, like the tail of a sacrificial animal,[339] and that he returned to God the whole completely acceptable sacrifice of his life. But there was one thing that cast a pall over their joy: they feared that he might wish to remain unreconciled to his son Louis, for they knew that a wound frequently cut open and cauterized brings more bitter pain to the one who receives it. Nevertheless, trusting in the invincible patience that he always practiced, they kept gently tapping on his mind through his brother Drogo, whose words he would not want to spurn. At first he did display bitterness in his soul,[340] and after thinking for a while and gathering what little strength he had left, he tried to spell out how many and how great were the inconveniences he had suffered from him and what he deserved for acting in such a way against nature and the teaching of the Lord. "But," he said, "because he does not wish to come to me to give an account of himself, I do what is mine to do: with you and God as witnesses, I forgive him every sin he has committed against me. It will be for you to warn him that if I have forgiven him wholly for his wicked deeds, he should not forget who led his father's gray hairs to death with sorrow and, in doing so, has despised the teachings and admonitions of our common father, God."

(64) These things said and done, he instructed—for it was the eve of the Sabbath—that the night Office be celebrated before him and that his breast be fortified by the wood of the holy cross; as long as he could, he signed with his own hand both his brow and his chest with that same sign, but when he became weak, he asked with a nod that this be done by his brother Drogo.[341] He spent that whole night without any bodily strength but with his mind at rest. On the next morning, which was Sunday, he ordered the Sacrament of the altar to be prepared, the Office of the Mass to be celebrated by Drogo, and Communion to be given to him at his hand, as was the custom.[342] After

339. Cf. Leviticus 3:9. The point seems to be that the temple priest sacrificed every possible bit of the animal, even the tail and its fat.

340. Cf. Esther 4:1.

341. Cf. the accounts of Charlemagne's death in Einhard, c. 23, and Thegan, c. 7. Ermoldus, page 146, says very little on the subject.

342. By custom, Charlemagne received communion from his archchaplain.

this he was offered a little something warm to drink. After he had drunk a little of this, he bid his brother and the others who were there to take thought for the care of their own bodies, for he would hang on as long as it took them to refresh themselves.

As the moment of his death approached, he drew Drogo close by joining his thumb to his fingers, for he had been accustomed to do this when he summoned his brother with a sign. He approached with the rest of the priests, and Louis commended himself with such words as he could manage and also with signs, asked to be blessed, and requested that those things be done that are customary at the departure of the soul. After they did this, as many have related to me, he turned his eyes to the left, and with as much strength as he could muster, as if he were a little angry, he said, twice, "Huz, Huz," which means "Be gone!" It was clear that he saw some evil spirit whose company he wished to have neither alive nor dead. Then, having raised his eyes to heaven, the more threatened his gaze, the more joyful his appearance, so that he seemed to differ not at all from someone who was laughing. Having departed in such a way from the end of this life, he went to his rest happily, as we believe, as has been truly said by a truth-speaking teacher: "He cannot die badly who has lived well."[343]

He died on the twentieth of June in the sixty-fourth year of his life.[344] He ruled over Aquitaine for thirty-seven years and was emperor for twenty-seven years. After his soul departed, the emperor's brother Drogo, the bishop of Metz, along with the other bishops, abbots, counts, vassals, and a large mass of clergy and people took the emperor's remains and with great honor had them transported to Metz, where he was nobly buried in the basilica of St. Arnulf, where his mother was also buried.

---

343. Augustine, *De Disciplina Christiana*, 12.13, Corpus Christianorum 46 (Turnhout, 1969), 221.
344. He was actually sixty-two or sixty-three, but a number of sources make the same mistake the Astronomer does.